D1571988

A HISTORY OF
Garfield County

A HISTORY OF

Garfield County

Linda King Newell
Vivian Linford Talbot

1998
Utah State Historical Society
Garfield County Commission

ISBN 0-913738-37-9
Library of Congress Catalog Card Number 98-61317
Map by Automated Geographic Reference Center—State of Utah
Printed in the United States of America

Utah State Historical Society
300 Rio Grande
Salt Lake City, Utah 84101-1182

Contents

GENERAL INTRODUCTION vii

INTRODUCTION   A Bit Like Heaven ix

CHAPTER 1   Shaping the Land 1

CHAPTER 2   The Ancient Ones:
Prehistoric and Historic Native Americans .. 20

CHAPTER 3   Early Trade and Exploration 39

CHAPTER 4   A Precarious Beginning:
Settling Panguitch 57

CHAPTER 5   Garfield County and Exploration
of the Colorado River 93

CHAPTER 6   Settlements on the Upper Sevier River 108

CHAPTER 7   Colonizing along the Escalante
and Paria Rivers 127

CHAPTER 8   Establishing Garfield County 168

CHAPTER 9   Garfield County Ushers in a New Century .. 197

CHAPTER 10   The First Decades of a New Century   233

CHAPTER 11   The Great Depression to
               Post-War Recovery   283

CHAPTER 12   Garfield County at Mid-Century   317

CHAPTER 13   Change amid Controversy   352

APPENDICES   385

SELECTED BIBLIOGRAPHY   399

INDEX   407

General Introduction

When Utah was granted statehood on 4 January 1896, twenty-seven counties comprised the nation's new forty-fifth state. Subsequently two counties, Duchesne in 1914 and Daggett in 1917, were created. These twenty-nine counties have been the stage on which much of the history of Utah has been played.

Recognizing the importance of Utah's counties, the Utah State Legislature established in 1991 a Centennial History Project to write and publish county histories as part of Utah's statehood centennial commemoration. The Division of State History was given the assignment to administer the project. The county commissioners, or their designees, were responsible for selecting the author or authors for their individual histories, and funds were provided by the state legislature to cover most research and writing costs as well as to provide each public school and library with a copy of each history. Writers worked under general guidelines provided by the Division of State History and in cooperation with county history committees. The counties also established a Utah Centennial County History Council to help develop policies for distribution of state-appropriated funds and plans for publication.

Each volume in the series reflects the scholarship and interpretation of the individual author. The general guidelines provided by the Utah State Legislature included coverage of five broad themes encompassing the economic, religious, educational, social, and political history of the county. Authors were encouraged to cover a vast period of time stretching from geologic and prehistoric times to the present. Since Utah's statehood centennial celebration falls just four years before the arrival of the twenty-first century, authors were encouraged to give particular attention to the history of their respective counties during the twentieth century.

Still, each history is at best a brief synopsis of what has transpired within the political boundaries of each county. No history can do justice to every theme or event or individual that is part of an area's past. Readers are asked to consider these volumes as an introduction to the history of the county, for it is expected that other researchers and writers will extend beyond the limits of time, space, and detail imposed on this volume to add to the wealth of knowledge about the county and its people. In understanding the history of our counties, we come to understand better the history of our state, our nation, our world, and ourselves.

In addition to the authors, local history committee members, and county commissioners, who deserve praise for their outstanding efforts and important contributions, special recognition is given to Joseph Francis, chairman of the Morgan County Historical Society, for his role in conceiving the idea of the centennial county history project and for his energetic efforts in working with the Utah State Legislature and State of Utah officials to make the project a reality. Mr. Francis is proof that one person does make a difference.

ALLAN KENT POWELL
CRAIG FULLER
GENERAL EDITORS

Introduction

A BIT LIKE HEAVEN

The people of Garfield County are fiercely attached to their communities and the scenic land which surrounds them. Lifelong county resident Marilyn Jackson admits it is not quite heaven, but believes it comes close:

> How do you describe heaven? Does it have blue skies with beautiful mountains? Are there streams and lakes with tall pines and wild flowers on the countryside? Are there valleys where lush grass grows and winter snows glisten in the sunlight? Is it picturesque with every hue of the rainbow, and has four distinct seasons? Are the climate and soil just right for growing? Are there minerals and natural resources abundant? Is it free from earthquakes, tornados, war, crime and turmoil? Are there friendly neighbors and [a] good standard of living?[1]

Settling the rugged canyons and high valleys of the county was a monumental task for the hardiest of pioneers. Beginning with the men and women who first settled Panguitch in 1864, each generation overcame obstacles and hardships to provide for themselves and their posterity a better and more prosperous life. Today, eight towns dot the varied landscape of Garfield County. Panguitch, the county seat, is the largest, with 1,444 residents in 1990, and is the gateway to one of the nation's most scenic wonders—Bryce Canyon National Park. Tropic, with 374 inhabitants, sits at the foot of Bryce Canyon and provides warm hospitality to those who venture east beyond the park into the vast beauty of what is called "Color Country." South of Tropic is Cannonville (population 131) on the edge of Kane County's Kodachrome Basin with its sculpted red rock. Henrieville (population 163) is three miles east of Tropic on Utah's scenic byway, Highway 143, that leads from Bryce Canyon to Capitol Reef National Park, the southern part of which is also in Garfield County. Farther east are the towns of Boulder and Escalante, with populations of 126 and 818, respectively. Located in the heart of Garfield County, these two towns sit in the Escalante Basin, at the edge of mountains with the same names as the two towns. Boasting a heritage of five and six generations of Mormon immigrant ancestry, both communities have evolved into oases for the modern-day traveler. The water from the eastern slopes of surrounding mountains drains into the Colorado River and Lake Powell, traveling through the Glen Canyon National Recreation Area. Sitting on the north and south ends of the county are Hatch (population 103) and Antimony, the county's smallest town, with 83 people.

Garfield County has a history of mining, logging, ranching, and farming—producing cattle, sheep, timber, fruits, and vegetables. Because of the distance to larger population centers, manufactured goods and services have always been more costly in the county than in more densely populated areas. Some families whose ancestors had homesteaded their land relinquished it in the hope that obtaining grazing permits would be more economical than maintenance costs of owning the land. After World War II, growth generally was limited to what the area's natural resources could sustain, and many people—especially the young—left to find work in factories and industrialized cities. Once independent and self-sufficient, families struggled with increasing restrictions on surrounding public lands because their economy was based on natural resources. Controls on the lands that have traditionally provided these resources created problems for many residents. Today the county has new life, however, and anticipates the continued expansion of tourism, which is now the county's largest industry.

An estimated 90 percent of those who visit the county are drawn there by Bryce Canyon National Park. Many return to see Garfield's other scenic sights, hike in its canyons, fish in its streams, hunt in its mountains, raft through the Colorado River's Cataract Canyon, explore the county's history, and marvel at its ancient Anasazi and Fremont rock art and archaeological sites.

Those who live in Garfield County, whether they be oldtimers or newcomers, feel a sense of place among its red rocks and mountains. They value the land and its history—their history. It is the hope of the authors that their efforts in researching and writing this book will do justice to both people and place. This history is intended to supplement the several fine town and county histories that have been published in the past. It is hoped that it will augment those works by providing in one volume an overview of Garfield County's history that is as accurate as possible and accessible to the general Utah population and the schools of the state. Readers should not expect to find detailed family or town histories here, but, rather, selected examples and accounts of some of those who helped build the county.

Both authors have roots that go deep in Garfield County history. Vivian L. Talbot's father was born in Panguitch. One of her great-grandfathers was William Orton, an early county settler. Her husband was also born in Panguitch; his family was part of Panguitch's first and second settlement. Linda King Newell's grandfather George Davies and his first wife, who are buried in Escalante, raised ten children on Boulder and Escalante mountains. He later had the first U.S. mail contract between Junction and Escalante. Her grandmother Emma Carson Morrill Davies lived at the Blue Springs fish hatchery with her family early in the twentieth century. Several aunts and uncles made their homes in the county, and Linda grew up with fond memories of summer visits to Escalante to see Woolsey cousins. As a college student, she worked three summers at Bryce Canyon Lodge. Over the years, both authors have maintained a keen interest in Garfield County and its people.

This book could not have come to fruition had it not been for people from each town who gave us access to photographs, family histories, town histories, and other historical materials. They include Fay Jepsen of Boulder, June Shakespear of Tropic, Dorothy Leavett of Cannonville, Marilyn Jackson of Escalante, Beth Allred of Hatch, Dorothy Houston of Panguitch, Teora Willis and Jeanie Chynoweth of Henrieville, and Nancy Twitchell of Tropic. We thank each one for collecting, writing, and sharing so much information. We also thank Karl C. Sandberg for sharing his history of Widtsoe.

Garfield County Commissioner, Louise Liston, has been especially helpful and patient, as has Camille Moore and others who work in the county commissioners' offices, especially Donna Guida.

We appreciate the encouragement, help, and gentle prodding Kent Powell of the Utah State Historical Society has given us from the beginning. He and Craig Fuller started us out on firm ground by providing us with a list of historical sources that held information relevant to this project. We thank Richard A. Firmage for his fine editing of the manuscript.

Finally, we thank our husbands, Jack Newell and Grant Talbot, who have accompanied us on many research trips to Garfield County, offered suggestions on the manuscript, and, in Grant's case, researched many historical details we were able to include. We also appreciate their love and support throughout the entire project.

ENDNOTE

1. Marilyn Jackson, "The Unraveling of a 'Shurtz Tale': An Epoch of Escalante Excitement," 1994, unpublished manuscript in possession of authors.

GARFIELD COUNTY

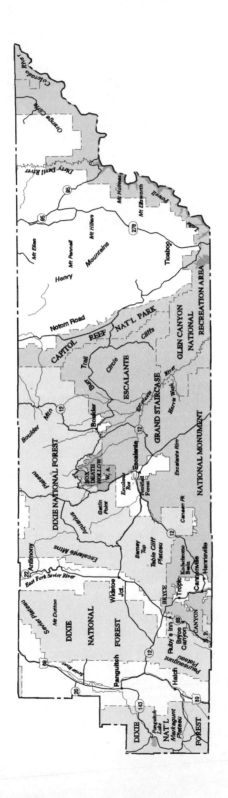

INDEX MAP

CHAPTER 1

SHAPING THE LAND

Garfield County as presently constituted is the fifth-largest Utah county in terms of land area, with 5,158 square miles, and claims both the Great Basin and the Colorado Plateau as part of its geological legacy. From the high country of Garfield's western lands tiny streams and springs give birth to the Sevier River, which gathers the interior waters of Utah's high plateaus into the Great Basin. The river's name is based on the Spanish name, *Rio Severo*, meaning severe and violent river—a suitable description for the sections of the river that tumble through rugged canyons on both ends of Garfield County.[1]

The longest river completely contained within the boundaries of a single state, the Sevier's main fork begins as a spring above Long Valley Junction in Kane County. It winds its way north through Garfield, Piute, and Sevier counties before curving south around the upper reaches of the Pahvant Range in Millard County to end in Sevier Lake. The lake is shallow, but it expands during occasional wet cycles; in drier years the river disappears into an alkaline flat. The

Sevier River drainage system marks a transition between the Great Basin and the Colorado Plateau physiographic provinces.

The Colorado Plateau begins near where the Wasatch Mountains end—at Mount Nebo in Juab County. From there it extends south into Arizona and east into Colorado. Plateau is a French word meaning a tray or flat place—a somewhat odd name for a region that has high country with altitudes of over 11,000 feet and canyons that plunge to 2,900 feet in elevation. The Colorado Plateau, however, was not so named because it is flat, but because of the general flatness of its underlying rock strata.[2] The streams and creeks that drain this region's high country feed into the Colorado River. There are plateaus on the Colorado Plateau with names like Sevier, Aquarius, Paunsaugunt, and Kaiparowits that extend into Garfield County, and mountains including Escalante, Boulder, and the Henrys.

Garfield County reaches to the heart of the Colorado Plateau, stretching from its western edge on the lip of the Great Basin to the Colorado River some 137 miles to the east. This strip of land, approximately forty-three miles from north to south, is known for its steep mesas, forested plateaus, imposing cliffs, barren slick rock, whimsical rock formations, and stream-cut gorges and canyons. It is diverse in its topography, magnificent in its scenery, and colorful both in its geology and its history.

The landscape itself tells the beginnings of that history, which goes back millions of years. Buried beneath Garfield County's Boulder and Escalante mountains are layers of rock laid down up to 550 million years ago by repeated encroachments of a great western sea, sedimentary erosion deposits carried and shaped by wind and water, and volcanic lava flows and intrusions. The Colorado River, which defines the county's eastern boundary, cuts through and reveals some 330 million years of rock deposits that form those layers.

A little over four miles above the northeast corner of Garfield County, the Green River joins the Colorado. These two grand rivers—indeed, the upper Colorado above the confluence was at first named the Grand River—begin high on the alpine ridges of the Continental Divide. The waters of the Green River flow from the Green Lakes in the Wind River Range of western Wyoming. The lofty peaks of Rocky Mountain National Park give birth to the upper Colorado River. Literally hundreds of springs, brooks, streams, creeks, and washes feed the rivers along their often meandering, sometimes raging, courses, cutting downward through millions of years of rock deposits. Major John Wesley Powell called the deep gorges of the Colorado River "a book of revelations in the rock-leaved Bible of geology," and he was "determined to read the book."[3]

The Paleozoic Era (570 to 245 Million Years Ago)

About 300 to 280 million years ago, toward the end of the Paleozoic (old life) era of geological reckoning, central and eastern Utah began to evolve from a relatively flat, water-covered, stable area to one of incredible activity. In just a few million years a huge mountain range, called the Ancestral Rocky Mountains, pushed up from the earth, extending from New Mexico to Wyoming. A branch of that range curved westward into east-central Utah to form the Uncompahgre Uplift, which rose to elevations of some 12,000 to 15,000 feet. As the range ascended, it displaced a vast sea that had washed back and forth across Utah for some 200 million years. As the sea receded, a huge basin, called the Paradox Basin, formed over central and southeastern Utah, roughly between the Uncompahgre Uplift and what is now the Waterpocket Fold region in Garfield County. An estuary of the Gulf of California extended northward to the Needles area in present-day Canyonlands National Park, on the San Juan County side of Cataract Canyon. Sediment from the rapid erosion of the Uncompahgre Uplift washed into the Paradox Basin, repeatedly depositing layers of limestone, sandstone, and shale, depending upon the nature of the environment over the millenia—limestone being generally deposited when the area was covered by water; sandstone being deposited from eroded sediments of the highlands surrounding the basin when it was dry land; shale, a hardened mud, during transition periods.[4] According to Utah geologist William Lee Stokes:

> The Paradox Basin was nearly hemmed in by highlands to the north, northeast, and east and by shallow barriers or sills along the other sides. . . . The rim of the southwestern margin of the basin, which is now known as the Four Corners area, was almost at sea

level, so any slight rise of the ocean allowed seawater to spill into
the basin and any lowering cut off the supply of water. The spill-
way was a favorable place for the growth of marine organisms
which tended to build up large banks or shoals of limy material.
The large amount of organic material also restricted circulation of
water in and out of the basin and later, when buried, became a
favorable reservoir for oil and gas.[5]

The diverse and abundant sea and plant life of the layer after
layer of rock laid down through this Pennsylvanian period of geological development is evident in Garfield County. The alternating
beds of sandstone and limestone, compressed by further deposits of
the geologic eras which followed, are visible today where the
Colorado River has carved Cataract Canyon to reveal a slice of
Garfield County's geological history. Displayed within its depths, near
where Gypsum Canyon enters from San Juan County, is the oldest
exposed rock in the county or, for that matter, in the three-county
area that includes all of Canyonlands National Park. These rocks
from the Pennsylvanian period were formed some 350 million years
ago. This same formation represents the youngest rocks on the rim
of the Grand Canyon as the Colorado River cuts farther south and
west.[6]

During this time, Garfield County, together with the entire
southwestern portion of present-day Utah, lay near the equator. The
sun beat fiercely on the land and sucked dry the water from the western bench regions of the Pacific Ocean that had washed over the area.
The moisture that fell on the Uncompahgre Uplift acted in concert
with the wind to erode the highlands and deposit their load in the
Paradox Basin, burying the remains of the earlier abundant plant and
animal life. Many fossils, including those of both vertebrates and
invertebrates, are found in the upper strata of the Paleozoic era
deposits.

Among the rock formations of the Permian period (285–245
million years ago)—the last 40 million years of the Paleozoic era—
Kaibab Limestone was formed. This formation, which contains oil
and natural gas, extends into the Upper Valley Oil Field of Garfield
County and the Virgin and Washington oil fields in Washington
County. The Upper Valley Field is located a few miles southwest of

the town of Escalante between Escalante Mountain and the Escalante Rim. It is estimated to hold approximately 25 million barrels of oil. In the White Rim Sandstone of Wayne and Garfield counties (located within a triangle formed by the Green, Colorado, and Dirty Devil rivers) is an extensive deposit of tar sands—oil impregnated sandstone. An estimated 6.5 billion barrels of oil, in strata from five feet to more than 300 feet thick, are trapped in this porous rock.[7] The modern-day importance of these deposits will be discussed in a later chapter.

Mesozoic Era (245 to 66 Million Years Ago)

During the early part of the Mesozoic (middle life) era the ancient Pacific Ocean continued its periodic spread inland over broad mud flats to lap at the edge of the Ancestral Rockies. Then the sea, which had moved back and forth across most of Utah for the previous 300 million years, slowly withdrew to the western boundary of present-day Garfield County. This was the beginning of a gradual 220-million-year shift of the Pacific coastline to its current location. A barrier of some sort—perhaps mountains, low hills or even a gradual bulging of the earth's crust—developed along eastern Nevada, keeping the ocean back and forming a semienclosed basin between the barrier and the Ancestral Rockies. For the first time in some 230 million years, none of Garfield County was submerged by the sea.

As the climate warmed, the land dried again. During the Triassic period—from 245 million to 208 million years ago—the prevailing north and northwesterly winds moved, rearranged, and sculpted enormous sand dunes, forming a Sahara-like desert that extended from central Utah far into Colorado, Arizona, and New Mexico. Canyonlands National Park boasts some of the most conspicuous displays of rock from this period found anywhere in the state. Virtually all the deeper gorges as well as the access roads in the park negotiate through the red and white sandstone formations from this period. The same formations continue along the Colorado River for the length of the entire eastern boundary of Garfield County—from Cataract Canyon through the Circle Cliffs.[8]

A wetter climate returned for a time, and streams meandered through the canyon country of southern Utah. Shallow lakes and

Ripple rock found along the Waterpocket Fold in Garfield County. (Utah State Historical Society)

mud flats left deposits of silt which eventually hardened into sedimentary rock known as the Moenkopi Formation—reddish brown shale, gypsum, sandstones, and "ripple rock." Exposed portions of this formation cut across Garfield County from the Circle Cliffs in Kane County northwest along the Waterpocket Fold into Wayne County. Tracks of small lizard-like reptiles can be found in the Moenkopi Formation.

About 220 million years ago a mudstone called Chinle Shale began to form. Volcanos spewed ash and rock over the area, covering and eventually helping petrify some of the trees, some of which can be found along the Circle Cliffs. In the younger deposits of Chinle Shale and Kayenta Sandstone, dinosaur tracks become more common, their size increasing over time. Some stream channels cut during this time yield uranium deposits. A number of these deposits occur in the Shinarump Conglomerate in the Circle Cliffs.

The wind and water erosion of the Ancestral Rockies east of

Garfield County and the Mesocordilleran Highlands in western Utah provided much of the Triassic sediment of the Colorado Plateau 245 to 208 million years ago. The volume of eroded material was so immense that, according to one researcher, it "not only filled and smoothed over the ancient Paradox Basin, but also began to bury the mountains themselves. By the close of the Triassic Period no surface remnants of the Uncompahgre Uplift remained in Utah."[9]

Triassic formations of both hard and soft layers are found, with the harder rock forming cliffs and the softer deposits creating slopes of eroded material. Wingate Sandstone, the most prominent of the harder formations, is evident as the highest ridge along the Waterpocket Fold. It forms miles of nearly impenetrable cliffs surrounding the Burr Trail as well as those that cross the Flint and Shafer trails in Canyonlands National Park. Chimney Rock Canyon in the Garfield section of Capitol Reef National Park provides another example of Wingate Sandstone. Below the Wingate cliffs, a plateau of Kayenta Sandstone extends along the white cliffs of Capitol Reef.

During the next 64 million years, which encompasses the Jurassic period of the Mesozoic era, three distinct environments succeeded one another, each leaving its geological mark on the Garfield landscape. First came another period of a dry desert environment, where winds sculpted sand dunes of enormous size. Continental drift slowly rotated and moved the land northward, far from its original latitude. The dunes became the cross-bedded Navajo Sandstone, white to pink in color, that dominates the scenery of the present-day Escalante-Boulder road and extends the length of the Escalante River. The Glen Canyon rock formations also came from this period, as did the Great White Throne in Zion National Park and Rainbow Natural Bridge.

In the second phase, a radical change in the environment took place as a great sea descended from Canada to cover the dunes and deposit a layer of Carmel Limestone. This layer thins considerably as one moves east until it disappears at the Colorado River. Erosion has exposed it from Cannonville and Henrieville south, and then west through Kane County. It is also evident in highway cuts on the eastern edge of Boulder Mountain toward Hanksville and near the Singletree Campground. The Hole-in-the-Rock road follows a backbone of Carmel Limestone from the present-day town of Escalante to the Colorado River.

The third phase brought a warm tropical climate that resulted in the Morrison Formation, which at one time covered an estimated 750,000 square miles of the western United States. Salt Wash Sandstone and Brushy Shale are two prominent subdivisions of the Morrison Formation in Utah. Within the Salt Wash Sandstone are found significant uranium deposits on the Colorado Plateau. A strip of Brushy Shale lies along the eastern flank of the Henry Mountains. It was in this third phase that the dinosaurs flourished, although they had existed for millions of years previously. The Morrison Formation is probably the most-studied geological formation in the world due to the great number, variety, and importance of its fossils.

An episode of uplifting, or mountain building, called the Sevier Orogeny occurred during the latter part of the Mesozoic era. The relatively narrow uplift stretched from southwestern Utah and eastern Nevada to Idaho and Wyoming. It is most striking along the Sevier River Valley, from which the orogeny takes its name. Immense slabs of rock, thousands of feet thick, pushed from west to east across the underlying formations. According to one geologist:

> As the great sheets of rock slowly moved over the material beneath them, they bent, buckled, and cracked until they came to rest as a shattered and contorted mass. New thrust faults periodically developed beneath older ones and the whole stacked sequence would move again. One by one, over millions of years, sheets of tortured rock piled one upon another like the shingles on a roof.[10]

About 140 million years ago the last invading sea came in from the east and southeast, dividing North and South America into separate land masses. Stretching from the western Sevier River Valley to the Mississippi River, this sea pushed, flattened, and covered vegetation, sand, and mud while depositing sediments.[11] The sand and mud would become the Dakota Formation, exposed in a narrow strip along the Waterpocket Fold and circling east to the Henry Mountains. It is also the oldest rock visible in Bryce Canyon, where it is between 200 and 300 feet thick and dates back 95 million years. The Bryce formation is not actually a canyon; it is a series of fourteen large amphitheaters intricatly carved from the Paunsaugunt Plateau to depths of 1,000 feet or more. Fossils in the Dakota Formation at Bryce tell the story of the area's evolving plant and animal life, with evidence of a wide variety of vegetation, snails, clams, fish, turtles, crocodiles, and small primitive rodent-like mammals.[12]

The lush vegetation also formed seams of coal. An estimated three to seven billion tons of coal are believed by some to be in the Kaiparowits coal fields of Garfield and Kane counties. Another large coal field is in the Henry Mountain area. The sea's shores periodic advance and retreat over millions of years resulted in alternate layers of shale and coal in the area today. As the streams and rivers flowing from the highlands on the western edge of Garfield County deposited their loads of sediment in the sea, the smallest particles washed farther out to settle into the mud of the deep sea. These deposits became the Tropic Shale that forms the natural huge amphitheater where the towns of Tropic, Cannonville and Henrieville are located today. Coal seams left by luxuriant vegetation also appear between layers of the shale in this area, indicating the periodic rise and fall of the water.

During one of the periods of shallow seas about 85 million years ago, the Straight Cliffs Formation began as sandy beaches on top of the Tropic deposits. Later layers came from brackish swamps, riverbeds, and floodplains. As the sea periodically receded and advanced it washed sand along its shores, which became Wahweap Sandstone. In making its final retreat, the ocean left shifting river systems, swamps, and alluvial plains throughout eastern Utah that continued to shape the landscape. Snow high on the Sevier Orogenic Belt to the west melted into braided streams and rivers, carrying debris and sediment across vast floodplains to bury the Wahweap Sandstone and create the Kaiparowits formation of Bryce Canyon and the Kaiparowits Plateau. (Kaiparowits is said to be an Indian word, and it appears to have a number of meanings, depending on which tribal interpretation is used. The most common translation is "Big Mountain's Little Brother"; another is "Home of our People." A third is "One-Arm," a name given to Major John Wesley Powell, who lost an arm at the Battle of Shiloh during the Civil War. Novelist Zane Gray's Wild Horse Mesa is said to be the Kaiparowits Plateau.)[13]

At Bryce, most of the sandstones that covered the Tropic Shale

during this period have been stripped away by erosion. Only a few
outcrops of Straight Cliffs Formation, Wahweap Sandstone, and
Kaiparowits deposits remain at the lower levels in the southern part
of the national park. They appear as brownish-gray rock and sediment interspersed in layers of sandstone and mudstone; but they record an ancient and strikingly different landscape from the cool high
plateaus and vibrant canyons of today.

These rocks reveal an ancient coastal lowland where rivers flowed
east into the vast sea. Small dinosaurs wandered along the rivers
through lush jungle, feeding on primitive plants, each other, and
other animals. Insects buzzed while furry rodent-like mammals
escaped the heat of the tropical sun and the humid air in burrows
and under lush foliage. Turtles alternately sunned themselves on rot-
ting logs and wandered through the ooze of the swamps.[14]

Cenozoic Era (66 Million to the Present)

During the transition between the Mesozoic (middle life) and
Cenozoic (new life) eras, the dinosaurs disappeared from the surface
of the earth. No one knows with certainty what catastrophe killed
these huge reptiles some 65 million years ago, but, whatever it was, it
affected the entire planet for tens of thousands of years. Clam fossils
from 106 locations around the world indicate that some 70 percent
of the mollusk species were wiped out at nearly the same rate from
New Zealand to Alaska during the same period that the dinosaurs
disappeared.[15]

Meanwhile, other forces were acting to further shape Garfield
County. The first 30 million years of the Cenozoic era were marked
by the rise of Capitol Reef, the Waterpocket Fold, the Circle Cliffs,
and the San Rafael Swell. The Uinta Mountains in northeastern Utah
also were lifted during this time, with lakes forming between them
and the Colorado-Wyoming Rockies. As the mountains eroded, they
provided sediment that entered the lake bottoms, and some sediment
washed south to Garfield County as the river systems continued to
develop.

The fanciful towers, castles, rock gardens, and pillars carved by
wind and water from the multicolored Claron Formation deposits at
Bryce Canyon began between 50 and 60 million years ago. A long,

Bryce Canyon formations. (Utah State Historical Society)

narrow body of water referred to as Flagstaff Lake extended from the Uinta Basin south between the San Rafael Swell and Circle Cliffs uplift and the Sevier Orogeny. Either an arm of Flagstaff Lake or another lake of this same period extended over much of present-day Washington County. Equally large bodies of water also were located in Wyoming and Colorado. The few scattered fossils in the resulting rock formation from the period are predominantly freshwater snails and clams. Pink sandstone layers interspersed through the Claron Formation were most likely laid down during dry periods when evaporation took more water out than the streams provided. During these times of a low water level, the rivers and streams washed sand and gravel over the earlier muddy limestone deposits.

The Claron formations of Bryce Canyon and Cedar Breaks have their genesis in the deposits washed into these ancient lakes. The pink hues come from iron oxide and manganese in these sediments. For millions of years, the lakes repeatedly contracted and expanded, leaving a diverse rock record. Differences in the rate of weathering produces parallel grooving in the rocks. Layers richest in lime are more resilient to erosion and form ridges, while the lime-poor beds are more indented and eroded.

About 40 million years ago molten rock from deep within the earth combined with and melted light-colored continental rock, producing a silica-laden magma that built into great volcanos. Massive eruptions from these volcanos rained ash across the landscape of western North America. Smaller volcanic intrusions, some of them rich with copper, iron, gold, silver, and other ores, began to push upward. Volcanos spilled ash and lava, while Utah and the surrounding regions begin to bow upwards, lifting slowly to some 5,000 feet above sea level.

As the plateaus pushed upwards, the Colorado River and its tributaries cut downward into their canyons. Lava flows that covered the Markagunt (Paiute for high land of trees), Sevier, and Aquarius plateaus provided them with a hard basalt protective cover, guarding them against the massive erosion taking place to the south and east. In the middle of this volcanic activity, clusters of volcanos pushed up through the underlying sedimentary rocks.[16] The Henry Mountains were thus born, as were the La Sal Mountains near Moab, Navajo Mountain south of Lake Powell, and the Abajo Mountains west of Monticello.

The Henry Mountains rise from the center of the triangular land mass formed by the meeting of the Colorado River and the Waterpocket Fold to the south and the Wayne County line to the north. They are not a range but are simply a group of five individual mountains formed by small igneous intrusions that punched through the older layers of rock 25 million to 35 million years ago. The distance between the northernmost peak of Mount Ellen to the southernmost summit of Mount Ellsworth is only about thirty miles. A circle of eighteen miles radius includes the whole group.

The most northerly and highest of the Henry Mountains is Mount Ellen (elevation 11,508 feet). From its two-mile crestline spurs descend in every direction. To the south, lies the 7,857 foot Penellen Pass from which Mount Pennell rises to 11,232 feet. Both mountains are guarded on their west flanks by a continuous ridge of exposed Navajo sandstone. On the southeastern side, Mount Pennell slopes to the Pennell Creek Bench, which separates it from Mount Hillers (elevation 10,650 feet). Mount Holmes (7,930 feet) and Mount Ellsworth (8,150 feet) stand close together at the southernmost end of the Henry Mountains on the brink of the Colorado River.[17]

The fissures on Mt. Ellen and Mt. Pennell have produced small amounts of copper with gold. Some gravel washed from the mountains contain bits of placer gold. The uranium and vanadium ores in the area predated the volcanic activity.

The Henry Mountain peaks of today project high enough above the desert floor to wring out what moisture is left after clouds cross the high plateaus to the west, giving them a comparatively generous supply of rain. The slopes of the highest peaks are rich with vegetation and timber, and springs abound from their flanks. The smaller mountains and the foothills are less generously watered and have few plants.

About 24 million years ago, block- and detachment faulting began, and the Hurricane, Wasatch, and Sevier faults developed.[18] The Duchesne and White rivers that began on the southern slope of the Uinta Range, and the Gunnison River of the Rockies, all drained into the Henry Mountains Basin and south into the Kaiparowits Basin.

Panguitch Valley was formed when the Sevier Fault split the Markagunt Plateau on the west and the Paunsaugunt Plateau on the east. The valley between provided a natural course for the Sevier River and its tributaries. Much of the land today consists of alluvial deposits; the valley is strewn with volcanic stones and rubble washed from above. There is, however, about 7,000 acres of good bottomland composed of the rich silt deposited in the valley by the gentler currents of the Sevier River.

The area that stretches directly east from the Sevier River consists of high tableland that were fractured and lifted from the valley floor by the great faults. The plateaus include areas that range from 400 to 1,800 square miles and rise to more than 11,500 feet in elevation. They provide long barriers along the valleys that stretch for miles. Masses of volcanic rock, sometimes reaching a thickness of 5,000 feet, cap these great tablelands. Some of the underlying sedimentary layers are so deeply buried that they are seen only in the deepest gorges.

Toward the end of the Tertiary period (around 5 million years

ago), the Green River reached the Canyonlands area and flowed into
the Henry Mountains Basin, spilling over on the south end. As the
river began its downward cut through the multiple layers of Mesozoic
and Paleozoic rock, the Colorado Plateau began a slow tilt upward to
the north, due to great pressures from deep inside the earth. As the
slope of the land increased, the Colorado River, no longer slowed by
huge lakes, became one of the "most erosive streams on earth."[19] Two
million years ago, it began carving its inner gorge.

The river's tributaries also became highly erosive, cutting deeper
and deeper into the land as they moved to join the Colorado. The
most prominent of these streams in Garfield County are (from north
to south) the Dirty Devil, North Wash, Hall's Creek, and the
Escalante River. Along their routes a landscape of Navajo Sandstone
stands nearly naked, stripped by erosion of its Jurassic, Cretaceous,
and Tertiary period rocks.

The Escalante Basin extends in a southeasterly direction to the
Colorado River, between the Straight Cliffs and the Kaiparowits
Plateau to the south and the Circle Cliffs and the Aquarius Plateau to
the north. The majestic Aquarius Plateau with its Boulder Mountain
rises over 9,670 feet, making it one of the world's highest forested
plateaus. The Escalante River extends more than a hundred miles to
the Colorado River (although the distance actually is closer to fifty
miles as the crow flies) through some of the most spectacular, least-
explored country in the continental United States.[20]

The Garfield Landscape Today

A large network of nearly two dozen creeks and washes mean-
ders into the Escalante River, forming the Escalante Basin. Those on
the southwest beginning at the town of Escalante down to the
Colorado River are Phipps Canyon, Harris Wash, Collett Wash,
Scorpion Gulch, Fools Canyon, Coyote Gulch, Willow Gulch, Soda
Gulch, Davis Gulch, Clear Creek, and Indian Gulch. From the
Colorado River back toward town are Fence Canyon, Cow Canyon,
Stevens Canyon, Georgie Canyon, Lower (East) Moody Canyon,
Upper (Middle) Moody Canyon, Wide Mouth, Silver Falls Canyon,
Horse Canyon, The Gulch, Deer Canyon, Boulder Creek, Calf Creek,

Cottonwood Canyon, Osbourne Canyon, Sand Creek, Death Hollow, and Pine Creek.

The wanderings of these watercourses through the cross-bedded Navajo Sandstone have resulted in giant alcoves, box canyons, gorges, waterfalls, natural bridges, and arches. The natural bridges and arches are Escalante Natural Bridge on the south wall of Escalante Canyon just south of Sand Creek; Maverick Natural Bridge in a tributary canyon of Phipps Canyon; Phipps Arch in Phipps Canyon; Stevens Arch (the largest in the Escalante Basin), at the mouth of Stevens Canyon; Lobo Arch in Coyote Canyon; Coyote Bridge a mile farther downstream; and, about four miles farther, Jug Handle Arch; Broken Bow Arch, on the north wall of Willow Gulch; and Nemo Arch and Moqui Window in Davis Gulch. Today the canyon floors harbor wildflowers and grasses, ferns and willows, trees and shrubs, and have become a haven for hikers.

The climate of Garfield County ranges considerably from the high Escalante and Boulder mountains to the canyon depths. The prevailing western winds traveling across the Great Basin are forced to altitudes of over 10,000 feet as they cross the plateaus of Garfield County. The highlands act to condensate the moisture and extract it from the wind-driven clouds. Descending from the higher lands into the warmer regions below, the now-dry winds actually extract moisture from the lower altitudes rather than adding to the humidity.[21]

The rainfall in the inhabited valleys of Garfield County is variable from year to year and place to place, but it is sparse compared to that received by the plateaus, requiring irrigation for lawns, gardens, and farms in the summer months. The average valley precipitation is around twelve inches a year, with an average low of about seven inches and the average high between fourteen and twenty-two inches. The plateaus act as reservoirs to collect the precipitation; the water then makes its way to the Sevier and Colorado rivers in scores of rivulets and creeks. Numerous springs, fed by the rain and snow in the high country, dot the base of the plateaus.[22]

Temperatures average between 30 and 40 degrees Fahrenheit in winter and 85–90 degrees in the summer at the towns of Boulder and Escalante. The Tropic, Henrieville, and Cannonville areas tend to be a bit warmer year-round, while Panguitch is often colder. Temperatures there can vary as much as fifty or sixty degrees in a single day. One early resident of Panguitch maintained with a wink that Panguitch was not as cold as everyone said it was—he could only remember one summer when there were no leaves on the trees.[23] Others have commented that the climate there is "nine months of winter and three months of damned cold weather." A mid-century traveler through the valley wrote that Panguitch is "where in summer they have the best winter climate in the world."[24] While exaggeration is the prerogative of old-timers, the official record shows a more realistic, but still cold, picture. Panguitch is subject to a relatively dry northwesterly flow and is surrounded by mountains and highlands that take much of the remaining precipitation and keep the valley area drier than might be expected for such a high elevation. Still, the climate can be most harsh—temperatures can drop to a low of thirty or more degrees below zero in winter and soar to the nineties in summer, and summer frost is not uncommon. Mean low temperatures in January are about 5–6 degrees, with highs averaging 38 degrees. In July average highs are in the low 80-degree range, lows average 45 degrees. The growing season is short, with only an average of 76 consecutive frost-free days.[25]

The high plateaus receive about twenty-five inches of moisture a year. Although the first major snow usually falls in late September or early October, snowfall has occurred in all twelve months. Patches of snow commonly are still evident in late June. Violent summer thunderstorms and severe lightning often accompanied by hail are not uncommon and can cause dangerous flash floods in the washes of the dry desert below.

Large mammals such as mule deer, elk, antelope, black bear and cougar make their homes on the higher tablelands in summer, many of them migrating to lower elevations in the winter to find feed. Beaver lodges dam small streams, while coyotes and bobcats range widely. Marmots, rabbits, weasels, chipmunks, skunks, and ground squirrels are also common. The last free-roaming herd of buffalo in America make their home in the Henry Mountains at the present time.

Among the many birds of Garfield County, both bald and golden eagles are occasionally seen soaring high above the landscape.

Goshawks also thrive in the forested areas. Merriam turkeys, an introduced game species, live on the east side of Boulder Mountain. Brook, rainbow, and cutthroat trout are plentiful in the county's lakes and streams, while hybrid species have been planted in Blind and Cooks lakes. Mosquitos and horseflies torment hunters, fishermen, campers, and hikers in the high wet places, while scorpions keep them alert in the drier lowlands. Rattlesnakes can be found from mountaintop to canyon bottom.

The vegetation of areas is influenced by both altitude and availability of water. In the lower desert areas where water is scarce, so is plant life; plants there include sagebrush, various cacti, paintbrush, rabbitbrush, ricegrass, ephedra, and other plant life common to the western deserts. In the deep canyons where streams and springs run most of the year, wildflowers, grasses, and watercress are often found. Between 5,000 and 7,000 feet elevation the landscape changes. A variety of small bushes and shrubs intermingles with the sagebrush and rabbitbrush. Blackbrush and shadscale become common. Greasewood grows in the more saline low areas. Utah juniper begins at around the 5,000-foot elevation and is joined by pinyon pine at about 6,000 feet. A transition zone of western yellow pine and gambel oak starts at around 6,800 feet, and by 8,000 feet Douglas fir and white fir flourish. Narrowleaf cottonwood, red-barked birch, and chokecherry thrive along the edge of streams. Transition-zone shrubs include antelope brush, manzanita, serviceberry, and big sagebrush.

Between 8,000 and 9,500 feet in elevation aspen, blue spruce, white fir, and Douglas fir are the most common trees. In a few places limber pine, a particularly hardy high-altitude species, spreads its rugged branches. Shrubs include the hardy chokecherry and snowberry. At elevations above 9,500 feet only the most rugged, storm-resistant trees survive: alpine fir, Englemann spruce, limber pine, and the granddaddy of all trees, the bristlecone pine. In the Great Basin bristlecones can be found at scattered high elevations, and some bristlecones are more than 4,600 years old—the oldest-known living things on earth. Dendrochronologists have located even older dead bristlecone pines in California and Nevada, with rings dating back more than 12,000 years, making them contemporaries of the Paleo-Indians who roamed the Garfield landscape in millenia past.

ENDNOTES

1. John W. Van Cott, *Utah Place Names* (Salt Lake City: University of Utah Press, 1990), 335. Both Van Cott and Halka Chronic in *Roadside Geology of Utah* (Missoula, MT: Mountain Press Publishing Company, 1990) note that some sources incorrectly credit Brigadier General John Sevier of Kentucky as namesake of the Sevier River.

2. Dean L. May, *Utah: A People's History* (Salt Lake City: University of Utah Press, 1987), 8–9.

3. Mary C. Rabbit, "John Wesley Powell: Pioneer Statesman of Federal Science," *The Colorado River Region and John Wesley Powell,* Geological Survey Prefessional Paper 669 (Washington, D.C.: United States Government Printing Office,1969), 3.

4. William E. Stokes, *Geology of Utah* (Salt Lake City: Utah Museum of Natural History/Utah Geological and Mineral Survey, 1988), 86.

5. Ibid., 87.

6. For seventy miles above the confluence of the Green and Colorado rivers, the Colorado meanders, dropping an average of only 1.3 feet per mile. Through forty-mile-long Cataract Canyon the river follows a more direct course, dropping an average of ten feet per mile. Before the construction of Glen Canyon Dam, as the river left Cataract Canyon near the southeastern corner of Garfield County, its course again slowed and twisted, dropping only about 1.5 feet per mile for another 180 miles through Glen Canyon on its way to the Grand Canyon.

7. Stokes, *Geology of Utah,* 103. See also Bradley G. Hill and S. Robert Bereskin, eds., "Oil and Gas Fields of Utah," Utah Geological Association Publication No. 22, Salt Lake City (1993).

8. Stokes, *Geology of Utah,* 101.

9. Ibid., 105–6.

10. Nicholas Scrattish, *Historic Resource Study: Bryce Canyon National Park* (Denver: United States Department of the Interior, 1986), 2–4.

11. Stokes, *Geology of Utah,* 132.

12. Scrattish, *Historic Resource Study: Bryce Canyon,* 2–4.

13. Van Cott, *Utah Place Names,* 211.

14. Scrattish, *Historic Resource Study: Bryce Canyon,* 2–4.

15. David Jablonski and David M. Raup, "Selectivity End-Cretaceous Bivalve Extinctions," *Science* 268 (21 April 1995): 389–91.

16. Grove Karl Gilbert, *Geology of the Henry Mountains* (Washington, D.C.: Government Printing Office, 1880), called the mountains laccolites (more commonly known as laccoliths). Although Mount Hillers is a true laccolith, the other four peaks are stocks. Stokes, *Geology of Utah,* 185.

17. Gilbert, *Geology of the Henry Mountains,* 2–3.

18. Block faults are where a block of the earth's surface has two or more sides on which breaks, or faults, occur. Detached faults run nearly horizontal and are usually formed by the down-thrust of regular faults, causing the upper crust to slide across lower rocks. See Chronic, *Roadside Geology,* 302–3.

19. Stokes, *Geology of Utah,* 191.

20. Much of the information for the Escalante Basin comes from the chapter written by Edson B. Alvy in Nethella Griffin Woolsey, *The Escalante Story: 1875–1964* (Springville, UT: Art City Publishing Co., 1964), 1–18.

21. John Wesley Powell, *Report on the Lands of the Arid Region: With a More Detailed Account of the Lands of Utah* (Washington, D.C.: Government Printing Office, 1879), 151.

22. Ibid., 130–36.

23. As told to Linda K. Newell by her father, Foisy E. King.

24. Walter Kirk Daly, "The Settling of Panguitch Valley, Utah: A Study in Mormon Colonization" (Master's thesis, University of California, 1941), 23.

25. Mark Eubank, *Utah Weather* (Salt Lake City: Weatherbank, Inc., 1979), 217.

CHAPTER 2

The Ancient Ones

PREHISTORIC AND HISTORIC
NATIVE AMERICANS

As early as 12,000 years ago humans inhabited Garfield County and the surrounding area of the American Southwest.[1] A variety of cultures have come and gone, including the Paleo-Indian big-game hunters (12,000–7,000 B.P),[2] the Archaic hunter-gatherers (8,000 B.P.–A.D. 500), the agricultural Fremont and Anasazi cultures (A.D. 200–1300), and the Ute and Paiute peoples during more recent time periods. Cultural stages in which these prehistoric peoples traversed the mountains and canyons of the Garfield landscape are known to researchers as the Paleo-Indian, Archaic, Formative, and Protohistoric stages. Although archaeologists assign dates to various cultural periods, these dates are considered general in nature, as prehistoric peoples did not wake up one morning and decide to alter their culture and economy. Change in some cases may have been abrupt, but most cultural and economic changes likely took place over many generations.

Paleo-Indian Period: 12,000–7,000 B.P.

The term Paleo-Indian refers to people of Asian origin whose

20

ancestors crossed the Bering Strait land bridge between modern-day Siberia and Alaska sometime before the end of the last Ice Age 12,000 years ago. Divided chronologically into three subphases, the Paleo-Indian period includes the Llano (12,000–10,500 B.P.), Folsom (11,000–9,000 B.P.), and Plano (9,500–7,000 B.P.) subphases.[3]

Evidence of the Paleo-Indian period in central and southern Utah is scarce, consisting mostly of isolated artifacts. To date, there is little evidence of their long-term occupation in Garfield County, but Paleo-Indian projectile points found in the San Rafael Swell area, southeastern Utah, and near the Circle Cliffs just east of Boulder, imply that these people passed through the future county's region. Folsom point fragments have also been found near Escalante. In addition, collectors reportedly have found Folsom points near the town of Koosharem, fifty miles northwest of Boulder.[4]

The Llano subphase is characterized by the Clovis projectile point, distinctive long spearheads named for the New Mexico site where they were discovered. Since the Clovis point is a unique artifact used by Clovis hunters, the Llano culture is often referred to as the Clovis culture, evident throughout much of the Intermountain West and southwestern United States.[5] Many of the excavated Clovis sites outside of Utah have yielded the remains of mammoths, but no such association between mammoths and Clovis people has been verified in the state. Rock art sites in Garfield County, however, depict mammoth-like figures, suggesting that humans and mammoths inhabited the region during the same time period.[6] Two such pictographs are found between the Escalante River and Fifty Mile Mountain.[7] Clovis people also subsisted on other animals, including bison, horses, camels, wolves, saber-toothed tigers, sloths, antelope, bears, and jackrabbits, as well as a variety of plants.[8] Little is known about Clovis social organization, but evidence suggests that Clovis peoples likely traveled in small bands of related individuals following the movements of herds they hunted.

The Folsom subphase followed the Llano, with some overlap in time, and is characterized by a change in primary prey from mammoth to bison, and a change in artifact technology. The Folsom projectile points are smaller than the Clovis; they are also thinner and have a more pronounced concave base and basal ears.

Fremont Pictographs in North Wash near Hog Spring. (Utah State Historical Society)

In many areas of the United States, although not in Utah, Folsom points are often found with kill sites of the extinct longhorn bison. In Utah, however, there are widely scattered sites where Folsom or Clovis points have been found, including Garfield County in the upper region of the Escalante River drainage system and near the confluence of the Dirty Devil and Colorado rivers.[9]

Subsistence during the Plano subphase remained similar to that of the Folsom—primarily big game with an emphasis on bison. Two characteristics, however, separate the Plano from the Folsom culture: the use of mass-kill hunting techniques and the introduction of new varieties of projectile points. Mass kills involved driving a herd of bison over a cliff, into a box canyon, or into other natural traps. This technique required greater cooperation than did those hunting methods employed by Clovis or Folsom hunters. The amount of meat and hides obtained from mass kills must have been astounding at times. For example, of about 200 bison killed on one occasion, about seventy-five percent of the skeletons show evidence of the animals being butchered. This hunt probably yielded over twenty-six tons of meat, two tons of edible internal organs, and nearly three tons of fat, without taking into account the weight of the hides.[10] It is not surprising that the two most plentiful bison species of the period became extinct during the Plano subphase, giving way to the surviving modern bison.[11]

Archaic Period: 8,000 B.P.–A.D. 500

Archaic refers both to a period of time and a way of life. As the climate became more arid through the Paleo-Indian period and into the Archaic period, vegetation patterns and animal distributions came to approximate those of today, and the Archaic peoples exploited a larger variety of local plant, animal, and other natural resources. Thus, the term "hunters and gatherers" is often used to describe Archaic peoples.

Based on stone-tool analyses, Archaic cultures appear to have occupied the Escalante River drainage for a considerable time. Interestingly however, archaeological studies of the Glen Canyon area and the Escalante River indicate that this part of the state was not intensely occupied until late in the Archaic period.[12] Archaic peoples lived and worked in small, kin-related groups, following annual or seasonal migration patterns of game animals and the availability of plant food. The variety of resources they used is reflected in the Archaic people's tool kit. Small grinding stones, manos and metates, as well as mortars and pestles, were used in processing plant foods. Archaic people made a great variety of projectile points and stone tools, as well as rope, mats, sandals, harpoons, fish hooks, snares, baskets, nets, split-twig figurines, and other items from plant and animal materials.

Another tool used by Archaic people was the atlatl, or spear thrower. There is evidence of its existence in Europe as early as 25,000 years ago, and it was likely a weapon of the New World Paleo-Indians. Because Archaic peoples used dry cave sites, many atlatl specimens from this period have been preserved in them.

A basic atlatl resembles a giant crochet hook, and the tool varied in length between fourteen and twenty-eight inches. A dart or spear could be fitted into the hook or notch near the far end. The handle often had finger holes or leather loops to help keep the atlatl in the hand during a throw, propelling a spear much farther and harder than was possible with a human arm alone. Atlatl darts or spears were usually made in two parts, the main shaft and the foreshaft. The foreshaft was shorter and held the projectile point, fitting into a socket drilled in the main shaft. When the point penetrated an animal, the main shaft would fall away and could be retrieved by the hunter and refitted with another foreshaft for a second shot. A fletching of feathers was glued or tied to the shaft for more accurate flight.[13]

During the Archaic period tool types varied substantially because of regional differences in resources and strategies for obtaining food. The large number of projectile points from this period indicates that these early people were relatively numerous and widespread on the Paunsaugunt Plateau between 8,000 and 1,500 years ago.[14] Caves and rock shelters were important places of abode for the Archaic people. Prime locations in Garfield County included Captains Alcove, Dust Devil Cave, and Sand Dune Cave, located south and southeast of the Circle Cliffs.

Maize agriculture was introduced to the area sometime between 3,500 and 2,500 years ago, probably from Arizona and northern Mexico. Although hunting and gathering activities of the Archaic people continued in scattered areas of the Colorado Plateau region, the cultivation of corn and squash increased, requiring a more sedentary life. The adoption of agriculture brought to a close the Archaic culture in Garfield County, the Colorado Plateau, and the Southwest.[15]

Formative Period: A.D. 200–1300— Anasazi and Fremont Cultures

The Formative, or Late Prehistoric, period, in the Southwest refers to the block of time between the introduction of pottery and the development of the bow and arrow (about A.D. 200–500) and the advent of the Protohistoric period (about A.D. 1300). The Formative period is characterized by more sedentary cultures, population growth, the appearance of villages, and an agricultural economy supplemented by hunting and gathering. Its technological innovations included ceramic vessels, adobe and masonry structures, and irrigation agriculture.[16]

Although Formative cultures in the Southwest include a number of diverse and widespread groups, two particular cultures inhabited the Escalante River drainage and surrounding area—the Anasazi and the Fremont. The Coombs Site in Boulder, now the Anasazi Indian Village State Park, lies in a transitional zone between the Virgin and Kayenta Anasazi and the San Rafael Fremont peoples.

Anasazi is derived from a Navajo word meaning "Ancient Tribe," "Ancient Ones," or "Enemy Ancestors."[17] The Navajo understood that an older people had inhabited the Southwest and that these people were somehow foreign to them. What the Anasazi called themselves, however, is lost in time. There is no clear history of the term Moqui Indians, the namesake of the Escalante High School mascot and numerous canyon-wall storage structures, often referred to by locals as Moqui houses. References to "Moqui houses" or "Moqui steps" more accurately refer to structures built by prehistoric peoples of the Anasazi and Fremont cultures.

Within the Anasazi and Fremont cultures there is a sequence of development and economic activity—a progression from hunting and gathering to increasing dependence on domesticated crops; the increased use of color to enhance the aesthetics of their pottery; trade expansion; and the adoption of corn, beans, squash, and other culti-vated crops. Nevertheless, the earlier Archaic activities of harvesting plants, hunting animals, and collecting raw materials also continued to be practiced.[18]

A number of general characteristics help define the Anasazi. Their use of pottery probably came through contact with the Mogollon culture farther to the south. The most common pottery construction was a method with the inside and outside surfaces scraped smooth. The pots were gray initially, with designs of black paint added later. The Anasazi also developed white pottery, either produced by reducing air flow during firing or from the application of a white slip. As expertise increased, some areas began producing black-on-red, black-on-orange, red-on-orange, and several combi-nations of these colors to produce a multicolored pottery. By about A.D. 1000 gray pots exhibit a textured, corrugated surface. The inte-rior surfaces of the vessel were scraped smooth, but exteriors retained the corrugated pattern of pinched construction coils.[19] At Coombs

Village is found a variety of pottery made by Anasazi people living along the Virgin River drainage, pottery made by Kayenta Anasazi of northeastern Arizona, pottery from the Chaco and Mesa Verde Anasazi from the Four Corners regions, and pottery from the Sevier and Emery Fremont cultures of central Utah.[20]

Although dry farming, which relied on direct rainfall, was common, the Anasazi also often placed garden plots in areas where runoff from showers would supplement normal precipitation. The Anasazi also developed ditches, check-dams, and other water-control devices to lessen the uncertainty of farming in marginal environments. The remnants of many of these earthworks have been identified from aerial photographs. Boulder Creek, Harris Wash, and other well-watered and fertile areas of the upper Escalante River provided excellent locations for Anasazi and Fremont people to establish small horticultural villages.[21]

The Anasazi employed stone masonry and adobe construction for communal structures of contiguous, flat-roofed rooms. Other structures include pithouses, or subterranean living quarters. Communal structures ranged in size from several small units, which could house a few related families, to larger villages with hundreds of living and storage rooms. Kivas, or subterranean ceremonial rooms, appear later in the development of the Anasazi culture. Large trash areas, or middens, contained discarded materials and burials. One Native American described this seemingly strange combination of artifacts:

> Corn cobs and husks, the rinds and stalks and animal bones were not regarded by the ancient people as filth or garbage. The remains were merely resting at a midpoint in their journey back to dust. Human remains are not so different. They should rest with the bones and rinds where they all may benefit living creatures—small rodents and insects—until their return is completed. The remains of things—animals and plants, the clay and stones—were treated with respect. Because for the ancient people all these things had spirit and being. The dead become dust; and in this becoming, they are once more joined with the Mother. The ancient Pueblo people called the earth the Mother Creator of all things in the world.[22]

The Anasazi also made particular styles of axes, grinding stones, and tools for cutting scraping, pounding, piercing, and digging. Ornaments of shell, bone, stone, and turquoise were also common. Trails, roads, and signal points provided communication between villages, allowing information and goods to be exchanged more easily.

Within the Anasazi culture, several regional variants have been identified by archaeologists. They include the Chaco of northwestern New Mexico, the Cibola of the upper Little Colorado River drainage, the Mesa Verde of southwestern Colorado and southeastern Utah, the Kayenta of northeastern Arizona, and the Virgin of northwestern Arizona and southwestern Utah. Regional variants prominently associated with the Coombs Site at Boulder's Anasazi State Park include the Kayenta and Virgin Anasazi variants.[23]

Although the cold snowy winters of the Paunsaugunt Plateau discouraged permanent settlement, Bryce Canyon breaks to the east into warmer valleys where people could build more permanent homes. By A.D. 700 Anasazi were living in villages in the Paria Valley. In the warmer summer months they used the high plateau for game, food plants, and timber.

About A.D. 1300 the Anasazi culture appears to have undergone a reorientation.[24] Greater numbers of people continued to concentrate in fewer localities. The small villages that earlier typified the Anasazi all but disappeared, giving way to large plaza-oriented pueblos housing as many as 2,000 persons. By the beginning of the 1600s, the Pueblo peoples occupied approximately their present locations.[25] It is likely that moving Anasazi populations mixed with already established peoples, producing a culture with the semblance of earlier Anasazi cultures but also showing a mixture of traits in its material culture, architecture, and social and religious practices.

The Kayenta and Virgin variants are particularly important to the history of Garfield County and are found at Boulder's Coombs Site, as is the Fremont. Kayenta refers to a major branch of the Anasazi bounded by the Grand Canyon to the west, Monument Valley to the east, the modern Hopi mesas to the south, and the Canyonlands region of southern Utah to the north.[26] Throughout much of their development, the Kayenta Anasazi lived in pithouses and/or small pueblos that may have housed an extended family or several closely

related families. The Kayenta built two types of villages. The first were
found mostly on mesa tops and consisted of stone masonry, jacal, or
adobe, architecture, and pithouses grouped around a central plaza.
The second type were cliff dwellings, which often consisted of a living
room, a grinding room, and several storage rooms constructed
around a common courtyard. Later the Kayenta built large cliff
dwellings containing several suites of rooms, probably the most
famous of which are Betatakin and Keet Seel, located in Navajo
National Monument in northern Arizona.

A hallmark of the Kayenta Anasazi was their fine pottery—finely
painted black-on-white and black-on-red wares.[27] They also produced artistically stunning multicolored pottery. The descendants of
the Kayenta eventually occupied the area at the southern edge of present-day Black Mesa, Arizona. Today these people are known as the
Hopi.

In Utah, Kayenta influence is evident from the Glen Canyon area
north through Garfield County and the Escalante River drainage,
past the Henry Mountains to the east side of the Wasatch Plateau,
and northwest on the Kaiparowits Plateau. The small, scattered settlements that characterize Kayenta occupation in the general area often
contain features such as masonry and jacal rooms, storage granaries,
slab-lined hearths, retaining walls, and pithouses. Less common, but
also present, are check dams, towers, potsherds, remnants of stone
tools, and rock art panels.[28] Ridges and other elevated locations over-
looking draws and sage flats seem to have been favored locations,
though the people also utilized rock shelters and shallow caves.

The Escalante Valley and surrounding hills contain a number of
these sites. Along today's Utah Highway 12 around the old Riddle
Mill are found granaries, stone tools, arrow- and spearheads, knives,
scrapers of varying styles, and rock art. The petroglyphs on the ledges
feature handprints and representations of mountain sheep, zig-zag
lines, circles, stick figures of men—some with horned headdresses,
shields, and bows and arrows. Five miles west of the town of
Escalante, near the confluence of North Creek, Main Canyon, and
Upper Valley, are other pictographs and petroglyphs. Other area sites
are also close to water sources, including a large campsite north of
the town near where Pine Creek meets the Escalante River. Stone gra-

naries are still visible up Alvey Wash on the west side of the canyon. Brigham Young University researchers have excavated a prehistoric village near Bailey Wash. The site has numerous rock art forms—handprints, geometric forms, animals, men, and marks, some of which appear to be tallies.

The prehistoric peoples who occupied these sites made various styles of projectile points—some show very crude workmanship, others were very finely chipped by expert craftsmen. The pottery found in these areas is primarily gray ware, although some pieces show black designs, and a few black-on-red sherds can also be found.

The Virgin River drainage has long been considered the core area of the Virgin Anasazi. This group extended north and east across the Zion National Park uplands, east toward the Kaiparowits Plateau, south to the Colorado River, and west along the Muddy River in Nevada.[29] Although similar to the Kayenta, these peoples may have lived in scattered family farmsteads during the summer and gathered in villages during the winter. The Virgin Anasazi were initially defined on the basis of their pottery types.[30] Some archaeologists argue that they are derived from the Kayenta group, who may have migrated to the Virgin River area, maintaining close contacts with the Kayenta while developing a separate cultural tradition.[31]

The Fremont culture derives its name from the Fremont River drainage in east-central Utah, where archaeologist Noel Morss first recognized a cultural group distinct from the Anasazi. Further study by archaeologists recognized the Fremont as a separate tradition, similar to the Anasazi in some ways but not an Anasazi subdivision.[32]

The Fremont occupied the northern half of the Colorado Plateau and the eastern portion of the Great Basin in Utah and western Nevada from about A.D. 500 to 1250. There are three differing views on the origins of the Fremont: 1) Virgin Anasazi people migrating northward merged with or displaced Archaic populations, 2) the Fremont are derived from the northwestern Plains people who acquired traits from the Anasazi; and 3) the Fremont are derived from existing Archaic populations, the most favored theory.[33]

Through remains of pottery, projectile points, rock art, architecture, and means of subsistence, archaeologists have classified the Fremont into different variants.[34] The San Rafael Fremont, one of five variants of the Fremont culture in Utah, was located roughly between the eastern flank of the Sevier Plateau and the Colorado River, and between Garfield County and the Book Cliffs in northeastern Utah. Small garden plots, similar to those of the early Anasazi, were important to the economy of the San Rafael Fremont. The other variants of the Fremont are Sevier Fremont, Uinta Fremont, Parowan Fremont, and Great Salt Lake Fremont. Variants of the Fremont elsewhere relied more heavily on the harvest of game and the gathering of wild plants for food and other resources.

Settlement and subsistence patterns and material culture differed between the Great Basin and Colorado Plateau Fremont people. The Fremont culture depended more on hunting game and gathering seeds and plants than did their Anasazi neighbors to the south. Sites near lakes or marshy areas seem to have been more oriented toward fishing and other water-based resources than toward farming. For the Fremont Indians living in upland areas, maize, beans, and squash horticulture became more important. Upland Fremont villages tended to be relatively small and were often built close to perennial streams. The people lived in both pithouses and surface structures, though pithouses were the most distinctive structure. Kivas are not found at any Fremont sites.

Fremont pottery is a gray ware, constructed by a coil and scrape method, as is Anasazi pottery. Plain gray is the predominant type, but variations include scoring, incising, and applique. Some of the corrugated and painted wares of the Fremont of Garfield County and southern Utah were probably influenced by design and construction techniques of the Anasazi.

Certain cultural traits are unique to the Fremont. For example, one-rod-and-bundle basketry construction is so characteristic to the Fremont culture that some archaeologists believe it can be defined by such basketry alone.[35] Another peculiarity of the Fremont is their footwear. In contrast to the yucca sandals worn by the Anasazi, the Fremont preferred moccasins constructed from the hock of a deer or mountain sheep leg, referred to as a dew-claw moccasin. Troughed metates having a shelf at the closed end (called Utah metates) are often a feature of Fremont sites, as are well-shaped stone balls. Clay figurines—some quite detailed and ornate—are common with

Fremont people. These trapezoidal-shaped figurines or dolls often have hair bobs and necklaces. Similar figures are depicted in Fremont rock art, often with elaborate headdresses, body ornamentation, and shields.

Fremont rock art in Garfield County is widespread, extending from the upper reaches of the Escalante River drainage south to the Kaiparowits Plateau, east towards the Henry Mountains, and southeast to the Glen Canyon-Lake Powell area. Prominent rock art sites are found along the Escalante River and its tributaries, particularly in the area of the Escalante-Calf Creek confluence and on the sandstone cliffs along the trail to Lower Calf Creek Falls. Other sites include The Gulch along the Burr Trail and Muley Twist Canyon in the southern part of Capitol Reef National Park.[36]

Although the regional rock art is predominantly Fremont, motifs and design elements attributed to earlier Archaic peoples are also present. Some bighorn sheep forms and abstract geometric designs indicate Anasazi influence.[37] An accurate number of rock art sites in Garfield County is unknown; nevertheless, such sites likely number in the thousands.

When describing the traits distinctive of the Fremont, it is important to keep in mind that they were a people able to adapt to many different kinds of environmental settings. Thus, their living patterns varied to a wide-enough degree that there is no single set of artifacts or material remains that identifies the Fremont people.[38]

Much of Garfield County lies between the known territories of the Colorado Plateau Fremont and the Virgin and Kayenta Anasazi. As a result, many of the prehistoric sites in the county hold physical evidence of both the Fremont and Anasazi culture, including the Coombs Site in Boulder, the Bull Creek sites (about fifty miles northeast of Boulder), Circle Cliffs sites, Escalante River drainage sites, Kaiparowits Plateau sites, and other sites near Ticaboo. At many of these sites there is a mixture of Fremont and Anasazi characteristics.[39] In general, as one moves north and west from the Glen Canyon/Lake Powell area Anasazi features diminish and more classic Fremont features become more common.[40]

The Fremont did not last much, if at all, past A.D. 1250 and were probably contracting and consolidating their habitations after A.D.

1150.[41] Archaeologists do not know for sure what happened to the
Fremont people after about A.D. 1300. Some suggest they were ancestors to the contemporary Paiute, Ute, and Shoshoni, but linguistic
studies clearly show that those Numic-speaking peoples migrated
east across the Great Basin from the Owens Valley area of California.
A more plausible theory is that the Ute, Paiute, Goshute, and
Shoshoni Indians displaced the Fremont culture. Still another view
is that the Fremont moved to the northern plains and that their
ancestors today are the Plains Apache. A fourth theory suggests that
the Fremont, like the Anasazi, drifted south in response to deterio-
rating environmental and social conditions.[42]

Until further evidence of cultural continuity between the
Fremont and contemporary Native American peoples of Utah and
Garfield County can be established, the fate of the Fremont people
will remain a highly debated topic among archaeologists as well as a
campfire mystery.

Protohistoric Period: A.D. 1300–1776

Roughly at the time the Fremont disappeared from Utah, Numic
speakers began arriving. Numic is a branch of the Uto-Aztecan family of languages that developed in the western United States and
northern Mexico.[43] The living descendants of the Numic-speaking
peoples are the Northern and Southern Paiute, the Ute, Shoshone,
and Goshute. At the time of European contact, they occupied the
Great Basin—from the Rocky Mountains to the Sierra Nevada of
California, and from central Idaho south to the Colorado River.

The probable homeland of these Numic peoples appears to have
been somewhere in the vicinity of Death Valley in the extreme southwestern corner of the Great Basin. Based on archaeological finds,
some researchers believe that scattered Numic populations occupied
that part of the Great Basin as many as 5,000 years ago. These people
were so successful in adapting to their own harsh desert setting that
the territory vacated by the Anasazi and Fremont—some of which
was better watered—appeared every bit as desirable to the Numics as
their more arid homeland.[44]

Evidence of early Numic peoples in Garfield County is widespread. Campsites with stone rings, Numic ceramics, and Desert

Side-notched projectile points are evident in areas along ridges that might have provided good access through the Escalante River drainage, Bryce Canyon, and in the canyons around Boulder. There have been many Paiute artifacts found on the Pansaugunt Plateau, and at least five sites on the Paria Plateau contain Paiute brownware pottery. The Numic in more southern areas of Utah, including Garfield County, had contact and trade with the Hopi, as is evidenced by small quantities of black-on-yellow Hopi pottery in the area.[45]

Eventually, three main groups of Paiutes lived in this region between the Colorado River to the east and the Markaugant Plateau on the west. The Antarianunts lived near the northeastern tip of the Henry Mountains; the Kaiparowits lived from the Escalante River to the upper Sevier River valleys, overlapping with the Panguitch group, whose land included Panguitch Lake. On the west side of the Cedar and Beaver mountains were the Cedar and Beaver Paiutes. These larger groups consisted of a number of small bands which traded with each other and sometimes intermarried.

These Southern Paiutes, like other Numic peoples, had a hunting-and-gathering economy and exploited seasonally available resources. They used a wide variety of plants. The women, who did most of the gathering, would beat seeds from a variety of plants into cone-shaped baskets, winnow the seeds, and then place them on flat stones next to a flame to parch. Later they could be ground, made into a mush, or baked as bread in the fire's ashes. The plateaus also yielded a reliable source of roots and berries. Pine nuts, which are high in both protein and fat, were a staple. They gathered the cones in early fall, roasted them to force them open, then stored the small nuts for the winter.

Panguitch Indians were one of the few Southern Paiute groups who fished extensively. Although some groups supplemented their diet with sporadic corn agriculture, the Panguitch and Kaiparowits Paiutes did not. They did, however, use bows and arrows. Small game such as rabbits (hunted by individuals or caught in nets in group drives), wood rats, mice, gophers, squirrels, chipmunks, birds, and snakes were part of their diet. Although large game did not comprise a significant portion of the Paiute diet, they did have access to deer and mountain sheep.

Their tools included cone-shaped plain brownware pottery (sometimes decorated with fingernail slashes), well-made basketry, mats and bags, rabbit nets, digging sticks, grinding stones, and the Desert Side-notched projectile point. The basic warm weather garment for both men and women was a double apron of skin or plant fiber. In colder weather they wore rabbit-fur robes and simple leggings. Shelters usually consisted of wickiups constructed of bent willow and cottonwood branches with an over-lay of brush or juniper branches.[46] They also utilized rock shelters or open sites on sand dunes.

The Numic people organized into small family bands. In the autumn several groups would unite to harvest pinyon nuts and hunt deer, which they then cached to help get them through the harsh winter. Late winter and early spring often were times of near or actual famine. During summer the groups dispersed to springs and other perennial water sources, capitalizing on the many foodstuffs available; but sometimes they would gather for a communal hunt or rabbit drive.

The Numic peoples' ways of life would at first slowly but gradually change with the coming of outsiders to their lands. Early in the 1600s, the Spanish pushed north from Mexico in search of gold and new trade routes. They had little influence, however, on the Southern Paiute culture until well after Catholic priests Francisco Garces, Francisco Atanasio Domínguez, and Silvestre Vélez de Escalante recorded the first contact with them in the 1770s. Changes then became much more drastic and rapid.

ENDNOTES

1. This chapter is based on material written by Todd Prince, park manager at Iron Mission State Park in Cedar City, Utah. From 1989 to 1993 he held the museum curator position at the Anasazi State Park in Boulder, Utah.

2. Contemporary archaeologists and anthropologists use the term "Before Present" (B.P.) to identify ancient time spans. It is the same as saying "years ago."

3. F.R. Hauck, *Cultural Resource Evaluation in South Central Utah, 1977–1978* (Salt Lake City: Bureau of Land Management, 1979), 77.

4. For artifact typology see Betsy L. Tipps, *The Tar Sands Project: An Inventory and Predictive Model for Central and Southern Utah*, Cultural Resource Series 22 (Salt Lake City: Bureau of Land Management, 1988), 79. For the San Rafael Swell see two articles by G.W. Tripp, "A Clovis Point from Central Utah," *American Antiquity* 31, no. 3 (1966): 435–36; and "Bill Mobely Does It Again!" *Utah Archaeology Newsletter* 13, no. 1 (1967): 16. For southeastern Utah see Alice. P. Hunt and Dallas Tanner, "Early Man Sites Near Moab, Utah," *American Antiquity* 26, no. 1 (1960): 110–17; Lamar Lindsay, "Unusual or Enigmatic Stone Artifacts: Pots, Pipes and Pendants from Utah," *American Antiquities Section Selected Papers* 2, no. 8 (1976): 107–17; Lloyd M. Pierson, *Cultural Resource Summary of the East Central Portion of Moab District, Cultural Resource Series 10* (Salt Lake City: Bureau of Land Management, 1981); and Floyd W. Sharrock and E.G. Keane, *Carnegie Museum of Collections from Southeastern Utah*, University of Utah Anthropological Papers 57 (Salt Lake City: University of Utah Press, 1962). For Circle Cliffs see Alan Schroedl, "The Archaic of the Northern Colorado Plateau" (Ph.D. diss., University of Utah, 1976). For the Escalante area see Hauck, *Cultural Resource Evaluation in South Central Utah*. Summaries of Paleo-Indian points found in Utah are in James M. Copeland and Richard E. Fike, "Fluted Projectile Points in Utah," *Utah Archaeology* 1, no. 1 (1988): 5–28; and Alan Schroedl, "Paleo-Indian Occupation in the Eastern Great Basin and Northern Colorado Plateau," 1–15.

5. Hauck, *Cultural Resource Evaluation*, 76.

6. David B. Madsen, Donald R. Currey, and James H. Madsen, "Man, Mammoth, and Lake Fluctuations in Utah," *American Antiquities Section Selected Papers* 2, no. 5 (1976).

7. Hauck, *Cultural Resource Evaluation*, 321–32.

8. Linda S. Cordell, *Prehistory of the Southwest* (Orlando, FL: Academic Press, 1984), 131; Jesse D. Jennings, ed., *Ancient Native Americans* (San Francisco: W.H. Freeman and Co., 1978), 1–42.

9. Copeland and Fike, "Fluted Projectile Points,"

10. Joe Ben Wheat, "A Paleo-Indian Bison Kill," in *Early Man in America* (San Francisco: W.H. Freeman and Co., 1973), 88.

11. Jennings, *Ancient Native Americans*, 35.

12. Berry and Berry, "Chronological and Conceptual Models of the Southwest Archaic" *Anthropology of the Desert West: Essays in Honor of Jesse D. Jennings, University of Utah Anthropological Papers* 110 (Salt Lake City: University of Utah Press, 1986), 253–327; and Schroedl, "The Archaic of the Northern Colorado Plateau."

13. See Richard N. Homer, "A Mathematical Typology for Archaic

Projectile Points of the Eastern Great Basin" (Ph.D. diss., University of Utah, 1978).

14. William D. Lipe, "Anasazi Communities in the Red Rock Plateau," in *Reconstructing Prehistoric Pueblo Societies*, William A. Longacre, ed. (Albuquerque: University of New Mexico Press, 1970), 84–139; Steve Dominguez, Dennis Danielson, and Karen Kramer, *Archeological Survey of Trail Maintenance, Revegetation, and Prescribed Burn Areas in Bryce Canyon National Park* (Lincoln, Nebraska: National Park Service,), 11.

15. Berry and Berry, "Chronological and Conceptual Models," 319. Traditional estimates of maize introduction to the Southwest place the event in the 4,000–5,000 B.P. range. More recent research suggests that new data places the event around 2,500 B.P.

16. Cordell, *Prehistory of the Southwest*, 182; Tipps, *Tar Sands Project*, 18.

17. Kathleene Parker, *The Only True People: A History of the Native Americans of the Colorado Plateau* (Marceline, MO: Walsworth Press, 1991).

18. See Jesse D. Jennings, *Prehistory of Utah and the Eastern Great Basin*, University of Utah Anthropological Papers 98 (Salt Lake City: University of Utah Press, 1978).

19. Robert H. Lister and Florence C. Lister, *Those Who Came Before* (Globe, AZ: Southwest Parks and Monuments Association, 1989).

20. Robert H. Lister and Florence C. Lister, "The Coombs Site," 53.

21. Good discussions of prehistoric agricultural diversity and water control can be found in Suzanne Fish and Paul R. Fish, eds., "Prehistoric Agricultural Strategies in the Southwest," *Anthropological Research Papers* 33 (Tempe: Arizona State University, 1984); and Anne I. Woosley, "Agricultural Diversity in the Prehistoric Southwest," *The Kiva* 45, no.4 (1980): 317–35.

22. From Leslie Marmon Silko "Landscape, History, and the Pueblo Imagination," 83–84, as quoted in Shelley J. Smith, et al., *Intrigue of the Past: Investigating Archaeology* (Salt Lake City: Bureau of Land Management, 1992), 74).

23. For non-technical books about the Anasazi see Donald G. Pike, *Anasazi: Ancient People of the Rock* (New York: Harmony Books, 1974); Dewitt Jones and Linda S. Cordell, *Anasazi World* (Portland, OR: Graphic Arts, 1985); Gary Matlock, *Enemy Ancestors* (Flagstaff, AZ: Northland Publishing, 1988); Richard J. Ambler, *The Anasazi* (Flagstaff, AZ: Museum of Northern Arizona, 1987); Lister and Lister, *Those Who Came Before;* Parker, *The Only True People;* and Gilbert R. Wanger, *The Story of Mesa Verde National Park* (Mesa Verde National Park, CO: Mesa Verde Museum Association, Inc., 1991).

24. Ambler, *The Anasazi*, 4.

25. William D. Lipe, "The Southwest," in *Ancient Native Americans,* Jennings, ed., 375.

26. Jones and Cordell, *Anasazi World,* 30.

27. Ibid., 32.

28. Tipps, *Tar Sands Project,* 20–21.

29. Deborah A. Westfall et al., *Green Spring: An Anasazi and Southern Piute Encampment in the St. George Basin of Utah,* Cultural Resource Series no. 21 (Salt Lake City: Bureau of Land Management, 1987), 8.

30. A summary of these early investigations can be found in James H. Gunnerson, "Plateau Shoshonean Prehistory," *American Antiquity* 28, no. 1 (1962): 41–45.

31. The term "Western Kayenta" is still preferred by some authors, while others refer to the Virgin as a minor cultural tradition. Recent work by Gardiner F. Dalley and Douglas A. McFadden, *The Archaeology of the Red Cliffs,* and *The Little Man Archaeological Sites,* Cultural Resource Series no. 17 (Salt Lake City: Bureau of Land Management, 1985), together with Barbara A. Walling et al. "Excavations at Quail Creek," Cultural Resource Series no. 20 (Salt Lake City: Bureau of Land Management, 1986), and Westfall et al., *Green Spring,* provide excellent examples and basis for argument that the Virgin developed independently and can be distinguished on the basis of architecture, ceramics, and apparent anomalies in religious practices and trade. Also see Kevin Rafferty, "The Virgin Anasazi and the Pan-Southwestern Trade System, A.D. 900–1150," *The Kiva* 56, no. 1 (1990): 3–24.

32. Lipe, "The Southwest," 326–401.

33. See James H. Gunnerson, "The Fremont Culture, A Study in Culture Dynamics on the Northern Anasazi Frontier," *Papers of the Peabody Museum of Archaeology and Ethnology* 59, no. 2 (1969); Noel Morss, "The Ancient Culture of the Fremont River in Utah," *Papers of the Peabody Museum of American Archaeology and Ethnology* 12, no. 3 (1931); Aikens, *Fremont-Promontory-Plains Relationships,* University of Utah Anthropological Papers 82 (Salt Lake City: University of Utah Press, 1966); Jennings, *Prehistory of Utah and the Eastern Great Basin,* 155; and John P. Marwitt, *Median Village and Fremont Culture Regional Variation,* University of Utah Anthropological Papers 95 (Salt Lake City: University of Utah Press, 1970). Although the development of Archaic populations into the agricultural Fremont seems reasonable, David B. Madsen and Michael S. Berry, "A Reassessment of Northeastern Great Basin Prehistory," *American Antiquity* 40, no. 4 (1975): 391–405, suggest a gap of 1,000–2,000 years between the

late Archaic and early Fremont. Additional dating of early Fremont sites should eventually resolve this issue.

34. See David B. Madsen, *Exploring the Fremont* (Salt Lake City: Utah Museum of Natural History, 1989).

35. For further discussion of Fremont basketry see James M. Adavasio: "Fremont Basketry," *Tebiwa* 17, no. 2 (1975): 67–76; and idem. "Prehistoric Basketry," in William C. Sturtevant, ed., *Handbook of North American Indians*, vol. 11, *Great Basin*, Warren D'Azevedo, ed. (Washington D.C.: Smithsonian Institution, 1986), 194–205.

36. Kenneth B. Castleton, *Petroglyphs and Pictographs of Utah, Volume Two: The South, Central, West and Northwest* (Salt Lake City: Utah Museum of Natural History).

37. Polly Schaafsma, *The Rock Art of Utah* (Cambridge, MA: Harvard University,).

38. Madsen, *Exploring the Fremont*, 24.

39. Madsen, in *Exploring the Fremont*, 42, suggests that a definite cultural affiliation cannot be assigned to such sites. He half-jokingly, and perhaps half-seriously, prefers to call them "Freazi" or "Anamonts."

40. Hauck, Cultural Resource *Evaluation*, 83; Madsen, *Exploring the Fremont*, 42.

41. Lipe, "The Southwest," 386.

42. See Gunnerson, "Plateau Shoshonean Prehistory," 41–45, and "The Fremont Culture;" David B. Madsen, "Dating the Paiute-Shoshone Expansion," *American Antiquity* 40, no. 1 (1975): 82–86; Tipps, *Tar Sands Project*, 23; and Aikens, *Fremont-Promontory-Plains Relationships*.

43. Jennings, *Prehistory of Utah and the Eastern Great Basin*, 235. The Numic-speaking groups include three closely related pairs of languages that cover a vast area.

44. Aikens and Witherspoon, "Great Basin Numic Prehistory," 15.

45. Hauck, *Cultural Resource Evaluation*, 84. See also Lipe, "Anasazi Communities in the Red Rock Plateau."

46. Westfall et al., *Green Spring*, 10.

CHAPTER 3

EARLY TRADE
AND EXPLORATION

The Spanish Explorers

The traditional date for the beginning of the historic period in the southwestern United States is 1540, when Spanish conquistadors, led by Captain Garcia Lopes de Cardenas, discovered the Grand Canyon and claimed for Spain the entire American Southwest. A number of Spanish explorers and traders followed, penetrating northern and central Utah, beginning with Father Estevan Perea in 1604.[1]

By the mid-1600s Spaniards were trading with Utes as well as raiding them for slaves on the eastern Colorado Plateau. The Spanish settlers in Mexico and New Mexico of this era found the less-docile tribes like Utes, Apaches, and Navajos difficult to govern and Christianize, but they could—and did—have some measure of control over them through slavery. Thousands of Native Americans were sent into the mines of northern Mexico and to the haciendas of the landed gentry of New Mexico where they toiled away their lives in hopeless bondage.[2]

Bryce Canyon in August 1916. (Utah State Historical Society)

Although there is little or no evidence of any long-term settlements of Utes in the Garfield area, their hunting grounds crossed
Garfield County from Panguitch Lake to the Colorado River. For the
most part, small bands of Paiutes lived along the Sevier River from
present-day Marysvale south through Garfield County. Just south of

Bryce Canyon in Kane County is a region around Skutumpah Creek where Ute, Paiute, and Navajo lands overlapped. Members of all three tribes were acquainted with Bryce Canyon. The Paiute legend for the creation of this natural wonderland tells of lizards, birds and other animals that occupied the land and could turn themselves into human forms:

> They did something that was not good [and] Coyote turned them all into rocks. You can see them in that place now . . . some standing in rows, some sitting down, some holding onto others. You can see their faces, with paint on them just as they were before the became rocks. The name of that place is Angka-ku-wass-a-wits [red-painted faces].[3]

A change in relationships between the various groups of Numic peoples was also taking place. Utes saw social and economic benefit in trading with the Spanish from New Mexico. At first, furs, buckskin, and dried buffalo meat constituted the items of exchange. The Spanish, however, were interested in more than furs—they wanted to expand the lucrative Indian slave trade. By the early 1760s tribes between the Wasatch and Rocky Mountains were being exploited by New Mexican traders from Taos and Santa Fe. Small bands of Utes that traditionally had little political cohesion combined under war chiefs whose power rested on their ability to acquire and keep horses for their followers. They eventually learned that if they engaged in the slave trade themselves their own people were less likely to be sold into bondage. Consequently, they would become the scourge of the Goshute and Southern Paiute bands as they raided their camps for women and children to trade to the Spanish.

In 1776 a party of Spanish explorers headed by two Franciscan priests, Francisco Atanasio Domínguez and Silvestre Vélez de Escalante, traveled into much of Utah in a failed attempt to find a new route overland from Santa Fe to the newly established missions in California. The expedition journal indicates that they were "following the Ute Trail" and "the old slave route." Members of the party spoke the Ute language well enough to communicate with the bands they encountered.[4]

Although members of the Domínguez-Escalante expedition

never set foot in the Garfield County region (they circled far around
it), no less than seven place-names in the county would eventually
honor Silvestre Vélez de Escalante: the town of Escalante, Escalante
Canyon, Escalante Mountain, the Escalante River, Escalante Basin,
and Escalante Natural Bridge.

Eventually most of the Numic Indians, except for the Western
Shoshone and Southern Paiute, obtained horses either from the
Plains tribes or from the Spanish. With the introduction of the horse,
the Ute and Northern Shoshone became much more mobile and efficient at hunting large game and at raiding and warfare. Trade and
contact with distant peoples, including the Spanish, became easier
and occurred more frequently. Tepees made of hide and poles
became common, as horses enabled the people to transport cumber-
some materials with greater ease.

Meanwhile, Spanish explorers continued to seek trade in Utah.
Maurice Arze and Lagos Garcia led a company of seven men to the
Great Basin and the *San Sebero* (Sevier) region. In 1821 Utah became
part of the territory of the Mexican government when they won
independence from Spain. The newly liberated Mexicans lost no time
in taking over the trade and mining enterprises of the Spaniards, continuing contacts between Santa Fe and the Indians in Utah until after
the Mormons reached the Salt Lake Valley.[5]

The first American to travel overland to southern California,
frontiersman Jedediah Smith, is credited with rediscovering the
Sevier and Virgin rivers. Many subsequent traders, but by no means
all, followed the route of the Domínguez-Escalante party. Several
groups either came or left Utah through the southern regions on
what would become the Old Spanish Trail. By the mid-1830s it had
become an established trade route between Santa Fe and California.
It had numerous variants, but the main route traveled northwest
from Santa Fe, crossed the Colorado River near Moab, and forded the
Green River near the present town of Green River. From there the
trail swung southwest and split at Fremont Junction. One section—a
later short-cut—snaked west through Salina Canyon and then followed the Sevier River Valley south through future Sevier and Piute
counties.

The other route took the Forsyth Valley to the Loa-Fremont area then crossed west to Otter Creek. It traced the creek south through Grass Valley along the eastern side of today's Piute County until it met the Sevier River's East Fork north of Antimony. The two trails came together at the junction of the East Fork and the main flow of the Sevier River.[6] From there Spanish caravans continued south with their captives and other trade items, following the river across the northwestern corner of future Garfield County from Circle Valley (in Piute County) south to the present site of Orton. There the trail curved west and then south along Bear Creek and up onto the Markagunt Plateau, which forms Garfield's western boundary.[7] The trail followed Little Creek down the other side of the mountain near the present town of Parowan before meeting the Domínguez-Escalante route near present-day Cedar City.

Utes, Navajos, and Mexicans frequently used another trail from the south through Garfield County for their raids on Paiute camps. They came into Utah at the Crossing of the Fathers (also known as Ute Ford, now submerged by Lake Powell) where the Domínguez-Escalante party forded the Colorado River on their return trip to Santa Fe. From there the raiders went up the Paria Valley, into Tropic Canyon, through the northern part of Bryce Canyon, and over the Markugunt Plateau to the Great Basin trails.

A story persists today that one party of Spanish traders tried to cross Boulder Mountain and got caught in early snow north of the Escalante River. Bitter cold and starvation took the lives of nine of them before spring thaws finally allowed the survivors to leave the mountain. Later settlers reportedly found nine grave markers, which were visible for many years before being "obliterated by shifting sands."[8]

Trappers and Traders

In 1830 mountain men William Wolfskill and George C. Yount led a group of twenty trappers the entire length of the Old Spanish Trail—the first documented group to do so. They traveled the eastern half of the loop through central Utah. Somehow they missed the turn in the trail where it snaked up Bear Creek and down Red Creek to present-day Paragonah. They continued along the Sevier River through Garfield County near the present site of Panguitch and on to the 9,000-foot Markagunt Plateau, where they ran into trouble. According to their account:

> Our trappers, with much toil, reached a strip of Table land, upon a lofty range of mountains, where they encountered the most terrible snowstorm they had ever experienced. During several days, no one ventured out of camp. There they lay embedded in snow, very deep, animals and men huddled thick as possible together, to husband and enjoy all possible animal warmth, having spread their thick and heavy blankets, & piled bark, and brush wood around & over them. . . . After the storm subsided and the weather had softened, Yount & Wolfskill ascended a lofty Peak of the mountains for observation. In the whole range of human view, in every direction, nothing could be discerned, in the least degree encouraging, but only mountains, piled on mountains, all capped with cheerless snow, in long and continuous successions, till they seemed to mingle with the blue vault of heaven and fade away in the distance.[9]

The explorers eventually found their way into Little Salt Lake Valley, where they killed the last of the four cattle they had brought with them for food. From there to California they lived on mule and horse meat, some of which "was very poor."[10]

During the next two decades traffic on the trail—including the slave trade—peaked, even though California and New Mexico had passed anti-slavery laws in the 1820s. Trading caravans as large as 200 people traveled the Old Spanish Trail. The traders wore varied apparel. Elaborately embroidered jackets and vests adorned with silver bell-shaped buttons contrasted with the scanty buckskin loincloths of the captured Indians. As the traders began their journey from New Mexico, they first swapped guns, blankets, and trinkets with Navajos in exchange for horses. The poorer-grade animals could be traded later as food to "Digger" Indians, as some of the Indian groups of the desert areas were later labeled, whose only trade commodity was often their own children. (Both Paiute and Goshute Indians were referred to as "Digger" Indians because they commonly dug in the soil for bulbs and roots in their endeavors to find food in the harsh semiarid lands they inhabited.) Along the way, the traders also purchased captives from Ute bands who had taken women and children in hit-and-run raids on the unmounted Paiutes and

Goshutes. In California the New Mexicans traded the captives for more horses or sold them for cash—the top rates reportedly being "$100 for a boy, and from $150 to $200 for healthy girls, who were in greater demand as house servants."[11] The slave trade was a profitable business.

After about 1840 contact with Europeans became increasingly frequent, dramatically affecting the native inhabitants of the Garfield region. Traders and fur trappers had been in and out of southern Utah for decades, frequently using parts of the Spanish trails. Often they sent pelts to Taos with the New Mexican caravans. Although these men were not ones to leave a written record of their experiences, it is highly probable that some of them obtained their furs from along the Sevier River and the waterways in Garfield County, since mountain men traveled throughout the West in search of beaver, which was in high demand to make fashionable tophats. The streams of southern Utah never yielded a high numbers of furs, particularly beaver, however. The trappers soon moved on to other territories and eventually to other occupations as the fur trade dwindled by the early 1840s.

Mormon Exploration

Although John C. Frémont's scientific exploration of Utah for the U.S. government in 1843–44 did not take him into the Garfield region, his report published in 1845 had far-reaching implications for the eventual settling of the future county. Frémont, an army topographical engineer assigned to "furnish a scientific description of the Far Northwest," traveled through northern Utah in 1843 on his way to California. The return trip followed the Old Spanish Trail from Los Angeles to Parowan and then proceeded up the present-day Interstate 15 corridor to Utah Valley. Frémont and his men exited through Spanish Fork Canyon, cutting across future Wasatch, Duchesne, and Uintah counties into Colorado and from there on to Independence, Missouri.[12]

Frémont's report became particularly important to leaders of the Church of Jesus Christ of Latter-day Saints (Mormons or LDS), who were seeking a place of refuge for their beleaguered followers. The church had been organized by Joseph Smith in New York state in

1830, and had moved to Nauvoo, Illinois, by way of Ohio and Missouri because of harassment and persecution. In June 1844, the Mormon's prophet had been murdered. His successor, Brigham Young, and other church leaders found Frémont's description of the Great Basin pivotal as they considered options for resettlement of their people.

Eventually, with the coming of the Mormons to the Inter-mountain West in 1847, livestock and farming settlements would encroach on traditional lands that once supported the region's Native Americans. And while the slave trade would ultimately end, European diseases—including smallpox, influenza, and measles, for which the Native Americans had no immunity—would cut a swath of death through their communities.

Between July 1847 and the beginning of 1850, the arrival of thou-sands of Mormon immigrants to the Salt Lake Valley made it imper-ative for their leaders to find new sites for settlement. In addition, thousands of forty-niners heading for the gold fields of California soon passed through the Salt Lake Valley. Miners bought mules and supplies and then moved on, but those in wagon trains intent on set-tling in California sometimes hired Mormon guides to take them via the new southern route to avoid being caught by winter in the Sierra Nevada like the Donner-Reed party of 1846. This route followed part of the Old Spanish Trail, which some Mormon Battalion members had traveled from San Diego to Utah in 1848, returning from California after serving in the U.S. Army during the Mexican War. They had been the first to take wagons over the route, which would eventually be known as the "Mormon Corridor" (roughly following today's Interstate 15).[13] Mormon church leaders soon decided that they needed to know more about the land south of Utah Lake.

The Parley P. Pratt Expedition

Brigham Young stated in March 1849: "We hope soon to explore the valleys three hundred miles south and also the country as far as the Gulf of California with a view to settlement and to acquiring a seaport."[14] That same month he also asked the newly formed Legislative Assembly of the Provisional Government of the State of

Parley P. Pratt who led an exploring expedition to Southern Utah in late 1849. (Utah State Historical Society)

Deseret to commission Parley P. Pratt to explore the central and southern portions of Utah with a party of fifty men.[15]

Pratt, already known for his competent leadership, chose his men carefully. They each needed skills and talents that would aid in the success of the expedition. Among his choices were John Brown, William Henrie, and Joseph Mathews, who were expert hunters; Robert Lang Campbell, a seasoned clerk and camp historian; William W. Phelps, an accomplished surveyor; and Dimick Huntington, an experienced scout with a uncommon aptitude for trading and conversing with the Indians. Some of those chosen were Mormon

Minute Men; others, like Isaac C. Haight, had been with the Mormon Battalion. In age, the men ranged from eighteen-year-old Alexander Lemon to Samuel Gould, who was seventy-one.

The expedition was to "maintain a complete record of soil conditions, topography, vegetation, streams, timber, pasture lands, and all other natural resources" necessary to locate new settlements. They were also to return with specific recommendations for town sites. It was quite a task, considering the expedition began its winter journey on 24 November 1849, with deep snow covering much of the route, and were to return in February. They would be the first Mormons to enter future Garfield County.

Twelve large wagons lumbered out of Cottonwood Creek in Salt Lake Valley at noon on 24 November under cloudy skies. Each wagon, pulled by two yoke of oxen, carried food, blankets, tools, Indian trade items, and other necessities. One carriage, a brass field cannon, and thirty-eight saddle horses and mules, along with a number of cattle, were part of the procession which would swell to forty-seven men, three less than had been planned, by the time they left newly settled Provo. The caravan would follow old Indian trails and part of the Old Spanish Trail where no wagons had ever been. And they would cut new trails within the wilderness of southern Utah.

Snow and cold temperatures, often well below zero, would plague the explorers much of their journey. They traveled through Utah and Juab valleys, then turned east through Salt Creek Canyon to the Sanpete Valley and the two-week-old settlement of Manti. There, five more men volunteered to join the expedition, bringing the total to fifty-two and adding two more wagons. They followed the Sevier River through future Sevier and Piute county regions, crossing craggy passes in deep snow and freezing cold, and crossing into the Garfield County area on 15 December. There they camped in the south end of Circle Valley along the Sevier River.

Robert Campbell described the terrain before them in his journal: "The Valley terminated in an impassable canyon, and an abrupt chain of mountains sweeping before and on each hand, and the river rushing like a torrent between perpendicular rocks."[16] The wagons remained at that site for two days while several members of the group searched for a trail either to the south or west that would take them out of the valley. The Ute chief Wakara (Walker) had told them a week earlier that there were no passes over the mountains to the east of the Sevier River, and, even if there were, the dry and inhospitable country on the other side would not grow corn.

Sometime after dark on the second day, John Brown, John Bankhead, and Robert Campbell arrived back in camp with mixed news. They had discovered a route, which Campbell declared "very difficult, but not impassable, winding over a succession of canyons with steep ascents and descents, nearly perpendicular in places, with rocks and cobblestones all the way." At the conclusion of the report the rest of men reportedly shouted a loud, "We can go it!" Campbell lightened the task ahead with a song, which he sang to the men before the bugle called them to prayers.

> We've found out the trail boys,
>   Where over we go;
> It lies thro' the mountains,
>   Deeply covered with snow;
> It's rough rocky road,
>   The route we have been;
> But there is plenty of deer,
>   For them we have seen;
> We looked away far beyond,
>   But nothing could we see;
> Save the blue expanse of ether,
>   So clear and so free;
> But to a high Mountain,
>   Some of us did go;
> And we spied out a trail,
>   Where the Mountains can go. [17]

The next morning, 17 December, the party divided. The first group started ahead to clear rocks and timber from the route, while the remaining men readied the wagons and started them over Brown's Pass, newly named for its discoverer, John Brown. Hampered by the steep, undulating terrain and four to six feet of snow, the lead party made only seven and a half miles; the rear company traveled only four and a half miles.

The most difficult and temper-trying day since leaving Salt Lake

Valley was 18 December. The trailbreakers at times dismounted to stamp and pack the snow to make a trail for the horses and wagons; at other times they opened narrow passages with picks and shovels or cut through the six-foot snowdrifts. The forward company retraced their tracks several times to help lower the wagons with ropes over the steepest and most precarious sections. By nightfall the rear group had traveled only two miles beyond the forward company's encampment the evening before. The lead group camped on the other side of the ridge just north of present-day Spry.

The next day the party turned west. When a temporary impasse made it seem as though they could go no farther, some of the men became disheartened. Even when they were on their way again, the men were too cold and tired to exhibit good spirits and dispositions turned ugly. Schyler Jennings brandished a club at Dan Jones, swearing at him for allowing his horse too close to the wagon Jennings was driving. Pratt jumped into the fray, ordering the men to stop, then scolded all who had "enmity towards their brethren." After he finished the chastisement, he and three others climbed into the wagon to pray for forgiveness.[18]

That night they camped on the western edge of Garfield County. On 20 December, the expedition passed into Iron County near where today's Utah Highway 20 links the east and west corridors of the state. Parley P. Pratt and John Brown had located the pass leading into Parowan Valley and the Southern Route. Had they done their exploring in the warmer months they would doubtless have found the more passable Old Spanish Trail through Sevier, Piute, Garfield, and Beaver counties.

The expedition explored along the modern I-15 route as far south as present-day St. George. From there they looped northwest through Snow Canyon, then north along the edge of the Escalante Desert, before turning east to Cedar City to meet the Southern Route again. They started home facing deep snow and temperatures as low as thirty degrees below zero.

The Southern Expedition traveled some 700 miles in a little over two months, with the first members of the company arriving back in the Salt Lake Valley early in February 1850. Some of the men experienced permanent injury from frostbite, but none died. Although one might question the wisdom of such an undertaking in the worst possible time of year, the information Pratt and his men brought back with them proved valuable. Within fifteen years, thirty-seven towns had been located on sites Pratt had recommended in central and southern Utah. Undoubtedly, some of these sites would have been settled regardless of Pratt's report, but the achievements of the Southern Expedition combined with later exploring endeavors to open Garfield County to settlement in 1864.

The John D. Lee and John C.L. Smith Explorations

In 1851 Mormons began building communities and forts south of Utah Valley—the first being Parowan beginning in the third week of January. They laid out towns and built homes along the same creeks and rivers that native peoples had used for thousands of years before them. They explored the mountains and valleys for timber, game, and minerals. During the first week of June 1852, eight men from newly settled Parowan responded to the invitation of a Paiute chief, Quinarrah (Kanarrah), to visit his camp over the mountain to the east of the new settlement. The eight men were John Calvin Lazell Smith, John Steele, John D. Lee, John L. Smith, John Dart, Solomon Chamberlain, Priddy Meeks, and F.T. Whitney. [19] John D. Lee led the small group up Center Creek onto Prince Mountain, where they had a clear view to the west into the Parowan Valley. To the east they could see Panguitch Lake—the first recorded sighting of the lake and this portion of Garfield County.

Panguitch Lake is a beautiful freshwater lake in a rugged forested area eighteen miles south of where the town of that same name would be settled. The name of the lake and the creek that flows from it comes from the Paiute word *pawguh'uts* and the related Goshute word *Pawngweets,* both meaning "fish" or "big fish." Trout were so abundant in the lake that the natives had only to walk along the shore and spear them to have a plentiful supply. The Goshutes from near the Utah-Nevada border and the Paiutes from the Parowan-Panguitch area occasionally visited each other's lands. Nearly every person in these two bands would later be massacred by a company of U.S. soldiers while the Indians camped together at Spring Valley, between present-day Baker and Ely, Nevada. [20]

John D. Lee who was among the first to explore Panguitch Lake and the Upper Sevier River. He built a home in Panguitch. (Utah State Historical Society)

The explorers followed Indian trails nine miles down the mountain, where Chief Quinarrah welcomed them to his village of about a hundred Paiutes near Panguitch Lake. With John D. Lee as their interpreter, the men from Parowan traded flour and bread for fish. When they refused to trade gunpowder, Quinarrah became angry, saying they "were not the friends" they claimed to be. Although Lee had a difficult time interpreting all of the long speech that followed, he clearly understood that the chief was "very much displeased."[21]

Tense moments followed as the guests' eyes darted around the area looking for the quickest, safest exit. Lee, however, calmed Quinarrah before a retreat became necessary and succeeded in gleaning information about the land that lay below them along the course of the Sevier River. Although the visit to Panguitch Lake was short, the party of explorers returned to Parowan impressed with the possibility of settlement in the four-mile-wide, timber-covered valley, and determined to explore the area further.

With John C.L. Smith as their leader, a group of seven men left Parowan on 12 June 1852 to examine more closely the Sevier River Valley and to find the headwaters of the Rio Virgin, the lower portions of which had been investigated by them the previous January and February. The men were Priddy Meeks, John C.L. Smith, John Steele, Francis Whitney, Solomon Chamberlain, John Dart, and John D. Lee.[22] This time they followed the Old Spanish Trail at least part of the way up Little Creek to the summit; they then crossed over into Panguitch Valley. Upon scouting the area, they found water plentiful and ample land for farming. John Steel wrote: "There is a good chance for a small colony . . . some 50 or 100 families, who might wish to go into the lumber trade, as this is good country for timber." He also noted that "some very handsome, open kanyons, with plenty of poles, house logs, and saw timber, and good water" lay to the east.[23]

For the next two days the party traveled south along the west edge of the Sevier Valley to Assay Creek, passing from present Garfield County into today's Kane County, where they found the headwaters of the Sevier River's East Fork. John C.L. Smith in his report to the *Deseret News* stated: "There can be a good wagon road got from the Sevier country, to this point. There are plenty of hops and timber, and some handsome places for settlements in the narrow but fertile bottom of the stream."[24] Circling through the southeast portion of present-day Zion National Park and back north through the present town of Toquerville, the explorers arrived back in Parowan on 24 June 1852. They completed their 336-mile trek in only twelve days, reporting their travels in a letter to the *Deseret News* two days later.[25] It would take ten more years, however, for Mormon pioneers to bring their wagons and cattle into Panguitch Valley, which John Steele had described so promisingly.

Parowan men would continue to make trips to Panguitch Lake for fish to augment the town's meager food supply. These excursions would become particularly important in years of poor harvest due to grasshoppers or low water supply, or both.

John C. Frémont's Fifth Expedition, Winter 1853–54

Assigned to locate a central route across the continent for the Union Pacific Railroad, John C. Frémont mostly traversed Spanish trade routes. In the winter of 1853–54, however, he and his men crossed the Green River near the mouth of the San Rafael River and followed it to a river that would later be named the Fremont. They then crossed over the Awapa Plateau south of Fish Lake and down Grass Valley to the Sevier River. Fighting deep snows and bitter cold, the men wandered for three days through the same northwest corner of future Garfield County that the Parley P. Pratt expedition members had found so difficult. With snow "up to the Bellies of the animals" and sub-zero temperatures, they struggled to break trail. Wrote one: "None of us had shoes; some of the men had raw hide strapped round their feet, while others were half covered with worn out stockings and moccasins. We were reduced to rations of dried horse meat."[26]

On 7 February 1854 they found a pass (now named Fremont Pass) into Buckskin Valley and to Parowan. One man had died, several more had to be carried in. They had eaten nothing for two days. Frémont wrote: "At Parowan the Mormons treated us very kindly; every family took in some of the men, putting them into clean, comfortable beds, and kind-faced women gave them reviving food and pitying words." In a letter he wrote, "The Mormons saved me and mine from death by starvation."[27] Some of these same Mormons would be the first settlers in Garfield County in 1864.

ENDNOTES

1. Rick J. Fish, "The Southern Utah Expedition of Parley P. Pratt: 1849–1850" (Master's thesis, Brigham Young University, 1992), 119, identifies eleven Spanish expeditions into Utah before the Domínguez-Escalante expedition of 1776.

2. L.R. Bailey, *Indian Slave Trade in the Southwest* (Los Angeles: Westerbe Press, 1966), flyleaf.

3. Clifford C. Presnath, "The Legend of Bryce Canyon as Told to the Park Naturalist by Indian Dick," *Zion and Bryce Nature Notes* 8 (March 1939), as quoted in Nicholas Scrattish, *Historic Resource Study: Bryce Canyon National Park,* 7.

4. Fish, "Southern Utah Expedition," 8.

5. Ibid., 14.

6. The town of Junction, which is the Piute County seat, gets its name from the junction of the Sevier River and its east fork about a mile east of the town.

7. John W. Van Cott, *Utah Place Names* (Salt Lake City: University of Utah Press, 1990), 244.

8. Lenora Hall LeFevre, *Boulder Mountain and Its Peoples* (Springville, UT: Art City Publishing, 1973), 5.

9. William B. Smart, *Old Utah Trails* (Salt Lake City: Utah Geographic, 1988), 45–46.

10. Ibid., 46.

11. Bailey, *Indian Slave Trade,* 146.

12. Fish, "Southern Utah Expedition," 24–28. See also John C. Frémont, *Report of the Exploring Expeditions to the Rocky Mountains in the Year 1842 and to the Oregon and North California in the Years 1843–44* (Washington, D.C.: Gales and Seaton, 1845), 272–74.

13. Fish, "Southern Utah Expedition," 39, 41–52. Captain Jefferson Hunt, formerly of the Mormon Battalion, had been sent back over the route to get supplies for the immigrants the first winter the Mormons were in the Salt Lake Valley. Even though most of the stock he purchased died on the return trip, he knew the trail and was one of the Mormons who took California-bound wagons across it.

14. Journal History, 9 March 1849, LDS Church Archives.

15. Brigham. H. Roberts, *Comprehensive History of the Church of Jesus Christ of Latter-day Saints,* vol. 3. Reprint (Provo, UT: Brigham Young University Press, 1965), 485. Pratt was a member of the legislature and was present at the session. See also Fish, "Southern Utah Expedition," and Parley P. Pratt, *Autobiography of Parley P. Pratt* (Manchester: James Jones, n.d.).

16. Robert L. Campbell, Journal, 15 December 1849, Historical Department, Church of Jesus Christ of Latter-day Saints (hereafter cited as HDC), Salt Lake City, Utah.

17. See ibid., John Brown, Journal, and Journal History, for 16 December 1849, all in HDC.

18. Journal History, 18–19 December 1849; Campbell, Journal, 18 December 1849.

19. Ida Chidester and Eleanor Bruhn, *Golden Nuggets of Pioneer Days: A History of Garfield County*, 9. Chidester and Bruhn give the Paiute chief's name as Ow-wan-nop, while Wayne K. Hinton gives it as Quinarrah in *The Dixie National Forest* (Cedar City, UT: U.S. Department of the Interior, n.d.).

20. LaVan Martineau, *Southern Paiutes: Legends, Lore, Language, and Lineage* (Las Vegas: KC Publishing, 1992), 60, 160. Martineau says the soldiers—who caught the Indians unaware and massacred men, women, children, babies, and even the dogs—may have been from Camp Floyd, Utah, or from Camp Douglas.

21. *Deseret News*, 7 August 1852. See also Journal History, 26 June 1852, and journals of John Steel, Mahonri Moriancumer Steel, and the Priddy Meeks. Thanks to Fred Esplin for a typescript of the Meeks journal.

22. Priddy Meeks, Journal, 56.

23. John Steel, Journal, 33.

24. *Deseret News*, 7 August 1852.

25. Ibid.

26. As quoted in Herbert E. Gregory, "Scientific Explorations in Southern Utah," *American Journal of Science* 248 (October 1945): 532–33.

27. Ibid.

CHAPTER 4

A Precarious Beginning

SETTLING PANGUITCH

To George A. Smith

Owing to the decreases of our wheat crop this past season through the scarcity of water, several of the brethren have made an exploration on the Sevier due east from this place, and report having found an excellent valley capable of sustaining as large a number of inhabitants as Parowan Valley with good and abundant facilities for a thrifty settlement. Estimated distance 45 miles from P[arowan]. Party reporting wish to know of us if they can have the privilege of settling in said valley. . . . We do not feel to decide upon a matter of so much importance without consulting Prest Young through Your agency.

Your early favor in an answer either for or against will be thankfully received by Your Brethren in the Truth.

Wm H. Dame
C.C. Pendleton[1]

Panguitch's First Settlement, 1864–66

Within a month of the above letter to George A. Smith, fifty-four families left Beaver and Parowan, traveling forty miles over the mountain to build a new community. They hacked a road through the difficult mountain terrain of Little Creek Canyon, reaching the twenty-five-mile-long Panguitch Valley on 16 March 1864. That night the lead party of five families—Alfred and Mary Caroline Hadden, with seven of their eight children; the Jens Neilson and Riley Moss families; John R. and Jane Coupe Robinson, with six children; and John's brother Timothy Robinson—stayed at the junction of Panguitch Creek and the Sevier River. Timothy Robinson was married to Alfred and Mary Caroline Hadden's daughter, Julia Ann, who had just given birth to a son on 3 March in Paragonah. Most likely she did not accompany her husband on this first trip but came shortly after. The following day other families began arriving to join in the founding of the new settlement. They named it Fairview, which the legislature would later change to Panguitch.[2]

The settlers found ample water and began to plant crops in the rich soil near Panguitch Creek, which drained the clear natural reservoir of Panguitch Lake located in the mountains to the west. They divided the land east and south of town into forty-acre fields, with a four-rod lane around each field. They would eventually fence the entire tract, which was about ten miles long. Alfred Hadden immediately set about surveying a canal (later called the South Field Ditch) to bring water from the creek to the fields south of the town. Alex Matheson dug the canal with the help of a plow and four sturdy oxen. But the planting progressed slowly; only one out of every three families had a yoke of oxen, and some of those teams were needed to drag logs to the town site. Even with the early spring start, all the crops would not get planted in time to mature in the high altitude before winter. Meanwhile, Edward Dalton of Parowan proceeded to survey the town and parcel off lots.

Organizing a branch of the LDS church, Parowan Stake President William H. Dame and his counselor Jesse N. Smith appointed Jens Neilson as bishop, Jesse Louder as first counselor, and Daniel Matheson as second counselor. Thomas Gunn would serve as chorister. Jenkins T. Evans and Alex Matheson became the first "ward teachers." The women's Relief Society would not be organized until 1873; at that time, Myra Mayall Henrie became president, Phoebe M. Sevy and Sally Parmer were her counselors, with Mary A. Marshall secretary and Margaret Warner treasurer. This first LDS Relief Society in Garfield County boasted 118 members.[3]

Hastily built "brush shanties and cellars" served as shelters for the families until they could build more substantial homes, but first they erected a tithing house and a hewn-log meetinghouse.[4] Fear of Indian attacks soon forced the new arrivals to turn their building efforts to the construction of a fort in the eastern section of the town. They built their log houses adjoining each other around a five-acre-square plot—known today as Panguitch's School Square. The doors and windows faced inward, with small portholes on the back walls where residents could peer out into the valley. A guardhouse stood at the fort's center, and sentries watched over the safety of the community and its stock at night. A stockade made of closely set posts provided night protection for the animals and formed the fort's northwest corner. The eighteen-by-twenty-foot meetinghouse formed its southwest corner, serving as church, school, and community center. Each side of the building had a door and two windows. A large stone fireplace at the north end provided both heat and light, with tallow candles adding their glow to that of the fireplace. The smoothed split-log floor offered a fine surface for members of the community to waltz or dance a jig, accompanied by the town's five musicians—three of them fiddlers.[5]

Amid the planning, planting, and building, other important milestones of the community took place. On 26 August, Hans and Magdelina Nielsen Christensen welcomed a son they named C. Franklin, the town's first-born child. Two more babies, both girls, would be born that winter: Cornelia to Julia Ann and Timothy Robinson on 30 January 1865, and Lydia to the George Mumfords in February.

At an official elevation of more than 6,600 feet, the residents of Panguitch would forever be at the mercy of short growing seasons and harsh winters. The winter of 1864–65 was exceptionally cold and snowy—and it came early. Deep drifts closed the passes before the townspeople could get their meager wheat harvest to the flour mills in the closest settlements of Gunnison (115 miles north) or Parowan (40 miles west). The women at first used coffee mills to grind what little wheat they had. As those implements wore out they resorted to

William and Charlotte Talbot. William participated in the "Quilt Walk" the
winter of 1864–65. (Courtesy Grant R. Talbot)

metate stones similar to those they had seen Indian women use. What they couldn't grind, they boiled. The few fish the men caught and the occasional small game they could kill provided some relief, but it was not enough to satisfy the hungry community.

In the face of possible starvation, a party of seven men—Alex Matheson, William Talbot, Thomas Richards, Jesse Louder, John Butler, Thomas Adair, and John Paul Smith—left for Parowan to get supplies for the hungry Panguitch families. They took only one light wagon pulled by two yoke of oxen, but they still had to abandon it when the animals bogged down in the heavy snow at the head of Bear Valley. From there, even breaking trail became impossible, so the men resorted to laying quilts in front of them, walking across one, then spreading another, and so on, until they reached Parowan. Alex Matheson recorded the story:

> At one time we were about to give up but we had a little prayer cir-
> cle and ask God for guidance. We decided if we had faith as big as
> a mustard seed we could make it and bring flour to our starving
> families. So we began our quilt laying in prayerful earnest. In this
> way we made our way over the deep crusted snow to Parowan. The
> return trip was harder with the weight of the flour but we finally
> made it to our wagon and oxen and on home.[6]

Another group left for Manti and didn't fair much better. They had to cross the Sevier River nearly a dozen times, almost losing their teams when they broke through the ice.[7] When supplies finally got through "the children laughed and cried for joy to be privileged to eat real bread."[8] The residents of Panguitch all survived the first winter. This called for a celebration.

On 16 March 1865, the anniversary of their arrival in the valley, the town had a party. Julia Robinson remembered, "We had pies made of bulberries and service berries and the Bishop made forty gallons of beer. We had plenty of chickens and other things to eat that were good, molasses cakes & etc. We had plenty of old time music." John and Emily Louder, John Hatch, Sid Littlefield, and Saul Wardle were the musicians for the always popular dancing.

Spring's warm temperatures also brought the first tragedy to the little village. Alfred and Isabella Paxton Whatcott were English con-

verts to the Mormon church. They immigrated to America with a
small son and daughter, having buried another daughter before leaving England in 1863. On 3 October of that year, while they camped
in Parley's Canyon before descending into the Salt Lake Valley,
Isabella gave birth to another son. The Whatcotts took up sheep
ranching at Parowan and from there went to help settle Panguitch.
On 11 May 1865 the swollen Sevier River claimed the life of Alfred
Whatcott when he tried to cross it with a herd of cattle. It took three
weeks before the water subsided and his body was found. When his
widow gave birth to their fourth child five months later, she named
him Alfred, after his father.

The Black Hawk War

At the time of the settlement of Panguitch, several bands of
Paiute Indians occupied the surrounding lands. A small group lived
east of Panguitch in the Widtsoe area; their Paiute name was
Yuhnguh' Kawduhtseng, or "Porcupine Sitting People," because of a
nearby mountain of that same name. The *Awvo'utseng,* or "Semi-cir-
cular Cliffs People," occupied the Bryce Canyon-Cannonville-Tropic
area. To the north lived two other bands of Paiutes. One was known
as *Togoo'vahtseng,* which some sources say meant "Sand People,"
although others believe the word meant "swampy"—an interpretation that fits the wetlands along the Sevier River. They inhabited the
Circle Valley region and the adjacent mountains, extending into
Garfield County to the area around Spry. Over the mountain, immediately to the east of their hunting grounds, the *Paw goosawd
Uhmpuhtseng,* or "Water Clover People," occupied the length of Grass
Valley, extending into Garfield County south of Antimony. In the still
unexplored eastern reaches of future Garfield County lived the
Tuh'duvaw Duhts'eng, or "Barren Valley People," in the Escalante area
and the *Untaw'duheutseng* people of the Henry Mountains. Chief
Ow-wan-nop's band, known as *Pawdoo' Goonuntseng,* or "Water Up
People," ranged from Panguitch to Parowan Valley to the west. The
Mormons called them "Parowan Indians" and named both Parowan
and Paragonah after them.[9]

The winter of 1864–65, so difficult for the new settlers, devas-
tated all of these bands. The unusually deep snow took its toll on the

Chief Black Hawk. (Utah State Historical Society)

wildlife that served as their winter food staples. Almost daily storms
continued through most of April. Franklin H. Head, the territorial
superintendent of Indian affairs, wrote, "The Indians are extremely

poor, and like other people, will steal before they will starve." Farther north, in Sanpete Valley, some Utes had become hostile, stealing cattle and killing whites. Indian tribes throughout Utah, most of whom at first had welcomed the Mormons, seeing them as a new resource, now saw them as intruders on their lands who were driving game from traditional hunting grounds. By 1866 Brigham Young both recognized and sympathized with their plight:

> [We] occupy the land where they used to hunt the rabbit . . . and the antelope were in these valleys in large herds when we first came here. . . . they could catch fish in great abundance in the lake in the season . . . and live upon them pretty much throughout the summer. But now their game has gone and they are left to starve.[10]

However sincere Young's sympathy may have been, it was late in coming. A year earlier, the Ute chief Black Hawk, determined to drive the intruders out, had forged a war alliance among most of the bands throughout the territory, including Navajos who came into Kane and Washington counties to trade. Black Hawk himself reportedly said that "none of his warriors had any grievance against the settlers" and that the raids were "forced by starvation of his people.[11]

Traditionally, the Utes and Paiutes preferred to trade with settlers for food or other needs, rather than raid them.[12] The Paiutes, who, for the most part, did not have horses, usually walked into the Mormon settlements to beg or trade for food. As Black Hawk and his warriors began to raid Mormon communities, stealing livestock and killing whoever tried to stop them, cultural misunderstandings and clashes arose even between the friendly Indians and the settlers. Tragedy resulted on both sides.

While most of the Black Hawk War took place in central Utah, Indian troubles began in the south early in 1865 when Navajos crossed over from Arizona and raided Kanab, stealing horses. The men at Panguitch began carrying their guns at all times. John Louder organized an independent company of twenty-five Panguitch men he called Minute Men. Louder served as captain until Colonel George A. Smith arrived to officially organize the militia on 21 March 1865. The men elected Louder to continue as their captain, Alex. G. Ingram as captain of the guard, and Alexander Matheson as sergeant.

Some seven miles north of Panguitch near Lowder Spring (a misspelling of the Louder family name), a company of seventy-six Iron County militiamen under the command of Major Silas Sanford Smith built a small fort early in 1866.[13] Fort Sanford offered a measure of protection from Indians for the settlers as well as anyone traveling the Old Spanish Trail or along the Sevier River. Since Lowder Spring was a warm spring, unusual for that area, it offered comfort not normally found in the Garfield area. The men built the eight-foot-high walls from juniper posts which they planted in a vertical stockade style, enclosing five acres with good grass so livestock could be protected. They also dug a deep ditch around the perimeter to prevent attackers from scaling the walls.

On 22 April John Louder visited friends at Fort Sanford. With orders to "take in all straggling Indians in the vicinity," William West and Collins R. Hakes rode out from the fort to intercept two Indians, Santick and Shegump, they had seen duck hunting across the river. The Indians objected, saying they wanted to talk to Louder, whom they trusted. The whites said that Louder was at the stockade. Santick and Shegump started for the fort, but West pulled his horse up to block them. At that point one of the Indians grabbed the bit of West's horse and the other fired, hitting West in the shoulder. In the ensuing struggle Hakes killed Santick.

From the fort Louder could see the trouble and rode to aid his men, wounding the escaping Shegump in the shoulder. Although Louder tracked the wounded man about four miles to a rock outcropping, darkness forced him back to the fort. The next day, his father, Jesse Louder, and three other men picked up the trail and found where Shegump had met other Indians who helped him to safety.[14]

The following day, 24 April, Major Silas Sanford Smith, under orders from General George A. Smith, told Captain Louder to take some fifteen men to the Paiute Indian camp above Panguitch and take the Indians there prisoner. Louder and his men were to hold them at Panguitch until they received further orders. The Panguitch residents had previously traded with these Indians and even knew some by name. Louder later wrote:

> On approaching the Indian camp we thought it best to divide the
> party, so as not to excite the Indians. We did so, coming in at inter-
> vals. Old Doctor Bill, one of the occupants of the camp became
> very excited when I asked for their guns, and began looking
> around for his gun. . . . At this juncture another Indian [named
> Red Lake] came in with his gun in his hand. Coming up to me, he
> pretended to hand it to me, but in doing so, he . . . turned the
> muzzle towards me. I caught the gun in my left hand and hurried
> off on my horse.[15]

Meanwhile, Doctor Bill had secured his bow and shot an arrow
into James Butler's ribs. As the Indian reached for a second arrow, a
shower of bullets felled him. Butler turned to see Louder struggling
with Red Lake. With the arrow still protruding from his side, he went
to rescue his friend, firing once with his double-barrel gun, killing
Red Lake.[16]

The militia were finally able to "arrest" the remaining Indians.
Whether they held them there or took them to Panguitch is not clear,
but the following day the soldiers buried the dead. None of the
settlers were killed and there is no account of how many of the
Indians died other than Doctor Bill and Red Lake. Louder recalled:
"We kept [the Indians] for a considerable length of time, until we
received orders from Colonel Dame to liberate them, and they were
consequently turned loose."[17]

On 1 May 1866 Brigham Young issued orders that the residents
of Sanpete County and communities south along the Sevier River
and into Kane County gather into groups of at least 150 men to protect their families and livestock. This, coupled with the two clashes
with the Indians in Panguitch Valley, triggered the decision to abandon the town of Panguitch. Leaving crops in the ground, new homes,
corrals, and the unfinished fort with all its buildings, the pioneers of
Panguitch packed up their wagons that same month. Some took
refuge at Fort Sanford for a short time; among them were John and
Jane Mills Paxton Ramsey and Jane's four children and their families,
including widowed Isabella Paxton Whatcott and her three sons.
Finally, believing it impossible to return to friendly terms with the
Indians, the soldiers and families living at the fort also evacuated that

post. It was never used again. Eventually farmers would salvage the poles of the stockade to build houses, outbuildings, and fences.

The extended Mills-Whatcott family left Fort Sanford for Kanosh, Millard County. Others from Panguitch trekked back across the mountain to Parowan, and some eventually scattered to other communities. Among those who stayed in Parowan were John and Emily Teressa Hodgetts Louder.

Few of the original settlers would ever return to live in Garfield County. One exception, the Timothy and Julia Ann Hadden Robinson family, went to Kanosh for several years and then to Iron County before eventually moving back to Garfield County. Eighteen-year-old Enoch Wardle, a single man with no family attachments, would also return; however, at the breakup of the original town, he headed south to Utah's Dixie, where he mustered into the First Brigade of the volunteer cavalry company of the Iron Military District.

By June all the settlements from Gunnison to Kanab had been abandoned. Black Hawk and his warriors, gathered from allied bands across the territory, continued in their efforts to drive the whites from their land or at least to raid their livestock herds.

The James Andrus Military Expedition, 1866

On 15 August 1866, under orders issued by Brigadier General Erastus Snow, Captain James Andrus and his First Brigade of Cavalry of the Iron Military District, Nauvoo Legion, left St. George in search of marauding Indians. Instead, they found the beautiful Garfield high country. Andrus had orders to cross the unexplored region along the west side of the Colorado River from the Kaibab Plateau (then called Buckskin Mountain) to the confluence of the Green and Colorado rivers. The full company consisted of sixty-two men in five platoons.

Andrus sent eighteen of the troops under the command of Lieutenant Joseph Fish north to Parowan and then across the pass to the Sevier River. They continued on to the headwaters of the "Pah Rear" (Paria) River, where the two groups were to rendezvous. The remaining forty-six men accompanied Andrus across the Arizona Strip to Kanab before turning north to the unexplored reaches of Escalante and Boulder mountains. Of these men, five would return

to make homes in Panguitch: Samuel Adair, David Cameron, Jesse
Crosby, John Houston, and Hyrum Pollack; eighteen-year-old Enoch
Wardle, who had been among the first settlers at Panguitch and had
signed on with Andrus after the community was evacuated, also
returned. Another soldier, twenty-one-year-old John Taylor Lay,
would live out his life in Escalante.

Each soldier had a horse, two revolvers, and a long-range rifle. A
pack animal for every two men carried their forty days' supply of
rations and equipment.[18] Both groups were to find and reprimand
any hostile Indians and appease the friendly Paiute and Kaibab
Indians. At the same time, Andrus had instructions to discover all he
could "of the facilities and resources of the country," and prepare a
report of his findings. This report of the central and eastern portion
of today's Garfield County gave an important first description of the
rough canyon country which sloped eastward from the rim of the
Great Basin and the high plateaus of the Colorado River. The troops
thus helped create the first known map based on actual exploration
of the region.[19]

The military reconnaissance mission proved to be especially useful to the future settlement of Garfield County. But, in dealing with
the Indians, Captain Andrus, according to some sources, proved to
be better at reprimanding than at appeasing. Stories of his inhuman-
ity to the Indians have passed down through three tribes. One
Shivwits member said that Andrus "used to kill Indians and was a
very mean man towards them, while others were good."[20] For
example, earlier that year, the company had searched along Kanab
Creek for Navajos who had killed Dr. James M. Whitmore and Robert
McIntyre near Pipe Springs in Kane County on 8 January 1866.
Instead, they found an innocent band of Paiutes, whom Andrus and
his men killed, including women and children.[21]

The first four days of the 1866 expedition took the troops along
the Arizona Strip and then northeast to the town of Kanab, which,
like Panguitch, was deserted because of the Black Hawk War. There
they found the buildings and parched crops undisturbed. They then
traveled northeast up Johnson Canyon. The miles covered thus far by
Andrus and his men were familiar to most of them. By 7 August, the
company had entered into new terrain. On Friday, 24 August, they

camped near the mouth of Henrieville Creek on the border of future
Kane and Garfield counties in the upper valley of the Paria River in a
small, circular basin about twenty miles in diameter. From their camp
the men could see west to the Pink Cliffs of the Paunsaugunt Plateau
which form Bryce Canyon. To the northeast they viewed the weath-
ered, striped face of Table Cliff Plateau jutting two thousand feet
higher than the rim of Bryce Canyon. To the east over rocky hills lay
Kodachrome Basin, and beyond they could see a slender finger of the
Kaiparowits Plateau pointing north to the headwaters of the
Escalante River.

Franklin Benjamin Woolley, who wrote the report of the expedition, described this basin, where three small towns—Tropic,
Henrieville, and Cannonville—would eventually nestle:

> The Valley sides are Sloping, excepting near to the Mountains,
> where they are generally precipitous, covered with scrubby cedar
> and pinion pine cut up by rough deep kanyons and gorges, run-
> ning from the mts. to the Pah Rear [Paria]. The immediate mar-
> gins of the Streams and the beds of dry washes are narrow . . . and
> subject to sudden floods. Most of them dry up in the summer sea-
> son. Along the margin of the main stream and Some of the
> branches are narrow bottoms of fertile land, not in sufficient quan-
> tity to Sustain any large settlements, if there was even a certainty
> of water during the dry season. The streams rise from small springs
> in the heads of the washes, close under the mountain . . . and
> afford small spots of hay and meadow land.[22]

Andrus sent out two scouting parties on Saturday to find a practical route out of the basin; one came back with a successful report—
they had discovered a passable glade to the southeast. Woolley
explained that except for where they had entered the valley, the
"passes are all high; and for a large portion of the year impracticable
owing to the Snows, which fall here very deep in winter."[23] Neither
scouting party had seen any sign of Indians, but Indians were quietly
watching the soldiers.

On Sunday Lieutenant Fish and his men arrived in camp. From
Parowan they had traveled over the wagon road to the abandoned
buildings and fields of Panguitch, which languished in the same
untouched condition as Kanab's. Continuing south along the Sevier

River six miles, they turned east up Red Canyon, and roughly followed the route of present-day Utah Highway 12 through the future
site of Cannonville to the Andrus camp about three miles farther
south. Fish declared the entire trail to be passable by wagons in summer.

Upon regrouping, the troops weeded out fourteen lame and inef-
ficient animals and chose six men, Elijah Averett, Albert Beebee,
George Isom, Charles Pinney, Hyrum Pollack, and Frederick Rugg, to
take them and some surplus equipment back to St. George. This
group left at two o'clock on Sunday. At the same time, the main party
broke camp and moved seven miles up Henrieville Creek to a place
where several seams of coal were visible in the hillside. They called
this camp Coal Point.

The expedition had hardly settled in before Beebee, Pinney, and
Rugg came limping into camp. The men returning to St. George had
gone only six miles before two Indians deemed them sufficiently vulnerable to attack. They killed Elijah Averett, who was in the lead.
George Isom took an arrow in his left shoulder as the rest scrambled
for cover in the junipers. In their retreat, Hyrum Pollack became separated from the other men. He remained hidden until he saw the
Indians leave with the horses, then started hiking back toward camp.
Meanwhile, the other fleeing men hid the wounded Isom in some
timber and hurried to get help.

Twenty-five of Andrus's men set out immediately to find and
"punish the Indians." Only a mile and a half from camp they met
Pollack, who pointed them in the direction he had seen the Indians
go. Although the soldiers eventually recovered twelve of the horses
with their packs still intact, the Indians, whom they thought they had
cornered in a cave, escaped into the night. The next morning the men
found and buried Averett's body, then recovered the wounded Isom,
who was "much exhausted from fatigue and exposure." The canyon
in Kane County where Elijah Averett was killed now bears his name
and his grave is marked today by a round stone marker inscribed
"E.A. 1866."[24]

On Tuesday, 28 August, the brigade broke camp and began
climbing the steep, blue clay hills, known as "The Blues," to the
Aquarius Plateau above. After rescuing a horse that had slipped off

the mountainside and having their teeth rattled by a ferocious thunderstorm, the green highland of Upper Valley Creek proved a welcome sight—even in the rain. Woolley wrote that the "Scenery at once changes as if by magic, to a beautiful park, green grassy meadows, groves of timber on sloping hill sides, streams of clear cold mountain water shedding into a Small open Valley forming the Center of the picture, very refreshing after the barrenness of the Pah Rear Side."[25]

The next day, the militiamen followed Upper Valley Creek six miles before coming to a steep canyon with an old Indian trail leading down out of view. "Having no guide and the gulch appearing very rough," Andrus decided it best to swing north in search of a pass that would steer them around the deep washes and canyons. Woolley described their path as "the roughest Country we had yet passed over." They had to shoot one horse after it tumbled fifty feet over a cliff, breaking its shoulder. That night they camped on Birch Creek (which they called Cottonwood Creek) and woke to the glitter of heavy frost on their bedrolls and equipment.

On the last day of August they entered what they would call Potato Valley. Ten years later, in 1876, a group of Mormon settlers would lay out the townsite of Escalante where the Andrus expedition camped that night. Describing the Escalante River, Woolley wrote enthusiastically that the "stream affords about as much water" as the east branch of Rio Virgin just below Springdale. He estimated the valley, which he believed could be cultivated, to be about a mile wide and six miles long, "level, easy to irrigate, fertile [with] facilities surrounding it for the support of a thriving settlement of one hundred and fifty families. Climate and elevation about the same as Long Valley on the Rio Virgin." In exploring the surrounding area, the men found "Fuel and timber abundant, excellent range for cattle, hay accessible in valley at Timber Park, within distance of 10 to 12 miles. We have found wild potatoes growing from which the Valley takes its name."[26]

Difficult as getting onto the plateau had been, trying to get across it and down the other side proved even more challenging. The militiamen detoured several miles southeast trying to cross the Escalante River gorge, finally giving up and turning back to Potato Valley. From there they followed Pine Creek up through what is today the Box Death Hollow Wilderness Area, then, as Woolley recorded, they "commenced to ascend the rim of the basin by steep rough difficult Kanyons and side hills. Camped on mountain side at Quaking asp Springs."

The following day the party's route paralleled what is now the U.S. Forest Service road across the Aquarius Plateau to the top of Boulder Mountain. From the summit the men scrutinized the route over which they had come. Wrote one: "This view satisfied us entirely of the utter impracticability of any trail crossing the basin from Potatoe Valley, N.E. or S.E. either to the Mountains bordering it or to the river."[27]

On Sunday, 2 September, the men traveled about nine miles across Boulder Mountain until about noon, at which time they emerged from the pine forest onto "a high bold promontory"—either Bown's Point or Deer Point on the southeast rim. Woolley described the grand panorama that stretched out before them for hundreds of miles from the northeast to the southeast:

> Immediately under us and down the black volcanic precipice . . . more than a thousand feet below are three Small lakes surrounded by groves of timber beautifully Situated on A Small plateau . . . that seems to have sunk down from the upper level of the mountain. These lakes may at one time have been the craters of now extinct volcanoes. Below these to the S.E. is the Colorado Plateau stretching away as far as the Eye can see a naked barren plain of red and white Sandstone crossed in all directions by innumerable gorges [and] Occasional high buttes rising above the general level, the country gradually rising up to the ridges. . . . The Sun shining down on this vast red plain almost dazzled our eyes by the reflection as it was thrown back from the fiery surface.[28]

About twenty-five miles to the east loomed a mountain range that Woolley called by its Indian name: "Pot-Se-Nip" (or Pat-Se-Nup); others referred to the peaks as the unnamed mountains—and, indeed, they remained the last mapped and named mountains in the continental United States. Three years after the Andrus party viewed them, John Wesley Powell would name them the Henry Mountains

Looking from the Aquarius Plateau to Boulder Mountain. Capitol Wash domes are in the background. (Utah State Historical Society)

in honor the secretary of the Smithsonian Institution, Joseph Henry, who had helped finance his expedition.

In reading the rugged landscape, Andrus and his men mistook the Fremont River for the Green River, and Upper Halls Creek for the Colorado River. Woolley estimated they had traveled about 260 miles from St. George. "Being Satisfied that the Mouth of Green River the point of our destination was in sight before us, and that we were as near to it as it was possible for us to get," wrote Woolley, "and that there were no trails leading in that direction, we unanimously agreed that we had carried out so far as practicable that portion of our instructions, and commenced our return at 3 P.M. of Sunday Sept 2d [1866]."[29]

Since the incident in which Elijah Averett had lost his life, they had seen no fresh signs of Indians, although they did record crossing and sometimes following a number of Indian trails. They descended the mountain into lower Wayne County and traversed the Awapa

Plateau, entering Grass Valley in present-day Piute County a few miles above today's Antimony. There they thought a small community might be established. At Circleville they found another empty town, the wheat ripe for harvest, but no one to do the work. The Old Spanish Trail took the militia on a final swing across the northwest corner of Garfield County before they traveled up Bear Creek to Parowan and then back to St. George.

In his final report to Brigadier General Erastus Snow, Andrus thanked his men for "their hearty Co-operation in the Campaign, and "the Almighty" for "the blessings . . . extended to us on our journey; much of the way being through an indian country rough Mountains and without trail or guide. [We] attribute our safety to his overruling Providence."[30]

During the Black Hawk War, an estimated seventy whites lost their lives. There is no count of Indians killed, but Native Americans suffered many more casualties. Black Hawk finally made peace with his Mormon neighbors in the fall of 1867, and in 1868 he and other Indian leaders signed a peace treaty. Some raiding and killing by scattered renegade groups continued, however, until 1872. That year, 200 federal troops came to the assistance of the settlers.

Panguitch's Second Settlement

Interest in establishing a permanent community at Panguitch did not fade during the years of Indian unrest. Hope for the town's eventual resettlement continued, as is evidenced by an article that appeared in the *Deseret Evening News* on 11 April 1870. The newspaper published correspondence received from Parowan regarding a Monday evening meeting held there on 8 April at which Brigham Young presided: "President George A. Smith spoke respecting the breaking up of Pangwitch, stating that there was not time to settle it again."[31]

During the late summer and early fall of 1870, A.M. Musser, who also spoke in favor of resettlement at the Parowan meeting earlier that year, led church leaders including Brigham Young, his counselor George A. Smith, Apostle Erastus Snow, and others on an expedition to visit the colonies in southern Utah. They took a route south through Juab and Millard counties to Parowan. At Parowan the party, which had been traveling with some twenty guards, swelled to forty-three, including Parowan bishop William H. Dame and others from Beaver, Iron, and Washington counties. Bishop Dame outfitted the company with the necessary provisions, bedding, cooks, teams, and wagons. An odometer fastened to the axle of Brigham Young's carriage marked the miles.

Leaving Parowan at first light on Monday, 5 September, the group traveled forty-one miles up Center Creek and over Prince Mountain along the same route the first party to explore Panguitch Valley had taken nearly twenty years earlier. They wound their way "through some beautiful small valleys and oases," past Panguitch Lake—which they noted teemed with trout—and down into the valley "to the well located but temporally abandoned town of Panguitch" before sundown.

Musser described the next day's journey through the southern end of the county:

> From where we nooned . . . (at the last crossing of the Sevier, a most delightful spot) to near the rim of the great Basin, we passed over and through a paradisaic country. . . . It is a valley gently undulating, covered with grass and dotted with springs and "seaps" which form a small stream that courses through the valley and empties into the Sevier River. Timber is abundant and so easy of access, that teams can be driven amongst it without roads being made.[32]

Following this southern Utah tour, Young directed George W. Sevy, who resided at Harmony in present-day northern Washington County, to bring his two families and take charge of the resettlement of Panguitch. The *Deseret News* then published the following notice from Sevy early in 1871: "All those who wish to go with me to resettle Panguitch Valley, will meet me at Red Creek [near present-day Paragonah] on the 4th day of March, 1871 and we will go over the mountain in Company to settle that country."[33]

The trip "over the mountain" took less time than earlier treks, as the company of about twenty-five men and two women went a few miles north of Paragonah and then followed Little Creek to Bear Valley over what was a well-established portion of the Old Spanish

Trail.[34] They arrived in the valley on either 18 or 19 March. The new settlers found the valley without snow, the abandoned fields dry and dusty, and the homes and other buildings and clearings much as the first settlers had left them in 1866.[35] Apparently the Indians had left everything completely alone; even some crops were still standing.

During 1871 approximately 120 men, most with families, came to live in Panguitch. Of these, only about a half-dozen from the first colonization eventually returned. They included John Lowe Butler II, John Hyatt, Sidney J. Littlefield, Riley Moss, William and Charlotte Newman Talbot with their five children, James and Sarah Jane Snyder Dickenson with their family, and Enoch and Mary Mortensen Wardell. The settlers decided that former residents could reclaim their property or sell it, but, in the meantime, land and dwellings should be divided among the newcomers.[36]

Of necessity, those who arrived with the second settlement occupied homes built by the original colonizers, which were no more than cabins within the old fort. David Shakespear was ten years old in 1871 when his family came to Panguitch from Springvalley, Nevada. His father had "bought a house in the fort and twenty acres of land in the south field from one of the men who had left." Within two miles of town they found plenty of firewood and grass for their animals, Shakespear reported, and continued, "We found deer and other game in abundance, and the lake and streams were well stocked with fish."[37] One of the first tasks of the settlers was to dig a culinary water well in the center of the fort so they no longer would have to use the creek water, which they deemed "very unsanitary" after the domestic animals had also used it. Albert DeLong, W.D. Kartchner, and James and Samuel Henrie were the first to build homes for their families outside the fort. Isabelle Henrie, Samuel's wife, recalled that moving into her new two-room home was the "happiest time of her life . . . where she could work and be comfortable."[38]

In keeping with custom, a new LDS ward was soon organized within the resettled community. George Sevy became bishop and selected James Henrie and Meltiar Hatch as his counselors, with Joseph L. Heywood as the ward clerk. At least one member of the second settlement, William H. Packer, approved of Sevy's stewardship when he reported the bishop's "good work . . . in all phases of the

Joseph L. Heywood, resident of Panguitch, first U.S. Marshal in Utah, and head of a commission to establish Utah's territorial boundary. (Utah State Historical Society)

community."[39] A later arrival, James Y. Williams, agreed with Packer that Sevy was a "good man," but he thought the bishop "to[o] lenient to evil doers, yet it seems to be incorporated in his nature to be lenient and kind hearted to even the wayward and unruly."[40]

George Sevy's first wife, Phoebe Melinda Butler, did her part to assure the survival of this second settlement. Because yields from crops that first year were sparse, the townspeople took all their wheat to the bishop's wife. She boiled it and then distributed it as needed to the members of the community.[41] This grain they supplemented by butchering some of their cattle for food and sending men on horseback to Parowan for flour.

During the first fall of resettlement some of the residents established the Panguitch Cooperative Mercantile and Manufacturing Institution, modeled after the larger Zions Cooperative Mercantile Association in Salt Lake City. The founders of this organization were convinced of the "impolity of leaving the trade and comerce" of their city to "strangers."[42] At the first general meeting, the stockholders consolidated spiritual and economic power by electing Bishop George Sevy president; one of his counselors, Meltiar Hatch, as vice-president; Clarence Jackson, secretary; and James and Samuel Henrie and William LeFevre as directors. The institution employed ward clerk Joseph Heywood as its clerk and manager at a salary of 5 percent of the proceeds, which they later reduced to a more modest 3 percent.[43] Later, William Proctor and Martin W. Foy would also operate stores in Panguitch.

Agriculture became the basis of the Panguitch economy; however, the town's high elevation limited the types of crops settlers could grow, even though the first few winters were mild. In 1874, however, a severe winter killed a majority of the stock because the residents had not been able to grow and stockpile hay for winter feed. Potatoes, grains, meadow grass, and eventually alfalfa (usually two cuttings per year) proved to be the most successful crops, but this was determined only after much trial and error. For example, much of the wheat planted in heavy clay soil near the river froze in the early years; but those who planted in the south field (where the richer earth was more porous) seldom experienced that problem. Trouble also came with growing alfalfa until someone advised the growers to irrigate the fields late in the fall.[44]

Stock raising became the dominant occupation, and along with this the dairy industry also grew. Unlike those from the first settlement who had used Panguitch Creek as their only source of water for irrigation, the second group of settlers also tapped the Sevier River, even building a dam on it in 1873. This supplied sufficient water until 1883, when it became necessary to build a dam at the outlet of Panguitch Lake.[45]

In addition to such agrarian enterprises, other undertakings indicated progress in the community. The town established a post office, with William Kartchner as the first postmaster. John W. Norton set up a blacksmith shop in one of the houses in the fort. A harness and saddle shop operated by Joseph Marshall and William Hodget did a good business. James and Samuel Henrie brought a gristmill to Panguitch from Panaca, Nevada, and rebuilt it on Panguitch Creek about a mile from town. Riley G. Clark first ran the mill, but he died soon after it began production. James Dickenson then operated it for about the next twenty years, and the area became known as Dickenson Hill. Fathers baptized their children in the mill race and then took them into the mill or the Dickenson home to be confirmed members of the Church of Jesus Christ of Latter-day Saints.

The Houston and Cameron brothers combined their efforts and "built and operated a sawmill on the Mammoth"; and it was reported that they too "did a flourishing business." Panguitch Creek powered sawmills built by George Sevy, James Imlay, George Wilson, Joel Johnson, Allen and Ninian Miller, and Elijah Elmer. William and John Butler built a shingle mill along this same creek. An "up-and-down" sawmill was constructed at the mouth of the canyon on Panguitch Creek.

When the sawmills became operative, the settlers built plank homes and the new cooperative store.[46] Simon Lowell constructed his pottery shop near the sawmill and "turned out a great variety of first-class crockery." James Henry and Jesse Crosby had Riley Clark, Sr., build a tannery in 1875. It was operated first by Lorenzo Clark, then by Joseph C. Davis until a fire eventually destroyed the business.[47] Sometimes these early industries lacked skilled workers, the tannery being such an enterprise. According to Salt Lake City newspapers, shoemakers were badly needed in Panguitch. An article stated that the cooperative tannery had ample leather but that the community was virtually without shoes. This provided "a splendid opportunity to three good, steady shoemakers, Latter-day Saints, who want good homes, plenty of work, and abundance to eat, drink and wear."[48] Ril Clark, Jr., was one of several who answered the call and took the "fairly good grade of leather" processed at the tannery and made it up into boots and shoes." Eventually the shoe and boot shop and the tannery were incorporated into the Panguitch mercantile cooperative.[49]

In the midst of this growth, the town had some surprise visitors on 7 November 1874. A posse headed by United States Marshal William Stokes arrived with a warrant for the arrest of John D. Lee for murder and conspiracy in the Mountain Meadows Massacre—a tragedy that had occurred some seventeen years earlier in 1857 when Mormons and Indians treacherously killed more than one hundred emigrants on their way to California at Mountain Meadows in Washington County. Lee had been one of the Mormon leaders in the area at the time. The posse consisted of Thomas Winn, Thomas Le Fevre, Samuel G. Rodgers, David Evans, and Franklin R. Fish. Indictments for conspiracy and murder were also out for William H. Dame, Isaac G. Haight, John M. Higbee, Philip Klinginsmith and others.[50]

Stokes had been trailing Lee for some time. He at first started for Lee's Ferry at the crossing of the Colorado River but heard Lee had gone to Harmony and went there instead. Coming up empty-handed at Harmony, Stokes followed several false leads before he got word that Lee was visiting his fourth wife, Sarah Caroline Williams Lee, and her eleven children in Panguitch. Stokes recalled the lack of local cooperation: "I inquired of the citizens about Lee, but could learn nothing. Some said they never knew him, others that they had never heard of such a man, had not even heard the name."[51]

Undeterred, the marshal deputized all within his sight and ordered them to help find the fugitive. They surrounded and searched Caroline Lee's house to no avail. Stokes noticed what he thought was suspicious activity by some of the family around a hog

John D. Lee's home in Panguitch where he was captured while visiting his fourth wife, Sarah Caroline Williams Lee. The front log portion of the house is original. The sided back part was added later. (Utah State Historical Society)

pen behind the house and checked there. The posse found Lee hiding in the pen and arrested him. When Lee's son's spoke to their father of staging a rescue, Stokes made it clear that any such attempt would bring immediate death to Lee. Lee himself discouraged any acts of violence, remarking that a sufficient period of time had elapsed since the massacre that he felt he stood an excellent chance of having an impartial trial.[52]

Stokes and his men took Lee to Beaver, where he was tried on 23 July 1875. After this trial resulted in a hung jury, Lee was tried a second time in September 1876. This time the jury found him guilty of murder in the first degree. The death sentence he received was carried out in front of a firing squad on 23 March 1877, at the site of the massacre at Mountain Meadows. Many both at the time and since felt that Lee was a scapegoat sacrificed by Mormon leaders to end the affair and protect others from prosecution. Lee's family buried him in the Panguitch cemetery.[53]

Headstone at John D. Lee's grave in the Panguitch cemetery. (Utah State Historical Society)

The month following Lee's arrest, on 18 December 1874, the Panguitch United Order was organized by local LDS stake president Joseph A. Young as part of the Mormon church's endeavor to pro-

mote communal enterprises—a long-time church ideal.[54] The board
of directors chose George Sevy as president of the cooperative order,
with John W. Norton as first vice-president and James Imlay as second vice-president. In the course of its existence the order's enterprises included stock raising, dairying, freighting, smithing, milling,
and farming. However, the order did not prove to be very successful
and in less than two years it ceased to exist.[55] Frequent disagreement
and dissension among the participants caused some to question the
value of the order altogether. Alma Barney declared that the order
took "thrifty, energetic men and made lazy men of them."[56]

Other community institutions progressed, however. Most settlers
carried on an active barter system to augment their home production. William Talbot kept intermittent records of his own transac-
tions. His entries of 27 October 1879 indicate that he made wagons
and traded them for materials with which to construct additional
wagons as well as flour and other commodities for his family.[57] Mary
Heywood cultivated yeast—a much-needed trade item. She supplied
the whole town, exchanging one cup of yeast for a cup of flour.[58]

Although hard currency was not plentiful in the community, the
settlers found they could sell some of their products for cash in the
mining camps of Nevada, which allowed them to purchase items not
manufactured locally. Phoebe Sevy milked cows and then made butter and cheese. She sent these commodities along with lumber from
her husband's mill to Pioche, Nevada. She netted $400 from her first
shipment and was able to buy a "mattress of which she had long
dreamed . . . a feather bed with a good tick."[59] A number of other
women in the community also made butter and cheese for commercial purposes, and many were fine dressmakers and seamstresses.

Among the fine seamstresses in Panguitch, Annie Dowler Judd
provided a much-needed service for which she neither asked nor
received compensation—along with other women in the community,
she helped "lay out the dead." Her mother, Emily Adams Judd, introduced her to this service when Annie was only twelve. At that tender
age she held the light for her mother and the other women who
helped as they prepared deceased townspeople for burial. On one
occasion, Annie placed coins over the eyes of a corpse when the other
women were too reluctant. As a young wife and mother she contin-

ued to prepare the dead for burial, often staying up all night to sew clothes to dress the body. She rendered this service for forty-two years until she was seventy-four.[60]

In the spring of 1877 the new president of the LDS church, John Taylor, visited Panguitch with other church leaders. At the home of William David Shakespear, the leaders organized a new LDS stake on 3 April, with James Henrie as president, George Sevy and Jesse W. Crosby as counselors, and M.M. Steele, Sr., as clerk. The following August the stake held a quarterly conference and the members met in a newly completed meetinghouse.[61] It was probably at this meeting that the Retrenchment Society was organized in Panguitch. This society would foreshadow the Young Ladies Mutual Improvement Association (YLMIA) of later years. One of its goals was to help the young ladies of the territory put aside frivolous things and "retrench" to the more serious and pious things of life.

Within a few years of the resettlement of Panguitch, townspeople had developed lime and brick kilns. According to local resident Dorothy W. Houston, "Burning brick was a community affair, lasting three days."[62] Frederick Judd constructed the first kilns and fired the first brick and lime in Panguitch. He and Samuel Worthen, an excellent mason, began to change the town's face. Many of the early two-story, red-brick structures they built still stand, including the William and Louisa Lee Prince home, said to be the first brick house in the valley. At this writing, the home is a charming bed-and-breakfast establishment located on the corner of 200 South and 300 East. A number of Panguitch residents established two dwellings, one on their town lot and another on farm or ranch property, which they mainly used during the summer when their children did not need to be close to schools.

James Williams boasted in 1877 that Panguitch "had three good day schools all winter, very well attended, and conducted by their teachers in a very able manner."With no public funds available for schools, parents were assessed three dollars per child for each three-month term.[63] Under the supervision of Sophia Peterson the LDS Relief Society built a "nice and commodious brick relief hall," which teacher George Dodds used as a school room the winter of 1876–77.[64] Other early teachers included M.M. Steele, Sr., Myra Henrie, W.P.

An early brick house in Panguitch—renovated in the 1990s as the William Prince Inn.

Sargent, and his wife, Maria L. Sargent. In 1880 the Panguitch Cooperative covered its store, which had been made out of planks in 1873, with bricks.

Beginning in 1881 Frederick Judd started to make brick for the Panguitch LDS Stake Tabernacle. Joseph Heywood proposed the larger building in an LDS quarterly stake conference on 20 March 1880, "so people that so desired could attend church. M.M. Steele, Sr., was put in charge of building. George Dodds drew the plans." Construction of the building began in 1882. It would take ten years to complete. Samuel Worthen and his sons were the brickmasons. Alfred Riding designed the cornice and made the ball (which measured two feet in diameter) that sat on top of the seventy-nine-foot-high spire, which John W. Norton and son Albert fashioned in their blacksmith shop. John F. Sevy made the four-foot-long fish skewered on the spire. Two fourteen-year-old boys, John Steele and Oscar Prince, did most of the painting.[65]

Early Mormon settlers who practiced polygamy often had separate homes for their wives. This compounded the usual difficulties faced by women in such early rural settlements. When George Sevy came to the Panguitch Valley he brought two wives, having recently married the young daughter, Margaret Nebraska, of another Panguitch settler, James H. Imlay. According to her descendants, this was "a great trial" to Sevy's other wife, Phoebe Melinda.[66] However, as was the case with many others in similar circumstances, the challenges of establishing a new community and rearing a large family consumed her time, interest, and energies. Many such women took over the running of family farms and ranches. One of Phoebe's sons recalls that his mother awoke very early, would "warm a pan of milk, put bread in it, give each of them a spoon, and the children would surround a stool on which she placed the pan and they would have bread and milk for their breakfast while she was out doing the morning chores."[67]

George Sevy later took a third wife, had a ranch near Panguitch Lake, helped lead the Hole-in-the-Rock colonization of what became San Juan County, and eventually lived out his days in the Mormon settlement of Colonia Juarez, Mexico. Phoebe, however, despite her husband's entreaties, remained in Panguitch to look after their interests there and to be with her children as they grew to adulthood.

As with most colonization efforts, people in Panguitch worked long hours to create a thriving community. They also realized the value of recreation, amusement, and other activities to bring refinement and entertainment into their lives. Dances and theatrical productions became common, held at first in the old meetinghouse within the fort, then in a store they called the "Old Sow." When it burned down, they used the lower schoolhouse for recreational activities. The town had three main fiddlers, John Louder, Sid Littlefield, and Solomon Wardell. John's mother, Zilpha Louder, and John Hyatt could also help out when needed. Seth Johnson, Charles Pinney, Jesse W. Crosby, and Alma Barney took charge of theatrical productions. Henry Lynn, Sr., called the quadrilles "and danced as he called."[68]

The settlers always held a big celebration on the Fourth of July. Sarah Jane Montague supervised the making of the first flag in Panguitch in 1871. Several friends met in her home and sewed by candlelight to complete their work before the celebration.[69]

Thus, by the end of its first decade, it appeared that this second settlement of Panguitch would endure. The community continued to be the largest and generally the most prosperous within what later became Garfield County and was to become the county seat.

Panguitch Lake

Soon after the resettlement of Panguitch, a number of families moved to the Panguitch Lake area, where the summer grasses were especially favorable for dairy farming. Sometime in 1873 or 1874 Niels Peter Ipson constructed a dugout cabin on the north shore on land he had purchased through trade with the local Indians. He and his wife spent forty summers at the lake and were the first there to own a sailboat. Beginning in 1874 William Prince began homesteading a ranch in the vicinity.

James H. Imlay built a ranch at the mouth of Blue Spring Canyon along one of the streams that feeds the lake. Blue Springs is located in a lush, high valley a few miles south of the lake. The springs themselves are very deep and reach some fifty feet across and about seventy feet long. The clear water appears blue, and "articles such as a watch or coin are distinctly seen on the bottom." Although other streams feed into Panguitch Lake, according to locals, "none are so sure and steady as the Blue Spring." Samuel Henrie, Allen Miller, and Warren Sevy established their ranches there. Among the others who had ranches in the Panguitch Lake area were Seguine Cooper, Albert Haycock, Wallace W. Houston, John and Joseph Imlay, Brigham Knight, Bert Lameroux, Alma Lee, Sidney Littlefield, James Montague, James Pace, Cyrus and Enoch Reynolds, George W. Sevy, William Slade, Joseph Woods and Samuel Worthen.[70] Some of these men, like George Sevy, were polygamous and also kept homes and other families in the valley.

Ranches and dairy enterprises in the area boomed. It was reported that "thousands of pounds of butter, cheese and mountain trout were taken by these ranchers to the Silver Reef mines near St. George and traded for gold pieces." The sawmills around the lake provided lumber and shingles for these mines as well.[71]

In 1876 James Shepherd Montague built a seven-room hotel on the south shore. The Montagues soon gained fame for their warm hospitality. Later they added a dance hall to their operation that extended out over the water. The Montagues and Ipsons joined to produce a flourishing fish business. It was reported that they "caught and sold many wagon loads of fish. Other settlers fished through the ice in the winter, doing a good business for several years."[72] Panguitch Lake became a center of summer activity for many years to come. After the turn of the century, Mike Gillmore established a resort at Panguitch Lake, complete with cabins named for movie stars such as Tom Mix, Buck Jones, and May West. His guests awakened to a fog horn he blew each morning.[73]

ENDNOTES

1. W.H Dame and C.C. Pendleton to George A. Smith, Parowan, 16 February 1864, 2 Ms 1322, Box 6, fd. 12, HDC.

2. Unless otherwise noted, information on this first settlement of Panguitch comes from Ida Chidester and Eleanor Bruhn, *Golden Nuggets of Pioneer Days: A History of Garfield County,* 11–15.

3. Chidester and Bruhn, *Golden Nuggets,* 165.

4. Alexander Matheson, "The first settlement of Panguitch," no date, copy in possession of Dorothy Houston, Panguitch.

5. Julia Robinson to Sister Heywood, 20 December 1921, copy in possession of Dorothy Houston, Panguitch.

6. Emily Hodges, "Emily Hodges, wife of John Lowder [Louder] Life Story as told to Elenore Bruhn, 1916," copy from Beth Hurst. This expedition would later be commemorated in a poem by Roque Willard entitled "The Quilt Walk."

7. Joseph Fish, *Pioneers of the Southwest and Rocky Mountains* (n.p., n.d.), 292.

8. Chidester and Bruhn, *Golden Nuggets,* 12.

9. See La Van Martineau, *Southern Paiutes: Legends, Lore, Language and Lineage,* 154–62.

10. Brigham Young, "Remarks," Journal History of the Church of Jesus Christ of Latter-day Saints, 28 July 1866.

11. The F.H. Head quote is from Albert Winkler, "The Ute Mode of War in the Conflict of 1865–68," *Utah Historical Quarterly* 60 (Fall 1992): 302. The Black Hawk quote is from Kate B. Carter, *Our Pioneer Heritage* (Salt Lake City: Daughters of Utah Pioneers, 1968), 9:247.

12. Winkler, "The Ute Mode of War," 300.

13. George A. Thompson, *Some Dreams Die: Utah's Ghost Towns and Lost Treasures* (Salt Lake City: Dream Garden Press, 1982), 45. John W. Van

Cott, *Utah Place Names,* 114, gives the year the fort was built as 1864 and the number of soldiers as twenty-five, both of which seem to be in error.

14. The information about this encounter and the one following, which occurred near Panguitch, are taken from a document written by John Louder and published in Peter Gottfredson, *Indian Depredations in Utah* (Salt Lake City: Skelton Publishing Co., 1919), 190–91. The account in *Golden Nuggets* differs somewhat from Louder's.

15. Gottfredson, *Indian Depredations,* 192–93.

16. Chidester and Bruhn, *Golden Nuggets,* 13, seems to combine the incidents at Fort Sanford and the one at the Indian camp. Gottfredson, *Indian Depredations,* 144–45, tells of word being sent to Circleville that a "pretended friendly" had shot and killed a white man at Fort Sanford on 21 April 1866. This seems to be in error, as there is no record of anyone being killed at Fort Sanford, and the incident John Louder recorded and Gottfredson included on pages 190–92 puts the date of the skirmish as 22 April.

17. Gottfredson, *Indian Depredations,* 192–93.

18. C. Gregory Crampton, "Military Reconnaissance in Southern Utah," *Utah Historical Quarterly* 32 (Spring 1964): 148.

19. Ibid., 145–61. The report was written by Franklin Benjamin Woolley, whose family became prominent pioneers in southern Utah. The report and two accompanying documents, a map and muster roll, are in the Utah State Archives manuscript collection, Military Records Section, and are published in full in the Crampton article.

20. Martineau, *Southern Paiutes,* 65.

21. Three stories about Andrus were related to LaVan Martineau by southern Utah Indians. Two of the stories relate to the massacre of Paiutes described here. In each of these accounts there were two survivors. The first tells of an old woman named Tahdah'heets (meaning orphan) and her grandson Tony Tillahash, whose parents and siblings were all killed in the raid. The boy's anglicized last name means "the Beginning and End of a Family." Another story tells of two brothers who also escaped. The third story recounts an unprovoked firing by Andrus on two Shivwit Indians along the Santa Clara River at another time. Martineau, *Southern Paiutes,* 62–65.

22. Crampton, "Military Reconnaissance," 150–51.

23. Ibid., 150.

24. Ibid., 152.

25. Ibid., 153.

26. Ibid., 154. Potato Valley is not a name the expedition seems to have

chosen, suggesting that other explorers may have been there previously but that they only left word-of-mouth information.

27. Ibid., 155.

28. Ibid., 158.

29. Ibid.

30. Franklin Benjamin Woolley was killed three years later, in 1869, near Victorville, California, by Mojave Indians. Crampton, "Military Reconnaissance," 146, 160.

31. Journal History, Friday, 8 April 1870.

32. "Correspondence," A. Milton Musser to Editor *Deseret News,* Journal History, 10 September 1870.

33. *Deseret News,* 28 February 1871.

34. Walter Kirk Daly, "The Settling of Panguitch Valley, Utah: A Study in Mormon Colonization" (Master's thesis, University of California, 1941), 41. Daly writes that the first two women were George Sevy's second wife, Margaret Imlay Sevy, a daughter of James Imlay, and Caroline Butler. Another source indicates that there were twenty-five "families" in Sevy's company. See *The Genealogy of the Descendants of George Washington Sevy,* compiled by Minerva Sevy Vance and Eileen Sevy Cluff (n.p., 1965), 21, copy in possession of Vera Sevy Peterson Fotheringham, Salt Lake City.

35. Chidester and Bruhn, *Golden Nuggets,* 17.

36. Mary Mortensen was known as Maren Nielsen in her native Denmark. For unknown reasons, after she came to the United States she was called Mary Mortensen. She and Enoch had a son born in Panguitch 2 April 1872. See "Wardell Life Sketches" in possession of Wendy Wardell Adams, Centerville, Utah.

37. David J. Shakespear, "A Short History of Panguitch," *Garfield County News,* 15 September 1938.

38. Chidester and Bruhn, *Golden Nuggets,* 18, 20.

39. *Deseret News,* 31 January 1872.

40. *Deseret News,* 16 March 1877.

41. Chidester and Bruhn, *Golden Nuggets,* 17.

42. Articles of Association and Minutes of the Panguitch Cooperative Mercantile and Manufacturing Institution, 1871–1938, film #LR 671924, LDS Church Archives.

43. Ibid. Two years later, M.M. Steele was elected secretary.

44. Shakespear, "A Short History."

45. Daly, "The Settling of Panguitch Valley," 45.

46. Shakespear, "A Short History."

47. Chidester and Bruhn, *Golden Nuggets*, 17–19, 59.

48. *Deseret News*, 11 July 1877.

49. Shakespear, "A Short History"; Articles of Association and Minutes of the Panguitch Cooperative Mercantile and Manufacturing Institution.

50. See Daly, "The Settling of Panguitch Valley," 55. Daly gives the date of the arrest as 9 November 1874, but Juanita Brooks, in *The Mountain Meadows Massacre*, gives the date as 7 November.

51. Daly, "Settling of Panguitch Valley," 58.

52. Ibid.

53. Ibid., 57.

54. Minutes and Records of the United Order of Panguitch, manuscript #LR 671923, LDS Church Archives,.

55. Ibid. The last date of recorded minutes is 22 March 1876.

56. Ibid., 15 March 1875.

57. William Talbot, journal and ledger, holograph in possession of Grant R. Talbot, Centerville, Utah.

58. Chidester and Bruhn, *Golden Nuggets*, 61.

59. Vance and Cluff, *George Washington Sevy*, 23.

60. Annie Judd's granddaughter, Helen Seaman Linford, of Cedar City, Utah, told this story to Vivian Talbot. Linford also related that Mormon Indian missionary Jacob Hamblin was one of Annie's customers; she sewed him a suit.

61. Chidester and Bruhn, *Golden Nuggets*, 18; *Deseret News*, 22 August 1877.

62. Dorothy W. Houston, unpublished Panguitch history, 1993, 3, copy in possession of the authors.

63. In the Minutes of the Panguitch Cooperative Mercantile and Manufacturing Institution the stockholders met in a schoolhouse as early as 30 October 1871. There is further mention of the Panguitch United Order meeting at a "lower school house " on 12 November 1875 and at an "upper school house" on 26 January 1876. At least the first of these structures was probably built during the first settlement.

64. *Deseret News*, 16 March 1877; see also *Garfield County News*, 15 September 1938.

65. This building was torn down in the 1930s in spite of the protests from the local Daughters of Utah Pioneers and other Panguitch residents. Chidester and Bruhn, *Golden Nuggets*, 175, 307–8.

66. Vance and Cluff, *George Washington Sevy*, 22.

67. Ibid.

68. Chidester and Bruhn, *Golden Nuggets,* 192.

69. Ibid., 61.

70. Ibid., 216–19.

71. Ibid., 217.

72. Shakespear, "A Short History of Panguitch."

73. Information from Marilyn Jackson, Escalante resident and historian.

CHAPTER 5

GARFIELD COUNTY AND EXPLORATION OF THE COLORADO RIVER

While Panguitch was being settled for the second time, important events were taking place in the eastern portion of the future county. John Wesley Powell led two scientific explorations of the Colorado River, the first in 1869 and the second in 1871–72. These expeditions had several purposes. Powell wanted to know if the Colorado River could be navigated, and, in the process of discovering that feasibility, he intended to gather as much scientific information as possible about the area's geology, anthropology, and plant and animal life along the river.

At the conclusion of these two expeditions, Powell sent his brother-in-law, Almon H. Thompson, to explore and name the tributaries to the Colorado River. The reports that came from these monumental scientific explorations would serve as a guide to the region for generations to come.

The John Wesley Powell Colorado River Expeditions (1869, 1871–72)

Although Native Americans, early explorers, trappers, and settlers

The "Emma Dean" with John Wesley Powell's chair on top. (Utah State Historical Society)

had crossed the Colorado and Green rivers, no one was known to have ventured into the section that runs from the confluence of the Green and Colorado rivers to Grand Wash below the Grand Canyon and lived to tell about it. Earlier explorers, trappers, and military expeditions in search of practical railway routes saw no reason to go beyond the confluence. After reaching the junction of the two rivers in 1859, Captain J.M. Macomb of the U.S. Army commented, "I cannot conceive of a more worthless and impracticable region."[1] The leader of an earlier southern scientific expedition in 1857–58, Joseph C. Ives, had stopped at the Colorado River to look over its vast canyons below. "Ours has been the first," he wrote, "and will doubtless be the last party of whites to visit this profitless locality. It seems intended by nature that the Colorado River, along the greater part of its lonely and majestic way, shall be forever unvisited and undisturbed."[2] John Wesley Powell and millions who have followed have surely proved him wrong!

At Powell's birth in Palmyra, New York, on 24 March 1834, his parents named him John Wesley, hoping he would become a minister. But the young man did not follow the wishes of his anti-Mormon father; instead, he became a teacher, soldier, professor, explorer, scientist, director of the United States Geological Survey, and a friend of the Mormons.

A slim, wiry man, Powell stood five feet seven inches high with his boots on. He had a light complexion, grey eyes that smiled when he did, an unruly head of thick auburn hair, and a cropped beard. The right sleeve of his shirt hung empty, his arm a casualty of the Civil War, in which he had reached the rank of major in the Union Army.

He was a thirty-five year-old professor of geology at Wesleyan University when he and ten men with four boats pushed off the bank of the Green River on 24 May 1869, ready to plunge into the "Great Unknown" reaches of the Colorado River and its main tributary. The townspeople of Green River, Wyoming, cheered them off. Major Powell, Bill Dunn and Jack Sumner led in the smallest craft, the sixteen-foot *Emma Dean*, named after Powell's wife and made of pine. For much of the voyage Powell would ride as look-out in a chair strapped to the top of this boat. Next came Walter Powell, the Major's brother, and George Bradley in the *Kitty Clyde's Sister*; they were followed by the *Maid-of-the-Canyon*, with Andy Hall and William "Billy" Rhodes Hawking at the ores. Two brothers, Orvel G. and Seneca Howland, together with Frank Goodman brought up the rear in the *No Name*. These three latter boats were each twenty-one feet in length.

When the expedition reached the confluence of the Green and Grand rivers on 17 July, they had passed through numerous rapids

Francis Marion Bishop, cartographer for the Powell expedition. (Utah State Historical Society)

and canyons, lost the *No Name,* a third of their bed rolls, much of their food, and part of the scientific equipment. They camped at the confluence for four nights, exploring, taking scientific measurements,

Repairing one of the Powell Expedition boats at the mouth of the Muddy River. Individuals from left to right are W. Johnson, F.S. Dellenbaugh, and J.K. Hillers. (Utah State Historical Society)

and taking stock of their supplies. "The flour has been wet and dried so many times that it is all musty and full of hard lumps. We make a sieve of mosquito netting and run our flour through it, losing more than 200 pounds by the process," wrote Powell. "Our losses . . . leave us little more than two month's supplies, and to make them last thus long we must be fortunate enough to lose no more."[3]

On the morning of 21 July, they started again with a new air of excitement—they were on the Colorado River. Four miles later the river swept them into future Garfield County and down Cataract Canyon. Before they stopped to sleep that night on a narrow, rocky strip of beach, they had run numerous rapids, portaged three more, swamped—but rescued—the *Emma Dean,* lost three oars, and only made eight and a half miles. All the boats leaked from their poundings against the rocks of the turbulent canyon. The next afternoon they made camp at a larger beach. There they found a pile of driftwood, which they used to make new ores. Powell and a companion climbed 1,500 feet up the canyon wall to some dwarf pines to get pitch to patch the leaks. On the evening of 23 July, Powell reflected on their journey and contemplated what lay ahead:

> There are great descents yet to be made, but if they are distributed in rapids and short falls, and they have been heretofore, we shall be able to overcome them; but may be we shall come to a fall in these canyons which we cannot pass, where the walls rise from the water's edge, so that we cannot land, and where the water is so swift that we cannot return. . . . How will it be in the future?

On the 27th they stopped again to repair leaks and also succeeded in killing two mountain sheep. That night they feasted: "And a feast it was! Two fine young sheep! We cared not for bread or beans or dried apples to-night; coffee and mutton are all we ask," wrote Powell.

After eight days of battle with river and rock, the tempestuous river finally calmed and turned west. Before them lay a range of unmapped, unexplored mountains. Powell named them the Henry Mountains. A short distance farther, he signaled the men to turn up a stream entering from the west. One of the group who had gone ashore shouted, "Is it a trout stream?" Bill Dunn shouted back, "No, it's a dirty devil." Powell considered the Dirty Devil an appropriate name for the river.

Another canyon lay around the next day's first bend. Powell called it Glen Canyon for the many tree-lined glens at the mouths of the numerous creeks that entered the river. About 200 feet above them on the left wall they could see the ruins of an old Indian struc-

ture. Climbing to it, they found flint chips, arrowheads—some perfect, others broken—and pottery fragments scattered "in great pro-
fusion." The structure had walls of carefully laid and mortared stone.
On a nearby cliff face were "many etchings." Fifteen miles downriver
they found more ruins.

That evening, at a camp about three miles farther, Powell decided
to climb to the top of a rock outcropping above the camp to see if he
could get a better look at the country. Near the top he was surprised
to find stairs cut in the red rocks. Farther up he came to "an old, rick-
ety ladder" standing against a twelve-foot wall. Powell supposed this
to be a look-out point for the ancient people who had once inhabited this canyon.

The next day, 30 July, the Powell expedition passed out of future
Garfield County. Today, the waters of Lake Powell have climbed the
walls of Glen Canyon to bury the secret coves and elegant grottos that
Powell described with such appreciation and reverence.

A hundred days after departing from the town of Green River the
Powell expedition exited the Grand Canyon on 29 August, minus
three of its crew. The day before, William Dunn and the Howland
brothers looked downriver at another treacherous chasm strewn with
boulders—Separation Rapid, as it was later named. Sure the expedition could go no farther on the water, they elected to climb out of the
canyon. Powell would later be told that Shivwits Indians, mistaking
them for miners who had abused an Indian woman, killed the trio
after they climbed over the rim of the Grand Canyon.

Powell's second expedition was a combination river and overland
expedition. Although Powell took no formally trained scientists with
him, his brother-in-law, Almon H. Thompson, would become a first-
rate topographer, as would the expedition's artist, seventeen-year-old
Frederick Dellenbaugh. Powell hired Jack Hillers as a teamster, but
the German immigrant had more valuable talents and became the
survey group's photographer.

In preparation for this second voyage, Powell arranged to have
supplies carried in at several strategic points along the river. He contracted with Indian agent and Mormon missionary Jacob Hamblin
to carry supplies down the Dirty Devil River to its junction with the
Colorado River. Hamblin did not go far enough north in search of

John Wesley Powell with a Southern Utah Native American. (Utah State Historical Society)

the headwaters of the Dirty Devil, however. Instead, he traveled down another river, which Thompson would later name the Escalante, that was some forty miles southeast of the Dirty Devil. After following its narrow, rugged, twisting canyon for fifty miles, Hamblin could go no farther. He retreated to report back to Powell that the river was not passable to the Colorado. He took the supplies by another route farther south to the Crossing of the Fathers, now submerged by Lake Powell.

The second Powell expedition started at Green River, Wyoming, on 22 May 1871. During the course of the trip, Powell left and rejoined his men a number of times. In his absences he returned to Washington to seek additional funding, visited his wife, Emma (whom he had left in Salt Lake City), explored the area of future Zion National Park and other areas of southern Utah, and traveled to Indian communities with Jacob Hamblin.

Major Powell was on the river with his men from 2 September to 10 October from Green River, Utah, to the Crossing of the Fathers, and thus traced the eastern boarder of Garfield County again. When he was away, he delegated the command to Almon H. Thompson. With his field headquarters in Kanab, Thompson would spend the next six years surveying and mapping the Arizona Strip and southern and east-central Utah—including most of Garfield County.

Of the two Powell expeditions down the Colorado River, the first became the most significant and best-documented. The records of the two expeditions were combined into one report, but Powell neglected to even name the men who were part of the second trip. The crew of Powell's 1871–72 expedition consisted of Major Powell's cousin, Clem Powell, his brother-in-law, Almon H. Thompson, Frank Richardson, Frederick Dellenbaugh, S.V. Jones, J.F. Steward, F.M. Bishop, Andrew Hatton, and photographer O.E. Beaman. Some of them, including Dellenbaugh, left valuable accounts of the second expedition.

Almon H. Thompson's Scientific Explorations, 1871–1877

In 1871 when John Wesley Powell began his second expedition, the eastern two-thirds of Garfield County—from the Aquarius Plateau and the northern tributaries of the Escalante River to the Henry Mountains and the Colorado River—remained the last great unmapped wilderness of the American West. At the end of the second expedition, Powell instructed Almon H. Thompson to survey and map the tributaries of the Colorado River below its confluence with the Green River, and to give names to the many unnamed fea-

John E. Weyss, an artist with the George M. Wheeler Survey, made the first
illustration of Bryce Canyon—a pencil drawing in 1878. (Utah State
Historical Society)

tures of this unusual landscape—a task which took nearly six more
years. With Kanab as their base, Thompson, with eight other men to
assist him, set to work.

The exploring party made its way to the Paria River, following it
to its headwaters below Bryce Canyon. They called the plateau that
caps the Pink Cliffs to the north Table Top Plateau (known locally as
Barney Top), and the stream which emerges from it was named Table
Cliff Creek—later named Henrieville Creek after settlement of that
town in 1878. Apparently the party did not venture into the Bryce
Canyon area that would one day become a stunning national park.
Edwin E. Howell and Grove Karl Gilbert of a rival survey expedition
led by Lieutenant George M. Wheeler stumbled onto the pink cliffs
and spires in 1872 and provided the first recorded depiction of the
intricately carved fairyland:

> We came suddenly on the grandest of views. We stand on a cliff
> 1,000 feet high, the "Summit of the Rim." Just before starting
> down the slope we caught a glimpse of a perfect wilderness of red
> pinnacles, the stunningest thing out of a picture.[4]

John E. Weyss, an artist with the same survey, made the first illustration of Bryce Canyon—a pencil drawing. The following year Thompson and F. S. Dellenbaugh returned to the area and climbed into Bryce Canyon from the south near Rainbow Point.

On 18 November 1876 T.C. Bailey—also of the Wheeler group—would walk out onto Sunset Point while surveying a guide meridian. He penned one of the most vivid early descriptions of the canyon:

> The surface breaks off almost perpendicularly to a depth of several hundred feet—seems, indeed, as though the bottom had dropped out and left rocks standing in all shapes and forms as lone sentinels over the grotesque and picturesque scene. There are thousands of red, white, purple, and vermillion colored rocks, of all sizes resembling sentinels on the walls of castles; monks and priests with their robes, attendants, cathedrals, and congregations. There are deep caverns and rooms resembling ruins of prisons, castles, churches, with their guarded walls, battlements, spires, and steeples, niches and recess, presenting the wildest and most wonderful scene that the eye of man ever beheld, in fact it is one of the wonders of the world.[5]

From Henrieville Creek the Thompson survey group continued up "The Blues" to Potato Valley, camping in one of the "green grassy meadows" Franklin Benjamin Woolley had lavishly written of in his military report seven years before. After climbing to the summit of a white sandstone ridge just east of present-day Escalante townsite, Thompson recognized the river Jacob Hamblin had earlier thought was the Dirty Devil while trying to get supplies to the second Powell river expedition. This river cut a course southwest of the Henry Mountains, while the Dirty Devil joined the Colorado River some forty miles to the northeast. Thompson recalled, "Believing our party to be the discoverers, we decided to call the stream Escalante River in honor of Father Escalante, the old Spanish explorer, and the country it drains, Escalante Basin." The nearby stream that feeds into the Escalante River they named Pine Creek. The Escalante River and its basin drain a 8,840-square-mile area. From the ridgetop Thompson described the scene before him:

> We found we were on the western rim of a basin-like region 70 miles in length and 50 miles in breadth and extending from the

eastern slope of the Aquarius Plateau to the Colorado River. A
large portion of this area is naked sandstone rock traversed in all
directions by a perfect labyrinth of narrow gorges, sometimes
seeming to cross each other but finally uniting in the principal
[river channel] whose black line cut its way to the Colorado River
a few miles above the mouth of the San Juan River.[6]

After locating the Henry Mountains on the horizon and verify-
ing their position in relation to them, they selected a route to the
Colorado River. It took them to the foot of the Aquarius Plateau
(which they named after the water-bearer constellation for its multiple lakes and streams), then across the main ridge of the Waterpocket
Fold. They affixed that name to the huge geological region because
of the many natural hollows and water-filled tanks there that supplied them with water. As they approached the Henry Mountains, the
men surprised a small band of Paiute Indians who hid in the brush
in fright when they saw that the intruders were white. Finally an old
man braved an approach. The explorers rewarded him with a few
gifts they carried with them for just this sort of an occasion.

Thompson and his men continued on around the south end of
the Henry Mountains to the mouth of the Dirty Devil River. The boat
they had cached there the year before remained water worthy. Four
of the men took the craft down the Colorado River to its junction
with the Paria River, where they beached it and eventually made their
way back to Kanab. The rest of the party, led by Thompson, back-
tracked to Potato Valley and resumed the work of surveying, mapping, and sketching the features of the Aquarius Plateau, the Henry
Mountains, and the numerous springs and creeks that drained them.

When Powell discovered and named the Dirty Devil River on 27
July 1869 he had no idea where its headwaters were located, nor did
he know that it had two main forks. Consequently, when Thompson
and his men later explored the river from its upper tributaries in
Wayne County to its mouth, they called it the Fremont River from
the head of the south fork to where it empties through a narrow
canyon into the Colorado River. The north fork he named Curtis
Creek. Confusion over the names persisted for a number of years.
Today the north fork is known as Muddy Creek, and the south fork as

the Fremont River. Where they join near Hanksville they become the Dirty Devil.

When Thompson chose to name another tributary Tantalus Creek he chose well. The creek begins as a spring high on the Aquarius Plateau near today's Bowen Reservoir and cuts through the Waterpocket Fold. The mythological Greek gods punished the sinful Tantalus by causing a lake's waters to recede whenever he tried to drink from it. During the warm months of summer Tantalus Creek is absorbed into the sand or evaporates before it reaches the Fremont River.[7]

In 1872 Thompson took his survey team up Pennellen Pass, which cuts between the two highest peaks of the Henry Mountains— Mount Pennell and Mount Ellen—but he did not survey that area on this trip.

The Powell survey team received new distinction when E.E. Howell joined it in 1874 and Clarence E. Dutton and G.K. Gilbert signed on in 1875. It was Gilbert and Walter H. Graves who conducted a scientific study of the Henry Mountains in 1875–76. In the years between Thompson's first visit to the Henry Mountains and this survey a number of frontiersmen also had visited the area to no avail in search of minerals or land on which to farm or graze their stock. Gilbert's report declares the Henry Mountains virtually useless for any practical purpose:

> The physical conditions of elevation and aridity which have caused it to be so deeply carved . . . have rendered the region [nearly inaccessible] and have made it a desert, almost without economic value. . . . There is timber upon their flanks and . . . coal near at hand, but both are too far removed from other economic interests to find the market which would give them value. It is only for the purposes of grazing that they can be said to have a money value, and so distant are they at present from any market that even that value is small.

At the conclusion of his report, Gilbert declared, "No one but a geologist will ever profitably seek out the Henry Mountains."[8]

In 1879 John Wesley Powell issued his *Report of the Lands of the Arid Region of the United States, with a More Detailed Account of the*

Lands of Utah, which included the results of Almon H. Thompson's explorations from 1871 to 1877. In this report, Powell laid out a program for the orderly development of the West in general and Utah in particular. Since only a small portion of the region could be farmed (even by employing irrigation through cooperative investment and labor), Powell recommended that the land not be settled in the customary patterns of the more arable eastern and West Coast regions. He believed that the terrain should determine the shape of the tracts of farmed land, not an artificial grid.

The high timberlands, according to the report, were more valuable for their forests than for farm acreage and should be protected from fire. Since pasturage was sparse and would require large sections of land to sustain grazing, Powell recommended that farms and ranches be at least 2,560 acres and should include reliable water sources and small areas of irrigable land. He expressed his concern over expected settlement and its impact on water resources by suggesting that reservoir sites be selected and set aside for future irrigation needs. For example, Dutton, in his part of the report, estimated that a dam at the Panguitch Lake drainage point would expand the lake to an area of six or seven square miles, increasing its depth by some twenty-five feet.[9] Powell estimated, however, that only 2.8 percent of the plateau region could be irrigated. And during the next hundred years, in fact, the construction of dams and canals only increased the irrigated acreage by about two-tenths of 1 percent.

Looking at Garfield County today with its placement of communities near waterways, its six small reservoirs, its logging and ranching industry, and its access roads to scenic wonders, one would have to conclude that the stewards of the land, both private and public (though they are often at odds with each other), have been reasonably faithful to John Wesley Powell's vision of the settlement of this semiarid region.[10]

ENDNOTES

1. As quoted in Herbert E. Gregory, "Scientific Explorations in Southern Utah," *American Journal of Science* 248 (October 1945): 537.

2. Ibid., 528.

3. John Wesley Powell, *The Exploration of the Colorado River and Its*

Canyons (1895; reprint, New York: Penguin Books, 1989), 211. The information for Powell's journey through Garfield County comes from Powell's report cited above; William L. Rusho, *Powell's Canyon Voyage* (Palmer Lake, CO: Filter Press, 1969); John Wesley Powell, *Report on the Lands of the Arid Region of the United States, With a More Detailed Account of the Lands of Utah* (Washington, D.C.: Government Printing Office, 1879); Mary C. Rabbit, "John Wesley Powell: Pioneer Statesman of Federal Science," in *The Colorado River Region and John Wesley Powell,* U.S. Geological Survey Professional Paper 669 (Washington, D.C.: United States Government Printing Office, 1969); and William Culp Darrah, *Powell of the Colorado* (Princeton: Princeton University Press, 1951).

4. Herbert E. Gregory, *A Geologic and Geographic sketch of Zion and Bryce Canyon National Parks* (Zion-Bryce Natural history Association, 1956), 25.

5. Bailey's 1876 field notes are in the Public Survey office. A copy of Kirkpatrick's undated excerpt is in the Bryce Canyon National Park library files, BRCA # 350.

6. Almon H. Thompson, Diary, as quoted in Nethella Griffin Woolsey, *The Escalante Story: 1875–1964,* 24.

7. John W. Van Cott, *Utah Place Names,* 148; and Powell, *Lands of the Arid Region,* 157.

8. Grove Karl Gilbert, *Geology of the Henry Mountains* (Washington, D.C.: Government Printing Office, 1880), 2. This report was published a year after Powell's main report.

9. Mary C. Rabbitt, "John Wesley Powell," 10. See also Powell, *Lands of the Arid Region,* 144–46.

10. Over a hundred years after the U.S. Geological Survey mapped Garfield County, Rick Crawford and some companions were hiking near Escalante and found a rusty cylindrical canister. Inside they found a note which read: "Department of Interior, U.S. Survey of Territories, Second Division Geological and Geographical, J.W. Powell in charge, A.H. Thompson surveyor of party. This first was visited on the 27th day of July, 1875." See Marilyn Jackson, "Hikers Discover Powell Exploration Notes Near Escalante," *Garfield County News,* 5 December 1985, 1.

CHAPTER 6

SETTLEMENTS ON THE UPPER SEVIER RIVER

W ithin a year after the second settlement of Panguitch southern Utah pioneers began to establish additional townsites in close
proximity to the upper Sevier River. In some cases their efforts
proved to be tentative and misguided, as they chose locations inca-
pable of sustaining economic prosperity or even a reasonably comfortable existence. High elevations and their associated short growing
seasons and extremely cold winters combined to discourage many
newcomers. But those who stayed found ways to adapt their livelihoods to the harsh conditions. Perhaps they felt compensated for
their struggles as they daily viewed the surrounding beauty and
enjoyed its peaceful influence. Of these early settlements, only two
have endured as towns to the present, but the other villages contributed to the overall settlement of the area.

Hillsdale

In an effort to find an ideal location for a sawmill, two mill-
wrights, George Deliverance Wilson and his brother-in-law Joel Hills
Johnson, brought their families and other settlers to the east bank of

the Sevier River in 1871 and established a community. Hillsdale, named either for Johnson or in memory of his mother, is about nine miles south of Panguitch and six miles north of present-day Hatch. Besides the extended Wilson and Johnson families, other early settlers included the Alveys, Asays, Cloves, Fredrick Cooke, the Degraws, William W. Eagar, David Fredrick, the Henries, Brigham Knight, Henry King, the Martineau brothers, the Merrills, Jacob Minchey, Jesse Perkins, the Pinneys, Teancum Pratt, the Schows, Andrew S. Siler, Leveret Vanleuven, Henry White, James V. William, and the Workmans.

The pioneers surveyed their townsite south of the mill in August 1872 after being instructed to do so by ecclesiastical authorities.[1] Although the site fulfilled the promise of adequate water to power the mill and accessible timber for building the town, the high elevation—almost 7,000 feet—also meant long, cold winters and short growing seasons.

Johnson and Wilson had arrived in the region from warmer climes—the Mormon Dixie and Muddy missions, respectively. The two were relatively advanced in years for the tasks of beginning a new settlement, Johnson being almost seventy years old and Wilson sixty-three.[2] George Wilson had been a member of the Mormon Battalion and had crossed the plains on foot three times—once with the battalion, then returning back east to get his family and bring them west. Two of Johnson's sons, Seth and Nephi, came to help settle Hillsdale and also had an impact on the community's progress. In fact, descendants of both Wilson and Johnson remained in the Hillsdale area throughout its relatively brief history.

For a number of years the town's social life—church and community meetings, Sunday School, dances, and other events—revolved around a sawed-log home belonging to Nephi Johnson. Eventually the townspeople built a log house specifically for such purposes, and it became the town hall, church, school, and center of most social functions. An old Hillsdale Ward ledger includes a record of donations of lumber and labor between the years 1879 and 1881, and perhaps this is when residents constructed the community building.[3] Among the earliest schoolteachers were Martha A. Wilson, Seth Johnson, William Lumar (or Lewman), and an "old Welshman" named James A. Williams. One of Seth Johnson's sons described the old log schoolhouse:

> On the sides of the building the desks were hung with hinges to the wall. A bench made of a slab of plank was the seat with no back. A large fireplace was in one end of the room and on cold days we were sometimes allowed to stand with our backs to the fire to get warm.[4]

Children generally attended school three or four months out of the year during the coldest part of the winter. When school was not in session they spent time helping with family chores, including the usual tasks associated with farming. One former resident, Lydia Johnson Henderson, recalled wash days when she was growing up in Hillsdale. She first went with her mother to gather sagebrush along the hillsides. After the brush was burned, they used the ashes to soften the water used for their laundry. She also remembered having to search the nearby hills for any dead sheep left behind from passing herds, "from which she secured wool to put in quilts and for other miscellaneous uses."[5] One of her brothers, Anthony, recalled a time when he was five or six years old. Their father had taken the children to a field he was clearing and wanted them to pile up the brush to be burned. The children worked with a marked lack of enthusiasm, but when lunch time came and their father spread out a quilt for them all to sit on they ate their stewed dried apples and loaves of bread with zeal. This prompted the father to remark, "You all seem to have a much better appetite than you have a 'work-a-tite.'"[6]

With the exception of the sawmill, Hillsdale residents engaged in few commercial enterprises beyond agriculture. Typically each family raised a few cattle, pigs, and chickens, and they planted hay and farmed wheat. Together with kitchen gardens, this became the basis of their subsistence economy. They took butter and cheese to Utah's Dixie area to trade for commodities unavailable at home. But the cold weather often hindered even these modest enterprises. One resident recalled that food often became so scarce during the winter that she and her brothers and sisters were "forced to live on cooked wheat and milk with sometimes a piece of bread."[7]

The winter of 1879–80 was particularly harsh. After a deep and early snow the water froze at the gristmill ten miles away before Hillsdale residents could haul their grain to be ground. Vegetables froze in their storage pits and cattle froze to death even though the men attempted to move them to lower ground. However, as Joel H. Johnson's grandson and namesake reported, even though "some ran short of provisions neighbor helped neighbor and by keeping the old coffee mill grinding grain, we were able to provide plenty of chaffy bread." Despite their circumstances, Johnson recalled a joyful Christmas in his home that included the retelling of the story of the first Christmas by the fireplace, carolers, homemade woolen stockings filled with meager but appreciated fare, a children's Christmas dance in the afternoon, and a "grownups" dance in the evening.[8]

Practically all of Hillsdale's citizens were members of the LDS church. Church authorities created a branch there of the Panguitch Ward in 1874 and Nephi Johnson served as the community's first presiding elder.[9] By 1877 Hillsdale had about thirty-five families, enough to form their own LDS ward on 15 August. Seth Johnson became bishop, and the residents of nearby Hatch Town and Asay became separate branches of this ward. Most of the early settlers were devout Mormons and eagerly hosted church leaders, including church presidents, when they visited Hillsdale. They contributed to the building of the St. George and Manti LDS temples, and leaders of auxiliary organizations carried out the programs mandated by church leadership.[10] Most of the children, when eight years old, were baptized in the millrace pond. Two of Seth Johnson's offspring recalled being baptized in the winter through holes cut in the ice because their father insisted that all his children be baptized on their eighth birthday.[11]

Seth Johnson was a Mormon polygamist, and he brought one of his two wives, Lydia Ann Smith, from Toquerville when he came to Hillsdale in 1872. His second wife, Martha Jane Stratton, and her children later joined them. Lydia's children recalled that the trip took less than a week in their wagons pulled by oxen. They left Toquerville on son Seth Alvin's eighth birthday and arrived in Hillsdale on daughter Mary Julia's tenth birthday. Lydia Ann was a practical nurse and midwife in addition to being proficient in the processing of buckskin and in making gloves and hats. The sale of her home-manufactured items along with butter and cheese helped her to be able to buy additional clothes and food for her family. Seth Johnson constructed one long house for his two families; Lydia Ann's family occupied one end and Martha Jane's the other. Both families met in the center of the house for meals and morning and evening prayers. Everyone worked together to cook meals and carry out other household tasks. Mary Julia, the oldest of twenty-five children from both marriages, recalled, "During all the years that I lived there I never remember hearing my father quarrel with either of his wives or of his wives quarreling with each other." She further stated:

> Mother was quite a nurse and Aunt Martha [her father's second wife] always thought when she was sick that there wasn't anyone she would rather have care for her than mother, and she was, as always, willing to do all she could for mother, or for either of the families that needed her help.[12]

Many of these residents of Hillsdale became discouraged over the years and slowly started to move away, in part because of the cold climate but also because of periodic floods that washed out dams and hampered irrigation efforts, eventually causing much of the farmland to dry up. Of the two founders of Hillsdale, George Wilson lived out his life there, dying in 1912. Joel Johnson, however, returned to the Dixie town of Bellevue (now called Pintura) in 1886. George Wilson then became local LDS bishop and later presiding elder as Hillsdale's population began to decline and the town once more became a branch of the church. By the 1920s the branch itself was dissolved and what few Hillsdale residents remained became part of the Hatch LDS Ward.

Today, some descendants of the early settlers together with other newcomers maintain a few summer homes in the area. The pastures and other farmland are still used for grazing, but most of what remains is a few old frame and rough-sawn-log houses, barns, and other outbuildings that give evidence that Hillsdale was once a bustling village established in a beautiful location.

Hatchtown

Besides Panguitch, Hatch is the only other enduring town along what is now well-traveled U.S. Highway 89. (In various records this community is referred to as Hatchtown, Hatch Town, and Hatch. This work will use the name Hatchtown when referring to the early settlement period prior to the town's relocation, at which time the residents officially changed the name to Hatch.) For those who live in this community and for its visitors perhaps the town's most striking feature is the spectacular view to the east at sunset. When the waning sun shines on the cliffs of the Paunsagaunt Plateau, which dominates the whole eastern side of the valley, the sight is truly breathtaking.

The settlement of other southern Utah and eastern Nevada communities affected the eventual founding of Hatchtown. In the early 1860s Brigham Young admonished LDS families to establish the Dixie Mission in the St. George area. Then, in 1867, he made additional calls to the Muddy and Western, or Eagle Valley, missions. The settlers in these regions suffered extreme hardships as they struggled to acquire even the basic necessities of life. Then, in 1870, the United States Congress revised the eastern boundary of Nevada, moving its borders one degree of longitude to the east. This took terrain from the western edges of both Utah and Arizona territories. The agrarian settlers of the Muddy and Eagle valleys now found themselves living in Nevada counties dominated by mining activities and governed by people not of their faith. In addition, the Nevada state government began suits against these Mormon residents for back taxes which they could ill afford to pay. Brigham Young released the settlers from their missions and advised them to return to Utah Territory. Many of the Muddy Valley people went to Long Valley; most of the Eagle Valley people relocated to either Panguitch or Long Valley. Both groups were encouraged to occupy dwellings in towns abandoned during the Indian hostilities of the mid-1860s.[13]

One of the settlements in Long Valley was Windsor, later called Mt. Carmel. About 1872 Joseph and Sarah Ann Pedric Asay established a summer ranch several miles north of Windsor, along a stream they named Asay Creek, one of the main tributaries near the head of the Sevier River. By the 1880 census six families resided in the area. Heads of families included Sarah Ann Asay (Joseph had died in 1879), her son Eleazer, Richard Gibson, James Little, Oliver Anderson, and John Jones. For a time this community was called

Aaron, after one of the Asay sons. Other very small settlements in the area of the upper Sevier River included Johnson, Castle, and Proctor; but these consisted only of a scattered ranch or two here and there, and organized communities never really developed. They were later absorbed into Hatchtown.

Asay, however, showed greater promise. Later arrivals Tom Jessup and Dan Leroy established a sawmill along the creek, and Joseph and Sarah Ann Asay's son Amos operated another sawmill and a shingle mill. Although the town's residents enjoyed little success in cultivating wheat due to the short growing season at that high altitude, they did harvest oats and wild hay. The area proved ideal for fishing and for grazing cattle, sheep, and horses. Eventually others came to the area to settle.

Jerome Asay, Sr., another of Joseph and Sarah Ann's sons, established a grocery and hardware store and later added a restaurant to accommodate travelers.[14] In 1887 Jerome applied to U.S. Post Office authorities to authorize the Asay post office. He served as the town's first postmaster in a log building located next to the rock house built by his parents. This office served about twenty-four families. Later the post office was transferred to the old Hatchtown location, but it still retained the name of Asay. The residents built a small log schoolhouse that also functioned as a church and public meetinghouse. Sarah Meeks, Rebecca Wilson, Mamie Foy, George Haycock, and Dicy Delong were among those who taught the children of Asay in this structure.

In the late 1800s one of the area sawmills burned down. This event, coupled with the usual trials engendered by a short growing season and severe winters, doomed the little town of Asay. One by one, area families began to leave. Some went only a short distance to the community of Hatchtown, however. Others relocated farther afield, until, by 1900, no one was left. For its founders, Joseph and Sarah Ann Asay, the rugged mountains, plentiful pasturage, and sparkling streams of the area "must have seemed a very beautiful and fertile country . . . after the hot, dry, desolate land of the Muddy."[15] It was not easy to eke out a living in the mountains, however.

Among those called to the LDS Dixie Mission was Meltiar Hatch, a veteran of the Mormon Battalion. He brought with him two wives,

Permelia Snyder Hatch and Mary Ann Ellis Hatch, and their families. Hatch had answered the call issued by Mormon church leaders to go to Eagle Valley, where he had served as a bishop. Following Brigham Young's advice, he took his families to Panguitch when the Nevada state boundaries were redefined. He began the move by taking Mary Ann and her family together with Permelia's boys to drive their stock to their new home. When he attempted to return for Permelia, however, winter snows in the mountains forced him to postpone his trip until late spring. Meanwhile, Permelia was confined to her bed gravely ill for most of this time, with only a sixteen-year-old daughter, Weltha Maria, and a kind neighbor to care for her and her four younger daughters.

Hatch did return to Eagle Valley for this family as soon as the snow melted from the passes in the spring. During the move to Panguitch, however, Weltha Maria was "thrown from the wagon and both wheels ran over [her] leg, breaking it in two places." She also suffered broken ribs, but finally both families were relocated in Panguitch.[16]

The people of Panguitch formed a co-op and gathered together a sizable herd of cattle. They decided to locate the animals about twenty miles south of town, and Meltiar Hatch and one of his sons took charge of this enterprise. They built a log home and corrals where Mammoth Creek tumbles down Cedar Mountain to join the Sevier River. Hatch brought his wife Mary Ann to live at the ranch. She cooked for the ranch hands and offered hospitality to newcomers and travelers alike.

Neils Peterson Clove and his wife Sophia Rasmussen also moved their family from Sanpete County to Hatchtown during the 1870s. Clove's full name was originally simply Neils Peterson; but, according to family tradition, he was encouraged to change his name by Mormon church president Lorenzo Snow due to the many people named Neils Peterson working on the Manti LDS Temple in Sanpete County. In selecting Clove he explained that in his native Denmark it meant "smart aleck." [17] Clove had two additional wives, Kareen Marie Jensen and Neilsanna Anna Johanna Nielson (a childless woman known as "Aunt Hannah"), whom he settled in Panguitch. He and Sophia built their home where the Hatch Reservoir would later

This log school, church, and recreation hall was built in old Hatchtown in 1893—one mile south of the present town of Hatch. (Courtesy Beth Allred)

be located. Because of the site's lower elevation, the weather proved a little milder, allowing them to establish the first garden in that locality. Clove, a shoemaker by trade, became well known for the lime that he burned in the Mammoth area. The lime was used in building a number of early Garfield County homes, including some in Panguitch. The two families of the Hatches and the Cloves formed the nucleus of what became the community of Hatchtown.

Abram Smith Workman and his brother Dave came from the Dixie Mission to work in the fields of Panguitch in 1878. They sought Clove out when they heard about his lime kiln. Impressed with the area, they relocated there with the Hatch and Clove families. Abram Workman later recalled:

> In the fall of 1878, a government man came from Beaver to inquire why the land in this section had never been filed on. . . . I helped survey the land in the area and located the 160 acres on which Brother Peterson [Clove] filed. I went with him to Beaver as a witness in the filing of his claim.[18]

Abram Workman later married Julia Hatch, a daughter of Meltiar and Mary Ann, and taught school in the area for a brief period.

In 1877, when Hillsdale received LDS ward status, with Seth Johnson as bishop, church organizations at Asay and Hatchtown became branches of the Hillsdale Ward. Presiding elders included Abram Workman, Aaron Asay, and James Dutton.

Abram Workman aptly described the Mammoth Creek area when he wrote, "The river had rapids and waterfalls, a better place for fishing than for farming."[19] Along with producing quality butter and cheese, the settlers gathered gooseberries, currants, and serviceberries to make jams and jellies, all of which they traded to the peddlers from Dixie who brought fruits and molasses in the fall.

In time Hatchtown attracted other settlers. By 1880 about 100 residents lived in or near the community.[20] Although Samuel Barnhurst died within a few months of his arrival to the Mammoth area in 1889, his widow, Anna Marie Jensen, played an important role within the community. She served as midwife, as postmistress of the Asay post office from April 1891 to February 1898, and as the Mammoth LDS Ward's first Relief Society president. Descendants of the families already mentioned, along with later arrivals including the Allreds, Riggs, Lynns, Sawyers, Burrows, Andersons, Huntingtons, and Elmers, swelled the ranks of Hatchtown residents. Within the next decade, these people would witness great changes when the Sevier River began to live up to its turbulent Spanish name.

Antimony

Although the community of Antimony has historic ties and close geographic proximity to Piute County, it is physically located within the borders of present-day Garfield County. The area's lush vegetation and abundant grasses induced settlement in the Antimony area. Albert K. Thurber and George Bean traveled through Grass Valley in early 1873 as part of a twenty-two-man peacekeeping mission to the Indians at Fish Lake. When they entered the valley, the tall grasses reportedly rubbed against the bellies of their horses, thus prompting the men to name the region Grass Valley. Near the present site of Antimony, Bean and Thurber caught several coyote pups and gave the name Coyote Creek to the stream running close by that emptied

An early photograph of Antimony. (Utah State Historical Society)

into the East Fork of the Sevier River. The name Coyote was later applied to the community established near this confluence.[21]

In 1873 Albert Guiser, the first white man known to settle in the area, established his ranch about a mile north of where Coyote Creek and the East Fork came together.[22] Others followed Guiser but, like him, did not stay long. In May 1875 Isaac Riddle, his son Isaac J., John and Joseph Hunt, Gideon Murdock, and Walter Hyatt of Beaver herded cattle and horses through the grassy tract and into John's Valley to the south. As superintendent of the Beaver cattle coopera- tive, Riddle later returned to the valleys with additional stock and cre- ated a small town he called Coyote near the mouth of Black Canyon. He is believed to have been the first Mormon settler in Grass Valley. Isaac Riddle was an early missionary associate of Jacob Hamblin in southern Utah. There had been some problems between a McCarty who settled for a time in upper Grass Valley and some Navajo Indian traders, which resulted in the deaths of three Indians in 1873. It might have been through Riddle's association with Hamblin and the latter's subsequent involvement in bringing about a peaceful solution to the incident that Riddle first became aware of the Grass Valley area.[23]

Later that fall, John Rice King of Fillmore also began herding stock in the area with some of his brothers. In 1876 King bought Albert Guiser's Grass Valley ranch and moved there with his wife Helen Matilda Webb and their family. Two of his brothers also bought land west of Grass Valley in Circle Valley in Piute County. That same year, King's sixty-three-year-old father, Thomas Rice King, following Mormon church directives, organized a family united order (communal cooperative) while yet residing in Fillmore. He and other members of his family decided to establish their order in Circle Valley just north of the Garfield line. Those who moved from the Millard County united order founded the settlement of Kingston, where most of them resided and took part in the experiment of communal living. Neither John King nor his sister Delilah and her husband Daniel Olson joined the order at that time; however, later they agreed to do so under pressure from their father and brothers.

John and Helen King chose to continue living in Grass Valley, or Coyote, as the area was known by both names. They planted the first crop of wheat in Grass Valley the following year.[24] King dug an irrigation ditch from Coyote Creek to bring water onto his land in 1878. Although early settlers struggled to establish themselves in this new location, the united order flourished in Kingston, which became the center of area commercial, social, and ecclesiastical activities.

Residents of Grass Valley participated in the united order enterprise as well. John King took charge of the horse herds while Culbert Levi King, his brother, took responsibility for the cattle herds. This necessitated Culbert's move in 1878 to Coyote along with his three wives, Eliza Esther McCullough, Elizabeth Ann McCallister, and Sarah Pratt. Most of the order's butter and cheese came from Grass Valley, and other families came to run sheep and farm the area. One humorous incident occurred while a man and an older boy were herding sheep in Coyote for the local united order:

> One night John Junior was taking his turn tending the sheep when the bears made a raid on them. A scaffold had been built upon which [the herders'] bed was made. The older herder became frightened and suggested they pray. While kneeling in prayer, the frightened sheep crowded under the scaffold, knocking it down.

The men fell amid the sheep and bears, but frightened the bears
away and no harm was done.[25]

Thomas Rice King died in 1879 at Kingston. Without his leadership, the united order began to flounder. It persisted, however, for
four more years, until visiting LDS church officials advised the people
to disband it. Many of its members moved to Coyote or just north of
there to Wilmont (considered part of Coyote). John and Culbert
King's brother Volney and his wife, Eliza Syrett King, were part of this
group.

Additional united order families who came to Grass Valley or
Coyote between 1879 and 1883 included widower Franklin Henry
Wilcox, who brought his nine-year-old son Frank Eber, his two-year-
old daughter, Kate Effie, and his mother, Catherine Wilcox Webb.
Catherine was a nurse. She already had three daughters residing in
the valley, at least two of whom, Helen Matilda Webb King and Lydia
Webb Huntley, also served as nurses.

Other early arrivals included George and Esther Clarinda King
Black, George and Inez Forrester Dockstader, James and Sophia (or
Eliza) Huff, Hans Jensen and his wives Louisa Mahitable and
Josephine, Peter Nelson, Niels Nielson, Mortimer W. and Christina
Brown Warner, Canute Peterson, Charles E. Rowan, Christian
Sorensen, John D. and Mary Theodotia Savage Wilcox, Walter and
Elizabeth Barrowmen Gleave, Albert Clayton, Archie M. Hunter and
his sister Jane Talbot, Bill H. Link, Angus and Edward McEdwards,
J.C. Jones, Dave and Josiah Nicholes, John Smoot, and John Steen.
Many of these settlers did not stay in Grass Valley more than a few
years, but others remained to establish permanent residences. The
first babies born to the new settlers of Grass Valley were Forrest King,
son of John R. and Helen King, born 1 April 1879, and the daughter
of James and Sophia (or Eliza) Huff.[26]

The years 1879 and 1880 brought interesting changes to Grass
Valley. Although the event was not recognized at the time as significant, in late October 1879 a group of pioneers passed through the
valley and camped near John King's place on Coyote Creek. These
fourteen people, who included five women and three children, joined
a larger group that came by way of Parowan and Panguitch and made

Grass Valley's one-room school where Antimony children were taught. Teacher Carrie Henrie is in the center of the back row. (Utah State Historical Society)

up the famous Hole-in-the-Rock expedition called to settle San Juan County in southeastern Utah.

For residents of Grass Valley the winter of 1879–80 proved to be most severe. An early blizzard forced some men who were rounding up horses to return to their homes without completing their task. They found the carcasses of some of these animals the following spring in the tops of pine trees, which indicated the depth of the snow that year.[27]

In the late winter of 1879–80, the children of Grass Valley began attending the Wilmont (or Wilmot) School in a one-room log building situated on "Clover Flat," one mile southeast of present Otter Creek Reservoir, just north of what came to be the Garfield-Piute county line. Archie M. Hunter, one of the few settlers not a member of the LDS faith, served as the first chairman of the school's board of trustees. Carrie Henrie taught these first students. Her salary and other school maintenance funds came from private donations. Since funds were limited, the children attended school only about five months out of the year. The schoolhouse served another function as well—in February 1880 twenty-five members met and organized the first branch of the LDS church in Grass Valley. John D. Wilcox became the local presiding elder.

Later the following spring someone discovered the chemical element antimony (or stibnite) up Coyote Canyon, about eight miles from the present town of that name. The bluish-white, brittle metal had been used by Indians to make weapons and tools. Whether or not they told the settlers about it is not known. Antimony's value, however, was as an alloy to strengthen lead and other metals. Since antimony alloys such as pewter expand when cooled, they retain fine details of a mold. Some modern-day uses of antimony alloys include in bearings, storage barriers, safety matches, and as red pigment in paint. The first mining company to utilize the ore in Garfield County was the Utah Antimony and Smelting Company, which American Antimony Company eventually bought out. Active mining of the element initially lasted only a few years, largely due to a drop in the price of the metal and the high cost of shipping it. However, mining activity would later enjoy a resurgence.

As was often the case in other early Utah settlements, life during the first few years often proved precarious. Except for the antimony mining, a sawmill run by James Huff up Coyote Canyon, and a couple of dairies, there were no other enterprises except ranching and subsistence farming. Since the cattle were able to feed on grass almost year around, the settlers did not raise hay.

The men helped one another get their crops in. The grain harvest often was not sufficient for their needs, in part because farm implements were few and often homemade. It was written that in the fall "They cut their grain with a cradle, raked it up with a garden rake, and bound it by hand. They didn't have twine to bind their grain, so they used a little bunch of grain to tie up a bundle."[28] Later, a Mr. Whittaker would come each season from Circleville with a horse-powered threshing machine to thresh the grain. According to Kate Effie Wilcox Jolley, when local residents ran out of flour during the harsh winter months, "they made their bread out of shorts, that is, a kind of leftover of the grain [the bran and coarse pieces remaining

Spry School about 1907. (Utah State Historical Society)

after grinding]. Sometimes they would gather pig weeds and cook them for greens to go with their bread."[29] To obtain other commodities one had to go to Kingston or places farther afield. Coyote had no stores, so many residents traveled to Fillmore or elsewhere to get supplies each fall.

Spry

In 1876 Daniel F. Tebbs moved his family six or seven miles north of Panguitch along what would become U.S. Highway 89. He located his farm in an area near the now-abandoned Fort Sanford, close to the warmwater Lowder Spring. Eventually a community developed there consisting of farms and widely separated homes in an area about five miles wide and ten miles long that ended at the mouth of Circleville Canyon. This settlement underwent several name changes through the years—Tebbsville, Cleveland, Orton, Bear Creek—finally, in 1908, the name was changed to Spry, in honor of Utah Governor William Spry.

Besides the Tebbs family, William LeFevre with two wives and their families moved to the area. Other early residents included the Veaters, Robinsons, Kesslers, and Wilcocks. These settlers and those who followed established some of the best cattle and dairy ranches in Garfield County, which have remained the only enterprises in Spry up to the present day. Daniel Tebbs served as the first postmaster in the district, operating the post office out of his house. The post office later moved to William Orton's home at the mouth of Bear Creek.

Daniel Tebbs functioned in several other capacities in the sparsely populated locale. He built the first log schoolhouse and became the school's first teacher, receiving his salary in produce and other goods. Jane LeFevre succeeded him. As was the case in other small settlements, residents held their church meetings, dances, and parties in the little schoolhouse. Tebbs donned additional hats as he became the fiddler and leader of community social functions. He is remembered in a verse from a song sung by the boys and girls during dances and parties:

> There's old Father Tebbs, who takes his old fiddle,
> Goes to the dance and plays "Yankee Doodle,"
> He pats his old foot, and he wiggles about,
> And plays the same tune, until the dance it lets out.[30]

These opportunities for social exchange brought all the area residents together. Whole families came in wagons and on horseback. When it was bedtime, the youngest children would normally be put to bed in a nearby home or on the benches of the schoolhouse. For the residents of Spry, life was uncomplicated—a true pastoral existence.

ENDNOTES

1. Effel Harmon Burrow Riggs, *History of Hatch, Utah and Associated Towns Asay and Hillsdale* (Beaver, UT: Hatch Camp of Daughters of Utah Pioneers, 1978), 341; and Stephen L. Carr, *The Historical Guide to Utah Ghost Towns* (Salt Lake City: Western Epics, 1972), 124.

2. Joel Hills Johnson was married four times, but it is unclear how many of his family members came with him to Hillsdale. His first wife, Anna P. Johnson, died in 1840. Later that year, Johnson married Susan Bryant. In 1845 he wed Janet Fife, and much later, after he emigrated west, he married Margaret Thrylkeld. See Joel Hills Johnson, "A Sketch of the Life

of Joel H. Johnson" in "The Seth Johnson Family History," compiled by James A. Ott in 1947. George D. Wilson probably came to the area with only one wife, Martha Ann Riste, who bore him eleven children. His first wife, Mary Ellen Johnson (Joel's sister), died in 1845. She had two sons, one of whom died shortly after birth. See Riggs, *History of Hatch,* 352.

3. See Riggs, *History of Hatch,* 344–45.

4. Joel H. Johnson, "Life Sketch of Joel H. Johnson," 1933, copy in possession of authors. This was the grandson of Joel Hills Johnson who helped settle Hillsdale.

5. Udell Jolley, "Life Sketch of Lydia Drusilla Johnson Henderson," in "Seth Johnson Family History."

6. Udell Jolley, "A Sketch of the Life of Anthony Stratton Johnson," in "Seth Johnson Family History."

7. Lydia Annie Johnson Wilson, "Life Sketch of Lydia Annie Johnson Wilson," 1933, copy in possession of authors.

8. Joel H. Johnson, "Life Sketch."

9. Ida Chidester and Eleanor Bruhn, *Golden Nuggets of Pioneer Days: A History of Garfield County,* 57; Riggs, *History of Hatch,* 341.

10. Riggs, *History of Hatch,* 342–45; Chidester and Bruhn, *Golden Nuggets,* 57–58.

11. Nephi Johnson, "A Sketch of the Life of Nephi Johnson," 1933, copy in possession of authors.

12. "A Sketch of the Life of Mary Julia Johnson Wilson"; Mary Julia Johnson Wilson, "Some Special Incidents and Stories I Remember About Members of My Father's Family," copy in possession of authors.

13. See Riggs, *History of Hatch.*

14. Carr, *Historical Guide to Utah Ghost Towns,* 125.

15. Quoted in Riggs, *History of Hatch,* 93.

16. As told by Weltha Maria Hatch in Riggs, *History of Hatch,* 14.

17. Riggs, *History of Hatch,* 20–21.

18. Ibid., 31.

19. Ibid., 32.

20. Chidester and Bruhn, *Golden Nuggets,* 107.

21. John W. Van Cott, *Utah Place Names,* 11. See also Larry R. King, *The Kings of the Kingdom: The Life of Thomas Rice King and His Family* (Orem, UT: Larry R. King, 1996), 91.

22. M. Lane Warner, *Grass Valley 1873–1976: A History of Antimony and Her People* (Salt Lake City: American Press, 1976), 6.

23. Ibid., 7; Pearson Corbett, *Jacob Hamblin Peacemaker* (Salt Lake City: Deseret Book Company, 1973), 367.

24. King, *Kings of the Kingdom*, 91.

25. Kate Carter, as quoted by Warner, *Grass Valley*, 13.

26. For names of early residents see Warner, *Grass Valley*, 14, 69–172; and King, *Kings of the Kingdom*, 152–53, 178–88.

27. Warner, *Grass Valley*, 18–19.

28. Ibid., 168.

29. Ibid., 167.

30. Chidester and Bruhn, *Golden Nuggets*, 53.

CHAPTER 7

COLONIZING ALONG THE ESCALANTE AND PARIA RIVERS

Lands beyond the East Fork of the Sevier River, where a number of Paiute Indians already resided, beckoned additional pioneers. Reports of lower elevations and a warmer climate brought the early settlers to the region. The unique physical features of the territory presented some interesting challenges to the newcomers as well as awe-inspiring vistas, however. In the vanguard were stockmen, but others soon followed, and together they created some enduring communities. The singular nature of the area's topography also served as a backdrop for one of the most interesting and harrowing migrations in the history of the American West, the Hole-in-the-Rock expedition.

Prior to permanent pioneer settlement in the area, the Kanarra Cattle Co-op had owned a ranch a few miles to the northwest of present-day Bryce Canyon at a place called Blue Fly. William S. Berry was the superintendent for the co-op. In 1874 he hired John Henry Davies to herd cattle in the Bryce area. Davies recalled how Berry and Isaac Riddle, head of the cattle co-op at Beaver, divided the country between the two companies. Riddle's outfit from Beaver ranged their stock north and east of Flake Bottoms down the Sevier River, and the Kanarra co-op ranged its animals south and west, including the head-waters of the Sevier River.

After Davies went to work for the co-op he spent the first few months breaking mules brought to the area from California by a trader known as "Spanish George." Berry's daughter, Louise, an experienced horsewoman, helped Davies break the animals. During the next five years that Davies worked for Berry he came into contact with the Paiutes living on the Kanarra co-op range and wrote that he became "pretty well acquainted with the adult members of the tribe."[1]

One group of about 250 Paiutes resided south and east of Bryce Canyon. As hunter-gatherers they obtained food from small game such as rabbits and chipmunks and they had learned to trap deer in the narrow canyon near Sheep Creek. Fall months found the Indian women gathering grass seeds used to prepare a type of flour. They mixed this with water to create a dough that they formed into cakes and baked on flat rocks or wrapped on sticks and roasted over a fire.

The presence of these peace-loving Paiutes living in what became the Cannonville and Tropic areas influenced early settlers in their names for such places as Indian Hollow and Squaw Flat. The white newcomers also took note that as tribal members moved about the area they left their sick and dying behind, seldom bothering to bury their dead. In the process of relocation Native American women could be observed walking single file along narrow trails carrying bundles of possessions or babies on their backs.

After settling in the area, the pioneers learned some of the Paiute language and customs. Some did what they could to ease the deprivation suffered by the Indians, which was in great part caused by the usurpation of their former lands and resources by the white newcomers. The settlers also noted periodic gatherings of the natives that some called pow-wows. One summer a large group got together at East Fork, with some of their number coming from as far away as the San Juan River region.

Navajo Indians occasionally came through the area, but they were not permanent residents. Some traveled along the upper Paria River. Another of the trails they used extensively went through today's Alvey Wash and Smokey Mountain Road to Glen Canyon. The trail took the Indians northwest to Fish Lake Mountain to hunt, trade along the way, and gather salt in the Redmond area, just north of Salina in Sevier County. Early white Escalante residents often observed these Indian movements.[2]

Escalante

The year 1876 represented the centennial of the founding of the United States, but for the residents of Escalante that year also marks the founding of their community. The town lies near the center of Garfield County, on the south side of the Escalante River between the confluences of the Upper Valley, Main Creek, and North Creek drainages on the west, and Pine Creek, Sand Creek, and Death Hollow on the east. The area would remain relatively isolated for many years because of its inaccessibility. As mentioned earlier, the first Mormons to traverse the area, members of a territorial militia from St. George led by James Andrus, once referred to it as Potato Valley. Although some attached to this militia group returned to Panguitch to live, they did not forget the valley. One of their number, John Taylor Lay, would live out the rest of his life in the area.

Jacob Hamblin had traversed portions of Escalante Valley in 1871 in his attempt to take supplies to the John Wesley Powell expedition. Powell had instructed Hamblin to follow the Dirty Devil River down to its confluence with the Colorado River, where he would meet Hamblin to pick up the provisions. But Hamblin mistook the Escalante River for the Dirty Devil, which actually lay some forty miles to the north.

In 1872, as a follow-up to Powell's second expedition, Almon H. Thompson led a group that made a study of what they called the Escalante Basin in honor of the early Catholic priest-explorer of the West.[3] In August 1875 Thompson encountered an exploration party, made up of James Schow, his brother Andrew, Samuel Henrie, Isaac Turnbow, and Thomas Heaps, all from Panguitch. These men had come to look over the valley after having been impressed by a report made by some explorers from Beaver who were in the area in late February.[4] They were looking for a new location in which to settle, not under direction from LDS church authorities, as was the case with most southern Utah communities, but because they desired to find a place with a warmer climate and a longer growing season. According to Thompson's diary, he advised the men to call the new settlement Escalante in honor of Father Escalante, who many erroneously believed came through the area in 1776.[5]

A number of Panguitch residents decided to move to Escalante the following spring of 1876. Josiah and Alice Woodhead Barker were on their way from Salt Lake City to St. George during the fall of 1875 and heard of these plans while camped in Panguitch. Bishop Sevy talked of Potato Valley to the couple, and the warmer climate particularly appealed to Josiah because he suffered from rheumatism and had lived in cold and often damp locations such as England and Cache Valley, Utah. Sevy also told the Barkers that several Panguitch residents were building a road that fall through Johns Valley over Escalante Mountain in preparation to relocate in the spring. Josiah and his son Peter decided to help. They worked alongside Alma Barney, William Henry Gates, Albert Delong, Henry Heaps, Dan Justet, and Edwin Twitchell until the winter weather of December became unbearable.

In preparation for the move, a group of men had also dug irrigation ditches in Potato Valley from the Escalante River to take water to what would be their north fields. The following February, Barker impatiently decided to begin the move to Escalante with his family, including daughters Mary Alice and Mariah, sons Peter, James, Josiah, and William, and a friend of Mary Alice, Kate Jacobs. When the party reached John's Valley it began to snow, making it tremendously difficult to travel over the mountain and make the descent into the valley. Mary Alice Barker, who rode in the first wagon, received the distinction of being the first white woman in the valley.

Soon after the Barker family's arrival came Thomas and Susannah Goldthorpe Heaps and their family. This early encounter was likely the beginning of a romance between Peter Barker and Eleanor Heaps, which culminated in marriage the following October, the first such union in the new community. The first group to arrive included Andrew P. Schow (previously appointed by Bishop Sevy to take charge of the colony), with his wives Annie Jeppesen (also recorded as Jesperson and Jepperson) and Mary Ann Perry and Annie's four children; David and Catherine Justet Stevensen and their

The road to Escalante about 1900. (Utah State Historical Society)

three sons; Don Carlos (Carl) and Elizabeth (Betsy) Shurtz with one child;[6] William and Mary Elizabeth Heaps Alvey (the daughter of Thomas) and four children; and Isaac Turnbow. Another party soon followed. It included James and Annie Hansen Schow and their five children; Morgan and Elizabeth Richards; John Taylor; Joseph H. Spencer (a half-brother to Thomas and Henry Heaps), with his wife, Jane Ellen Haslem, and four children; and Willard Heaps, the twelve-year-old son of the earlier arriving Thomas Heaps.

By mid-summer additional settlers arrived, including Henry Heaps, Sr., and his wife Susannah Turner; their daughter Alice with her husband, Onizime (Lacey) Laramie; Philo and Lucy Allen; John and Jane Moody; Dan and Nellie Justet; Brigham and Tyresha Woolsey; Edward and Lydia Wilcock; Darius (Di) Shirts and wife Margaret; David B. and Lydia Catherine Adams; George Coleman with wives Jane and Maria; and Albert Delong. In addition, Edwin Twitchell came from Beaver without his wife Vesta, who complained they had moved too many times. She decided to remain where she was until she was sure her husband wanted to stay in Potato Valley. When her fruit froze in June 1876, however, she changed her mind and joined her husband in Escalante. Philo Allen earlier had been a bodyguard to the Mormon prophet Joseph Smith. Edwin Twitchell and another early settler to Escalante, Lacey Laramie, originally came west as part of the 1849 gold rush to California.

Mary Elizabeth Hall, who arrived that first year with her husband, Job, described the equipment and livestock typical of that brought by all the pioneers:

> All our goods were in the covered wagon. A plow was tied outside. There was a wooden crate filled with chickens, tied and resting on two poles stuck out from the back of the wagon. The boys drove the pigs, sheep, cows, and extra horses along the trail.[7]

The colonizers first decided to locate their community on the north side of Escalante Creek (which ran from west to east through the valley) because water was more accessible there. After only a few weeks, however, Josiah Barker suggested that the south side of the creek offered more land on which to establish the community. Even though they had already brought some of the northern area under cultivation and dug some canals, the residents decided Barker was right and moved across the creek.

The town plan followed the typical Mormon farm village plat of a grid pattern with wide streets and large lots. Josiah Barker, an experienced surveyor, located the North Star while situated on top of what became "Meeting House Hill" at 100 South and Center streets. The men surveyed 160 acres for the town, which included streets six rods wide (about thirty-three feet) and eighteen blocks of lots, each block containing five square acres. The blocks were subdivided into four lots of one and one-quarter acres each. The land they had begun to cultivate on the north of the creek was used to grow alfalfa.

Each head of a family received twenty acres of farmland, two and one-half acres of alfalfa, and a city plot. Those practicing polygamy received two parcels.[8] The men drew lots to determine their land; other land was claimed on the basis of "squatters' rights." Eventually the early arrivals as well as those who came later homesteaded additional acreage in the upper Potato Valley and on what they called the South Desert. Many families adopted the practice of establishing ranches in the canyons, where they spent their summers. During the winter months they moved back to town, where their children attended school.

The residents lived in willow huts and wagon boxes until they could build more permanent homes. By the first winter a few had made dugouts on the north side of the creek. A dugout was made by digging a hole about six feet deep and twelve feet square. Settlers then covered the hole with cottonwood poles placed at about a 20° angle; they then placed bundles of rushes between the poles and secured them with willows, both of which grew profusely along the creek bank. Finally they shoveled about a foot of dirt on top to help keep out the cold.[9] The soil contained enough clay and lime for the walls to be firm enough to whitewash for a neater appearance. Securing lumber to build permanent homes had to wait until roads could be built into the canyons.

That first summer the appearance of makeshift structures and pole fences indicated settlement progress in the valley. By 4 July 1876 the residents had built a bowery of poles, willows, and tree branches to use for church services and to celebrate the 100th birthday of the nation. When a flag ordered from Panguitch did not arrive in time for the celebration, the citizens used an Indian blanket to fly from their flagpole. The festivities included patriotic speeches and songs, and the settlers dampened and tramped the ground to prepare for their dance in the evening.

The coming of the 24 July Pioneer Day celebration that year inspired Mary Ann Schow to sew an American flag. On this occasion, dinner was served to 140 residents and Paiute Indians. The villagers held dances on the sand near the banks of the Escalante River until they could build more suitable accommodations.

The Escalante pioneers had abundant timber in the canyons around their settlement and soon began building log homes. In 1877 Henry J. White built the area's first sawmill, on North Creek.[10] Residents also found a high grade of clay in Pine Creek. Carl Shurtz and Joseph Spencer used sun-dried adobes to build their first homes. But after experiments were made with the nearby clay and firing bricks in a kiln, the bricks became preferred. Two brothers, Joshua and Ephraim Hawkes, built the first brick homes in the town just before the turn of the century, and many others would follow in the next decade. Over fifty of these sturdy homes still stand today as monuments to their makers.

At first the wild, or "blue," potato, wild strawberries, choke-cherries, elderberries, gooseberries, and red currants supplemented the settlers' diets. According to Alberta Liston, wild onions also grew in the area, as did watercress and asparagus. Soon the rich, fertile soil yielded corn, wheat, and other small grains planted by the settlers, and each family also planted a vegetable garden.

When the grain was ready to harvest, Brigham Woolsey and William Henry Deuel helped cradle it. They threshed the grain by flailing it upon the ground or by driving horses and oxen over it. The villagers employed Indian women to winnow the grain. The residents ground their grain into a coarse flour with hand coffee mills. Finally, in 1879, James McInelly, Sr., installed a gristmill just northwest of the town. At first, he could only produce whole-wheat flour, but later both he and Edward Wilcock, who built a sawmill on Corn Creek, installed sets of burrs at their mills to produce fine white flour.

The settlers preserved their meat, usually venison, by "jerking" it. They did this by cutting the meat in strips, immersing it to soak in a boiling brine of saltwater, and then hanging it to dry.[11] Carl Shurtz performed this task one fall as a favor to a local Indian known as Pete, who somewhat reluctantly left a doe he had killed with Shurtz. When he returned a few days later he found the venison jerky already done and preserved for the winter. He was so delighted that for several years thereafter he brought an animal to Shurtz each fall to be jerked.

The soil and climate in the valley were well suited for growing molasses cane. Molasses and honey produced locally sufficed as sweetening for a community hungry for sugar. Once, after Brigham Woolsey and his sons finished processing forty barrels of molasses, a flash flood reportedly washed the product of their labors down the Escalante River, prompting wonder whether local residents consid-ered changing the river's name to the Sweetwater after that.

Water played a major role in the destiny of Escalante, and, indeed, became a limiting factor in the size to which the community could grow. Irrigation came by way of a canal built the first summer of settlement. The canal was a 380-foot-long tunnel through a sand-stone ledge. It not only supplied water for crops but for culinary pur-poses during the summer months. In the winter the settlers used what they called "lizards" for transporting water, an apparatus made

A pioneer homestead in Escalante with the original cabin and later house. (Utah State Historical Society)

of boards on a runner with a V-shaped front. Barrels filled with water rode upon these lizards from the creek to area homes. Later, the residents dug wells; but the wells produced extremely hard water with a high concentration of iron.

Settlers of Escalante formed their first irrigation district on 4 June 1877 at a meeting held in the home of Andrew Schow. Some 80 percent of the citizens attended, electing Schow to be the district's president and Josiah Barker as clerk. This organization built some small dams on the Escalante Creek, but all of them eventually washed out. A more permanent and successful structure came several years later.

Even before the first settlers arrived, Philo Allen, Sr., and his son Edmund had brought cattle into the area. They kept them in Main Canyon the winter before colonization began. Later, Hyrum Fowler, Llewellyn Harris and his son James, Reuban Collett, Silvester (Vet) Williams, Rob Wilson, Joe Lay, and brothers Rufus and Martin Liston all brought herds of cattle into the valley.

Except for stock raising, which also included sheep, economic enterprise was somewhat limited in the young community. Also, because of Escalante's relative isolation, its residents needed to be self-sufficient. Most families produced their own wool, which was washed, carded, spun, dyed, and knitted into garments. They made candles, soap, lye, yeast, dyes, and rennet for cheese making. What they could not or chose not to produce or manufacture themselves they generally bought from Martin Foy, who hauled supplies from Panguitch that he traded for hides and wool. Betsy Goodwin sold mostly sweets and notions from the home she shared with her husband, Isaac. From about 1879 to 1884 Reuben Collett maintained a store in his home. Other early merchants in Escalante included Edward Wilcock, Thomas Heaps, Josiah Barker, and Victor Bean. Local merchants and individual settlers often traded with Indians. In the fall, Navajos would cross the Colorado River and come into town to trade their blankets and rugs for horses.

Beginning in 1881 the second postmaster, Robert Allen (David R. Adams being the first), had a small store in his home and used part of the space for the post office. George Coleman, Willis Thompson, Dick Wilson, and Joseph S. Barney carried the mail during early years of settlement.

Local craftsmen included cabinetmaker James McInelly, carpenter Joseph Fordham, stonemason Morgan Richards, and blacksmiths Daniel Adams, Isaac Allen, and J.R. Porter. Job Pitcher Hall, despite being crippled, made and sold boots and shoes and wove baskets of creek willows. Lacey Laramie, another early shoemaker, reportedly had "a good sawed-log shop west of his home." Job Hall, along with his brother Charles, made barrels, which the settlers used for hauling water and as containers for molasses, vinegar, pickles, cider, and other liquids. Ephraim and Joshua Hawkes as well as Adelbert and Monroe Twitchell made lime and brick for the community.

Those living on ranches in the canyons during the warm months made butter and cheese to trade for other commodities. They utilized the cool, clear springs in the area in the processing. One author gave a fine description of the physical arrangements and the procedures carried out in this home industry:

The Escalante Public School in 1963 when it was being used as a warehouse. (Utah State Historical Society)

Most of the ranch houses were built with three separate log rooms in a line, kitchen, bedroom, and dairy. The dairy, called the entry, was usually in the middle and had only three walls. In it there would be a rock furnace on which a galvanized vat was placed to keep the milk at the right temperature. The vat would hold about 40 gallons of milk that would make a 30 to 40-pound cheese. . . . Instead of the furnace some of the women used only a stove with a large new wash tub for heating the milk. Cheese making was a painstaking process involving just the right amount of rennet, coloring, and salt, the right temperature (with no thermometer) and very careful handling of the curd to keep the precious cream from escaping.[12]

Usually the women took charge of this summer enterprise, helped by older sons and daughters, while the men remained in town

Escalante's Main Street in 1940. (Utah State Historical Society)

to look after orchards, gardens, and nearby fields. The presence of Indians in the area caused these women and children great concern, even though there were probably not more than a dozen Native Americans residing in the vicinity.

Women in the community had a variety of additional money-making projects and enterprises. Mary Ann Schow, Kate Deuel, and Elizabeth Griffin wove and sold straw hats. Rachel Lay and her children earned money by weaving carpets on her hand loom from fabric strips brought to her by her customers. She earned twelve and one-half cents a yard, or about twenty-five cents per day, for her work. Louise "Luie" and Willis Thompson also engaged in rug and carpet weaving.

The pioneers built their first schoolhouse of logs during 1876–77. The structure was thirty-six by eighteen feet and became the center of public functions until 1885. Jane S. Coleman and Mary Ann Schow taught the ninety pupils who attended school that first year. Andrew Schow organized the first drama company in Escalante as well as the first brass band, in which he played his cornet. Mary Ann Schow provided additional music on the organ she brought with her

The Relief Society Building in Escalante. (Utah State Historical Society)

to the valley. Other local musicians included Jeremiah Stokes, Darius (Di) Shirts, and Joseph Fordham.

With the exception of Edward Wilcock's success at setting broken bones and treating cases of typhoid and pneumonia (which he normally did free of charge), midwives provided the only medical care in the community during the settlement years. It is estimated that Susannah Heaps delivered more than 800 babies, and it was said that whenever the children saw "Grandma" Heaps with her "little black bag" they knew a baby was on its way. Some children even believed that she kept the babies in her bag, but they could never get a look inside to confirm their suspicions. Henry Laramie, son of Alice and Lacey Laramie, was the first baby born in the valley. Etta Moody, daughter of John and Jane Moody, was the first baby girl delivered in Escalante.

The Bishop's Storehouse in Escalante. (Utah State Historical Society)

Two other midwives also treated early settlers. Ann Morris Butler Rice continued to practice even though she was already sixty-one years old when she moved to Escalante. Sarah Caroline Williams Lee, the fourth wife of John D. Lee, served the residents for two or three years. In 1899–1900 Mary Alice Shurtz completed a course in obstetrics under Dr. Ellis Reynolds Shipp in Salt Lake City. Her training proved invaluable, as she practiced medicine in the area for more than thirty-five years, delivering more than 600 babies in Escalante. Members of the LDS Relief Society also assisted in caring for the ill, especially when there was too much sickness for the midwives to handle during times of epidemics.

Even before Escalante received LDS ward status the local women had a Relief Society organization, which was organized on 13 March

The Co-op Store in Escalante. (Utah State Historical Society)

1877. Mary Ann Perry Schow, a plural wife of Andrew, became president, with Susannah Heaps and Lydia C. Adams as her counselors. The minutes of the first meeting list seventy-one women as members of the new organization. In addition to the usual compassionate service performed by such a society, the members raised money to assist emigrating Mormon converts from England and to help build a meetinghouse. They also fenced a lot for a widow at a cost of forty-two dollars.[13]

The first LDS Escalante ward was created on 5 August 1877. Andrew P. Schow became bishop, a position he maintained for thirty-five years. His initial counselors were Edwin Twitchell and David B. Adams; Henry White served as clerk. The Schow family recalls that a neighbor who lived across the street from the bishop owned a nice white-topped buggy. It was reported that "each Sunday morning he would drive the buggy to his childrens' homes to pick up the families and take them to church, . . . after he got all of them to church, he would go home and sleep."[14]

Normally in these tranquil communities of Southern Utah a peace officer had little to do. Deputy Sheriff Reuben Collett, who filled this position from 1877 to 1881, encountered an exception to the norm on 30 November 1878. Late that evening, John F. Boynton rode into town from Escalante River Canyon near Calf Creek and confessed to the deputy that he had killed his partner, Washington Phipps, that morning. Collett took Joe Lay and William Deuel with him to check out Boynton's story and found Phipps's body about fifteen miles out of town. After burying him in a shallow grave, they placed heavy rocks and the dead man's boots on the mound.

The killing shocked the townspeople, who had often seen the two partners (and seemingly good friends) on the numerous trips they had made to town, where they usually camped in Henry and Susannah White's yard. Boynton and Phipps ran a herd of horses east of the community and eventually decided to split up over some differences. They divided their stock and lived about a mile apart on the river. According to Boynton, that fateful morning Phipps came into his camp brandishing a club and threatening to use it. After several warnings, which Phipps did not heed, Boynton shot him, ostensibly in self-defense. After holding a hearing in Escalante, Collett turned Boynton over to the authorities in Parowan, then the county seat for the area. After a preliminary hearing in December and a trial the following March, the court discharged the defendant and allowed him to go free. Boynton then returned to Escalante, where he concluded his business and then left the area for good. Local historian Nethella Griffin Woolsey reported that "for some people the thought of that lonely grave and the violence that produced it adds eeriness to the weird shapes in the canyon."[15]

Before Garfield officially became a county or Escalante had been incorporated as a town, local Mormon church leaders usually functioned as community leaders as well. After some trying times and in spite of its relative isolation Escalante's population grew steadily. Within six years of settlement it boasted 441 citizens. The natural beauty of its surroundings would contribute to the community's success as well as to its problems in future years.

Cannonville

Serving as the gateway to the intriguing Kodachrome Basin Utah State Park just across the Kane County line, Cannonville is located in the upper Paria Valley at 5,800 feet, a slightly lower elevation than that of some of its neighbors. The first group to use the area to graze livestock were part of the Kanarra Cattle Co-op. Then, in 1874, David O. Littlefield and Orley Dwight Bliss arrived to establish homes in the vicinity of where Henrieville Creek empties into the Paria River. Other settlers arrived the following year. The residents called the settlement Clifton (Cliff Town) because of its view of the Pink Cliffs and other rock formations in the locality. Ebenezer Bryce had emigrated from Scotland to New Jersey with his parents when he was a boy of fourteen. According to one source, he decided to go west in his late teens, later becoming a member of the Mormon church. Bryce came to the Paria Valley with his wife, Mary Ann Park, and their seven sons and three daughters.[16] He soon became frustrated with the sparse water supply at Clifton and moved his family upstream to Henderson Valley, calling it New Clifton. He and Daniel Goulding fenced about 200 acres of land there and dug a canal seven miles long to bring water from Pine Creek near Escalante Mountain to irrigate their land. Goulding brought fruit trees and grapevines from Pleasant Grove in Utah County. The two friends also built a road to nearby timbered areas to cut logs and firewood. The road terminated in a huge amphitheater that locals called Bryce's Canyon. Later, when the spectacular area that bore his name became a national park, someone asked Bryce what he thought of the area where he used to ranch. "Its a hell of a place to lose a cow," he replied. The Bryce family, who had originally moved to the area because of Mary Ann's poor health, would only stay until 1880 before moving on to Arizona.

The uncertain water supply made it difficult for the early settlers to survive. During July and August 1877 water came down the streambed only at night in the upper Paria Valley. The people scooped the lifegiving liquid from small pools into barrels for the next day's use; they hauled drinking water from Bryce Spring. In late 1877 the residents still at Clifton decided to relocate their townsite about 1.5 miles upstream.[17] Settlers dismantled their homes (basically

Ebenezer and Mary Ann Park Bryce. (Courtesy June Shakespear)

ten log cabins) and their school/meetinghouse and reassembled them
at the new location. They named the new community Cannonville
after LDS apostle George Q. Cannon. Some have said that the town

The double log cabin built by Ebenezer Bryce in Old Clifton. The cabin has been moved to Tropic. (Utah State Historical Society)

should have been called "Gunshot," because it was too small for a cannon.

In addition to the Littlefield, Bliss, and Bryce families, other early arrivals included former Mormon Battalion member James L. Thompson and his sons John Orson, James Brigham, William Samuel, and Joseph; Jonathan Packer and his son Nephi; additional members of the Littlefield family (Waldo and his sons Dave, Edward, and Sam); Joseph Spencer; William J. Henderson, Sr.; George and John Ingram; John H. Dickson; Ed Clayton; Morrison Mecham; and Lacey Laramie, as well as wives and other family members of many of the above.[18]

Although the new townsite proved more promising than the first site, the pioneers faced obstacles over and above those normally associated with establishing settlements in virgin territory. After the drought conditions they had previously known, the water they were able to bring from the Paria River was plentiful, but soil in the upper

A view of Cannonville. (Courtesy Dorothy Leavitt)

valley washed out easily. Erosion presented a constant challenge to the settlers; however, with hard work and ingenuity, the people were able to maintain their water supply. A lifelong resident described one such effort, which involved building a small dam:

> The irrigation diversion dam was made by cutting, dragging and placing trees across the creek and filling behind them with brush, rock and earth. The ditch was dug by horse-drawn scraper, pick and shovel and much sweat. They were short of engineering skill but they surveyed it with a carpenters level, using what sense the good Lord gave them, and they made do.[19]

It would be more than a decade before the residents of Cannonville would have a more dependable source of water—one coming all the way from the East Fork of the Sevier River. This project also made possible the settlement of Tropic, located about five miles north of Cannonville.

A rumored gold rush within Cannonville's first two years presented residents with another challenge. Prospectors came to the region in large numbers and an early winter isolated the community and caught the gold seekers unprepared. Many of them built dugouts to live in, but they had difficulty finding sufficient food. Local LDS church leaders instituted a distribution program to which Cannonville residents contributed from their already meager stores. They also organized hunting forays and shared the game with the stranded prospectors. A proud Cannonville resident later reminisced: "By generous, careful, cooperative effort, not one life was lost from want of food; but by Spring, not one person was carrying any excess body fat either."[20]

Although Cannonville would always remain essentially an agricultural community specializing in stock raising and fruit growing, some residents established other enterprises. For instance, Joel Hills Johnson brought some mill iron to the village to construct a sawmill, as he had a few years earlier in Hillsdale. Building the first carriage track for the mill required weeks of sweat and toil. An ox team brought in the steam boiler and engine, which furnished the power required. Oxen then hauled water to the boiler in barrels. At last the residents had their sawmill.

William J. Henderson saw the need for a store. He built a one-room structure of sawed logs from the mill, native stone for the foundation, and pine shakes he made himself for the roof. After completing his store, Henderson drove a wagon pulled by a four-horse team to Parowan for supplies; the journey over and back took eight days. Residents of Cannonville now had ready access to spices, sugar, raisins, freshly milled flour, harness and shoe leather, some basic hardware such as nails, wire, pans and knives, cloth and sewing notions, pencils and slates, and even candy and gum. With money being scarce, many residents used the barter system to obtain desired commodities. Without banks in close proximity to Cannonville, Henderson formed his own coins from a set of dies he owned. Along with his name, the inscription on the coins read, "Genl. Mdsde. Cannonville, Ut." Other southern Utah businesses such as the Hatch

Mercantile, the S & C Mercantile, and the Southern Utah Equitable
Company in Panguitch used their own scrip as well.

Town historian George W. Thompson related an incident illus-
trating the wisdom and diplomacy that Henderson possessed as the
town shopkeeper:

> One day one of the good sisters came to the store with a pound of
> butter. Mr. Merchant asked what she would like and she said she
> really didn't want anything except a small favor. She said a mouse
> had drowned in her cream. She got it out all right and the cream
> wasn't hurt a bit so she churned it but she didn't quite want to eat
> the butter. Would he please trade her someone else's pound of
> butter for it? It wouldn't matter to them for they wouldn't know
> the difference. While she was looking at the new cloth, he took her
> butter behind the counter and changed wrappers on it with
> another pound he had in stock, then, when she was ready to leave
> he gave her own butter back. Like she said, she didn't know the dif-
> ference so she was happy.[21]

Local residents obtained some special items from Native
Americans—particularly Navajos. South of Cannonville, following
the Paria River to the Colorado River, was Lees Ferry, the only
crossing of the Colorado for miles. As a result, many Navajos followed a well-worn trail between Utah and Arizona territories that
led them through the community of Cannonville. They liked to
trade at the local store and brought their mats, rugs, and blankets—
all beautifully woven from fibers of yucca, cane straw, and wool.
They often brought mustang ponies that they caught from wild
herds and then broke and trained for purposes of trade. Residents
of Cannonville and the Native Americans usually got along quite
well and the white settlers became accustomed to the frequent presence of the Indians.

One local woman in particular did not view Indians as a threat.
Nine Indians rode up to Matilda Willis Thompson's home one day
while she was kneading bread. Her frightened children ran to the
house to hide behind their mother's skirts. Forcing their way through
the door, the Indians demanded food. She said they would have to
wait until she finished baking the bread, but one eager intruder
reached for a handful of dough. Matilda quickly grabbed a knife and

brought it down, just missing the man's arm; she told him that if he tried that again she'd cut off his hand. She demanded that he and his friends go outside and wait. Amid the laughs and jeers of his companions, the offending Indian retreated to wait outdoors as he was told. Matilda finally brought out two freshly baked loaves and some meat for her uninvited guests and watched as they ate it with pleasure. From then on the Indians showed great respect for this frontier woman and would even leave some venison at her door when they happened to be passing by.[22]

When area residents could build more permanent homes, most of them used native stone for basements, cellars, and foundations, similar to that used by William Henderson for the general store. They mixed sand and lime for their mortar. By burning the plentiful limestone in adobe kilns the settlers had a ready supply of lime for the mixture. Juniper wood from the hills supplied ample fuel to fire the kilns. During the early years these pioneers usually made their own nails, either from hard wire or from square metal bar stock about one-eighth inch square. They heated the metal in a fire, cut it to the desired length, and then hammered it on an anvil to create a head on one end and a point on the other. Cooling the metal in cold water completed the process. They also used wooden pegs and dowels to hold building members together.

As was typical of all pioneers, the key to survival in Cannonville was self-sufficiency. Settlers made most of their commodities, including furniture, mattresses, candles, soap, and medicines. Of necessity, they also created their own entertainment. For instance, box-lunch auctions preceded many of the dances; the lunches were made by the girls and bid on by the boys. The funds generated usually went toward a civic improvement project. As George Thompson wrote, "Who brought which box was supposed to be a secret but somehow there seemed to be a means of understanding among the young folks so the right couples got paired together." When it was time to start dancing, George and William Dutton, Joe Fletcher, and Will Ingram, all fine musicians, furnished the music. Between them they could play the violin (fiddle), guitar, harmonica, drum, piano, and horn. Nephi and Maiben Johnson called the dances.

In addition to dances, the settlers amused themselves with horse racing, horse-shoe pitching, and marbles. Even in winter they could usually find a bare, sunny spot on the south side of Henderson's store where they would have a satisfying game of marbles. Some members of the community looked for alternative recreation and found it at John Seaton's still, located downriver in one of the canyons where Seaton had made a dugout. Locally grown hops, barley, corn, and rye became the ingredients for his brew, and he drew customers from a wide area because of the quality of his product. Even those who did not normally imbibe called upon Seaton for "medicinal" needs.

As with most southern Utah settlements, Clifton and later Cannonville relied on the LDS church for early community leadership. Clifton became a branch of the Panguitch Ward in 1876, with Jonathan T. Packer as branch president. The following year, Cannonville Ward was organized, and Packer served as its first bishop. Packer's term was relatively short considering the times. Ira B. Elmer succeeded him, serving from 1880 to 1884. As the communities of Henrieville, Georgetown (located just over the border in Kane County), and later Tropic developed, these towns became branches of the Cannonville Ward until their populations increased sufficiently to establish their own LDS wards.[23]

A woman in such frontier communities required great stamina. When Drusilla Johnson married William J. Henderson and set up housekeeping in Cannonville, summer days dictated that she rise very early each morning to milk the cows and prepare breakfast. She then accompanied her husband to the fields to plant corn, potatoes, or whatever else was necessary. Eleven o'clock found her back at home to prepare the midday meal, following which she again returned to help William. At night she stayed home to catch up on household duties. Udell Jolley notes that his aunt often took in other children to live with her own offspring when their mothers died until other arrangements were made, a common occurrence in other early Mormon settlements as well.[24] Life in Cannonville was not easy for Drusilla or for any of her neighbors. The people mustered the energy to do what had to be done and still had a little left over to enjoy whatever diversion presented itself.

A scene near Henrieville in 1907. (Utah State Historical Society)

Henrieville

Another Paria Valley community, Henrieville, also received families relocating after they abandoned nearby towns like Clifton and an even earlier settlement named Wooden Shoe. The name Wooden Shoe is believed to come from the first white settlers in the area, who were from Holland and wore wooden shoes.[25] Early arrivals in the upper valley began to divert much of the creek water for irrigation, and, as a result, during an extremely dry spell from 1875 through 1877, little water reached the community of Clifton, contributing to its demise. While some of the Clifton settlers relocated to Cannonville, taking along their log cabin dwellings and schoolhouse, others located between what would become known as the Henrieville Wash and Henrieville Creek northeast of Clifton. They named their town for James Henrie, who presided over the Panguitch LDS Stake, of which this settlement became a part.

Like other settlers who had first arrived in the northern Paria Valley, they hastily built dugout homes in the area. Those in

Early members of the Henrieville Relief Society. (Courtesy Teora Willis)

Henrieville were made by digging into the side of a hill to create three sides of the dwelling. The fronts of the structures were made of hewn logs, and each included a door and small windows. Logs or boards were put across the top and then covered with brush and dirt to form a roof. Inside they built fireplaces, which were used not only to provide warmth and light but also for cooking purposes. Pioneers also constructed covered bins to store grain and other foodstuffs. These doubled as children's beds, on which they piled their quilts and bedding. Primitive though they were, the dugouts provided a measure of comfort and protection from the elements. In just such a dwelling the first baby born in Henrieville arrived on 5 July 1880 to Edwin and Sarah Francis Littlefield.

Although the townsite was not surveyed until 1883, Henrieville residents began to build conventional homes and lay out town streets in 1878. Brothers Dave, Edwin, Sam, and Sid Littlefield; the James and Joseph Ingram families; and the Thompson brothers—Brig, Jim, and Jack—together with their families, all helped establish the town. James Thompson and Dave and Louisa Littlefield completed the first homes in the community. By 1884 Daniel Goulding had moved to Henrieville with his two plural wives, Elizabeth and Fanny Pratten,

The Savage Ranch near Henrieville. (Utah State Historical Society)

who were sisters. Goulding built a home for each of them side by side on the south side of town. He became the town's first mayor. William Patterson (Pat) Willis also came with two wives, Almeda Roundy and Mary E. Merril, as did James Smith, with his wives Mary Susan and Elizabeth. Elizabeth did home nursing, and townspeople relied on her in times of sickness and childbirth. Both Pat Willis and Jim Smith came as stockmen; so too did Elige and Billy Moore; Sampson Chynoweth and his two sons; William Sears Riggs and his sons; brothers Moroni, Neil, and Ebenezer Savage; Bill Bryce (son of Ebenezer); Jim Pace; and William Jasper Henderson.

Henrieville was at first a part of the Cannonville LDS organization; it became a branch of that ward, with James Brigham Thompson as presiding elder. Elizabeth Goulding was the local Relief Society president. In 1887 the Henrieville Mormon residents organized into their own ward and Daniel Goulding became the bishop, holding that position until his death in 1905. The congregation met in a building they constructed for multiple use—church, community center, and local schoolhouse. Residents began building

Field sports ground at Pine Lake where Henrieville residents often held their Fourth of July Celebrations. (Courtesy Teora Willis)

this structure in 1881. Local men hauled logs from nearby canyons for the lumber:

> The logs were hewn to the square using a broad axe. A narrow pit was dug about seven feet deep and the logs were laid across the pit. Then using a long saw with handles on both ends (whipsaw), the logs were split in half. One man stood on the top of the log and pulled the saw up while a man in the pit pulled the saw down.[26]

The builders used these split logs for the walls. Men brought the rest of the lumber for the floor and ceiling and some of the shingles for the roof from a sawmill at Mammoth Creek, some fifty miles away. John Thompson and a companion made additional shingles by hand using a drurvin knife and fres—a slow and exacting work. They completed construction on the building by Christmas 1881. Fanny Pratten Goulding, the bishop's wife, became the first teacher in this one-room schoolhouse. The children used slates and slate pencils, as did the students in most rural communities at the time. Years later, a second room was added so the children could be divided into two groups according to age and grade.

Young women in Henrieville during the 1890s. (Courtesy Teora Willis)

Hanging in the belfry of the school was the bell that one resident characterized as the "heart beat of the town." At 8:30 A.M. the janitor rang the bell, indicating that school would begin in one-half hour. At 9:00 A.M. the bell pealed again, announcing that school had begun for the day. It sang out twice more to signal the start and finish of lunch hour. A popular Halloween prank was to climb to the belfry and tie the clapper in the bell so that it would not sound.[27]

The 24 July (Pioneer Day) celebrations were also held in this multipurpose building. At one of the first of these, the barefoot boys picked up large slivers in their feet during the afternoon children's dance. Since their feet were well callused, the slivers did not pose much of a problem; after pulling them out, the boys kept on dancing. Most of the girls, however, reportedly wore rawhide moccasins using an Indian pattern. One local Native American, called "Moccasin Bill," taught the young women how to make them. When sufficient hides were not available, old denim sufficed for making the upper parts of the moccasins.[28]

Local establishments included a post office and blacksmith shop, but Henrieville residents had to travel to Parowan for "store-bought" items until stores in surrounding communities were established. The post office started serving the community in 1883, and William Thompson became the first postmaster. For a period of about two years—between 1888 and 1890—local mail service was discontinued. When it was reestablished, Melissa Ingram had the job of postmaster. Her husband, Joseph, did much of the repair work for farmers in his blacksmith shop. An enterprising man, Ingram also made shoes in addition to farming.

Agriculture became the mainstay of all citizens of the community. They cultivated gardens, planted shade and fruit trees, and kept chickens, pigs, milk cows, and sheep. Some raised and bred livestock for a living. Women washed and carded wool for their family's clothing, and for quilts, rugs, and straw mattress covers. One problem that plagued local residents, as it did those in Cannonville, was controlling water, since their soil easily eroded away. Flood waters periodically came down the creek and washed out the dam, posing a constant challenge to local citizens. Despite the adversity and challenges, the industrious people carved out a pleasant community that sustained a limited though stable population.

Additional Settlements, Both Short-lived and Enduring

Individuals who played prominent roles in Garfield County events came from the community of Georgetown, a village and associated farms located over the border in Kane County. Like Cannonville, the colony was named for George Q. Cannon, the LDS general authority in charge of the area. Because its residents were initially part of the Cannonville LDS Ward and later one of its branches, they were effectively a part of the social and economic life in this most southern portion of Garfield County. Several descendants of Joel Hills Johnson of Hillsdale and Cannonville relocated to this community. They served in leadership positions in both the Cannonville Ward and the Georgetown Branch. By the turn of the century, however, drought conditions forced most Georgetown settlers to leave.

Another short-lived community in the upper Paria Valley was Losee, also known as Loseeville. Daniel Goulding, formerly of Clifton, sold his property to Isaac Losee and Orville Cox in 1886. A few other settlers arrived in the area—enough to justify a post office.

When the settlement became a part of the Cannonville LDS Ward, a Sunday School was organized for the residents, with Ephraim Collett as superintendent and Losee as presiding teacher. By the mid-1890s, however, most of the town's occupants had moved away.[29]

Two other enduring communities, Tropic and Boulder, joined the ranks of Garfield County towns. However, their settlement took place at a later time and will be treated in another chapter.

Hole-in-the-Rock

In the annals of western history there are numerous accounts of individuals who mixed poor decisions with inordinate capacities for courage, fortitude, or just plain pluck. When one adds the attributes of faith and devotion to a cause, there was no better collective example than the Hole-in-the-Rock pioneers. Their saga has been told and retold by historians, descendants, and local writers, but no matter how often it is heard, listeners are awed by the experience. This is an adventure in which the dramatic topography of southern Utah and the early residents of Garfield County both played major roles; and thus it is fitting that it be included in this history.

In late December 1878 at a stake conference in Parowan the call went out for several men and their families to travel to southeastern Utah to establish a colony, later known as the San Juan Mission.[30] The reasons for this migration included securing the region for Mormon colonization before others could do so and cultivating better relations with the Indians of the area. At this conference and a later one held in Cedar City the following March, local church leaders named those assigned to the mission and later made calls on an individual basis to others. In addition, many chose to become involved in the venture after church authorities issued a blanket invitation to anyone who wished to join the expedition. Still others, who had no intention of settling along the San Juan River, went with this group on their way to Colorado, Arizona, or other locations. As Bishop C.J. Arthur stated in a meeting held in Cedar City on 2 January 1879, no one was compelled to go. Instead, he "required all to use their agency as to whether they went or not, but advised all who were called to go with a cheerful heart."[31] Not everyone called went with the first group, but the vast majority of participants came from several locations in southern Utah.

An advance or exploring party left Paragonah on 14 April 1879. It consisted of twenty-six men, two women—Elizabeth Hobbs Harriman and Mary Elizabeth Fretwell Davis—and eight children. Some of these people would stay once they reached their destination; the others would return to report on the route taken. Silas S. Smith of Paragonah led the expedition, and Robert Bullock and Kumen Jones of Cedar City and James B. Decker and George B. Hobbs of Parowan acted as advance scouts. John C. Duncan assisted the scouts at times. The party took a southern route and crossed the Colorado River at Lee's Ferry. They went as far south as Moenkopi, Arizona, before heading northeast. In July they ended their journey on the banks of the San Juan River. There they established a settlement at what they called Montezuma, some miles north and west of the Four Corners point in present San Juan County.

Their journey had been difficult. The group determined that the route they took would be impracticable because of hostile Indians and an inadequate water supply for the larger party coming later in the year. Harvey Dunton and the Harriman and Davis families chose to remain in the San Juan Valley. Most of the rest of the company left on 19 August 1879 to return to Iron County. For the return trip, however, they chose to investigate a northern route. They traveled by way of present-day Moab and Castledale, following the Old Spanish Trail much of the way, down Salina Canyon to the Sevier Valley, through Bear Valley, arriving back in Paragonah by mid-September. Upon completion of the trek, the men had made a circuit of about 1,000 miles and helped complete several hundred miles of roads as they went. Still, they were not convinced that they had located a satisfactory route to the San Juan settlement. The northern route they thought was too long—more than 450 miles—and the goal was to reach the San Juan River in time to get crops planted so they could later be harvested before winter.

Due east of Parowan and almost in a straight line to the San Juan settlements only 200 miles away lay the community of Escalante. Surely, reasoned those heading for Montezuma, they should be able to establish a road by this route that would get them to their destination much faster.

Three men from Escalante played a role in the decision to choose this short-cut: Charles Hall, Andrew P. Schow, and Reuben Collett. All three had explored extensively the terrain east and south of their settlement. Hall is generally acknowledged as having been the first to discover the narrow cleft in the 2,000-foot cliff above the Colorado River which came to be called Hole-in-the-Rock. Schow and Collett, however, probably exerted greater influence in the decision the migrants made to choose this route. They had actually descended to the river, crossed it in a makeshift boat, and explored a few miles east—but, unfortunately, not far enough to recognize what treacherous country the migrants would eventually encounter. In addition, Schow and Collett were friends of Silas Smith, who took charge of the colonization effort.

The company traveled across difficult territory southeast of Escalante, with the Straight Cliffs and Fifty Mile Mountain on their right and the Escalante River drainage to their left. By late November 1879, 250 men, women, and children, with eighty wagons and over a thousand head of cattle, had gathered in camps between forty and fifty miles from Escalante. They were poised and ready to make the 1,200-foot descent down to the Colorado River and on to the San Juan but expressed dismay at what they found. After hearing the reports of two additional exploration parties, and influenced by the fact that heavy snows already blocked any retreat over Escalante Mountain to the west, the leaders made the decision to go on with what has been characterized by some as "the most foolhardy trip ever undertaken by man."[32] As Samuel Rowley wrote in classic understatement, "Before we left our homes we were told that the country had been explored, and that the road was feasible. But now we found that someone had been mistaken."[33] Remarkably, however, once they made the decision to push on, everyone pulled together to accomplish their task with a minimum of dissension and complaint.

The men of the company divided into three road-building crews, after having already established the thoroughfare some fifteen miles from Fifty-Mile Spring to the edge of the gorge. The first party worked at the head of the Hole-in-the-Rock to establish a wagon

Looking through the Hole-in-the-Rock to the Colorado River below. (Utah State Historical Society)

road down the sandstone cliffs; the second group extended the road from the cliffs to the Colorado River; the third crew crossed the Colorado and built a road up the east bank cliffs. In the meantime, Charles Hall and his sons, John and Reed, felled and cut to measure the logs needed for a raft to ferry the wagons across. They hauled the logs sixty-five miles from Escalante and lowered them down the cliff

face through Hole-in-the-Rock. They then put together their prefab-
ricated raft by the side of the river.

Without question, the first crew had the most difficult task.
Although many in this group distinguished themselves and proved
invaluable in constructing this difficult route, Benjamin Perkins was
especially noted for his engineering skill and ingenuity. Lamont
Crabtree, a Hole-in-the-Rock historian, described the feat:

> Construction consisted of cutting away a 40-foot drop-off at the
> top of the crevice, moving huge boulders, leveling high spots, fill-
> ing depressions, and widening crevice walls. To avoid the steep
> grades near the bottom of the Hole-in-the-Rock, the pioneers
> tacked their road onto the face of the north wall of the crevice. The
> tacked-on road was supported by oak stakes secured into holes
> drilled into the crevice wall at two-foot intervals.[34]

In addition to isolation and the usual challenges of winter, the
workers had little blasting powder. By 25 January 1880, after six weeks
of labor, all three crews had finished their projects. By now the leadership of the enterprise had fallen upon Platte D. Lyman, who had
been Silas Smith's assistant. Smith was constantly going back and
forth between the wagon train and the settlements trying to get supplies sent, enlist volunteer help for road building, and gain financing
from the Mormon church and the territorial legislature for creating a
passable route for others to use later.

The migrants came well provisioned for two months of traveling, but their odyssey would extend to six. While the men worked,
others in the camps faced additional challenges. Herds had to be constantly moved to find new forage. Supplies had to be secured and sent
on to the road builders. Additional food had to be brought in as the
travelers' supplies started to run out. The migrants also needed to
find or build protection from the cold and snow.

Until the mill water froze, Escalante residents did what they
could to supply flour, beans, corn, and other produce to the expedition members. Elizabeth M. Decker wrote on 19 January 1880, "We
have just sent our last five dollars to Escalante to get some pork and
Molasses."[35] Some of the pioneers complained that the townspeople
took advantage of their situation and raised their prices considerably,

even claiming that the villagers held a meeting prior to the arrival of the wagon trains to plan this strategy. But, in defense of the Escalante residents, their town was a mere three years old; the residents only had the food they raised themselves and what they had freighted in, which came at considerable cost to them due to their isolated locale.[36] Also, the migrants wanted to buy most of their meat from local farmers, since the herd they brought with them was intended for the nucleus of future herds once they reached the San Juan area. Despite these complaints, many residents of Escalante and Panguitch came to the aid of the pioneers on numerous occasions throughout their journey.

One of the migrants' coping strategies was to hold dances at what they called Dance Hall Rock, located near the Forty-Mile Spring camp, where the huge sandstone rock forms a large amphitheater with a reasonably smooth surface. Fiddlers in the company supplied the music, as the women, children, and those men who could be spared from their labors danced and tried to forget their deprivations and the awesome challenges that lay ahead. The pioneers also held regular religious services most Sundays and on Thursday evenings throughout the trek to the San Juan.

The extended length of the ordeal posed a particular hardship on expectant mothers. Three babies were born before the emigrants reached their destination. Little is known about the first of these babies to arrive—even the names of its parents are not known. The baby was born at or near Escalante and was either stillborn or died shortly after birth. Upon hearing of this tragedy, Escalante resident Mary Alice Barker Shurtz, who was also expecting her first child, took butter, eggs, and bacon to the grieving mother to trade for the layette she had so lovingly sewn for her child.[37] Mary Shurtz would know a similar grief, as her child only lived twenty-two days. The other two babies were Lena Deseret Decker, born at Fifty-Mile Camp on 3 January 1880 to James Bean and Anna Maria Mickelsen Decker, and John Rio Larson, born on Grey Mesa, east of the Colorado River, on 21 February 1880 to Mons and Olivia Ekelund Larson of Santaquin.

On 26 January 1880 the descent of the wagons began through Hole-in-the-Rock. By locking the hind wheels and attaching long ropes or chains to the rear axle, several men could pull back on the

Dance Hall Rock—near Forty Mile Spring southeast of Escalante where members of the Hole-in-the Rock Expedition gathered in late 1879. (Utah State Historical Society)

wagons to slow their downward progress. With one man driving each team, the wagons arrived safely at the bottom of the cliffs. The women and children walked down the perilously slippery trail.

One of the more heroic incidents of this operation involved the Joseph Stanford Smith family. Smith served as one of the road foremen and had seen little of his family for weeks. He remained in the gorge to help ferry the wagons across the 300-foot-wide river to where they could climb up the dugway on the opposite bank. When word came that all the wagons that had been camping near the top were down, Smith looked for his own family but could not see them. He hurriedly climbed to the top and found his wife and three small children alone. He was understandably furious that no one had helped his family while he was helping others.

His wife, Arabella "Belle" Coombs Smith, felt confident that she and her husband could get their wagon down alone. After checking all of their equipment, they settled their children on a folded quilt above the crevice. Their little boy, three-year-old Elroy, held his baby brother, George Abraham, between his legs, while their five-year-old sister, Ada Olivia, sat in front of them. Their mother kissed each one and told them not to move, not even to stand. She advised Ada to say a prayer. After their father assured them that he would shortly return to walk them down, the couple began their descent.

They tied one of their horses to the rear of the wagon to help hold the wagon back. Belle stood behind the horse and held him with another rope. The first lurch pulled the horse down to his haunches, but Belle held on and pulled back with all her strength, realizing that the weight of the horse would help slow the progress of the wagon. On the way down, she tripped and was thrown from side to side against cliff and boulders and dragged over jagged rocks that tore at her clothes and flesh, but finally they reached the bottom. When Stanford Smith got down from the wagon, he saw that his wife and horse were bruised and battered. Blood ran from Belle's leg; she and the horse literally had been dragged down the cliff. But the look on Belle's face warned her husband that—at that moment at least—she would not abide his sympathy. She hurried him back up the trail to rescue the children. He found them just as their mother had left them, the baby having fallen asleep in his brother's arms. Once reunited, the family headed out of the canyon toward the river just as a party of men came to aid them. With great effort, Smith managed to conceal his anger as the men assisted the family across the river.[38]

After climbing from the banks of the Colorado River, the wagon train had another ten weeks of travel over some of the most rugged terrain in the country. Winter weather continued to plague them as well, but they finally arrived on the banks of the San Juan River, about fifteen miles from Montezuma, in early April. Many of the group, refusing to go farther, stayed there and founded the community of Bluff. Others continued on to the already established settlement. A trip that was to have taken from six weeks to two months had taken six months. In retrospect, they would have been wise to have taken the northern route. Miraculously, however, everyone arrived safely; there were no fatal accidents and relatively few losses to their horses and other stock. Certainly if this had been a test of their faith, devotion, and obedience, they had acquitted themselves admirably.

ENDNOTES

1. See "Among My Memories—diary of John Henry Davies 1860–1947," in *Davies Family History 1831–1947*, compiled by Reta Davies (Ogden, UT: Davies, 1982), copy in possession of Marilyn Jackson, Escalante.

2. Information from Marilyn Jackson, Escalante.

3. Ida Chidester and Eleanor Bruhn, *Golden Nuggets of Pioneer Days: A History of Garfield County*, 92, says that the Thompson survey met a group of Mormons, Alma Barney, Orley Dwight Bliss, Edward Banker, and Smith Thurston in Potato Valley. Neither Thompson nor those with him, however, mention an encounter with these or any other men in 1872. The authors thank Jerry C. Roundy of Escalante for drawing this to our attention. Chidister and Bruhn also refer to Orley Dwight Bliss as Arlo D. Bliss. One of Bliss's plural wives was Harriet Josephine Lee, a daughter of John D. Lee and Martha Elizabeth Berry.

4. Nethella Griffin Woolsey, *The Escalante Story: 1875–1964* (Springville, UT: Art City Publishing Co., 1964), 26–27. Much of the information regarding the early settlement of Escalante was taken from Woolsey's book.

5. Marilyn Jackson, "The Unraveling of a 'Shurtz Tale' and an Epoch of Escalante Excitement," manuscript, 1992, 21, copy of manuscript in possession of the authors. Woolsey also quotes from Thompson's diary entry; see Woolsey, *Escalante Story*, 24–25, 28. For information on the Domínguez-Escalante expedition see Chapter Three.

6. According to Marilyn Jackson of Escalante, a descendant of Don Carlos Shurtz, the family surname was really spelled "Shirts" by everyone except Don Carlos (Carl) and his progeny. Their ancestor came from either Switzerland or Germany and the ancestral name was believed to be "Scherz." In Escalante, all those surnamed "Shurtz" or "Shirts" are related.

7. As quoted in Woolsey, *Escalante Story*, 55–56, 87.

8. According to a brief biography on Andrew P. Schow, he and Edmond Davis were the only settlers in Escalante with two wives, and neither of the second wives had children. Woolsey, however, wrote that George Coleman came with two wives. See Marilyn Jackson, "Notes on Andrew P. Schow," 2, and Woolsey, *Escalante Story*, 46.

9. Quoted by Helen Bailey Schow in Jackson, "Shurtz Tale," 27.

10. Chidester and Bruhn, *Golden Nuggets*, 94.

11. Woolsey, *Escalante Story*, 57.

12. Ibid., 110.

13. Ibid., 239.

14. See Jackson, "Notes on Andrew P. Schow."

15. Woolsey, *Escalante Story,* 411.

16. Chidester and Bruhn, *Golden Nuggets,* 289.

17. Andrew Jenson, *Encyclopedia History of the Church of Jesus Christ of Latter-day Saints (Salt Lake City: Deseret News Publishing Company, 1941),* 147.

18. Chidester and Bruhn, *Golden Nuggets,* 117.

19. George W. Thompson, "Cannonville History," manuscript, 1994, 3, copy in possession of authors. Unless otherwise noted, most of the historical background on this community comes from Thompson's work.

20. Ibid., 5.

21. Ibid., 8.

22. Ibid., 13.

23. Jenson, *Encyclopedia History of the Church,* 114.

24. Udell Jolley, "Life Sketch of Lydia Drusilla Johnson Henderson," in "Seth Johnson Family History," James A. Ott, compiler, 1947.

25. Much of the information concerning the settlement of Henrieville is taken from a history written by Zella Willis, a long-time resident of that community; the original is in the possession of Teora Willis of Henrieville. See also Van Cott, *Utah Place Names,* 402.

26. See "History of the Henrieville School," in possession of Nancy Twitchell, and Van Dorn Smith, "History of Henrieville School," original in possession of Teora Willis.

27. Ibid.

28. Diana Johnson, "The First White Men Come to Henrieville," 2–3, copy in possession of Teora Willis.

29. Jenson, *Encyclopedia History of the Church,* 147.

30. David E. Miller, *Hole-in-the-Rock* (Salt Lake City: University of Utah Press, 1959), 10.

31. Ibid., 12.

32. Marilyn Jackson, "Notes on Andrew P. Schow."

33. Miller, *Hole-in-the-Rock,* 54–55.

34. Lamont Crabtree, "Hole-in-the-Rock," in *Utah History Encyclopedia,* ed. by Allan Kent Powell (Salt Lake City: University of Utah Press, 1994), 258.

35. Miller, *Hole-in-the-Rock,* 76.

36. Helen Bailey Schow, "Sagebrush Mary," 5, manuscript, copy obtained by authors from Marilyn Jackson.

37. Miller, *Hole-in-the-Rock,* 48–49; and Schow, "Sagebrush Mary," 3–4.

38. Raymond S. Jones, "Last Wagon Through the Hole-in-the-Rock," *Desert Magazine* (1954): 22–25. Although the Smith wagon was the last of those camped near the cliff, other wagons at Fifty-mile and Forty-mile camps had not yet arrived at the cliff. See Miller, *Hole-in-the-Rock,* 118 n. 22.

CHAPTER 8

ESTABLISHING GARFIELD COUNTY

W hen an assassin's bullet struck down the twentieth president of the United States on 2 July 1881 early residents of the aforementioned communities in southern Utah could not have guessed it would have any particular connection to them. Not long after President James A. Garfield's lingering death that September, however, the Utah Territorial Legislature agreed to the formation of a new county in southern Utah that would eventually bear Garfield's name. National politics also influenced the creation, location, and management of community post offices. During the 1880s local schools were organized into a countywide system. The long arm of national government reached into the personal lives of many county residents as it attacked the Mormon practice of polygamy. The decade also produced a new settlement and saw numerous citizens of local towns within and outside of the county periodically gravitate to county locations of pristine beauty to assuage their hardships and trials.

The Birth of Garfield County

As early as February 1876 the territorial legislature had received a

James A. Garfield, twentieth president of the United States, for whom Garfield County was named. (Utah State Historical Society)

petition from William Sevy and other citizens of Panguitch, then in
Iron County, requesting that a new county of their own be formed.
The representatives sent the petition to the legislative committee on
counties for its consideration.[1]

It took several years before the Panguitch request bore fruit, but
on 8 March 1882 Utah's House passed a bill changing the boundaries
of Kane and Washington counties and creating Snow County. The
representatives selected this name in honor of Erastus Snow, a LDS
church authority who had figured prominently in the settlement of
southern Utah. The next day, Utah's upper chamber, or Council, initiated an act that changed the boundaries of Iron County. Later that
day, the Council received word through Erastus Snow that Governor
Eli H. Murray would approve the formation of the new county if the
representatives amended the bill and changed the name of the county
to Garfield in honor of the slain president. Snow moved to accept the
amendment; the Council passed it and sent the bill to the House,
which also approved the change. Later that night, 9 March 1882,
Governor Murray signed the bill creating Garfield County.[2] The legislature defined the boundaries of the new county essentially where
they are today, that is, with Piute and Wayne counties on the northern boundary, the Colorado River defining the eastern line, Kane
County the southern neighbor, and Iron County along the western
border. From north to south Garfield County measures forty-two
miles, from east to west it averages 124 miles in length. The county
comprises 5,234 square miles.

The legislature designated Panguitch as the county seat and
decided that Garfield would remain connected to Iron County for
legislative representation. Garfield also came under the jurisdiction
of the Second Judicial District of the Territory, headquartered at
Beaver, where court proceedings took place and prisoners were taken
to await trial. As officers of the county, the legislature appointed
James Henrie, probate judge, and Andrew P. Schow, Ira Elmer, and
Jesse W. Crosby as selectmen to organize the new county government
and to serve until regular elections that fall. These men appointed
additional officers mandated by the legislature. They included M.M.
Steele, Sr., county clerk; Jesse W. Crosby, county recorder; John
Myers, county treasurer; William P. Sargent, prosecuting attorney;

John E. Myers, sheriff; David Cameron and James B. Heywood, justices of the peace; William Alvey, justice of the peace for Escalante Precinct; Joseph Houston, constable; Enoch Reynolds, road supervisor; and Albert DeLong, poundkeeper of Panguitch Precinct.[3]

When Garfield County residents went to the polls the next year (1883), the following won offices: John Myers, treasurer; Robert P. Allen, assessor and collector; James A. Worthen, recorder; Erastus Beck, James Houston, and Allen Miller, selectmen; John M. Dunning, court clerk; David Cameron, probate judge; John Houston, prosecuting attorney; R.C. Pinney, coroner; Joseph Marshall, sheriff; James B. Heywood, superintendent of schools and county surveyor; Joseph S. Barney, constable for Escalante Precinct; James W. Pace, constable for Panguitch Precinct; Martin W. Foy and John E. Myers, justices of the peace for Panguitch Precinct.[4]

During the early years of territorial organization national politics and national political parties held little interest for residents of southern Utah communities. People did not divide along party lines, especially in local elections; usually voters had only one slate to vote for, and civic leaders were usually prominent LDS church leaders as well. Later, LDS voters favored candidates of the People's party; non-Mormons chose those running for the Liberal party. Voters in Garfield County as well as throughout the territory usually did not become members of the Democratic or Republican parties until the 1890s, at which time the local parties were disbanded and the Mormon church agreed to promote the national political parties as a condition of Utah statehood.[5]

Mail Service in Early Garfield County

National politics, however, did influence local affairs in early Garfield County when it came to locating post offices and naming postmasters in each community. Private homes housed the early post offices. At first, mail came to Panguitch through the Little Creek and Bear valleys from Parowan and Beaver. Beaver continued to be the distribution center for Garfield County until 7 August 1890, when the Denver & Rio Grande Western Railroad opened a spur from Thistle through Sevier Canyon to Marysvale in Piute County. As mentioned, William D. Kartchner served as the first postmaster of Panguitch. In

1878 John W. Norton succeeded him, having built an addition onto his home to accommodate the post office. With each succeeding change in presidential administrations came new people to this position. From 1889 to 1893 Susan B. Tebbs served the town as postmistress, the first woman to hold the job in the county.[6]

Hillsdale was the site of the second post office established in what became Garfield County when Seth Johnson was appointed postmaster in December 1872. Others followed Johnson until the Hillsdale office was closed in 1886.[7] After the closure townspeople received their mail in a sack delivered from Panguitch. In April 1887, however, the U.S. Postal Service allowed Jerome Asay to establish a new office in Asay (Aaron) and serve as postmaster. Even after the office transferred to Hatchtown, it retained the name of Asay. It was not until the town of Hatch relocated to its present site that the post office carried the town's name.

During the late 1880s and early 1890s Neils Ivor Clove, J.C. Barnhurst, Annie M. Barnhurst, and William R. Riggs succeeded one another in directing the Hatchtown post office. One of the early mail carriers from the area was Abram S. Workman. His contract specified that he carry mail from Panguitch to Kanab—a distance of about seventy-five miles. During the summer months this presented no real challenges, but winter was another story. Abram wrote: "It was a job to try the metal of any man. The mail had to go six days a week, no matter what the weather. . . . There were times when I got on snow shoes and, with the mail sack on my shoulder, went to face the weather."[8] He recalled deep snow and drifts that sometimes piled up to ten feet. Although he did not specify how much he earned, he did say that when he got a new contract after his first term of four years expired he received an additional $450 per year. At that time there were few jobs that paid in cash, so he figured he made out quite well.

In Escalante the townspeople lacked regular mail service for the first three years of the town's existence. As various citizens made the sixty-three-mile trip to Panguitch they would bring back with them any mail for other residents. On 2 January 1879 David R. Adams was appointed to be Escalante's first postmaster. Robert P. Allen succeeded Adams in 1881 and located the office in a store that occupied one room of his home. While Allen sorted the newly arrived mail the townspeople often gathered in his yard and used the occasion for impromptu entertainment, "complete with musical instruments." Allen then "would call out the name on each letter, and the owner or a member of his family would claim the letter at the small window."[9] After the establishment of the Escalante co-op store, clerk Rob Adams moved the post office to the store.

The first post office in the Coyote (Antimony) area was known as the Otter Creek Post Office. It was built at Clover Flat in the mid-1880s, about five miles north of the present town. Jim Forshey ran the office for a few years until it was moved to Wilmont, also located on Coyote Flat, just north of the Garfield County line in Piute County.[10] John D. Wilcox took over at this new location. Mail came by horseback once a week from Junction. It wasn't until 1896 that Antimony had its first post office in town, located about one block south of the present LDS chapel. Henry J. McCullough, son of Mormon Battalion member Levi Hamilton McCullough, became postmaster.[11]

As mentioned, Henrieville's first post office began serving the community in 1883 when William Thompson became the postmaster. Mail service there later was suspended for about two years, at which time local residents again received their mail from a combination post office/blacksmith shop when Melissa (or Melicia) Ingram was appointed postmaster and her husband, Joseph, ran the shop. For a period of time Seth Johnson carried mail from Panguitch to the upper Paria River Valley. On one occasion, as he was making a trip from Pahreah to Cannonville, he reached a part of the route that took him through a narrow canyon with perpendicular walls on either side. At a point called "Devil's Elbow" he encountered a flash flood. Hurriedly unhitching his horses from the wagon, he grabbed the mail sack and headed for higher ground. Upon reaching what he thought was a safe distance above the flood, he watched in alarm as the waters rose dangerously close to his perch. Just as they were about to reach him, the waters began to subside and he finally could continue on his way. As for his wagon, he surmised that "it was on the way to the Pacific Ocean."[12] Similar to almost everything else in the pioneering experience, mail service was fraught with hazards.

Education

Shortly after the creation of Garfield County, an administration headed by Superintendent of Common Schools James B. Heywood created six school districts on 1 May 1882.[13] The six included Cannonville, Clover Flat (Antimony), Escalante, Bear Creek (Spry), Hillsdale, and Panguitch. M.M. Steele and William P. Sargent served with Heywood as board members. Heywood was also a member of the county board of school examiners and functioned as the county surveyor as well. Each district had three elected school trustees, whose duties were "to superintend the school in their respective districts." These boards were concerned with the construction of schools and collecting taxes to support them. They hired the teachers, secured furnishings and textbooks, and provided fuel to heat the buildings.

Although the local boards had the power to levy school taxes, the main source of funds to pay teachers came from tuition—generally about three dollars for a ten-week term. In addition, the territorial government assessed three mills on the dollar in property taxes to help fund district schools.

In a report issued at the close of 1883, Heywood pronounced the Panguitch district to be in fairly good shape. There were two schools, with 160 students "taught by two competent teachers, with one assistant." He considered these schools to be well furnished with desks and supplies. He also stated, however, that the Hillsdale, Cannonville, and Bear Creek districts were supporting only about one term of school per year, that the teachers were underqualified, and that the district populations were scattered.

Hatchtown (presumably within the Hillsdale district) actually began holding school as early as 1879, when Abram S. Workman taught local children in one of the bedrooms of the Mary Ann Ellis Hatch home. He only taught for two months, however, and wrote that he "did not realize much from the venture."[14] Schooling resumed in Hatchtown in 1882 when the county and school districts were organized. Mary Ann Clove taught the children of Hatchtown in her own home periodically over the next several years. Some of the area's other early teachers included Lucy Windsor from St. George, Lizzie Bell (the first to teach in the new log schoolhouse), Rebecca Wilson,

James B. Burrow, and Adolph G. McClasky, "a small man of Spanish descent" whose students finally had "real" school desks provided by the school district. Both parents and children remembered James Burrow as one who believed in posting mottoes above windows and doors for the moral education of his pupils.[15]

In his report, Heywood judged the Escalante district, with a comparable population as Panguitch, to be operating on a sub-par level, as it had only one primary school in a poorly furnished house. The superintendent wrote, "There is evidence of lack of interest in this district, which, in my official visits, I have endeavored to improve."[16] Figures provided by Heywood indicate that by the end of 1883 there were 296 children between the ages of six and eighteen enrolled in county schools out of the 445 school-age children living in the county districts. Eight teachers taught these students. Their job would have been difficult at best, with an average classroom load of thirty-seven students for each teacher, and most taught multiple grades at the same time and in the same facility. Given that some teachers had fewer students than the average, many classrooms had an even larger student/teacher ratio. Interestingly—but not surprisingly for the period—male teachers earned nearly twice as much as their female colleagues. Men earned an average of $41.34 a month, compared to $25.20 for women. Unfortunately, Heywood's report does not critique the qualifications of those teaching in the county.

The superintendent also failed to include in his report the education situation in one of its districts during the time period—the district of Clover Flat (the Coyote, or Antimony, area). By 1883 the population in Coyote had increased to the point that residents decided to build their own schoolhouse, since the facility at Clover Flat was about five miles away. While the new one-room structure was under construction, local children attended school in a portion of the George Black home, with Esther Clarinda King Black teaching the classes. She, along with Joe Dameron, also taught in the newly completed school, referred to as both the Marion Ward School and the Coyote School.[17] This building was deemed insufficient by 1887. Across the road to the west the townspeople built a new edifice to serve as school, church, and hall for social gatherings. In her diary, Irene King recalled her reaction to this new school, which was a 28-

Cannonville School. (Courtesy Dorothy Leavitt)

by-40-foot building: "It looked mammoth to we children. . . . There were three windows on each side, about a 12 or 14 foot stage on which stood the neat, homemade pulpit and book cupboard." She also recalled that a Mr. Winters taught a singing school in the facility. Her description of the dances and entertainments that took place in the school revealed that they were similar to those in other small towns in the county and across the territory:

> John Smoot was a fine singer and entertainer. . . . One song we loved to hear him sing was "Coons, Have You Ever Seen My Sweet Susanne?" Aurella [Smoot] used to sing with him. Then John Wilcox, the town comedian and mimic, always gave comic readings and songs. . . . Many a time the sun would be coming over the mountain as we were going home.[18]

As for county school organization as a whole, the next few years saw John M. Dunning, James A. Worthen, and George Dodds succeed one another as district superintendents. Dodds especially had a reputation for being an outstanding educator. Educators in each district respected his ideas and professionalism. Serving as Dodds's assistant, John C. Swensen, who later became a professor of sociology at

Brigham Young University (BYU), related his impressions after touring the district schools in 1892. He mentioned, in particular, John Dunning of Cannonville as being "an effective old-time teacher. I recall very distinctly a twelve-tail switch in the corner of the room which aided materially in his discipline."[19] In addition to the other schools in the county, he visited the school in Escalante, taught at that time by Walter M. Woolf, who also later became a professor at BYU. Perhaps this fact can be seen as an indication that the quality of education in Escalante had improved since Heywood's earlier report. A half century later, Swenson wrote: "The schools at that time were somewhat ungraded and from our present point of view, somewhat primitive, nevertheless, they served a useful social and educational purpose."[20]

Superintendent George Dodds's statistical report for 1890 indicated an increase in students, with 496 enrolled out of 748 school-age children living in Garfield County. The students were taught by thirteen teachers; thus, the average student/teacher ratio had increased by one—to thirty-eight pupils per teacher. A seventh district had been added to the county. Although the record is not clear what that district was, evidence indicates it was Henrieville, since a later report lists that town among the seven districts.

In 1890 the Utah Territorial Assembly passed a law doing away with all tuition charges for schoolchildren aged six through eighteen. In addition, it passed a companion compulsory school-attendance law that specified that children between six and fourteen years of age had to attend school at least twenty weeks out of each school year. According to Effel Riggs, in Garfield County these provisions "literally filled the school house."[21]

Polygamy

The 1880s became one of the most disruptive but interesting decades since the Black Hawk War years of the 1860s, as confrontation increased between Mormon church members and federal officials over the Mormon practice of plural marriage. LDS church members considered the practice to be a divinely inspired tenet of their religion, but outsiders regarded it not only as an abomination but also as a violation of the law of the land. Although Congress had passed and President Abraham Lincoln signed the Morrill Anti-Bigamy Act in 1862, that law seemed only a minor threat to the practice of polygamy among LDS church members because it included few enforcement provisions. The nation also was preoccupied with the Civil War and then Reconstruction. But when the Mormon church decided to test the constitutionality of certain sections of the Morrill Act, the Supreme Court ruled against it, causing antagonism towards polygamy to intensify.

Congress subsequently passed, and President Chester A. Arthur signed, the Edmunds Act of 1882, which made unlawful cohabitation a misdemeanor, disfranchised polygamists, and prohibited them from holding public office or serving on juries. It also permitted counts of polygamy and unlawful cohabitation to be combined in the same indictment. Along with these provisions, a board of five presidential appointees, known as the Utah Commission, replaced election officers in the territory.[22]

Anti-polygamy raids on Mormon households began throughout the territory in 1884. It became a time of turmoil for many families, as fathers—and sometimes mothers—went into hiding, causing both emotional and financial hardships. Deputy U.S. marshals, who were paid well for apprehending polygamists, were determined in their efforts, and Garfield County Latter-day Saints were as committed to frustrating those efforts as were Mormons in other counties throughout the territory.[23]

Certainly not all the LDS families who lived in Garfield County were polygamous, but enough were to cause unrest for the residents when the federal government began to put teeth in the laws prohibiting the practice. Also, since most residents belonged to the LDS faith, they openly defended the practice against outside attacks. Most of the early prominent leaders in the various county settlements had more than one wife. George Sevy of Panguitch, Meltiar Hatch of Panguitch and later Hatchtown, Andrew Schow of Escalante, and Seth Johnson of Hillsdale and later the Cannonville area are just a few examples of polygamous Mormon men.

The Thomas King family that established the Mormon united order in Kingston had little experience with the practice. Thomas was sealed to another woman, Rebecca Henry, but the two never lived together as husband and wife. When asked why Thomas did not take another wife, his first wife, Matilda, replied that he "was never cut out for a polygamist—he don't know how to go about it."[24] A son, Thomas Edwin, lived in polygamy for a brief period; however, after his first wife died, leaving him with just one wife, he did not marry again. His brother John Robison and sister Delilah both had monogamous marriages. Although brother Volney wanted to adopt the practice, his wife, Eliza, made it clear that if he took another wife "he would still be left a monogamist."[25] Another brother, William, married Mary Ann Henry after the death of his first wife. When church leaders put pressure on him to take another wife or have his bishopric taken away he married Lucy White. Although Mary Ann acknowledged that Lucy was a good person, she could never be reconciled to living "the Principle," as plural marriage was known to Mormons, and at times made William's life miserable over the issue.

William King never went to prison over polygamy, although he was indicted by a grand jury in 1885. In 1886 he hastened off to a church mission in Hawaii. He was arrested when he returned in 1890 but pled guilty and was fined. He never served prison time or paid the fine.

Culbert King of Coyote was not as fortunate. He became one of the community leaders who went to prison for violating the Edmunds Act. Of all the King family he was the most active polygamist. He married and lived with three women, who together bore him twenty-four children. In 1885 Culbert attempted to hide out in the mountains to avoid capture by federal marshals after his indictment; however, he finally turned himself in to avoid harm coming to his family. Judge Jacob Boreman in Beaver, well-known for his active prosecution of polygamists, handed King the usual sentence of six months in the penitentiary and fined him $300 plus court costs. He served from 25 December 1885 to 28 June 1886. Future church president Lorenzo Snow and future apostle Rudger Clawson were numbered among his fellow inmates.[26]

At the time he was sent to prison, Culbert King served as bishop of the Marion LDS Ward in Coyote. John D. Wilcox then took over as presiding elder, since both of King's counselors were away from the area. Isaac Riddle, also a polygamist and the ward's first counselor, had left on an exploring mission for the church in Arizona, and James E. Peterson, the second counselor, had gone on a mission to the southern states. Wilcox presided in the area until Peterson could be recalled from his mission and assume leadership until King was released.[27] As with most inmates who served time for polygamy, Culbert King returned home to a hero's welcome—complete with a picnic and public speeches. To members of the LDS church, these men were martyrs for the faith, not ex-convicts.

Polygamous wives also sometimes suffered incarceration. This could occur when plural wives received a subpoena to testify against their husbands in court and then refused to take the oath or to give testimony. This prompted judges to find them in contempt of court, and U.S. marshals took them into custody. To avoid this scenario, many plural wives chose to go into hiding similar to that of their husbands.

About the time of the settlement of Cannonville, civil authorities aggressively sought out those practicing polygamy in the area. Apparently these federal marshals traveled about in "white-topped buggies [which were] light spring wagons painted red, with white canvas tops." Locals could see them from a distance traveling between the fields before they reached the community. The alarm quickly spread, so the hunted had time to hide. Some local Mormons did end up serving prison time for adhering to the Principle.[28]

A grandson of Martha Jane Stratton Johnson later wrote about his grandmother's situation. Martha, the plural wife of Seth Johnson, Sr., came to the Paria Valley in 1886 from Hillsdale. According to her grandson, she had to live in many "out of the way places under adverse conditions" as "she was in almost constant fear of being caught and taken to prison."[29] Indeed, records indicate that Martha Johnson lived at various times at Paria (Pahriah) and Georgetown in Kane County and at Cannonville and Tropic in Garfield County.

President Wilford Woodruff's Manifesto dated 6 October 1890 and issued because of enormous federal pressure on the Mormon church and its properties advised Mormons not to contract new polygamous marriages, and, although church members ratified the measure, many continued to live in polygamy. Some church leaders and members even contracted such unions after that date. This resulted in continued conviction and prison time for many of the offenders.

Some polygamous families made their own trouble. A case in point was shoemaker John M. Dunning, Garfield's first county superintendent of schools and the first county clerk. Dunning also published *The Cactus*, Garfield's first newspaper, and he had two wives, Lydia and Debbie. That these two women disliked each other was no secret in Panguitch. Soon after Dunning died unexpectedly in 1897 at age forty-two, Debbie moved with her children back to Beaver, where she had lived before her marriage. But the thought of John still being close to Lydia in Panguitch—albeit in the cemetery—rankled her. A *Salt Lake Tribune* reporter uncovered the story nearly a hundred years later:

> Debbie enlisted the help of a brother-in-law with a horse and wagon. They made the long trip to Panguitch, . . . and by dark of night dug up John Dunning, loaded him and his tombstone on the wagon, leaving the base of the stone in the cemetery where it still remains. . . . When the sexton went to the cemetery . . . the next day, he discovered the empty grave and went into town to report that someone had stolen John Dunning. The town was in an uproar. Lydia wanted the sheriff to go to Beaver and arrest Debbie for grave robbing, but he told her he couldn't do that because Debbie had been married to John, too.[30]

No one is sure how the gravestone, which was more than three feet high and weighed several hundred pounds, ended up in a canyon near Castle Creek, half buried in the sand; but that is where young David Herrell found it many years later while on a camping trip with his family. Carved in the stone were the words "John M. Dunning, Feb. 26, 1854, May 21, 1879." The Villa Park, California, family returned to the area on a later trip and decided to take the gravestone home with them, where it remained in their yard until 1989. At that time, they decided to return the tombstone to Panguitch, where it resides today.[31]

Boulder: A New Community for a New County

Once again the quest for virgin range for livestock stimulated the founding of another village in Garfield County—the town of

Boulder. Positioned the farthest east of any of the county's settlements, it has always been one of the most isolated towns in Utah.
This condition is rapidly changing today, however, because the community is located along upgraded Utah Highway 12, judged by many
to be one of the nation's most scenic highways.

As early as 1879 stockmen started to bring their herds to the eastern slope of Boulder Mountain, which was so named on Almon
Thompson's 1872 map. Nicoli Johnson, William Meeks, and Willard
Brinkerhoff drove their cattle from Richfield to this range. August
Nielson was among those who followed, and he built a corral of
aspen poles for the fall round-up. By the early 1880s the new rangeland beckoned several other herdsmen, including those tending cattle
belonging to LDS church cooperatives. In 1887 Wise Cooper and
John King helped Mack Webb of Oak City bring 300 head of horses
to the mountain area. Still later, Alma Durfey from Rabbit Valley
north of Boulder Mountain in present Wayne County brought in his
herd. After spending much of the summer on the mountain, the
horse herds drifted to rangeland at lower elevations southeast of the
mountain as winter arrived.

Meanwhile, dairying had become a lucrative enterprise in Rabbit
Valley, where the products produced found a ready market in
Richfield and Fillmore. Amasa Lyman and his family worked at one
of the dairies owned by Frank Haws. In September 1888 Lyman and
his wife, Rosanna, decided to take a break from their chores. They
saddled up two horses, brought along a picnic lunch, and went
exploring. Their travel took them south and east around Boulder
Mountain as they enjoyed the golden aspens against the backdrop of
green foothills. Eventually, after crossing Boulder Creek, they came
to the head of a long valley that stretched to the south. They stopped
beside a clear stream, and within the shade of pine trees they ate their
lunch and made the decision to return to this valley to homestead the
following spring.

Amasa Lyman and his twelve-year-old son Vern left Grover in
Rabbit Valley in April 1889 with a wagonload of supplies to establish
a new homestead. As they traveled through the foothills east of
Boulder Mountain, they first used a logging road and then followed a
cow trail, chopping down trees and removing numerous boulders to

An old postcard depicts a stake and rider fence near Boulder made from posts cut to clear the land. A few of these fences still stand which were described as "horse high, bull strong, and hog and sheep tight."

get their wagon through. Sam Shefield and a Mr. Myers from Colorado soon caught up with them with their own light wagon filled with provisions. Eventually the group encountered huge snowdrifts by Oak Creek that forced them to abandon their wagons, loading as much as they could on their horses. Shefield hefted a hand plow onto his shoulders and carried it into the valley. They reached a round-up corral at Pine Springs, where the Lymans decided to establish their homestead. Shefield and Myers continued on farther west and south to locate their own homesteads.

As Lyman and his son began clearing their land, they discovered an old ditch, undoubtedly dug by Native Americans years before. Father and son spent most of May lengthening the ditch, eventually diverting water from Deer Creek onto their chosen land. When warm weather continued, they left to recover their wagon and take it back to Grover to bring the rest of the family to their new home. The Lyman family then camped out all summer and planted alfalfa, field corn, and other vegetables; but the corn did not ripen before winter came.

Two other early settlers in the area, George Baker and Willard

Brinkerhoff, followed the Lymans to Rabbit Valley in October 1889. Baker had partial ownership in the corral at Pine Springs and offered its ponderosa pine logs to Lyman to begin building his cabin east of Deer Creek. Lyman also hauled some lumber from a sawmill in Rabbit Valley, and by December the family had a home with a dirt roof, a lumber floor, and a door—rather nice accommodations for such recently arrived pioneers.

Rosanna Lyman built a fireplace of flagstone and clay. During the winter local game they were able to hunt augmented their food supplies. Amasa spent the winter months reading to the children from the Bible and having them memorize scriptures. He also taught them songs and poems. Rosanna became skillful at making buckskin gloves and coats for her family and later sold some for profit. The following year, in September 1890, Rosanna gave birth to stillborn premature twin daughters and the saddened family buried them under a big pine tree on the homestead.

In the meantime, Shefield and Myers had explored the valley and foothills for a week. Myers decided to return to Rabbit Valley and thence to Colorado, but Sam Shefield staked his claim in what is now the central part of Boulder where the schoolhouse stands. The ground there had been previously cultivated by Native Americans. Indeed, just northwest of his land Shefield came upon ruins where he found pottery, arrowheads, and grinding stones strewn about the area.

Having brought corn seed with him, Shefield soaked it overnight and planted it the next day. He then built a small dam on Deer Creek and dug a ditch to carry water to his corn patch. Unlike that of the Lymans, his corn grew and ripened in time to harvest that year, the first successful corn crop grown in that valley by white settlers. Shefield also built a small cabin with a horse corral close by.

Sam Shefield became known for his generous nature, as he helped out many of his fellow settlers. On one occasion, during a harsh winter when the Lyman food supply ran dangerously low, their son Vern walked over the Death Hollow trail to Escalante. When he reached town he ran into Shefield, who purchased a 100-pound sack of flour for the family at the Riddle gristmill and loaned the boy a horse to take it back to his family.[32]

When George Baker and Willard Brinkerhoff paid a visit to the Lymans that first autumn of 1889, they decided to claim some land of their own. Lyman and Shefield rode with them to find a suitable location. Instead of a homestead plot, the two decided to each take up a desert entry claim of 640 acres, as provided for by the Homestead Act. Brinkerhoff chose an area in lower Boulder; Baker picked out some property to the northwest of his friend's place. The following spring they came back and made arrangements to have water diverted onto their land through ditches and a canal, accessing both Deer Creek and Boulder Creek. Although Brinkerhoff continued to come each spring to work his land, he never settled in the area. Finally, in 1897 he sold it to Baker's father, William Baker of Richfield.

In September 1890 George Baker averted a possible altercation with some Paiute Indians who took exception to white settlement in an area they used for hunting. Baker gave the roving band a pony as payment for the land, which seemed to satisfy them. Before winter set in Baker had the men who dug his canal help him raise his log cabin. The following spring he brought lumber to complete his home. In 1891 Baker brought his wife, Amanda Jensen Baker, with their four daughters and one son to the Boulder area to live. Eventually Baker had to relocate his residence to higher ground to the north when the area around his house became too swampy and his orchard suffered from poor drainage.

Along with George and Amanda Baker came Franklin and Wilhelmine (Minnie) Smith Haws and their family, who staked a claim for themselves. Although the land was north of the Baker entry, with land on both sides of Boulder Creek, Frank Haws built his family's cabin close to that of the Bakers so when he was away riding the range his family would not be alone. That same year, the men built a road from Haws's pasture to the Baker property. Minnie Haws served the community as midwife for many years. She not only helped deliver babies but also cared for mother and child for ten days free of charge.

George Baker's brother, Henry, also took up land in the Boulder area. He came in 1891 and began to clear land and grow alfalfa. He built a two-room log house, complete with fireplace and a garden spot nearby. Although Henry Baker came each summer to tend to his

Wilhemine (Minnie) Smith Haws, a midwife and, with her husband Frank, among the first settlers of Boulder. (Courtesy Fay Jepson)

acreage, his wife, Hannah Ramsay Baker, and three sons did not leave Richfield and come to live in the home until 1897. A very proper lady who never appeared in public without hat and gloves, Hannah Baker insisted that the new community be called Boulder at a meeting held at the schoolhouse to discuss the naming of the settlement.

Hannah Baker's mother, Elizabeth Ramsay, also came to live with the family. A handcart pioneer to Utah, in her declining years Mrs. Ramsay had mental lapses, at which times she thought she was still taking a handcart to Zion. The Bakers had a small express wagon which she would commandeer and pull down the road to the Haws residence. Minnie Haws's daughters would meet her along the road and help her get to their mother's place, where some tea awaited her. After her third cup of tea and a visit with Minnie, she would return home, with young Ralph Haws keeping an eye on her from a discreet distance.[33]

Other early settlers in Boulder included Frank Haws's mother and stepfather, John and Sariah Hilman Haws Safely. Safely was known by locals as the "old Union soldier" because he fought in the Mexican War. Frank Haws's sister and her husband, Dora and Fred Simons, and their children also came to upper Boulder, where they settled on a homestead next to the Safelys. When William Baker bought the Brinkerhoff desert entry, more of his children moved to Boulder. The elder Baker never did live there himself, but he subdivided his land for his offspring, who included Ruth Rio and her husband, James C. Peters, who came during the 1890s. Other siblings and their mates followed later. Willis and Louise Thompson, William and Harriet Elmer Osborn, and Christian and Mary Justett Moosman were additional early settlers who remained long enough to have an impact on the new community of Boulder.

Another settlement southwest of the town's present site, an area called Salt Gulch, was homesteaded by Ben McGath and his partner, a well-educated German named Jabours; Cal and Josepha Shefield Gresham, who was Sam's sister; Warren and Margaret Aveline McCartney Ogden and their family of six; and John and Sally May Stringham King and their three children. These last three families had been living in Escalante. The Kings were known for their friendly hospitality; John especially had an outgoing personality and keen sense of humor.

Salt Creek became the main source of irrigation water for the Salt Gulch settlers. William Osborn, Jr., and Warren Ogden constructed a wagon road to Sand Creek, where they installed a whipsaw they had acquired. With this they made lumber for a flume that carried water from the head of Sand Creek across a lava bed and to a ditch they dug to their acreage. Warren and his sons also rebuilt some wagon roads in the area, making the trip from Escalante less hazardous.

Sparsely populated Boulder had no school, a fact that concerned its residents. In October 1892 the Lymans decided to move to Escalante so that their children could be educated. Rosanna Lyman and her daughters made a large quantity of cheese that year, so the family felt they could afford the move. However, the road to Escalante was treacherous and made for a very difficult trip. By the spring of 1894 the family decided to move back to Boulder; they were worried

Ice Cutting in Boulder. The ice was cut in the winter and packed in sawdust and lasted throughout the summer to provide the only refrigeration available. (Courtesy Fay Jepson)

about holding on to their land as more settlers moved into the valley. The return trip seemed even more difficult than the one two years before, partly because Rosanna was pregnant. When they finally made it to their cabin door the family rejoiced to be "home" again. On 10 October midwife Minnie Haws helped in the delivery of a baby boy to Rosanna and Amasa Lyman, the valley's first birth of a white child who lived.

Meanwhile, the Haws and Baker families traveled each fall to Thurber (known as Bicknell since 1924) in Rabbit Valley in order that their children could attend school. Each spring they came back to Boulder. On one return trip the Haws brought an organ wrapped in quilts to protect it on the bumpy mountain road. Finally, during the spring of 1896, Frank Haws, Amasa Lyman, and George Baker made the trip to Panguitch to meet with school superintendent George Dodds. They told Dodds they wanted to remain on their land in Boulder but that they needed schooling for their children. Dodds assured them that in a year or two the county would be able to build them a schoolhouse and supply them with a teacher. The three men

Boulder's first post office was in this home. (Utah State Historical Society)

declared that if the county could send a teacher they would have a schoolhouse built by fall.

Sam Shefield donated to the community the piece of ground where he had built his cabin and corral in order that the one-room log schoolhouse could be built in central Boulder; he then relocated to what was known as Upper Boulder, on the west side of Deer Creek. Amasa Lyman, George Baker, Frank Haws, Willis Thompson, Chris Moosman, Sam Shefield, and the older boys in the settlement contributed labor to the project. Each father built the desks for his own children. There were long wooden benches, some built lower for the smaller children. Nineteen pupils attended classes taught by John Houston of Panguitch from November to the end of March. The students rode horses from their homesteads to the school, bringing their lunches in buckets.

As was the case in other Garfield communities, the schoolhouse became the local meetinghouse and social hall for church, parties, and dances. Frank Haws and John Safely played music for the dances, which generally lasted until the ladies served supper at midnight. The

Mail carrier Franklin Hansen ready to leave Boulder for Escalante. (USDA Forest Service)

adults lingered to visit over coffee and dessert while their little children slept on quilts laid out on the floor next to the wall.

Boulder's isolation created ongoing problems when it came to mail service. Townspeople were dependant on visiting relatives, friends, and even strangers to bring letters into town. Although most mail eventually reached its destination, the settlers finally decided to take matters into their own hands. The men took turns once a month carrying the town's mail on horseback to Escalante, where they collected the incoming mail and personally delivered it when they returned. Boulder residents had to wait until 1902 to finally get their first post office.

The LDS church did not have any organization in the settlement until church president Lorenzo Snow authorized Victor E. Bean, who was moving to Boulder from Richfield, to begin a Sunday School in 1898. Members and non-members attended the meetings and sang songs together. A few times Sunday School was held in the homes of Salt Gulch settlers, sometimes even in those owned by non-Mormons. After these meetings everyone ate dinner together. They especially enjoyed those meals prepared by Margaret Ogden, who was an exceptional cook. Administration of LDS ecclesiastical affairs in Boulder came under the direction of the Thurber Ward in Wayne Stake during this early period.

Panguitch Lake

About the time Garfield County was organized, great changes were occurring south of Panguitch—around the lake from which the community derived its name. Many residents involved with the second settlement of Panguitch located second homes and ranches around Panguitch Lake. They built a crude dam across the outlet of the lake to enlarge the capacity, with the intention of storing some water from the spring runoff.[34] They also cleared the surrounding land, creating wide meadows and pastures ideal for dairy and sheep herds. Along with the dairy products from the vicinity, mountain trout from the lake and the many streams that fed it became a lucrative—seemingly inexhaustible—export for the residents.

As the lake developed into a more important source of irrigation water for Panguitch residents, they replaced the old dam in the 1880s with a masonry structure several feet high. Over the years its height has been increased from time to time to ensure greater storage capacity, benefiting especially those farming the south and west fields of Panguitch.

During that same time and into the early 1890s, Panguitch Lake also became important as a recreational center for residents of the county and for visitors from more distant locales. Those employed at the Silver Reef mines, long-time customers of the bounty from the lake and surrounding dairy ranches, began to come in large numbers to vacation at the lake, where they usually camped on the James S. Montague property to the south. The area soon became known as "Little Silver Reef." James Montague and his wife ran the first hotel in the area. Guests considered Mrs. Montague to be an excellent cook, and her trout dinners became well-known attractions.

The lake developed into a popular destination for Independence Day and Pioneer Day celebrants, with festivities lasting up to a week for each occasion. Southern Utah residents commemorated these holidays with other tourists, church dignitaries, and even some Indians, who were doubtless more intent on the festivities than the

Pioneer Day celebration at Panguitch Lake on 24 July 1894. (Utah State Historical Society)

occasions, neither of which they had much cause to celebrate. Local Native Americans, usually Paiutes, camped on a knoll not far from the white settlement and contributed to the festive mood by staging games and dances of their own. They welcomed white spectators to take part around their giant campfires.

Interest naturally spawned entrepreneurial activities related to recreation. A Mr. Fennemore from Beaver included a mile-long straight racetrack as part of a resort he established near the Montague Hotel. The track attracted racing enthusiasts from throughout the territory and surrounding states. Vacationers also attended foot races, prize fights, and wrestling matches. A group of prominent Panguitch men later formed a company that built a circular racetrack, complete with grandstand and stables. Three members of this organization, John F. Chidester, William T. Owens, Sr., and George E. Hanks, constructed a dance pavilion on the lake's south shore during the early 1890s; it was reputed to be the largest south of Salt Lake City. This trio also built Panguitch's first large dance hall. These men and other Panguitch musicians provided the music for large crowds of dancers, sometimes so many that they had to take turns coming to the dance floor. In addition to dances, the pavilion became the venue for plays and other entertainment, some presented by traveling stock companies, including the Stuts Company of New York City and the Colmenia Pratt and Redic companies.

Personal dramas also added to the lake's fame. On one occasion a leading lady of the Stuts Company, Mable Rico, almost drowned in the lake, perhaps in a suicide attempt. James Ipson, who was returning to his home on the north side of the lake after attending a dance, came upon an overturned boat and found Rico. After pulling the unconscious actress aboard his craft, he rowed back to the resort. She survived the ordeal.

Another drama did not turn out so happily. During a Pioneer Day celebration in 1895, a likable young Paiute known as Wint was enjoying himself and visiting with friends at a saloon by the lake. Before long, however, a group of drunken white men entered the saloon. One of their number, a man from Texas by the name of Frank Hagglestead, boasted that he was going to shoot Wint's hat off his head. In his inebriated condition he missed and the bullet entered Wint's head, killing him instantly. Hagglestead fled the scene.

Local authorities avoided a serious confrontation when they assured the local Indians that Hagglestead would be brought to justice. He actually turned himself in to authorities rather than risk apprehension and vengeance by the local Native Americans. After spending some time in the Panguitch jail, Frank Hagglestead was transferred to Beaver, where he received a sentence of sixteen years in the state prison and had to give assurance that he would leave the state after he served his term.

The residents of the lake made it their home during the summer months. To provide for their ecclesiastical needs, local Mormon church authorities organized a ward in the early 1880s under the direction of James H. Imlay. Thirty-five Mormon families met in the Montague home; William Prince served as the presiding elder.

Two circumstances brought an end to the huge popularity of Panguitch Lake. The first occurred in 1896 after Utah statehood when a law passed the first state assembly prohibiting horse racing and its associated gambling. This had been one of the lake's biggest draws. Then came the introduction of a different type of fish into the lake.

Concerned that the native mountain trout had been overharvested, the Utah Fish and Game Commission restocked the lake with chubs, which eventually filled the lake and ruined the trout fishing. Panguitch residents remembered the two game wardens who introduced chubs into the lake—their names were Walker and Sharp. Later, residents called chubs "sharp-walkers."[35] Interest in the lake declined in the area, and the resort and its buildings fell into disrepair. It would be several decades before Panguitch Lake enjoyed a resurgence in reputation. The lake, however, remained from a scenic point of view much as it did when Andrew Jensen described it in 1891:

> If the scenery from the shore or a neighboring peak is grand and awe inspiring, the view obtained from the center of the lake is doubly so. The transparent water, in which the mountains cast their shadows all around, the numerous crags, cliffs, massive rock walls, canyons, meadows, forests, and the cattle upon a thousand hills, which greets the eye in every direction, fills every admirer of the wonderful creations of the Almighty with lofty and sublime thought, and fills the heart with respect and reverence for Him who created "the heavens and earth, the sea and the fountains of water."[36]

In addition to the creation of a new community within Garfield County, towns that had been established earlier experienced healthy growth. By 1890 Panguitch boasted a population of 1,015 residents, Hillsdale 333, Escalante 667, and Cannonville 273.[37] Although no official population figures exist for Antimony during the 1880s, the Mormon church's Marion Ward in Grass Valley had 147 members divided among twenty-nine families in 1889.[38] Since not all residents within the valley were Latter-day Saints, the area's population figure would have been a little higher.

Within the next several years Garfield County would have two new communities established and one relocated. One of the new settlements endured; the other was short-lived. The next decade also produced statehood for Utah, thus bringing about additional changes in the county.

ENDNOTES

1. Journal of the Legislative Assembly of the Territory of Utah, Twenty-second session, 1876, 108, Utah State Archives, Salt Lake City.

2. Council Journal of the Twenty-fifth Session of the Legislative Assembly of the Territory of Utah, Salt Lake City, Utah, 1882, 251, Utah State Archives.

3. Ida Chidester and Eleanor Bruhn, *Golden Nuggets of Pioneer Days: A History of Garfield County*, 29.

4. Election results and copies of certificates of elections obtained from Utah State Archives and Records Service, Salt Lake City.

5. Walter Kirk Daly, "The Settling of Panguitch Valley, Utah: A Study in Mormon Colonization" (Master's thesis, University of California, 1941), 61.

6. Chidester and Bruhn, *Golden Nuggets*, 283–84.

7. Effel Harmon Burrow Riggs, *History of Hatch Utah and Associated Towns Asay and Hillsdale*, 304.

8. Ibid., 299.

9. Nethella Griffin Woolsey, *The Escalante Story: 1875–1964*, 197.

10. M. Lane Warner, *Grass Valley 1873–1976*, 18.

11. Ibid., Appendix, 17.

12. "Seth Johnson Family History," 17–18.

13. J. Oral Christensen, "The History of Education in Garfield County, Utah" (Master's thesis, University of Utah, 1949), 59.

14. Riggs, *History of Hatch*, 282.

15. Ibid., 215–16.

16. Christensen, "Education in Garfield County," 61.

17. Warner, *Grass Valley*, 21.

18. Ibid., 24.

19. Christensen, "Education in Garfield County," 64.

20. Ibid., 64.

21. Ibid., 65.

22. Stan Larson, ed., *Prisoner for Polygamy: The Memoirs and Letters of Rudger Clawson at the Utah Territorial Penitentiary, 1884–87* (Urbana: University of Illinois Press, 1993), 3–4.

23. Ibid.

24. As quoted in Larry R. King, *The Kings of the Kingdom: The Life of Thomas Rice King and His Family*, 131.

25. Ibid., 132.

26. Ibid., 134–36,

27. Warner, *Grass Valley*, 22, 142.

28. George W. Thompson, "Cannonville History," 6.

29. "Seth Johnson Family History," 3.

30. *Salt Lake Tribune*, 8 October 1989, 6B.

31. Ibid.

32. Lenora Hall LeFevre, *The Boulder Country and Its People*, 72.

33. Ibid., 29.

34. See Daly, "Settling of Panguitch Valley," 68–76, and Chidester and Bruhn, *Golden Nuggets*, 216–25.

35. Information furnished by Marilyn Jackson, Escalante.

36. As quoted in Daly, "Settling of Panguitch Valley," 75.

37. Allan Kent Powell, ed., *Utah History Encyclopedia*, 434–35.

38. Warner, *Grass Valley*, Appendix, 179.

CHAPTER 9

GARFIELD COUNTY USHERS IN A NEW CENTURY

Garfield County experienced widespread progress during the decade of the 1890s and the beginning of the new century. The Mormon church's Manifesto in 1890 officially discouraging polygamy among members of the LDS faith aided in this progress and was important in the territory's drive to achieve statehood. But gains also came about because of improvements in the county's infrastructure, communications networks, and economic base, as well as population growth from both natural increase and inmigration. With this came the establishment of Garfield's last enduring township in the early 1890s, the moving of an already established community, and the creation of another that experienced a rather brief history.

The transition from one century to another initiated needed changes to the livestock industry. As it did throughout the American West, the federal government involved itself in protecting county rangeland and watersheds by creating forest reserves. Ranching also contributed its share of interesting characters who influenced county development and history, perhaps the most notorious being the outlaw Butch Cassidy and his Wild Bunch.

Cabin at Eagle City in the Henry Mountains. This mining camp operated from about 1891 to 1911. (Utah State Historical Society)

Gold Mining in the Henry Mountains

Stories of gold discoveries in the remote Henry Mountains stirred some interest. Local lore says that a man named John Angrove first struck gold in Bromide Basin near the head of Crescent Creek "and was murdered for the wealth he found there." In 1889 Jack Butler and Jack Sumner located the gold seam that would become the Bromide Mine. A year later, two other men discovered another vein that became the Oro Mine. These two mines soon led to the development of mills on Crescent Creek that were processing gold ore worth $300 a ton. Other miners soon came, and the Ida and Alda mines sprung into existence, as did Eagle City.[1]

Eagle City boasted a saloon, store, hotel, and doctor's office. Riders from Butch Cassidy's Wild Bunch reportedly would visit the saloon, adding to the wild reputation of the town. As a young man, Charley Hanks delivered mail by pack horse a hundred miles across the San Rafael Desert from Green River to Eagle City. He then "carried gold bricks from the mills back to Green River. Although he remembered several close calls, he never lost a letter or a gold shipment to the outlaws who holed up there," according to one historian.[2]

As the miners sank mine shafts farther into the earth, water began seeping into the shafts at depths of about 300 feet. Mine owners decided to build a 3,000-foot-long drain tunnel, but they ran out of money before they got halfway through the project. Then, in 1911, the Bromide Mill burned down. This disaster combined with the flooded shafts and a shortage of labor to bring an end to the mining excitement in the Henry Mountains and Eagle City. The boom had lasted just over twenty years. One lone miner stayed in the area, however. Frank Lawler remained at Eagle City for sixty more years, digging and searching for the elusive wealth.[3]

The Founding of Tropic

The first community east of Bryce Canyon along Utah Highway 12 is Tropic. The town's residents considered a number of possibilities for its name. Jesse W. Crosby suggested Erastus—for LDS church leader Erastus Snow; someone else proposed the biblical name Ur; still another wanted it called Hansen, after Tropic's first bishop, Andrew James Hansen, but Hansen himself objected to that idea and suggested the name of Tropic because the area's climate, while not tropical, was at least warmer than that of Panguitch. Even Panguitch was not as cold as the high meadow country along the East Fork of the Sevier River between the two towns. Through the years Bishop Hansen would often be quoted as saying, "The coldest night I ever spent was sleeping between my two wives on the East Fork"; one was in Tropic, the other in Panguitch.[4]

The actual founding of the town of Tropic came about as a direct result of two water projects. First, John Hatch sold the water rights to Spring Creek and some springs west of the future town in 1889.[5] This was followed by construction of a canal about ten miles long that would take water from the East Fork of the Sevier River over the east rim of the Paunsaugunt Plateau and drop it 1,500 feet down to the upper Paria Valley.

Several earlier attempts to divert this water from the Great Basin drainage area to the Colorado River drainage system had failed.

One of the first stores in Tropic, also used as a cafe. (Courtesy June Shakespear)

William Lewman (Luman) and others revived interest in such a project in 1889. They formed the East Fork Irrigation Company of Cannonville, with Andrew J. Hansen as president, Abe Workman as vice-president, William Jasper Henderson as secretary, and K.A. Fletcher and William Lewman as directors. The company incorporated on 5 May 1889. It used revenue received from stock purchases to buy simple survey equipment and tools with which to dig the canal. Lewman, Henderson, Henry Mecham, Emery Mecham, and

Ole Ahlstrom completed the survey of the canal by early July 1889. The actual digging began in September of that year.

Anticipating the benefits of a reliable source of irrigation water, James Ahlstrom and Ole Ahlstrom built homes in the area in 1890 and 1891, respectively. They were followed by Charles W. Snyder and G.J. Simonds, but the actual organization of the community had begun when William Lewman, Andrew Hansen, and James Ahlstrom surveyed the townsite in the spring of 1889, shortly after the Cannonville meeting. It included sixteen blocks of four lots per block, each lot measuring about one and a quarter acres. The lots sold for $7.50, and this low price attracted additional settlers. William, John F., and Dan Pollock; John Ahlstrom; Joseph and James Robert Ott; Will Chatwin; George Shakespear; William and John Spendlove; Levison Hancock; Henry and William B. Mecham; John F. Manwill; Orin Mangum; Seth Alvin; Sena Schow Johnson; and Andrew Perkins all came to make their homes in Tropic.

Ole Ahlstrom listed thirty-nine men who worked on the canal. The builders, most of whom were or became residents of the new town, completed the canal by the spring of 1892, a remarkable accomplishment considering the tools they had to work with. Hansen recalled finding a group of people camped on the East Fork about the time the workers were ready to send water down the canal. He explained to them that water would be coming down near their campsite and suggested they move to higher ground. They didn't believe him, and he reported that he enjoyed hearing them shout expletives in the night when their camp flooded.

In modern-day vernacular, Garfield residents often refer to Tropic as being located "under the dump," meaning it is below "where the East Fork water was 'dumped' into the channel of Water Canyon, falling about 1,000 feet in less than two miles."[6] Others maintain that stockmen called the area the dump as they drove their livestock over the rim of the Paunsaugunt Plateau to take them to their winter range. As the water began to flow into the valley on 23 May 1892, residents of Tropic and other already established communities that would benefit from this new lifegiving water celebrated at the home of Caroline Hansen, A.J.'s second wife, with a feast of barbecued beef, veal, and mutton. One participant in the gala event recalled: "A country, they said, had been born, and so they sang out praises and prophesied great things about our future. . . . We danced all night til broad daylight and went home with the girls in the morning."[7]

The next year, 1893, the two water systems, Spring Creek and East Fork, came under the administration of the newly organized Tropic and East Fork Irrigation Company. Residents used the Spring Creek water for culinary purposes and for irrigating town lots from ditches dug along the streets. The water that came over the dump from the East Fork of the Sevier River irrigated the fields. For several years Seth Alvin Johnson served as watermaster for the company; he also served for a term as president.[8]

As had been the case with other communities in the Paria Valley, newcomers brought cattle and sheep herds with them as they established their new homes. Tropic was well situated between summer and winter ranges. These suitable conditions attracted Hyrum and Joseph Hilton and the Hintons from the Dixie area and brothers William and Henry Jolley from Long Valley. The depression of 1893 hurt the stockmen, but their animals could be traded for other commodities and thus they survived the hard times.

Despite the depression, 1893 saw the beginnings of a new enterprise in Tropic. A man from Iowa brought a load of fruit trees to the settlement and traded them for horses. These trees became the nucleus for fine orchards established within the community, especially the apple and plum orchards. Also, the Jolley brothers brought in several wagonloads of trees from Long Valley, and most of the townspeople planted some of them on their land. Residents also grew grains, alfalfa, and corn.

Tropic did not always live up to its name, however. Some years killing frosts in the last part of May or first part of June would ruin the gardens and fruit crops that year. Animals were also vulnerable. During the early spring of 1900, for example, when John Johnson and Maurice Cope were herding sheep for Ole Ahlstrom, it turned very cold and began to snow. By the next morning the snow was three feet deep and 300 sheep lay dead. In early May, men from Tropic arrived with teams and, by dragging trees behind them to make a path, got the remaining sheep out of the snow.[9]

A number of Tropic citizens including Thomas McClellan,

George William, and Joe Shakespear had homesteads in nearby mountains. Whole families would spend the summer months tending their dairy herds, milking the cows, and making cheese and butter to sell or trade.

The James Robert and Janet M. Johnson Ott family purchased the Yellow Creek Ranch, located about two miles from Georgetown, the village where Janet's parents resided. Their son, James A. Ott, fondly recalled spending most of his summers on the mountain with the family. He experienced adventures common to other children of that era and circumstance—enduring scary pranks of an older brother, getting bit by a rattlesnake, climbing boulder-strewn hills, searching for arrowheads, helping to milk cows and irrigate the fields, hunting small animals with a "flipper," or slingshot, and enjoying the bountiful yield from summer gardens—especially the watermelons and muskmelons, about which he wrote:

> We went often during the day and stuffed ourselves to the fill. . . . It was astonishing the amount of these things we could "put out of sight." Our clothes became so stiff with watermelon juice and dirt that about all we needed to do was to stand them in the middle of the floor at night and then run and jump into them in the morning.[10]

During these summers away from Tropic, the Ott children relied on one another for playmates; occasionally cousins visited. The isolation of Yellow Creek allowed their imaginations to flourish. Ott described other playtime activities:

> In the shade of the old cottonwood trees in front of the house we used spools to make wagon tracks over roadways and dugroads we constructed. We sometimes used onion tops put together and buried in the ground as pipe lines through which we ran water. We built corral and pasture fences out of little sticks and had shiny hard rocks for the cows and horses. Sometimes we built little rock houses and log cabins.[11]

Neither isolation nor hard economic times dampened the settlers' enthusiasm for recreation. Afternoon dances for the youth and evening dances for the adults furnished plenty of social interaction in the town of Tropic. John Pollock and David B. Ott played

First meeting house built in Tropic in 1895 for religious, educational, and social activities. (Courtesy June Shakespear)

their fiddles. A later dance "orchestra" included Jack Pollock on the violin, William Pollock on the accordion, Lizzie Pollock Reynolds on the drums, and Lizzie Mecham Barton and Hortense Cope Munson on the organ or piano. They even played some popular LDS hymns to which the participants danced. Horse races, wrestling and boxing matches, footraces, rabbit drives, and, when the snow was deep, sleigh rides, all provided needed diversion. Groups of young people would sing together on street corners. Newlyweds were given "bundle showers," social occasions when friends and family would gather together things they could spare and present the "bundles" to the newly married couples to help them set up housekeeping. Theatrical productions came under the direction of Alvin Seth Johnson and Charley Pinney. Most of these early events, along with church meetings and school, took place in the Johnson home. Nineteen children received an elementary school education beginning in 1892 from Phoebe Cox. Murray E. King and Sabina Chidester succeeded her as local teachers. The county organized the Tropic School District on 8 June 1893; John A. Spendlove, Levison Hancock, and William W. Pollock became its trustees.

At first, members of the LDS church in Tropic constituted a branch of the Cannonville Ward. By 1895, thirty-five families lived in the area, so on 23 May, when the town celebrated its birthday, Panguitch LDS Stake officers joined in the festivities and organized the Tropic Ward. Unlike present-day practice, the townspeople cast votes for their first bishop. They chose Andrew Hansen for the position, with William J. Jolley and Hyrum Hilton as his counselors. The members also laid the cornerstone for their first meetinghouse that day.

This event stimulated the purchase of a sawmill near Flake Meadows by the Ahlstroms, George Bybee, and Andrew Hansen. Their first order for lumber was for the proposed meetinghouse. When the men went out to cut logs for the mill, Louisa Bybee went along to cook for them. Under C.W. Snyder's direction, nearly everyone in town helped in one way or another to construct the building, which was made up mainly of two-by-six planks. When completed, as with other settlements in the county, the finished structure served multiple functions for the community.

With all the tourists flocking to Bryce Canyon today it is hard to believe that for a long time Tropic remained a fairly isolated community. An early road, built in 1893 into the valley, extended from King Springs and down through Little Henderson Canyon. One of the county commissioners, however, Allen Miller from Panguitch, refused to grant needed maintenance money for this steep road. According to a lifelong resident of Tropic, Wallace Ott, the commissioner looked grudgingly on those who left Panguitch to settle in Tropic because of the "climate." As far as he was concerned, the people there would just have to climb through the canyon. Among the those who had moved from Panguitch to Tropic in order to raise gardens and fruit trees were the William, Joseph, Richard, and George Shakespear families, the William Marshall family, and Heber and Frank Riding.[12]

Finally, in 1898, the state granted road funds, and Mahonri M. Steele, Jr., received the contract to lay out a road from the top of the dump down Tropic Canyon. Tropic resident John Ahlstrom, then serving as commissioner, secured additional funds to improve the existing road.

As Tropic grew and attracted more families, a rivalry of sorts developed between it and what remained of the east valley settlement of Clifton, where the mail for Tropic was sent. On 5 June 1893 Tropic's citizens asked the probate court in Panguitch to designate their community as a polling precinct. In spite of a protest by Clifton residents, after hearing testimony on both sides the court granted Tropic's petition. It appointed the following officers: Joseph Hilton, justice of the peace; John F. Pollock, constable; John A. Steele, road supervisor; and John A. Spendlove, Levison Hancock, and William W. Pollock as trustees for the new school district. Ira C. Schow became the first postmaster for Tropic.

According to the 1900 census, the population of Tropic had grown to 379. The residents felt they needed to devise further means of protecting their rights; they therefore decided to incorporate their town. They presented their petition of incorporation with ninety-six signatures to the court on 24 June 1902. After the request was granted, the following individuals acted as the town board: Andrew Hansen, president; William J. Jolley, Jr., Ole Ahlstrom, John Ahlstrom, and Hyrum H. Hilton as trustees; Joseph A. Tippets as town marshal and pound keeper, and Thomas R. Cope as justice of the peace.

Early business conducted by the board included the adoption of policies and regulations and the improvement of the town's infrastructure. By 1904 town officials even adopted a curfew policy that by today's standards seems rather strict: between 15 October and 15 March anyone under the age of sixteen had to be off the streets by 8:00 P.M. unless accompanied by an adult. During the warmer months the curfew hour was relaxed to 9:00 P.M. In October 1910 the town board addressed the problem of unsafe water conditions—they passed an ordinance prohibiting the watering of any horse or mule in town ditches if the animal suffered from distemper, glanders, or other diseases that could taint the culinary water. The board also began to plan toward installing a new water system, which they accomplished a few years later.

In 1893 Tropic had its own militia company, organized as part of the National Guard of the Territory of Utah. Company L, First Infantry, had a roster of seventy-five men, with John M. Dunning serving as captain, Andrew Hansen as first lieutenant, and George W.

Johnson as second lieutenant. This organization lasted only three years, however, being discontinued in 1896.

Residents of Tropic experienced a particularly devastating diphtheria epidemic during the winter of 1902–03. Before the disease ran its course, it had claimed the lives of fourteen children. Then, in early winter 1905, a scarlet fever epidemic broke out, taking the lives of other Tropic children. How many actually succumbed to the disease is unknown, but James Alvin Ott recorded that four children in his family, including himself, contracted scarlet fever, and two of his older sisters died as a result.[13]

Twenty years after its founding, the population of Tropic had stabilized and the community progressed along with its neighbors in the upper Paria Valley, remaining the largest of the three towns. Along with the businesses already mentioned, Ole Ahlstrom and Jedediah Adair operated early stores. Tropic also had a general merchandise store established by Seth Johnson. Later, another store was owned by Seth's son George and C.D. White. Two Johnson half-sisters, Janet Matilda Johnson Ott and Lydia Ann Johnson Jolley, were among the clerks at these establishments.[14] Such enterprises strengthened familial ties that remained important as the village grew. Although life could be precarious for its settlers, Tropic offered a close-knit community and peaceful atmosphere in the midst of scenic beauty.

Utah Statehood and Community Growth

After a half-century of petitioning the federal government, statehood became a reality for the citizens of Utah Territory on 4 January 1896. Residents throughout the county celebrated the occasion. Panguitch folks characterized their festivities as "the never forgotten celebrations," with flags flying and bands playing. They had a parade, attended a patriotic meeting, and danced into the night. Despite the day being the "coldest day of the year," people were proud and happy with high spirits.[15]

Residents of Cannonville, Henrieville, and Tropic came together for a statehood celebration at the newly completed meetinghouse/ community center in Tropic. Company L of the First Infantry of the Utah National Guard took charge of the festivities. One can assume that other villages within the county also celebrated the occasion.

Panguitch Main Street in the mid 1890s.

As the county seat, advances in all areas of society seemed more pronounced in Panguitch. For example, the first newspaper in the county began there. John M. Dunning's small four-page publication, *The Cactus* (later named *The Register*), came into being during the mid-1880s. It was short-lived, however, keeping the public informed for only about six months. Around the year 1895 Fred E. Eldredge arrived in the community and started publishing the *Panguitch Progress*. When he moved away in 1899, first M.M. Steele, Jr., and later Billy J. Peters took over the paper. Subsequent owners and editors included Elizabeth Worthen, Hans P. Ipson, Gladys and Winnie DeLong, and Fred M. Gavin. In 1908 Fred Eldredge retired to Panguitch and resumed ownership of the newspaper. When the *Garfield County News* under the editorship of Billy J. Peters, who also had recently returned to town, competed for readership in 1920, Eldredge sold out and moved to Marysvale, where he started another paper.[16]

The results of the November 1898 county elections also indicated political advances were being made—a woman won the position of county recorder. Mamie Foy holds the distinction of being the first woman to hold elective office in the county. It seems that she established a precedent, for thereafter women held that particular office term after term. In June 1902 Panguitch was split into two voter precincts, another sign of its growth.

The building of the Garfield County Courthouse in Panguitch represented another sign of progress. An imposing structure even today, the brick-and-rock edifice began serving the public in 1908. The county paid $425 for the lot and spent almost $11,400 to build the structure. The building committee that oversaw the project was comprised of John N. Henrie, James B. Heywood, and John Houston.[17]

Before the end of the 1890s Panguitch, like hundreds of small towns across America, had a fine brick library financed by millionaire Andrew Carnegie, with the usual agreement that the city would maintain and staff it. Lovisa Miller served the community as librarian for many years. Some said that not only did children go to the facility to borrow books but also "to have Mrs. Miller charm their warts off."[18] At this point in its history, Panguitch could boast of having more than thirty lovely brick homes, a brick LDS tabernacle, and other sound buildings for commercial and farming purposes.

Widtsoe (Adairville, Houston, Winder)

The history of Widtsoe could easily be characterized as a July Fourth skyrocket: in the beginning it produced no more than a sputter of promise; it then soared upward to become a spectacular display of growth and progress. Within two decades, however, its energy spent, it sank back to earth.

Located in John's Valley northeast of Bryce Canyon and along the East Fork of the Sevier River at the mouth of Sweetwater Creek, Widtsoe began as an area for local cattlemen to seasonally run their stock. According to Garfield County tax records of 1876, Mrs. John D. Lee, one of the wives of the recently captured Mormon leader (who was executed in 1877 for his part in the Mountain Meadows Massacre twenty years before), owned some of the land at Sweetwater Creek. Isaac Riddle, who in the course of his career seems to have ranched and run cattle throughout southern Utah, also established a ranch in the area. The location served as a regrouping place for the Hole-in-the-Rock pioneers in 1879. The 1890s county tax records list the area inhabitants as being "transients from Orderville."[19]

By the early 1900s John R. Campbell owned a ranch and had a large herd of sheep in the area. He sold some of his property to Jedediah Adair, who brought one of his wives, Julia Ann, to the area. They cultivated the land and successfully raised a variety of grains. This attracted other settlers, and by 1908 the Adairs had numerous neighbors who comprised the community of Adairville. It became the Tropic LDS ward's "Sweetwater Branch." Carl H. Mangum served as the presiding elder, with Orson Adair and John Tippetts as his counselors and John Campbell as Sunday School superintendent. After the arrival of still more settlers, the name of the community changed to Houston, in honor of the president of Panguitch LDS Stake, John Houston.

In 1910 Julia Adair donated forty acres toward developing a townsite in the midst of the ranches and farms. Following her specifications, the settlers surveyed the town to have streets five rods wide, blocks twenty rods square, with four lots to a block and all out-buildings to be located 100 feet from the streets. The newly surveyed town once again underwent a name change; this time it was called Winder to honor a counselor in the general presidency of the LDS church, John R. Winder. The settlement had moved beyond the "sputter" stage and was about to propel itself forward. In the meantime, there were also developments elsewhere in the county.

From Hatchtown to Hatch

Upon recommendation of the United States Geological Survey, the people of Hatchtown and Panguitch began excavation of a reservoir in the summer of 1894 or 1895. The site was a place called Flake Meadow, located on the Sevier River. (This is not the same Flake Meadow used by Tropic residents to acquire timber.) The citizens bought the Neils Peterson Clove homestead located above the damsite to use for water storage. Before they could complete the dam, however, high waters from the melting snowpack destroyed it. The need for water storage continued, and leaders of Piute and Sevier counties decided on a joint venture to construct a second reservoir at the same site. This time they used a concrete culvert, but once again the Sevier River refused to be harnessed. In late 1899 or the spring of

1900 the dam failed. Structures in the path of a possible flood were moved to higher ground.

Even after this second failure, the state continued to show interest in developing a water-storage facility in the area. Given the failure rate of the previous dams, however, such plans alarmed Hatchtown residents. In 1901 they made the decision to move their community to higher ground, away from the river channel. Their ecclesiastical leaders acted as their agents to buy just under 100 acres of land on which to locate the town. The land had originally been homesteaded by Thomas B. and Margaret Sawyer. According to a descendant of one of these citizens: "The local men laid the town off in streets and blocks. They used a homemade transit . . . and a chain was used for the marking process."[20] They surveyed ten blocks, each containing four lots. According to the sales agreement, the Sawyers had the first choice of a lot for their own house. They also selected the lot for the new church. When apportioning the remaining lots, the citizens used the following procedure: "After the survey, the blocks and lots were numbered and corresponding numbers placed in a hat. The citizens drew their lot numbers. Some trading went on due to price of lots and preference of location."[21]

The first home transferred to the new townsite belonged to Mary Ann Clove. Little by little, other structures followed. During the moving of the town, the residents experienced a remarkable display of cooperation and unity, which bolstered community solidarity and pride. They decided to drop "Town" from the name and call their new settlement simply Hatch. The move also inspired a petition to change the name of the post office from Asay to Hatch. The federal government granted this request on 23 January 1904. The post office became part of Abram Workman's store, another structure moved to the new site, and Workman served as postmaster. He had previously converted a little house he bought in the "old town" into his store— probably the first one in the community. On the new site he continued to stock some hardware items, kitchen ware, a limited selection of fabrics and groceries, including soda crackers and lemon biscuits, to meet the residents' basic needs. In addition, he had a dealership for a line of harnesses, wagons, and farm machinery.

One example of ingenuity and resourcefulness among the pioneers involved the relocation of Meltair Hatch's unique double log barn. The two barns had a drive-through area between them, with one roof covering the entire building. Each side matched the other perfectly in the length and notching of its logs. Hay could be unloaded on either side of the drive, and each building had stalls positioned on the east. By the time the town moved, Meltair Hatch had passed away, having died in 1895. Levi Sawyer, one of his sons-in-law, took charge of moving the structure. He numbered the poles from bottom to top, and "every section was labeled north, south, east or west. They were placed on a wagon in order and the barn was reconstructed to look as it did in the former location."[22]

All did not go smoothly as they moved the town, but the settlers tried to keep a sense of humor in the process. Thomas B. Sawyer recalled one incident:

> One day as we started up Alger Hill, things got on a bind; the logs in the house came apart. Everyone began to laugh as the logs, one after another, went rolling down the hill, leaving the roof settled securely on the wagon wheels. At first it looked like a lot of wasted effort, but the laugh was refreshing and we just pried the roof off our wagons and went out and got another log cabin.[23]

As monumental an enterprise as moving the town had been, cooperative effort for the benefit of all in the community was not new to Hatch residents. Beginning in the late 1890s a week or ten days was set aside each early spring to clean out irrigation ditches. All water users cooperated to clear weed growth, sand bars, and beaver dams from the channels in order to maximize water flow. After the relocation of the town, the residents formed the Hatch Farmers Improvement Association, a civic organization that undertook the betterment and upkeep of the community. Members donated time and resources to such projects as the creation and maintenance of roads and irrigation ditches.

During threshing season farmers also worked together, all sharing one threshing machine as well as the needed labor. Farm wives prepared ample meals of potatoes, meat, biscuits, rice pudding, and pies to feed the hungry threshing crews. As with almost every endeavor undertaken by settlers to bring civilized comfort to their communities, such tasks required the efforts of both men and women.

One woman in particular rendered great service to the people of Hatch. Like many relatively isolated communities, Hatch had no doctor, and the residents turned to midwives for their medical needs. Sarah Ann Asay became the first midwife in the Hatch area. She had remained in Salt Lake City to study midwifery from local doctors in 1867 when her husband Joseph and their sons were called to the Muddy Mission in present-day Nevada. A granddaughter wrote that the settlers recognized the "healing touch of her hands" and that she delivered 1,800 babies before she died in 1900.[24]

Other midwives in the Hatch area around the turn of the century included Anna Marie Barnhurst, Julia Hatch Workman, Sarah D. Anderson, and Julia Huntington. Soon after the town's relocation, a Dr. Garn also served the residents of Hatch for a time. But it wasn't until after 1911, when a Dr. Bigelow arranged a private hospital in Panguitch, that the people of Hatch had other regular medical options.

Sawmills and shingle mills played a major role in the early development of Hatchtown and continued to do so after relocation. The mills were located on Mammoth and Wilson creeks, and the Camerons, Hatchs, Wilsons, and Workmans operated these early enterprises.

The Hatchtown women did not have a LDS Relief Society organization until 1894, when they went to Asay to establish their association. Organizing other Mormon church auxiliaries eventually followed. Before the move, but after Hatchtown was organized into its own LDS ward, church members built a new chapel, finishing it in 1895. That same year, townspeople also began building a tithing office; they completed it the following year. In addition to religious services, the church building housed local dramatic productions, silent movies, and traveling troupes. For a time it became the schoolhouse as well, and residents installed a bell to call young people to classes and townspeople to other public gatherings. Local citizens moved both the church and tithing office buildings to the new town location. The two buildings were later sold and used for other purposes.

Hatch residents began to stake out dimensions for a new church building at their new location in January 1903, with a foot of snow on the ground. Members held meetings in the new structure by the end of the year, but work continued on the building over the next few years. In the process, Hatch church members sustained a new bishop in 1906, James B. Burrow. By 1908 the plastering was complete, and in 1910 the members added the chapel vestibule and bell tower. All the money and labor used in the chapel's construction came from Hatch residents.

By the end of the first decade of the 1900s the community of Hatch was securely established at its present location. Its citizens had managed to create enduring homes and institutional organizations to better ensure that their future needs and goals could be realized.

Stock Raising in the National Forests

As mentioned in previous chapters, many early settlers came into Garfield County in search of rangeland for their cattle herds. Others turned to stock raising when they realized that local climatic conditions precluded the growing of many crops. In the early years Garfield rangeland produced grasses and other forage in abundance. As a result, ranching became a profitable industry throughout the county, bringing moderate wealth to some and employment to many. But the business could also be fraught with hazards, both natural and manmade, and susceptible to the vagaries of nature and the marketplace.

The first substantial cattle herds, particularly in the eastern portion of the county, were brought in by members of cattle cooperatives. In time these gave way to individually owned herds. Some Garfield County men got into the stock business by working for those with established herds or by renting stock belonging to others. Edward Wilcock brought a leased herd of cattle from Parowan into the Escalante area; after three years he had a herd of his own from the natural increase.[25] Joseph Henry Linford began by herding sheep for James Showalter, a prominent stockman from Panguitch. During the winter the Linfords remained in town so their children could go to school; however, in the summer the family lived in a little house out at Showalter's summer range near Hunt Creek and the East Fork of the Sevier River, about twenty miles north of Bryce Canyon. Linford nicknamed the place "Poverty." His wife, Luella Rowena Orton, pieced many a quilt while out tending the herd in the relatively isolated region. After working for Showalter a number of years, Linford left Showalter's employ with 350 head of sheep and some grazing rights of his own, the basis of his livelihood until he sold out and retired years later.[26]

Until the first two decades of the twentieth century there was a ready market for wool.[27] Until around 1915 sheep shearers used hand clippers; a good shearer could shear about twenty head a day, but it was a back-breaking process. When gasoline-powered clippers were developed the operation became much more efficient. Professional shearers in the Escalante area included Albert Griffin, Dan Pollock, Frank Barney, Andrew (Bish) Schow, Mike Schow, and Will Alvey. The men began shearing in the early spring in the Dixie area to the south, then moved northward as the season progressed, finally ending up sometimes as far north as Idaho and Montana. These shearers took pride in the speed with which they worked. According to one local resident, Ronald Schow held the record, shearing 120 head in a day.[28]

For Cannonville residents, "shearing season lasted about a month and it was given about the same priority as a national holiday; even an excused absence from school." During this time, according to one local historian, men could find temporary employment as "shearers, wranglers, an equipment operator, tool sharpener, fleece tyers, carriers or trompers (usually school boys, sixth to eighth graders)."[29]

Garfield sheepmen had to take their wool to Marysvale to be shipped by rail. The magnitude of this operation was described by one author: The wool went

> by team and wagon . . . over nearly 100 miles of rough, partly mountainous road. The trip took ten days. Twenty to twenty-five wagons would travel together. . . . For the return trip wagons would be loaded with freight largely for Escalante merchants. Children were sometimes allowed to accompany their fathers. "Going with the wool" was considered a privilege by youngsters who otherwise never saw beyond the mountain, but they had to

endure being parched by the June sun that beat upon the smelly load of wool sacks.[30]

Stockmen made the trip to the railhead at Marysvale in the fall to sell their cattle. One resident of Escalante, David M. Woolsey, recalled seeing cattle herds stretched out as far as ten miles along the trail. For a time the cattle business prospered.[31]

During the winter, stockmen moved their herds to lower, warmer areas until spring. Many in the western part of the county used the west deserts of Utah for grazing. Those in the Boulder area brought their stock from the summer ranges on Boulder Mountain to the eastern desert areas near the Henry Mountains. Tropic herders brought their stock from the mountains to the north and ranged them as far south as the Wahweap, in southern Kane County and northern Arizona.[32] This necessitated the herders being separated from their families for extended periods of time and often entailed great physical hardship. But sometimes the monotony of staying with the herd involved unexpected adventure. Escalante resident and historian Marilyn Jackson related one such incident:

> In 1909, a stranger walked into the sheep camp of Hyrum Gates on the Escalante Desert. Word had reached the camp of a fugitive who had alluded [sic] Wayne county authorities and was being sought by a posse from Boulder. The man had killed a calf and ransacked a house, taking various things. The man was invited to eat with the sheep herders and was in the process of getting his plate filled, when the posse approached. The man grabbed his gun and ran, whereupon the officers called for him to stop. As he continued to flee, the officer fired his gun and the man dropped. [They took him] to Escalante where he died shortly afterward without identifying himself.[33]

A Garfield youth had an adventure of a different sort. Sixteen-year-old Vee Linford left Panguitch in the early spring to meet his family's incoming herd from the west desert, a trip of about twenty-five miles. On a lovely morning, with only wispy white clouds overhead, he began his journey. Provisioned with a lunch, a bag of oats for his horse, a warm coat, and a yellow slicker, he rode north of Panguitch about ten miles and then headed west towards Bear Valley.

As he gained elevation, storm clouds gathered, producing a cold rain, then "plastering sleet" which caused his wet clothes to freeze to his body. Unable to find shelter, he pressed on and climbed higher as an icy snow began to fall. He became lost and disoriented.

Linford decided to let his horse use her natural instincts and gave her free rein. Almost frozen, the young man dismounted, "hoping to walk some circulation into [his] numb body." He held onto his horse's tail, allowing the animal to guide him and break a trail through the snow. The animal wisely decided to head back home. Several times, suffering from fatigue, Linford longed to stop and rest. Becoming terribly sleepy, he squatted down from time to time in snow-covered sagebrush along the treacherous, downward trail. His horse seemed to sense the danger that her master could freeze to death, so she kept pushing him with her nose to topple him from his perch and get him walking again. Thus, they slowly made their way out of the canyon; finally, at 2:00 A.M., they reached a farmhouse at the mouth of the canyon and safety.[34]

While elements often conspired against the stockmen in their efforts to make a living, the amount of stock in the county increased faster than the range vegetation was able to recover. By the summer of 1903, after a period of drought, it was evident that

> the once rich meadows on the [Boulder] mountain had turned to dust beds. Herds of sheep were bedding by the streams and dying along the banks. Bones of cattle bleached on the dry benches. The cattle lingered around the mud holes. Those in a weakened condition would flounder in the mud and die. Poison weeds that grew after the better feed was gone added to the death toll of the starving cattle.[35]

By late fall the rains began to fall, washing precious topsoil away, but a good winter ended the drought. Stockmen, however, clearly needed to rethink their use of the land.

The stressed condition of ranges throughout the West helped cause the federal government to take steps to protect them along with the remaining forests and watersheds. In 1903 President Theodore Roosevelt created by proclamation numerous forest reserves, following precedents established in the 1880s and 1890s. These reserves

later became known as national forests. Among the areas so designated were the Aquarius, the Powell, the Sevier, and the Dixie
national forests in Garfield County.[36] The officers (later called
rangers) assigned to the various reserves took charge of regulating
activities there beginning in 1904. At various times since the forests'
organization the supervisors' offices have been located at either
Panguitch, Widstoe, Escalante, or at Cedar City in Iron County. At a
much later date, in 1944, all of the forest reserves in Garfield County
would be consolidated into the Dixie National Forest.

Many Garfield County citizens found employment administering these reserves, becoming supervisors, rangers, clerks, and administrative assistants. George H. Barney became the first supervisor of
the five districts of the Aquarius Reserve in 1903. He continued in
this position when the Aquarius became a part of the Powell Forest.
In 1905–06 Beaugard Kenner worked as the first supervisor of the five
districts of the Sevier Forest. Sylvans Collett supervised the Dixie
Reserve beginning in 1905.

With the creation of the forest reserves came the beginnings of
government control of grazing within these areas. At first such control proceeded slowly. In order to make an approximate count of animals using the forests, officials asked stock owners to apply for
grazing permits for as many head as they owned. For instance, in
January 1904 the Aquarius District granted permits for 75,000 head
of sheep and 12,500 head of cattle to graze on forest lands. This number decreased each year until the United States entered World War I
and the demand for meat and wool increased. Following the war the
numbers again declined and continued to do so.

During the early years of forest organization personnel created
some pasturage areas, ranger stations, telephone lines, trails, and
roads. Although early attempts at reseeding programs did not work
well, continued research and experimentation brought greater success to the practice in later decades. Reforestation also contributed to
the revitalization of the reserves. Periodic surveys of the forests that
assessed the quantity and health of the trees and the grazing potential
of the various areas helped forest officials plan the best use of available natural resources. Such studies eventually had an impact on the
number of stock-grazing permits the Forest Service granted and on

the times when the animals could be turned out onto forest lands. The studies also determined how much timber could be harvested and on what scale recreational facilities could be introduced. Much later, with the passage of the Taylor Grazing Act in 1934, rangeland deemed to be part of the public domain outside of national forests came under grazing control regulations as well. This land came under control of the Bureau of Land Management (BLM) after its organization in the 1940s.

To confront the issues dealing with new government controls, and in part because of their own personal economic interest in restoring the health of rangeland, Garfield residents formed several stockmen organizations. Among the first of these was the Escalante Cattle and Horse Growers Association, organized in 1907, with William V. Lay as president, Rufus H. Liston as vice-president, and Harry N. Cowles as secretary/treasurer. Its objective was to "promote and protect the business of raising cattle and horses upon and adjacent to the Powell National Forest," and members sought to cooperate with government officials of both the U.S. Forest Service and the U.S. Grazing Service. Its members handled such matters as "salting, vaccination and other treatment of disease in cattle . . . brand inspection, handling strays . . . watering places on [the] range, with reseeding," among other activities.[37] The early 1920s saw similar organizations formed, including the Boulder Grazing Association and the Hatch-Hillsdale Cattlemen's Association.

It is interesting to note that as the number of stock raised in the county began to decline so too did the population of Garfield County. Of course, stock reduction was necessary because the land could no longer sustain so many large herds; but the correlation also demonstrates how tied to the stock industry local people and businesses were until recent decades. When the stockmen suffered financially, so did the local economy, and this is what caused many families to move elsewhere. As an example, in 1922 there were 8,550 cattle and horses and 23,200 sheep in Escalante. The 1920 census shows the community with 3,608 residents. In 1963 there were 2,452 grazing permits issued for cattle and horses, none for sheep. The 1960 census records 702 residents in Escalante.

The rapid decline in ranching in the county can be attributed to many things, including inclement weather, severe late winters and early springs which took a toll on newborn stock, drought years, tough economic times such as those following World War I and during the Great Depression, government restrictions on grazing and increased grazing fees, predators, and, in more recent decades, competition in the marketplace from other states and abroad. These forces effectively eliminated the wool industry in the county by 1960 and threatened to bring about the demise of the cattle industry as well. Clearly, what enticed so many to settle in Garfield during its early period also led many to leave in later years. Residents could only hope that others would find alternative reasons to stay or to relocate to the county in the future.

Trees, Telephones, and Towns

In 1906 several Panguitch citizens formed the Garfield Mountain States Telephone and Telegraph Company. M.M. Steel, Jr., became president; Thomas Sevy, secretary; and Guernsey Spencer, manager of the company. Spencer came from Kanab and put in the poles, hung the telephone lines, and installed the switchboard in the Cameron home on the corner of Main and Center streets. Sadie Cameron became the county's first telephone operator. Officers chosen later included Thomas Sevy, S.O. Henrie, J.B. Showalter, J.J. Page, R.G. Clark, Dr. R.G. Clark, Jr., Benjamin Cameron, Sr., John Houston, John L. Sevy, and James Smith. Mountain States Telephone and Telegraph supplied the local company's customers with long-distance service. During this early period Mountain States Telephone & Telegraph (MST&T) often cooperated with rural communities when they formed their own telephone companies in providing long-distance service. It also offered technical assistance to the local entities and had a small equity interest in them. If after a period of time these local enterprises proved economically viable, MST&T would buy out the original investors and bring the local entities into its system. The Garfield company built an office of its own in 1910, and after several more years it became a part of the Bell Telephone Company and then joined with Mountain States Telephone and Telegraph.[38]

In May 1907 the Hatch Farmers Improvement Association negotiated a contract with the Garfield telephone company in Panguitch

United States Forest Service Employees using the first phone on the Dixie
National Forest about 1908. (USDA Forest Service)

to deliver phone service to Hatch residents. The association supplied 1,000 poles to bring the line south to the ranches beyond the summit, and by 1908 Hatch had a single telephone line to serve the community. Each time someone had a phone call, every telephone in the town rang. Effel Riggs described how the system worked:

> Each home had its own ring. James B. Burrow had a short, long and a short. A. S. Workman was given two shorts and a long. W. R. Riggs ring was three shorts. . . . It was often hard to get the line for an important message. Some folks, anxious to learn what was going on in the area, could not refrain from eavesdropping.[39]

Telephone communication for many other Garfield County residents paralleled the creation of national forests in southern Utah and the employment of personnel to administer them. In 1908 United States Forest Service employees completed a telephone line from Escalante to Teasdale in present Wayne County. By 1910 they completed the line to Boulder, then continued through the upper valley and on to Panguitch in 1912. An additional line went through Main Canyon and over the mountain to Antimony. The forest rangers who did most of the installation of the lines included Joseph and Hyrum Porter, R.F. Hall, R.H. Liston, and Josiah and Ambrose Shurtz. Individuals in the various communities served could connect to the Forest Service lines if they supplied their own poles, wire, insulators, and telephones.

Only three telephones existed in Escalante when Leander Shurtz, blind since birth, became the town's first telephone operator in 1913. Forest supervisor Henry Barney had one phone at his home, another served the Forest Service office, and Riddle's store had the third telephone. For twenty-six years Shurtz operated the Escalante system as it slowly expanded. He had a keen sense of hearing and in the days when subscribers were not assigned telephone numbers he could immediately recognize their voices. According to one resident, "you just took down the receiver, rang the bell, and said, 'Hello, Leander, give me my folks, please.' He knew who you were and what 'folks' you wanted."[40] Through his position Shurtz became acquainted with Gwen Partridge, a telephone operator at Panguitch. The two later married and operated the switchboard together in Escalante. Though

Leige Moore (left) and Myron Willis riding the range. (Courtesy Teora Willis)

the system seems primitive today, it was wonderful for these isolated communities to have access to the outside world.

Colorful Characters of the County— Law-abiding and Otherwise

Since many of the settlers in southern Utah made a livelihood running cattle or sheep, they seemed to acquire characteristics usually associated with the Old West of the resourceful, rugged individualist who spent extended periods of time with the herds, isolated from the crush of humanity. One such individual was Elige (Lige) M. Moore, longtime resident of Henrieville.

Moore came from southwest Missouri, having been born there in 1850.[41] His family lived near the infamous James family there and the children from both families often played together. But later in life Lige Moore took a different path from that of his friends Frank and Jesse James. As a youth he witnessed a Civil War battle that took place in the family's fields in which his father was killed. Two of Lige's brothers also died during the Civil War, reportedly while

fighting for the Confederacy at Gettysburg under General Robert
E. Lee.

After the war, still in his mid-teens, Moore gravitated to Texas,
where he spent some time involved in various enterprises with his
brother Thomas. Later, in Two Gun, Arizona, he rounded up a large
herd of horses and drove them to Utah. He crossed the Colorado
River at Lees Ferry and then went to the Paria area, where he traded
his horses for cattle. At first he located at Georgetown. He later
moved to Henrieville, where he spent most of the remainder of his
life. He and his wife, Amelia, had four sons and one daughter. Many
Mormons considered "Uncle Lige" to be one of the best "members" of
the LDS church who had not been baptized. He did not indulge in
some of the excesses normally associated with those who rode the
range. He was known for his generosity and earned the respect of his
associates. In later years, during the Great Depression, Wallace Ott
recalled Moore passing around his ten-gallon cowboy hat, one of his
hallmarks, at local horse races to gather money for a local departing
LDS missionary. He became the choice of his neighbors to represent
them on the advisory board of the local public domain land after the
passing of the Taylor Grazing Act in 1934. At age eighty-four he was
the oldest person in the United States to serve in that capacity.

Moore usually carried six-shooters and reportedly was a crack
shot. A Panguitch resident recalled that whenever Lige rode through
town he made quite a spectacle with his guns strapped on each side,
not a common sight in early twentieth-century southern Utah.[42]
Moore seldom wore his false teeth, however; he kept them in a leather
pouch tied to his saddle and declared, "Yes, that's just as close to my
mouth as I want to get them."[43] Besides raising cattle, he had a con-
suming interest in horse racing and was a racing judge at many of the
contests in and around the county. Tall in the saddle at six feet two
inches, Lige Moore appeared as the prototypical American cowboy,
even if he was not entirely representative of southern Utah stockmen.

Aside from the James brothers, Moore was said to have known
all of the notorious Robbers' Roost gang, including Butch Cassidy,
Matt Warner, Silver Tip Morgan, Blue John Evens, Tom McCarty, and
others.[44] Robert LeRoy Parker, alias Butch Cassidy, certainly had many
Garfield County connections. Born in Beaver in 1866, he was the first

Childhood home of Robert LeRoy Parker, known as Butch Cassidy, located in northern Garfield County south of Circleville. (Utah State Historical Society)

child of Maximillian and Ann Gillies Parker. The Parker family moved to Circle Valley in 1879 after Parker's father bought a homestead there. Although the closest town was Circleville, the property and the small two-room cabin that the family of eight occupied was actually in Garfield County.[45]

The family experienced some economic reverses, and, to help out, Ann Parker contracted to run a dairy for local rancher Jim Marshall about twelve miles south of the Parker farm. For two seasons Ann took her children and lived at the dairy, where they milked the cows and made butter and cheese. Marshall hired Roy, as Robert LeRoy was known, a fully grown and responsible youth, to work as a ranch hand. In this capacity the young man met Mike Cassidy, an older drifter who came to work on the ranch. Cassidy taught the young man how to handle guns, horses, and cattle. It wasn't long before Roy developed a hero worship for the older ranch hand and wanted to emulate his exciting life. Roy also learned the rudiments of rustling cattle and horses, an activity that Cassidy had apparently engaged in for some time. When the law got too close, Cassidy left the area.

Whether it was before or after Mike Cassidy's departure— sources differ—Roy Parker engaged with two other local men in putting their own brand on some maverick stock. In the end, all blame for the operation fell on Parker. He left the territory in 1884 when he was eighteen, never to live with his family again.

His route took him through the Robbers' Roost area, an infamous hideout of sorts composed of a maze of twisting canyons in the badlands of the San Rafael Swell area that straddles Garfield and Wayne counties located between the Dirty Devil River and the Green River's confluence with the Colorado River. Later on in his career outside the law Parker would come frequently with his gang and stolen stock to Robbers' Roost to hide from authorities. For some time after leaving Utah he worked at hauling ore for some mines around Telluride, Colorado. Eventually he met up with Tom McCarty and Matt Warner and the three men robbed the Telluride bank. Bank president and hydroelectric power entrepreneur L.L. Nunn headed a posse in pursuit. Nunn, who was a particularly good rider and had a fast horse, soon outdistanced the rest of the posse and caught up with the bandits. They reportedly quickly surrounded the diminutive bank president, disarmed him, stole his horse, and left him in their dust.

Roy Parker gave himself the name George Cassidy after his mentor Mike Cassidy and later dropped the George for "Butch" after working in Wyoming for a short period in a butcher shop. The targets of his depredations throughout the West (although never again in Garfield County, Utah) included large cattle operations, railroads, and banks—all of which he believed took advantage of the struggling homesteader. A sort of Robin Hood aura accrued to Cassidy, who was reportedly warned many times by residents throughout the region when law officers approached.

Only once did Butch serve time in prison. Ironically, he was falsely accused and found guilty of stealing horses in Wyoming. He was later pardoned after serving only seven months of a two-year sentence in the territorial prison at Laramie in 1894–95. Despite the

Robert LeRoy Parker, better known as Butch Cassidy, was Garfield County's most famous outlaw. (Utah State Historical Society)

relentless pursuit of various law agencies, including the famous Pinkerton detectives, he was never again incarcerated.

So many myths and legends surround the life and demise of Butch Cassidy that it is difficult to sort fact from fiction. Charles Kelly related the story of sixteen-year-old Harry Ogden from Escalante, who spent his savings to purchase a good horse and a sixty-dollar saddle. When out riding along the border of Robbers Roost in 1898, an outlaw on a jaded mount forced young Ogden off his horse, gave the boy a quick kick in the pants, then rode off on Ogden's animal. About three weeks later, Ogden received visitors at his home in Escalante. One of the men was Butch Cassidy, another was the outlaw who had stolen Ogden's horse and was still riding it. When Cassidy asked Ogden if he had lost a horse, the boy quickly identified it. Butch Cassidy then ordered the outlaw off the horse and told him "to start walking toward a distant gap in the hills and keep on going." He then said, "We don't have any room in this country for a man who will mistreat a young boy."[46]

Most who knew him described Butch Cassidy as an agreeable fellow with a sense of humor, generous with his associates, and quick to make friends with children. He also liked the ladies, and many apparently returned his affections. There is no documentation that he ever killed anyone, although some members of his loosely formed gang, called "The Wild Bunch," could not make that claim. One of the prevailing beliefs, and one perpetuated by the movie *Butch Cassidy and the Sundance Kid*, is that Cassidy and the Sundance Kid met their deaths in Bolivia when they were involved in a shoot-out with the local military in 1912. There is no question that the two went with Etta Place to Argentina and later were in Bolivia. However, many individuals claim that Cassidy returned to the United States—some say to California, others claim to the Pacific Northwest—and lived the rest of his life within the law under an assumed identity.[47]

Among those making the claim were members of his own family; his sister Lula Parker Betenson claimed that Cassidy came for a visit in the fall of 1925. On that occasion he told members of his family that a friend, Percy Seibert, from the Concordia Tin Mines near San Vicente, Bolivia, identified the two bodies as being those of him and Sundance. Cassidy figured Seibert did this so he could make a new start for himself without being chased by the law, either in the United States or in South America. Apparently he had expressed just such a desire to Seibert on several occasions.[48] In addition to his family's claims, many former associates in Wyoming insisted that Butch Cassidy returned there for a visit in the 1930s.

Some residents of Garfield County also claim that they saw Butch

Cassidy during the 1930s. In her autobiography, Emma Allene Savage Riddle recalled her experience:

> One day I went with Dad to visit Elijah Moore. There were several other men at his home when we arrived. Elijah introduced us to them and one of them was an outlaw by the name of Leroy Parker, alias Butch Cassidy. This was after Butch had been reported killed in Bolivia, South America. I was in awe of the man, thinking I had met a real honest-to-goodness outlaw.[49]

Wallace Ott told that Lige Moore invited him to come over to his home to meet Butch in 1937 or 1938.[50] Ott said Kenneth Goulding, Sr., was also present. Reportedly Butch rehearsed for those gathered how he came to lead his life. He told Ott that while attending a dance in Panguitch he got into a fight with the boyfriend of one of the girls he danced with. At first everyone thought Butch had killed the guy, rather than just knocking him out. He quickly fled town, followed by a posse. In Red Canyon he eluded his pursuers by detouring up a gulch in the dark; the posse rode on past him. Cassidy eventually made his way back to Circleville, where he packed up and headed for Colorado.[51] A draw in Red Canyon today bears Cassidy's name.[52] The sequence of his exploits as he reportedly related them to those gathered in the Moore home does not agree with what has been written by others, and so the stories and speculation continue.

Meanwhile, the fortunes for the Parker family in Circleville improved and the younger children and their parents moved to a brick home in town. Ann Parker, a devout and prayerful mother of eleven children, grieved for her eldest son and the life he led. Her daughter Lula believed this contributed to her mother's frequent "sick spells." One day in 1905 Ann became very ill. With no doctors in Circleville, her husband took her to Panguitch where one was available, although there was still no hospital in the town. Ann stayed in a hotel run by a Mrs. Crosby in order for the doctor to better monitor her condition. Her husband and daughter Lula helped care for her, but her illness, believed to be a heart condition, worsened; three weeks later she died. Her daughter wrote, "The people in Panguitch made her burial clothes. They were all so kind to us. We took her body home to Circleville in a buggy on a chilly, windy day."[53]

Garfield County can thus claim a legendary outlaw of its own. Little did county citizens realize at the turn of the century that a new medium of entertainment soon would come along to help perpetuate the legends and myths of the American West. Some of the county's breathtaking scenery would provide a backdrop for the filming of some of these popular dramas. In the meantime, other concerns occupied the people as America went to war and suffered through a devastating influenza epidemic. But all was not negative—the next two decades provided for many an affirmation of their hopes and dreams.

ENDNOTES

1. George A. Thompson, *Some Dreams Die* (Salt Lake City: Dream Garden Press, 1982), 77.

2. Ibid.

3. Ibid.

4. Ida Chidester and Eleanor Bruhn, *Golden Nuggets of Pioneer Days: A History of Garfield County,* 160.

5. Unless otherwise noted, information on the founding and early history of Tropic came from June Shakespear, "Tropic," copy in possession of authors.

6. Shakespear, "Tropic," 4.

7. As quoted in a chronology produced for Tropic's birthday celebration on 23 May 1979 by Michael Ferrin, copy in possession of authors.

8. Seth Alvin Johnson, "A Sketch of the Life of Seth Alvin Johnson," 1933, copy in possession of authors.

9. Shakespeare, "Tropic," 6.

10. James A. Ott and Virginia S. Ott, "A History of the James Alvin and Virginia Spencer Ott Family," 1966, 12, copy in possession of authors. Ott's account of his boyhood experiences is exceptional in content and style.

11. Ibid., 10–11.

12. Wallace Ott, interview with Linda K. Newell, Tropic, Utah, July 1993, tape in possession of authors.

13. See Ott, "History of the Ott Family," 2.

14. Janet Matilda Johnson Ott, "A Sketch of the Life of Janet Matilda (Johnson) Ott," 1933; Udell Jolley, "Life Story of Lydia Ann Johnson Jolley," c. 1933, copy in possession of authors.

15. Chidester and Bruhn, *Golden Nuggets,* 195.

16. Ibid., 210–11.

17. Fern H. Crawford, *Red Brick Homes and Other Buildings of Panguitch, Utah* (n.p., 1997), 8.

18. Ibid., 62.

19. See Stephen L. Carr, *A Historical Guide to Utah Ghost Towns,* 122; and Karl C. Sandberg, "Telling the Tales and Telling the Truth: Writing the History of Widtsoe," *Dialogue: A Journal of Mormon Thought* 26 (Winter 1993): 93–105. There are some discrepancies as to the order and time period when events took place in the settling and changing the name of Widtsoe among the sources named above and in Chidester and Bruhn's *Golden Nuggets.*

20. Effel Harmon Burrow, in Riggs, *History of Hatch,* 100.

21. Ibid., 101.

22. Ibid., 110.

23. Ibid., 105–6.

24. Ibid., 282.

25. Nethella Griffin Woolsey, *The Escalante Story: 1875–1964,* 128.

26. Robert H. Linford, "Biography of Joseph H. Linford," 2, copy obtained from the author.

27. See George W. Thompson, "Cannonville History," 23–24, unpublished manuscript, copy in possession of authors; and Woolsey, *Escalante Story,* 134–37.

28. Information provided by Marilyn Jackson.

29. Thompson, "Cannonville History," 24.

30. Woolsey, *Escalante Story,* 135–37.

31. Ibid., 137.

32. Shakespear, "Tropic," 8; Lenora Hall LeFevre, *The Boulder Country and Its People,* 237.

33. Material obtained from Marilyn Jackson, Escalante, Utah.

34. Vetta Linford, Memoirs, 1974, 6–9, copy in possession of the authors.

35. LeFevre, *Boulder Country,* 237.

36. For information on the national forests and livestock grazing activities in Garfield County see Chidester and Bruhn, *Golden Nuggets,* 250–61; LeFevre, *Boulder Country,* 236–42; Woolsey, *Escalante Story,* 137–246.

37. Woolsey, *Escalante Story,* 148–49.

38. Chidester and Bruhn, *Golden Nuggets,* 314.

39. Riggs, *History of Hatch,* 316–17.

40. Woolsey, *Escalante Story,* 209.

41. See "Still a Cowboy at 88 Years," *Tribune Intermountain Service,* 1938, 70–72, copy in possession of authors; and Ott, interview, 1993.

42. Recollections of Russell H. Talbot as told to his son Grant R. Talbot and subsequently related to the authors.

43. Ott, interview, 1993.

44. "Still a Cowboy," 71.

45. See Pearl Baker, *The Wild Bunch at Robbers Roost* (New York: Abelard-Schuman, 1965); Lula Parker Betenson as told to Dora Flack, *Butch Cassidy, My Brother* (Provo, UT: Brigham Young University Press, 1975); Charles Kelly, *The Outlaw Trail, A History of Butch Cassidy and His Wild Bunch* (New York: Bonanza Books, 1959); Larry Pointer, *In Search of Butch Cassidy* (Norman: University of Oklahoma Press, 1977). Pointer's is the most scholarly of these four volumes, providing complete citations, bibliography, and evaluation of evidence.

46. Kelly, *Outlaw Trail,* 168–69.

47. Charles Kelly believes the two died in Bolivia, but Pointer presents some compelling evidence disputing that theory.

48. Betenson, *Butch Cassidy,* 184–85.

49. Emma Allene Savage Riddle, autobiography, undated typescript, 1. The authors thank Nancy Twitchell for providing them a copy of this.

50. Wallace Ott, interview with Linda King Newell, 4 July 1995, transcript in possession of authors.

51. Ott, interview, 1993.

52. Butch Cassidy Draw is the first major drainage area east of the two tunnels that motorists on Utah Highway 12 pass through today.

53. Bettenson, *Butch Cassidy,* 164–67.

CHAPTER 10

THE FIRST DECADES
OF A NEW CENTURY

With the year 1910 came the heavenly display of Halley's Comet. It appeared on the western horizon "each evening about dusk with a fan-like tail growing wider and brighter as time went by." Many residents believed that on a particular night in late spring "this great fan would strike the earth and great destruction" would follow. Because of this fear, some reportedly were driven to commit suicide and some farmers even were reluctant to plant their grain that year.[1]

Residents of Garfield County remembered that two and a half years earlier another bright light complete with a long flaming tail had appeared in the sky. It grew larger and larger until it crashed to the earth three miles west of Antimony in what is known as Pole Canyon. As the meteorite fell, it sheared off part of a cliff and its impact created a huge hole that rapidly filled up with shale rock; the sound of its impact had resounded for miles around.[2] Now in 1910 could residents expect an occurrence far more serious? With the der-ring-do of youth, a group of young people in Hatch determined to spend the night of the expected calamity at the local reservoir. They wanted to see what would happen when the "great fan" hit the water.

Repairing the Hatchtown reservoir Dam in the winter of 1911–1912. (Utah State Historical Society)

With what might have been a mixture of disappointment and relief one of their number reported, "We waited until the hour had passed. No excitement whatsoever! Just a calm, lovely moonlit night!"[3]

Even though the immediate threat did not live up to their expectations, these young people actually had reason for apprehension—during the next two decades the drama of life would produce for them and others in Garfield County its share of excitement and tragedy. Like the rest of the nation, local residents felt the impact of U.S. participation in World War I and the worldwide 1918 influenza epidemic. But advancements in the structure of public education, increased population, the beginnings of economic exploitation of the county's most spectacular scenic attraction, Bryce Canyon, the advent of automobile ownership, and a dam failure all produced their share of excitement and progress.

Floods, Fires, and Other Natural Disasters

When one looks back on the adventure of these young citizens of Hatch, it seems only fitting that they should have gone to the reservoir to witness an expected tumult of nature. Within a few short years

Hatchtown dam site after the failure of the dam in 1914. (Utah State
Historical Society)

of their nocturnal vigil, the reservoir would indeed be the site of
wide-ranging destruction, although, gratefully, with no loss of
human life. The Utah State Land Board and state engineer, after
studying the suitability of the site for a dam, authorized the private
engineering firm of Jensen and McLaughlin to begin construction in
1906 of a third dam along the Sevier River. Despite concerns
expressed by the citizens of Hatch, this more sophisticated structure
was completed by November 1908 at a cost of more than $84,000.

Engineers soon discovered, however, that the water-control gates
in the culvert did not function properly. The water was supposed to
help raise the flood gates when the dam filled; but, instead, the pressure of the water made it impossible for the gates to open. The state
engineer determined that the gates would have to be dynamited loose
to allow the water to flow and relieve the pressure on the dam. The
resulting explosion shook the whole structure but achieved the
desired outcome. Workers later replaced the gates and repaired the
damage to the culvert and tower. However, the structural integrity of
the dam had been compromised. This, along with unstable soil conditions, a troublesome spring that the contractors failed to adequately

Governor William Spry (far right, looking down) visited Panguitch in 1914
after the dam at Hatch broke. (Utah State Historical Society)

deal with earlier, and overall poor design and construction doomed
the dam from the start.[4]

After several trying incidents and the constant efforts of townspeople to try to strengthen the dam, it became clear that a break was
imminent. By mid-afternoon on 25 May 1914 residents all along the
Panguitch Valley and north in the river's path were warned to move
to higher ground. The dam finally broke that evening. It carried with
it only one home in the relocated town of Hatch. Sam and Effel Riggs
had recently purchased the home and lived there with their extended
family. Riggs's mother, Priscilla, had just baked several loaves of bread
when the dam broke. Her ten-year-old son, Earnest, grabbed the box
of bread and ran with it to safety before the raging waters carried
their home away.

Those who had been critical of telephone service coming to the
valley now had reason to reconsider. Alice Syrett stayed at her telephone to send the alarm through to Circleville Valley until the floodwaters engulfed even the telephone lines. A ten-foot-high wall of
water began a devastating course, taking with it houses and out-
buildings farther downriver, "tossing them like egg shells upon the

Roller Mill in Panguitch was abandoned after it was damaged during the 1914 Hatchtown Flood.

foaming wave. . . . Crops were ruined, ditches and canals destroyed and in some places land was washed away and . . . mud was deposited over extensive areas," wrote one. Floodwaters reached the upper floor of the flour mill in Panguitch, "destroying the machinery, the stored wheat, and injuring the mill itself." The Fred C. Syrett home, a short distance east of the mill, was completely ruined by the flood, and the mill had to be abandoned. From that time until the present no flour mills have replaced it.[5] The cost of the damage throughout the valley was estimated at one-half million dollars. One notices that there is no dam or reservoir to the southeast of Hatch today, and it is not likely there ever will be again.

Another type of calamity that brought constant concern to early settlers of Garfield County was fire. Since most people built their homes and outbuildings of wood, and few ever painted them, the arid atmosphere caused the structures to become exceedingly dry. Methods of heating homes and cooking also increased the likelihood of fires. Only the fact that residents usually lived a little farther apart than did residents of cities kept flames from spreading to other buildings. People had no hope of putting a blaze out unless they discovered it early, since methods of bringing water to the fire were primitive. One could only hope to get loved ones out before it was too late.

One devastating fire occurred in Hatch in 1909. Jim Elder had obtained a job working on the new Hatch dam, and he and his wife, Rainy, built a two-room frame home in town. On a calm, sunny day, Rainy left the two older boys playing in the yard and eight-year-old daughter Theda watching her sleeping baby brother while she walked quickly to Jobe Hall's new store. As she arrived, someone shouted that her house was on fire. Running back home, she saw Theda "emerge from the smoke filled doorway . . . choking with smoke and dragging a blanket in which she carried a crying baby."[6] Many times such a scenario repeated itself throughout the early decades of county settlement.

The community-minded townspeople of Cannonville had their trials by fire as well. Not long after they enlarged and renovated their schoolhouse, all their efforts literally went up in smoke. Late one night in 1912 a resident discovered a fire in the school and spread the alarm. People came from all directions "pulling their clothes on and trying to keep untied shoes on their feet," but the fire proved too much for them. "The only water they had was part of a barrel, mostly ice, that had been hauled from the creek for drinking water for the children."[7] They saved very few school supplies and furnishings. One man did manage to pull the blackboard free of the wall, its frame charred but still intact.

Only momentarily daunted by such misfortune, Cannonville citizens began anew. An up-to-date structure replaced the old one and included three classrooms with ample windows, entryway, halls, and storage. The bell tower housed a bell of "excellent tone and range." When the old blackboard was installed in the new school, its charred trim reminded everyone of the schoolhouse fire. In the new school, "heat was provided from two large, gravity flow, coal-wood furnaces; each installed in its own concrete [pad] which protected the flue all the way through the building to the attic. They would not chance another fire," wrote one historian.⁸ Thus, out of the ashes, rose a modern building in which the residents took great pride.

Sometimes fires produced some immediate fringe benefits. Vera Fotheringham recalled just such a fire in downtown Panguitch during the early 1920s. The old Myers and Henrie Store had long since been converted into a movie theater, named the Elite and owned by Lyle and Elida Hatch. To take maximum advantage of the space, Lyle Hatch stored his potatoes underneath the stage. After the building caught fire, only the outer shell remained. However, when all the hot spots had cooled down, the "cooked" potatoes remained warm for days. Vera and many of her schoolmates made frequent stops to the burned-out theater and helped themselves to a delicious snack of roasted potatoes.⁹ The show house was rebuilt and served the community for several years as the Gem Theater.

Tragedy at Blue Springs

In 1908 the Utah Department of Fish and Game hired John "Jack" D. Morrill to operate a fish hatchery at Blue Springs that was designed to replenish Panguitch Lake and other fished-out waters in the area with rainbow and eastern brook trout. One contemporary described Morrill as "a very intelligent man and a very religious man [who] was kind to everyone . . . the same with his wife, Emma."¹⁰

Born in Kanarraville and raised in Parowan, Emma Carson met Jack Morrill in Junction, Piute County, where she had gone as a teenager to work in her adopted sister's hotel. She was eighteen and he twenty-two when they married in 1893. In 1908 Jack and Emma moved their four children (LaBaron, Belle, Melvin, and Clair) to Blue Springs, where they took up year-round residence. Although the family was often isolated by deep snows throughout much of the winter, they did have a phone that connected them to Parowan and to the Sevy Ranch on the Panguitch side of the mountain.

Emma gave birth to another daughter, Mildred, in March 1910 and another son, Ben, three years later. Her widowed mother, Hannah Waggle Carson, spent seven summers at Blue Springs with the family, helping her daughter with children and meals. During those beautiful summer months they entertained streams of visitors with a crank-type freezer full of homemade ice cream and "lots of

Emma Morrill and Children at Blue Springs in 1912. (Courtesy Barbara B. Burt)

fresh fish." The two women reportedly fed "people by the dozens." Emma would remember her eight years there as some of her happiest.[11]

Her husband, who had previously been a schoolteacher, home-taught their six children. When the oldest son, LaBaron, was twelve he was sent to Junction to live with relatives and attend a regular school. He had not been there long, however, when he became extremely ill with appendicitis. John and Emma were notified and hurried to Junction, where the boy died in his mother's arms.

Emma became pregnant with a seventh child in 1912. As the time for her delivery came closer, Jack took her to Parowan, where her sister, Alta Carson Pendleton, was to help with the birth. But Alta died unexpectedly just a few days after Emma arrived. Another sister, Rebecca Carson Miller, was also expecting a baby at that time, so with no one to care for Emma during her confinement the couple returned to Blue Springs, where the baby boy was soon born. He lived only three days. Jack built a tiny casket for his infant son and accompanied the body down the mountain to the Panguitch cemetery for burial.

The winter of 1915–16 turned particularly nasty, and the Morrill family was snowed in for most of December and January. According to one account, the fourteen-foot snowdrifts piled "almost to the eves of their porch." However, the family "happily spent its Christmas with a beautifully decorated tree and gifts long since carried from town." By 26 January the weather lifted. Eager to have mail from family and friends, Jack determined to go to the Sevy Ranch for mail the next day, as they had not had any mail for weeks. Emma wrote several letters for him to post at the ranch, including one to her sister Rebecca in which she expressed her uneasiness with her husband's venture.[12]

Emma watched Jack leave on horseback at 7:00 A.M. on Tuesday morning. She could see him ride across the large meadow to the ridge north of Blue Springs Valley, where the drifts became too much for the animal. Still in sight of the cabin, he tied his horse to a tree and proceeded on snowshoes down the mountain and past William Prince's summer ranch, leaving his warm outer coat strapped to the back of his saddle.

At the Sevy Ranch Jack found about twenty-five pounds of Christmas mail and packages waiting for his family. Rebecca Miller recalled that "he phoned Emma and told her he had made it all right, he had rested some, had his dinner and would start back about 2 o'clock. He thought he could reach home around 9 o'clock." By the time he left the ranch, however, a "terrible storm" had begun and the Sevys tried to persuade him to wait it out. Worried about his own family and certain he would be alright, he disappeared into the tempest. This storm proved so furious that it blew out a number of large windows in Panguitch. In the mountains, four feet of new snow fell on drifts already ten to twelve feet high.

An anxious Emma fought the snow and wind to the barn, where she did evening chores, milking their two cows, feeding the horses, and bringing in more firewood. For two days and two nights the family watched and waited as the storm raged, plunging temperatures as low as 23 degrees below zero. Emma and ten-year-old Belle, the oldest of the children, took turns around the clock cranking the telephone to try to get a message over the storm-damaged lines to someone in Parowan or at Sevy's Ranch to tell them Jack had not returned. At one point, Emma turned to Belle and said, "If you will stay with the children I believe I can put on those snowshoes and go out and find Daddy." This frightened the youngsters even more; they "cried and begged her not to go."[13]

Meanwhile, at Parowan, Clara Matheson Benson took over at the telephone switchboard for her sister on 27 January. The two women had just been discussing their concerns for the Morrill family because they not heard from them in six weeks. Clara hadn't been at the board five minutes when she noticed the little disc (which fell when someone rang in) quivering, but it didn't fall to make a complete signal. She quickly plugged in the connection and heard Emma crying and pleading, "Oh someone please answer me, any one please answer."

Clara steadied her own voice. "Aunt Emma, this is Clara, is there something wrong?"

"Oh thank God for you," Emma blurted. Then she informed Clara of Jack's venture and that he had not returned. The young telephone operator later wrote of her part in the drama:

> I told Aunt Emma to be sure and not hang the receiver of the phone up. . . . Then I told her my father, Simon A. Matheson, was eating dinner and I would call him to talk to her. He cautioned about the phone and told her to promise she wouldn't leave the house . . . and we would send help to her.[14]

Immediately after talking with Emma, Clara Matheson went for her sisters, Lizzie Carson Skougaard and Becky Carson Miller, so they could talk to her on the telephone and help keep her on the line.

Clara's husband, Philip Benson, began organizing a search party. At a mass meeting that evening, the opinion prevailed that the storm was too dangerous to send anyone out into it. According to Clara, "Phil was so angry he stood up saying, 'You in this building are all cozy and warm, but I am going to that family if I go alone. Is there any one with me?'" Three men—Fred Bruhn, John Dalton, and John C. Gould—agreed to join him. Simon Matheson gave Benson a telephone test set to carry on his back. They agreed on a set of prearranged signals to let Clara know where they were. "You can't hear us but we will hear you," he said. The searchers left at 5:00 A.M. the next morning.

With the telephone lines to Panguitch down, Clara and her father decided to send a telegram there for help. The telegraph message had to go from Parowan to Cedar City, then through a number of other stations to San Francisco and back through Salt Lake City to Panguitch. It cost $14.75—a hefty sum in those days. The telegram read:

> Parowan Utah
> Regardless of cost or distance and rush, John Morrill missing from Blue Spring Hatchery. Must have help. 4 Parowan men already gone.
>
> Simon A. Matheson
Clara M. Benson

When the message arrived in Panguitch, men there also organized a search party.

"The telephone closed at 10 P.M. but I told them I was going to stay," Clara remembered, "I could answer the switchboard as well as keeping in touch [with the searchers], and we had to keep talking to Emma and the children. . . . What a long day and night." At one point, little Belle came on the line and tried to talk through her tears. "Now listen, Belle," Clara told her, "stop crying and tell me so we can help."

"Mom has gone for the horse," she sobbed.

Simon took the phone and instructed her: "Call loud. Tell [your] mother to come back to the phone." When Emma returned, Simon made her promise she would not go out again.

Finally, the blizzard abated. Emma ventured outside for the first time since the storm began. She cleared a path to the barn and with an ax chopped the ice from the door. She climbed the ladder to the loft, forked down hay for the hungry animals, and milked the cows. Returning to the house, she again talked on the phone with Clara. When the searchers from Parowan reached the other side of the mountain just after noon, they plugged in their phone and heard Emma say to Clara, "Bless their hearts, I hope and pray they make it ok."

By late afternoon the men reached the ridge above Panguitch Lake. They could see two men carrying something toward William Prince's cabin on the west side of the lake. Frank Worthen and Ruby Syrett had found John Morrill's frozen body laying on one mail sack with another still strapped to his back. He had wandered in the blizzard until he fell face first into the snow, overcome by the intense cold. The Parowan men reached the Prince cabin a short time later, as did John Gould from Panguitch. They loaded the body onto a makeshift toboggan made from a "cheese board." Worthen and several men from both groups took the body to Sevy's Ranch.

Clara still sat at the Parowan switchboard when Worthen called with the news: "Hello, we found Morrill."

Emma, who was also listening, cried out, "Dead or Alive?"

"Dead," came the answer. Worthen hung up the receiver, not knowing he had told Emma of her husband's death.

Benson, Syrett and another Panguitch man went on to Blue Springs, reaching the Morrill family at about 11:00 P.M. The grieving Emma welcomed them with great relief and fixed them a warm meal. When they told her they wanted to take the family out to Panguitch, she begged them to leave them there; "she couldn't stand to think of the suffering they would have to go through to take her out," Clara wrote. The men found two pair of skis and some lumber in John's shop. They built a box large enough to accommodate the grief-stricken widow and the five children, piled hay in the bottom, and placed heated rocks in the blankets tucked around them, then started down the mountain. They pulled the sleigh themselves until Panguitch men with horses met them. One of the rescuers later recalled, "Mrs. Morrill never uttered a sound of discouragement or fear. She gained the respect of the men who so fearlessly were rescuing her and her children."

Quantities of food sent by the people of Panguitch awaited them at the Sevy Ranch: "whole hams, loaves of bread, whole cheese, wash boilers of hot coffee—were all results of the wholesome community spirit which existed," according to one account.[15]

John L. Morrill was buried in Junction, where Emma and the children continued to live. She later married widower George Davies, who carried the mail between Junction and Escalante for many years. They had two more children.

Turn-of-the-Century Medical Care

For assistance in times of illness or childbirth Garfield residents depended primarily on midwives. In Panguitch, Hannah Brandon

Shakespear, one of many who deserve mention, is said to have delivered 630 babies. Her charge of five dollars included the delivery and nine days of postnatal care. Mariah Schow and Ida Chatwin played a similar role during Tropic's early settlement years. When the town's LDS Relief Society was organized on 11 November 1895, many of the church women aided in the care of the sick and preparation of the dead for burial.

Midwives in the upper Paria Valley included Miriam Adelia Riding, known as "Aunt Dee," who traveled by horse and buggy to deliver babies in Cannonville, Henrieville, and Tropic. Just south of Cannonville, "Grandma" Nielson performed the same task. These women gained their practical knowledge mainly by experience. Gradually, however, midwives started to receive better training, and a number became nurses.

Panguitch did not have its first doctor until the 1890s when Dr. Moses Usher Campbell relocated to the town from New York for his health. Dr. J.J. Steiner followed, and he remained in Panguitch until 1904. His father then took over his position until Dr. R. Garn Clark could complete his medical studies and come home to practice. For thirteen years townspeople came to Dr. Clark, but in the end the opportunity to work in a regular hospital drew him to Richfield. Other doctors followed, most staying for only brief periods; an exception was Dr. M.W. Bigelow, who provided medical care to the community for many years. None of the towns in Garfield had a hospital, so the various doctors and nurses set up small clinics and hospitals in private homes.

Appendicitis, or inflammation of the bowels, as it was called, was a common affliction and created concern during these early times. Tropic's Jesse Jolley became the first resident of the county to live after an appendicitis operation; Drs. Garn and Cecil Clark performed the operation in Panguitch in July 1911. For setting broken bones, especially if an accident occurred during the winter when travel was impossible, Tropic residents usually went to Waldo Littlefield, a local resident without formal medical training but adept at this procedure. They called upon Sam Pollock to pull their teeth, another resident whose only professional credential was that he owned a pair of forceps. He often paid the patient a quarter for the tooth. Throughout the county, kitchen tables doubled as operating tables when doctors and dentists came through town to perform tonsillectomies or other procedures.

The Automobile Comes to Garfield

Excitement came to the county through a manmade source—the automobile. Although information concerning the date this mechanical marvel first arrived in most local communities is lacking, locals recollected who owned the first machines. Theodore Chidester introduced the automobile to Panguitch with his Model-T Ford around 1912. Soon after, George Hanks bought one and the two men began carrying passengers to the train in Marysvale—a business they conducted for years. Alma Barney and his son Newton entered a contest selling farm machinery and won a striking red Chalmers automobile from the Montgomery Ward company. Alma nearly lost his prize, however, when he took the car to Bryce Canyon. The primitive road ended abruptly at the canyon's edge, offering a sudden and spectacular view—so sudden that he almost drove over the brink. The early automobiles captured the interest of the town's young people to the degree that they were willing to pay a whopping fifty cents to ride around town in one.[16]

John Whitehead Seaman also owned one of the early cars in Panguitch. Seaman already had a certain distinction among his fellow citizens, and this acquisition simply added to his stature. A Union veteran of the Civil War, he had had the privilege of meeting President Lincoln, even serving as a member of the honor guard at the assassinated president's funeral. Seaman's passion was dancing. He willingly used his car to transport the town band wherever they played so he had an excuse to attend the dances. During his eighty-eighth year, the Republican Club of Utah invited him to speak during a Lincoln Day celebration. The trip took its toll, however, and he died on 17 February 1930, a few days after his return home.[17] In his lifetime this gentleman, along with other early arrivals, experienced much as the county advanced from a pioneer way of life into the wonders of the twentieth century.

Virginia Hardy Smith recalled that the first cars in Henrieville belonged to a Mr. Fife and a Mr. Ahlstrom.[18] Wallace Ott remem-

Fred Sargent and Joe Cherrington's Garage in Panguitch. (Courtesy Dorothy Houston)

bered that William Shakespear had the first and for a long time only car in Tropic. Like most early car owners of the county, Shakespear ordered his vehicle, a Model-T Ford, from a catalog; but Ott couldn't remember if it was from Sears, Roebuck & Company or from Montgomery Ward. Shakespear had to travel two days on the mail buggy to the railhead at Marysvale to claim his car. He spent a short time in that town learning how to drive his new acquisition, then started home. The drive to Tropic took two more days on the poor roads.

These early cars had only two forward gears, low and high. Shakespear used the low gear most of the time, once again because of the road conditions. As a result, the automobile made lots of noise, disturbing local horses and other stock. Ott's father reportedly had to "hold his mare by the bit to keep it from running away" whenever the auto went by. When Shakespear wanted to travel up the "dump" road to leave Tropic, he had to back up the hill, since the gas tank was located in the back of the vehicle and gasoline couldn't get to the motor if he traveled forward.[19]

Coming back down over the dump also presented problems. One time Shakespear's brakes went out and he stopped the car by steering

Building the road through Circleville Canyon about 1912. (Utah State Historical Society)

into a road bank, thus averting serious injury to himself, his wife, and family. Horses pulled the car home, and his wife, Matilda, "made new brake bands by sewing bib overall straps together. They worked fine, and lasted as long as the car, but he soon sold the car to Maurice Cope," according to a local historian.[20]

A crowd of children, with some grown-ups interspersed, greeted the first car to come into Escalante. A salesman known as "Candy" Smith made his grand entrance by automobile around 1914. Going down hills in town did not amaze the crowd as much as Smith's ability to go up them. Al Sherman probably owned the first car in the community, a Ford, but others soon followed, driving Fords, Maxwells, Stars, or Essexes. As automobile numbers increased, Charlie Weiss saw the need for an auto repair shop. He built and operated the first one in Escalante during the 1920s.[21]

The advent of vehicular travel also spawned road improvements. The U.S. Forest Service reconstructed the road over Escalante Mountain to Winder (Widtsoe), creating a better grade and a smoother surface. Still, where the road crossed the mountain at its lowest point the elevation was 9,200 feet. Travelers had little trouble making it over the mountain during mild weather, but it often became impassable during heavy rainstorms and in the winter. An improved route was still decades away.[22]

The people of Boulder had their first experience with an automobile when brothers Tom and Orin Barker arrived from Escalante after telephoning ahead that they were on their way. They drove a "stripped-down Model T Ford consisting of a frame, wheels, motor, and a seat. A roll of net wire was tied to the floor board." Each time the two came to deep patches of sand, Tom unrolled the wire and spread it over the road so Orin could drive across it. After rolling up the net, Tom hopped back in and off they went. Even though the Ford could make the steep grades on its own power, the trip took them eight hours. A crowd gathered at the schoolhouse to await their arrival and marveled as the Barkers rehearsed all the details of their journey. Prior to their return trip, "they roared away in a cloud of dust the full length of Boulder Valley, scattering chickens and frightening all the animals en route."[23]

Boulder's next encounter with mechanized travel occurred in April 1925 when four young men—Jody Griffin, Cal Shurtz, Emmitt Porter, and Theron Griffin—arrived in a cloth-top Model-T Ford. The men remained in town for Friday and Saturday night dances and further entertained the townspeople with their singing to the accompaniment of Percy Leavitt's accordion and Amanda Peterson's piano. By the following year residents of the community owned a half-dozen cars.

Publicizing Bryce Canyon

The coming of the automobile to Garfield County signaled the birth of a new industry—tourism. County residents had known the splendor of Bryce Canyon for decades, but the roads to the canyon were little more than wagon trails, and sight-seeing trips were hardly an option in the working world of pioneers. But the arrival of the automobile and the transfer of forest supervisor W.H. Humphrey from Moab to Panguitch on 1 July 1915 helped catapult the local scenic wonder to the nation's attention. Elias Smith, forest ranger of the East Fork Division, invited Humphrey to go with him to see the canyon. Although Humphrey "was loath to take the time right then . . . the ranger insisted." The first view of the canyon from the west

"Nooning" in Red Canyon on the road to Bryce Canyon 25 May 1916.
(Utah State Historical Society)

rim near Sunset Point stunned the new supervisor, who later referred
to it as "the most beautiful piece of natural scenery on the face of the
earth."[24]

"You can perhaps imagine my surprise at the indescribable
beauty that greeted us," Humphrey wrote. "It was sundown before I
could be dragged from the canyon view. . . . I went back the next
morning to see the canyon once more, and to plan in my mind how
this attraction could be made accessible to the public."[25] Humphery
assigned the task of publicizing Bryce Canyon to Mark Anderson,
foreman of the Forest Service grazing crew.

Anderson's first view of the canyon came early the next spring.
Immediately after returning to Panguitch he called the telegraph station in Marysvale, Piute County, and requested that a message be sent
to the district forest office in Ogden asking that George Goshen,
regional Forest Service photographer, "be sent down to Bryce Canyon
with movie and still cameras to take pictures of the grazing crew 'at
work' near the plateau rim." Goshen lost no time; he arrived in
Panguitch the next evening and worked all the following day. A stack

of photographs and the movie were sent to Forest Service officials in Washington and also made available to Union Pacific Railroad officials in Omaha, Nebraska.[26]

The first two descriptive articles about Bryce Canyon came out in the latter part of 1916. One was by a member of the grazing crew, Arthur W. Stevens, who wrote an article illustrated with Goshen's photographs for the Union Pacific publication, *Outdoor Life*. The second was an article for the Denver and Rio Grande Western Railroad's periodical *Red Book* dictated by Humphrey and published under the name of clerk J.J. Drew. Since this railroad had a spur as far south as Marysvale, Humphery tried to interest its owners in the tourism possibilities of Bryce, Zion, and Grand canyons, with Marysvale as the jumping-off station. He may even have hoped that the line would be extended on to Panguitch, which, however, never happened.

Meanwhile, a Panguitch couple, Clara Armeda (Minnie) and Reuben (Ruby) Carlson Syrett welcomed their first daughter to the world on 15 March 1916. For some time they had been looking for a place to start a ranch, and they began homesteading a quarter section near Bryce Canyon that May. "Most people in Panguitch thought the Syretts were foolish to homestead in such a desolate locale," wrote one observer. It was not until mid-summer that a Tropic rancher, Claude Sudweeks, stopped by to chat. He asked if they had seen Bryce Canyon. Ruby said they hadn't and asked what it was. "O, just a hole in the ground, but you ought to see it," came the reply. On a Sunday afternoon soon after Sudweeks's visit, the Syretts took their buggy to take a look at the canyon. Minnie recalled, "We were speechless, just stood and looked and looked. When we could talk, we could only whisper."

Later that summer friends from Panguitch began visiting the canyon at the Syretts' invitation. "We began to take our friends and advertise as much as we could, we thought everyone should see it," they said. Between 1916 and 1919 the deep snow and cold caused the Syretts to spend most of the winter months in Escalante, where the family had agricultural interests and Ruby helped run his brother's gristmill.[27]

Not long after the Syretts took up residence on their homestead, J.W. Humphrey secured fifty dollars from the National Forest Service

One of two mills at the Antimony mines in Coyote (Antimony) Canyon, about 1905. (Utah State Historical Society)

to build crude bridges over the East Fork of the Sevier River and the canal in the area. Homesteaders in the area donated most of the labor to construct a road to the canyon that would be passable in dry weather; but it was impossible to travel in wet conditions. The forest supervisor also arranged for another photographer to photograph Bryce Canyon. In Humphery's words, he "secured some of the best pictures taken up to that time" and made postcards from them. "These he placed on sale, and they added to the advertisement of Bryce Canyon." That same summer of 1917 the director of the Utah State Automobile Association, C.B. Hawley, drove to Bryce Canyon. He also came away impressed. As a result of Hawley's visit and later excursions by other Automobile Association officials, *Salt Lake Tribune* photographer Oliver J. Grimes came to take pictures of the canyon the next summer. He published a full-page article entitled "Utah's New Wonderland," which appeared in the *Tribune*'s Sunday magazine section on 25 August 1918. The article gave detailed directions for finding Bryce Canyon by automobile.

"Utah's New Wonderland" became the most widely read article on Bryce Canyon to that date and put the area on the road to national park status. In the midst of this optimistic enthusiasm for Bryce

Ruby and Minnie Syrett's first home in Panguitch. They began home-steading near Bryce Canyon in 1916. (Courtesy Ruby's Inn)

Canyon's potential as a tourist attraction, however, the realities of World War I preempted both local and national interest.

World War I

In terms of sacrifice, residents of Garfield County suffered comparatively little as America went to war in 1917; although, considering its population, a comparatively large number of the county's young men served their country. Since U.S. participation came late in the conflict and actual fighting for American troops was of relatively short duration, many young Garfield County men did not even leave the United States before the armistice. Local citizens did support President Woodrow Wilson's decision to enter the struggle. Many had to put their personal lives on hold when they volunteered for service. Those who stayed at home did what was asked of them to support the war effort.

James Alvin Ott, a twelve-year-old boy living in Tropic when the U.S. went to war, remembered learning patriotic songs in school and that everyone did without things that needed to be sent overseas. He wrote, "This economizing came to be called 'Hooverizing' after Mr. Herbert Hoover, then in charge, nationally. . . . There were liberty

The original Tourist's Rest established by Ruby and Minnie Syrett and acquired by the National Park Service in 1923. (Courtesy Ruby's Inn)

bonds to buy, wheatless and meatless days to observe. I got so tired of cornmeal bread and mush."[28] Alvin's older brother, Joseph Alma Ott, although not old enough to be drafted, cut short his education to volunteer for duty. In the fall of 1918 he got as far as Salt Lake City, ready to enter training camp, when the war ended. After being discharged, he returned home, never to resume his schooling again.[29] Seven young men from Tropic served honorably in the armed forces during World War I. All returned home safely.

All eight of those serving from Coyote (Antimony) also survived to receive honorable discharges. Their hometown became involved in the war, too. Even though the mining of antimony up the canyon had ceased long before the turn of the century, when the price of the ore started to rise in 1905–06 two companies resumed operations there. As mentioned earlier, antimony was valued as an alloy for strengthening lead and other metals. Local men helped build two new mills in Coyote Canyon, but only one ever operated. By the time they completed construction of a three-story structure, installed a crusher, and added an assay office the price of the ore once again

Peter LeFevre (sitting) leaving for World War I in 1918. (Courtesy Steve
Marshall)

plummeted—going from almost twenty-two cents a pound in 1906
to eight cents a pound in 1908. The beginning of the war, however,
caused the price to soar to a record of more than thirty cents in 1915.
Local antimony mines sent substantial amounts of ore to Marysvale
to be shipped on to ammunition plants before the mines began to
run out of the high-grade ore the plants required. By 1918 the price
had dropped substantially again, to under thirteen cents a pound,
ending the war-time "boom" in Coyote. In 1920, however, because of
the large amounts of ore taken out of the canyon, local residents
decided to rename their town Antimony.[30]

Other Garfield towns also saw their young men go off to war.
David Quilter from Henrieville had recently emigrated from Great
Britain. He served along with four other members of his commu-
nity. Quilter did not see action overseas but spent the war in
Washington state sorting lumber for building airplanes and training
new men.[31] Ten men from Cannonville served during the war;
Widtsoe sent twenty-five. Hatch contributed twelve men to the U.S.

fighting forces, with one man, Gilbert Yardley, dying while in the service.

As elsewhere in the county, young men in Escalante between the ages of twenty-one and thirty-one had to register for the draft during the war. Henry Barney took charge of the registration at the local meetinghouse. The first call-up required 5 percent of those registered. William Henry Richards and Ellis Shurtz were the first to go. The ward held a farewell party for them and gave each one a signet ring before they left on 4 September 1917. They did this for each group as they departed until the last inductions in October 1918. The draft eventually took forty-five young men from Escalante. Six of them were sent home because of various physical problems. Thirteen of the inductees saw service overseas, and one of them, William Henry Richards, died in action in France on 28 July 1918. His parents, William and Florence Richards, did not receive his body so he could be buried at home until three years later. One of the men who served from Escalante, Cliff Reynolds, later had seven sons, all of whom were in the military, serving either during World War II or the Korean War.[32]

Among all the towns in Garfield County that sent men to war, Panguitch residents made the greatest sacrifice; forty-seven went from that community and eight of them did not come back alive. James Dodds, Merlin Proctor, and Earl Riggs were killed in Europe and were buried there. Proctor's mother, Martha, eventually went to France with a group of war mothers to visit her son's grave. Henry LeFevre's body was returned home from France and buried in Panguitch, as were those of George Woodard, Christian Best, Douglas McEwen and Glen Miller.[33] The families of these young men sacrificed much. But even as the war wound down an even greater number of county residents experienced such sorrow.

The Influenza Epidemic of 1918–1919

The comparative isolation of Garfield County towns proved to be a mixed blessing when the worldwide Spanish influenza epidemic began in 1918. For two communities, at least, it kept the impact of the disease to a minimum. On the other hand, the lack of local trained medical help limited the care available to those who contracted the disease. From town to town so many became ill that some of the few not affected went among their neighbors offering what assistance they could.

In Tropic the townspeople took immediate steps to keep the flu from entering their community. They banned all public and private social gatherings, kept children at home from school, and prevented transients from entering the town. For a time these policies seemed effective, but during 1919 almost everyone in town came down with the flu at the same time, although it was a less deadly strain than that experienced in other communities.[34]

James Ott and his son Joseph Alma received word while they were out at their ranch that the rest of their family in town were down with the flu. Even though young Joe's mother, Janet Johnson Ott, advised him to stay outside, Joe entered the home and found everyone too sick to even get up for a drink of water or to make a fire. He assured his mother he would not get sick, and he went from bed to bed trying to meet each need. Happily, he was right. He rose often during the night to care for family members. Each morning he did what he could for them, then made the rounds to other homes of flu-stricken families in town. He fed and milked cows—some having been neglected for days—chopped and hauled wood, carried water, and gave food and medicine to the sick. When he returned home in the evening, he once again cared for his own family. Meanwhile, his father checked frequently on them but felt it wiser not to enter the home since someone had to work the farm and ranch.[35] According to Joe's younger brother, James, several townspeople died from the disease and perhaps more would have had not people like Joe stepped in to help.[36]

At Henrieville, the LDS Relief Society had Eda Willis Quilter and Audry Moore check on the sick of the community. Eda had recently married David Quilter in Salt Lake City after he was discharged from military service. He had been exposed to influenza while still stationed in Washington, where he saw many soldiers succumb to the disease. Upon returning home, after traveling by train to Marysvale, by buggy to Panguitch, and then on to Henrieville with the mail, the couple were quarantined. Even though Eda previously had a light case of the flu, her husband never contracted it from her or his army buddies. When she was released from quarantine she and Audry Moore made large pots of soup to take to the sick. When they arrived at Jim and Dorie Goulding's house, Jim Goulding was sitting in the middle of the bed holding his pregnant wife, who was dying. Two other Henrieville residents also died during the epidemic.[37]

In Antimony, John Reuben Jolley and his wife, Kate Effie Wilcox, witnessed friends and family succumb to the disease. As was the case in other Garfield communities, few in the town were well enough to help the very sick. Those who could help did farm and other outside chores, brought groceries to the stricken families, and performed other needed services. Despite this, four residents died from the flu— George Jolley, Arella Smoot, Thomas Ricketts, and Nephi Black. The death toll might have climbed higher had Antimony not had the part-time services of a doctor. Just prior to the epidemic a Dr. Moorehouse began to practice in nearby Junction. During the epidemic he devoted hundreds of hours to caring for the residents of Piute County towns as well as those in Antimony.[38]

Widtsoe was not immune from the spread of the disease. Adella Zabriskie recalled, "I look back with sadness on the influenza epidemic of 1918–19. We lost many young people at that time; nearly the whole town was down with it." She went on to say that her own family and that of Orrel Zabriskie did not catch the flu, so Orrel and her husband, George, "wore face masks and went to the homes, where they chopped and carried wood. They also brought water to the doors," leaving it outside on the porches.[39]

Like most citizens of that era, residents tried to help each other, particularly close friends. In some places outside the county, however, some people suffered because their neighbors were too frightened to help. Such instances do not seem to have been experienced in Garfield County, at least according to written memoirs.

Lillie Zabriskie Cuyler remembered big kettles of soup on the stove and pans of bread baking to help feed the sick. "Mother helped nurse several who had it, and one I remember who died in her arms was a Stoddard boy," Cuyler wrote. Another resident, Vird Barney, related how hard it was to dig graves fast enough. He remembered the time he and Richard Frederick Robinson, a "fine able-bodied young man," were digging the grave of Gertrude Young Bullock and

Robinson remarked, "One of these days you'll be digging my grave." He died three days later, and his friend Vird dug his grave.[40]

Although individual community figures are lacking, according to the U.S. Bureau of Census and Utah school census records, the number of deaths in the county increased substantially during 1918 and 1919. Deaths in 1917 totaled forty-three. In 1918 there were fifty-eight deaths, and in 1919 there were sixty-three. By comparison, after the epidemic had run its course, in 1920 deaths numbered only thirty-three. Only once in the next two decades did they rise above fifty again, and that was in 1923 when fifty-three residents died. However, by that time the population had increased by between 100 and 200 residents over what it was during the two epidemic years.

Although precise numbers are not available, old-time residents claim that Panguitch suffered a higher percentage of deaths and illness per capita than anywhere else in the county, perhaps even the state. During the winter of 1918, while residents celebrated the Christmas holidays, the flu arrived in that town. By the end of the first week in January the disease had overtaken most of the population. The call went out to surrounding communities to send help. Many, including two or three doctors, arrived from Parowan and other locales to take care of the critically ill.

Dr. Willard S. Sargent and his wife were in Philadelphia when she caught the flu and soon died. When he brought her body by train as far as Marysvale no one could be spared to help him take her body on to Panguitch or even dig her grave. He took her body back to Logan, where they had been living, buried her there, then came back to Panguitch to help the sick.

So many people died that residents had difficulty properly burying of the dead. Regular funerals were out of the question, so Sarah D. Syrett, Lovisa Miller, Leona Riddle, and Beulah Allen sewed burial clothing and prepared bodies for internment. Thomas Haycock and John C. Miller went to the homes of the deceased to remove the bodies and transport them to the cemetery. There Brandon Shakespear, Joseph Miller, and Arza Judd dug the graves. These people hardly had time to stop to eat during the worst of the epidemic. Death often came swiftly. One family lost three members in twenty-four hours.

Each day before seeing to his livestock, James L. Miller went to the cemetery to dedicate the graves. Postmaster L.C. Sargent closed the post office and took over those duties when Miller couldn't be there. Some burials even took place illuminated by automobile headlights. Adding to the town burden, the electric lights reportedly "froze up" during that cold January and no one could fix them.[41] Neither before nor since has the community of Panguitch experienced such a human toll. Fortunately, a few seemed immune to the disease and admirably performed many acts of service similar to those performed by residents in other Utah towns.

Only one community in Garfield County escaped the influenza epidemic. Isolated Boulder instituted a quarantine as soon as word came of the outbreak in Escalante. Visiting neighboring communities by town members was strictly forbidden. As a result, no one living in that valley caught the flu. Even Mercel Liston, living alone on his homestead in the area called the Draw, reported that no one in Boulder came near him when he brought the mail from Escalante. Several people in Escalante died from the disease, including Gilbert McInelly and his half-brother Leonard Fallis, Robert Barker, Chester Shurtz, Susannah Spencer Schow, Laura Lay Griffin, Eliza Alvey Porter, and Emma Roe Pollock. Emma's husband, Allen Pollock, only heard of his wife's death when he entered their home in Escalante after returning from the war. Gilbert McInelly's widow, Mildred, had four children to care for. Susannah Schow's husband, Andrew, was left with five children. The two surviving parents later married and combined their families and responsibilities.[42]

Once the crisis of the flu epidemic passed, residents of Garfield County had reason for optimism. Each community could point to its own marked advancements that had made life a little more pleasant and "civilized" for its citizens. Most of these improvements came about because of united efforts among townspeople; outside forces influenced other developments.

The Creation of Bryce Canyon National Park

Oliver J. Grimes, the *Salt Lake Tribune* photographer who had written about and lavishly illustrated Bryce Canyon in his earlier article, had become Utah Secretary of State to Governor Simon

Bamberger. Although he was unable to persuade the governor to assist in making the canyon more accessible (Bamberger reportedly once said, "I will build no roads to rocks!") Grimes did have more influence with the Utah Legislature, which passed a "Joint Memorial" on 13 March 1919 directed to the United States Congress. "On the public domain within the boundaries of the Sevier national Forest, in the Pink Mountain region, near Tropic, Garfield County, Utah," the document read, "there is a canyon popularly referred to as 'Bryce's Canyon' which has become famed for its wonderful natural beauty." The legislators reminded Congress of the state and federal governments' interest in protecting and preserving "natural attractions" and asked Congress to "set aside for the use and enjoyment of the people a suitable area embracing 'Bryce's Canyon' as a national monument under the name of the 'Temple of the Gods National Monument.'"[43]

A large group from Salt Lake City ventured south to see Bryce Canyon for themselves later that spring. Homesteaders Ruby and Minnie Syrett pitched a tent near Sunset Point and served lunch to the tourists. Ruby Syrett then went back to his ranch for more food and a half-dozen beds to set up under the pines. He and Minnie cooked breakfast for the campers the next morning. The meal was hardly over when more people began arriving. As one writer said, "Whether by design or chance the Syretts began accommodating tourists. They remained near Sunset Point until that fall."[44]

The following spring, Ruby and Minnie Syrett put up a number of tent houses for tourists to sleep in and got verbal permission from the Utah State Land Board to build a log lodge on part of the designated state school section in the area. They started construction of a lodge they called "Tourist's Rest." The building measured 30 by 71 feet and had a kitchen, storeroom, several adjoining bedrooms, and a large dining room with a stone fireplace at one end. The big double front doors acted as an informal sort of register where guests delighted in carving their names. Nearby the Syretts built a few small cabins and an open-air dance platform that, at 35 by 76 feet, was larger than the lodge itself. Ruby Syrett carved the center out of a large log, using it for a bathtub, and leaving the bark on the outside. The inside he painted white, "and people who bathed in it thought it a great novelty and talked about it for years."[45]

Ruby and Minnie Syrett were very good western host and hostess. Dressed like the real rancher he was, the genial Ruby greeted guests with a smile and a handshake, while Minnie combined her lively personality with courtesy and the serving of good food. But Tourist's Rest would be short-lived, as other forces moved to take advantage of the unique landscape.

Over the next four years negotiations between the State of Utah, the National Park Service, and the Union Pacific Railroad took place. Steven Mather, the first director of the National Park Service, urged Governor Charles R. Mabey and the Utah State Legislature to make Bryce Canyon a state park rather than a national park. A meeting was convened in Salt Lake City on 19 December 1921 to create a state park commission. The legislative Committee on Legislation and Geographic Boundaries sent a recommendation to the new commission that "Bryce Canyon be made the first of a series of state parks." Three years later, however, the state had failed to do anything more, and in 1924 Mather agreed to make Bryce Canyon a national monument administered by the National Forest Service.

Long and detailed negotiations with the Union Pacific Railroad would eventually result in a spur line being built from Lund to Cedar City, which would become the railroad company's center for its newly formed subsidiary the Utah Parks Company. From the Cedar City depot and the planned El Escalante Hotel (also owned by Union Pacific Railroad) across the street, tourists would be able to board buses that would take them on a loop through Cedar Breaks, Bryce Canyon, the North Rim of the Grand Canyon, and Zion National Park. Before this could happen, however, a road from Rockville to Mount Carmel had to be built, as did also an eight-mile section of road from Cedar Breaks to Mount Carmel. The latter was completed in April 1924.

The only road that connected Zion National Park to the Grand Canyon went south from LaVerkin to Fredonia, Arizona, seven miles south of Kanab. In 1927 a proposal to build a tunnel and connecting road through Zion National Park to the Marysvale-Kanab road was approved. The 5,600-foot tunnel cost $530,000 and took three years to build, but it cut the distance between Zion and Bryce from 149 to 88 miles.[46] Until these new roads could be built and old ones improved, however, tourist traffic was routed primarily through Marysvale by way of the Denver and Rio Grande Western Railway.

Three automobile touring companies met the mail train as it arrived at Marysvale each day. Marysvale resident Arthur E. Hanks conducted one-and-a-half-day tours to Bryce Canyon and a four-and-a-half-day trip to the Grand Canyon's North Rim by way of Bryce Canyon. Kanab resident H.I. Bowman had his headquarters in Kanab for a touring business that took in both Bryce Canyon and the North Rim. Only one company, Parry Brothers of Cedar City, served all four area scenic destinations: Zion, Cedar Breaks, Bryce, and the North Rim.

These tours, however, were not inexpensive for the 1920s. Parry Brothers charged eighty dollars per person for a five-day trip to the North Rim and Bryce. The company's eight-day grand loop tour of all four scenic locations cost $140. Union Pacific would eventually contract services from Parry Brothers to take rail passengers to these same destinations.

For its lodge at Bryce Canyon the railroad needed the water rights Ruby and Minnie Syrett had obtained for their Tourist's Rest camp as well as the land it occupied. The Syretts held the rights to two springs, Hopkins Spring and Shaker Springs (also referred to as Weather Springs). Union Pacific first offered to loan the Syretts $2,500 at 6 percent interest to pay off the debt they had incurred in building the camp, which they then could continue to operate until the Bryce Canyon Lodge was finished. At that time the railroad would move the camp at no cost to a new site with a five-year lease and free water (when available). Unhappy with the Union Pacific offer, Ruby Syrett prepared an inventory of his property, which he valued at $18,000—including water rights. The railroad countered with an offer of $9,000—excluding water rights. A flurry of offers and counter-offers took place in September 1923; finally, on 25 September, Ruby and Minnie Syrett sold Tourist's Rest and the water rights associated with it to Union Pacific for $10,000 and moved back to their ranch.[47]

Minnie Syrett remembered: "After being back at the ranch awhile, many of our old friends who had stayed with us at 'Tourist's Rest' came back and stayed with us at the ranch house so Ruby

Ruby and Minnie Syrett. (Courtesy Ruby's Inn)

decided to have something to make them comfortable." He divided
his fifteen acres of homesteaded land down the middle—north to
south—and convinced the engineers surveying the new road to the
canyon that the appropriate route lay on that line. They agreed, and
the Syretts began building Ruby's Inn. They first constructed a
sawmill to provide the logs.

On his frequent forays into the Escalante River drainage, Hole-in-the-Rock, the petrified forest near the town of Escalante, and other scenic highlights of Garfield County Ruby Syrett gathered rock and fossil specimens that he used in building a large open fireplace. This fireplace showcased petrified wood, dinosaur bones, shells, fossils, and colorful rocks. The Syretts kept a cheerful fire burning there which added "to the entertainment and [made] everyone feel welcome."

The establishment grew by stages over the years and Ruby's Inn became a renowned tourist stop, with "entertainment at night where the cowboys sing and recite and slides of the canyon were shown." Afterwards there were "old time dances with the cowboys leading out . . . and with tourists and everybody joining in." Ruby's Inn also provided a favorite local gathering place for family reunions, holidays, conventions, clubs, church outings, and dances.[48]

Meanwhile, construction of a lodge at Bryce Canyon was underway, with Gilbert Stanley Underwood, who designed the Yosemite Village project, as architect. Union Pacific park engineer Samuel C. Lancaster oversaw the project from his office in Cedar City. The lodge was located 700 feet from the rim, and Underwood's plan called for stone to be used up to the snow line, the rest of the structure being built from lumber. Union Pacific contracted with the Forest Service for $425 worth of timber to build the framework. Lancaster contracted with Ruby Syrett and Owen Orton to provide 200,000 board feet of lumber from Syrett's sawmill at a cost of $27.50 per 1,000 feet, and as many slabs as the building would require at five cents a linear foot.

Charles Church and Fred Worthen had the contract to provide building stone, which would be quarried only a mile and a half from the lodge site. The foremen would receive five dollars a day and the workers would be paid $3.20 a day. A progress summary sent to Union Pacific headquarters in Omaha on 15 July 1923 reported that the stone "breaks out from the quarry in the shape required for laying in the walls and it will not be necessary in any case to use a stone cutter upon it. [It] is to be laid up in a rough rustic style in cement and mortar, and can be done with the same common labor that is used for quarrying it."[49]

Construction started in the spring of 1924. By the end of that year the foundation work had been done, as had the skeletal frame construction for the building. By May 1925 the lodge, minus its stone facade, was virtually complete. It housed an office, lobby, dining room, kitchen, and bathroom facilities on the first floor. The second floor provided sleeping accommodations for overnight guests. Just when the stonework was done is not clear, but a wing was added the next year to provide more sleeping accommodations upstairs and a curio shop below; perhaps it was at that time that the stonework was done. In the summer of 1917 a recreation hall completed the structure. By that time five deluxe cabins and sixty-seven standard and economy cabins were also scattered among the trees, with concrete paths connecting them to the lodge. All electric wiring was placed underground. By 1929 there were ten more deluxe cabins added.

Bryce Canyon's status as a national park hung on three thorny issues: road access between it and Zion Canyon, acquisition by the federal government of the remainder of the state school land section on which the Syretts had first built their Tourist's Rest, and a change in the proposed name of Utah National Park to Bryce Canyon National Park. In a letter to a member of Congress dated 20 July 1927, Utah Governor George Dern stated "that the State of Utah will exchange the school section in question for some other section of land in order that Bryce Canyon may be made a national park." He also addressed the issue of the park name: first, changing the name to Utah National Park would negate the railroad's extensive and expensive advertising for Bryce Canyon National Monument; second, the name Utah National Park could just as well be used for any scenic attraction in the state; third, it implied that Utah only had one national park, when, in fact, Zion Canyon already had that designation.

Dern had no way of knowing that Utah would eventually have five national parks, three of which—Bryce, Canyonlands, and Capitol Reef—would occupy parts of Garfield County. The county would also embrace part of the Glen Canyon National Recreation Area and the Grand Staircase-Escalante National Monument. With the Zion Tunnel under construction and the state willing to trade the school

Fireplace and Welcome sign inside Ruby's Inn. (Courtesy Ruby's Inn)

land for another parcel, the way was cleared for Bryce Canyon to become a national park.

On 1 June 1925 Garfield County celebrated the opening of Bryce Canyon as a designated national park—although the area would not officially become one until 1928. Panguitch Mayor James M. Sargent met Governor Dern and his wife and hundreds of people from the north part of the state when they arrived in Panguitch for the festivities. After the appropriate welcome speech and response from the governor, the entourage, numbering 315 automobiles, moved toward Bryce Canyon. At the second tunnel in Red Canyon "they were halted by three brownies at a closed gate. These brownies, Kirk Daly, Thomas Marshall and Lavar Bateman were dressed in costume, turned up toes and all." From the top of the tunnel above the flower-bedecked gate hung a huge sign that read "Welcome to Utah's Fairyland." Then "fairies" appeared from everywhere, tying flowers and ribbons to the governor's car. One jumped onto the running board and asked Governor Dern, "Do you believe in fairies?" He replied that he did. "Then," she said, "Enter into Fairyland." The day, full of food, speeches, and entertainment, ended with a dance in

Panguitch. There would be other celebrations at Bryce Canyon, but none equaled the one that the local people planned and carried out that day.

In the summer of 1927 Assistant National Park Service Director Horace Albright laid out a plan for administrating Bryce Canyon in a letter to Steven Mather, first director of the National Park Service. Albright believed that Zion, Bryce Canyon, and Cedar Breaks could easily be combined into one administrative unit with headquarters in Zion. "One permanent ranger and possibly one or two temporary men in summer would be all that Bryce Canyon would need," he wrote. By January 1929 the implementation of Albright's plan had taken place, and "all rules and regulations for the government of Zion were made applicable for Bryce Canyon."[50]

The National Park Service hired Maurice Newton Cope as the ranger at Bryce. He had been a seasonal ranger there since 1925, working five months a year at Bryce and then moving his family to Tropic for the winter, where he taught school. In 1933 he became Bryce Canyon's first permanent park ranger, a position he held until he transferred to the warmer climes of Zion ten years later.

Grazing Rights in Bryce Canyon National Park

Not everyone embraced the national park status of Bryce Canyon. Stockmen had grazed their cattle and sheep in the park area since the 1860s, and those who held valid U.S. Forest Service grazing permits on that same land during the 1920s feared losing this valuable asset. They wanted the National Park Service to either allow continued grazing in the park or buy out their grazing rights. Permits had been issued to ranchers that extended into 1929, so the Park Service director gave the Forest Service authorization to oversee grazing in Bryce Canyon through that year.

In the transition years from 1928 to 1930 cooperation between the Park Service and Forest Service was particularly important. They put together a long-range "field agreement" in 1930 that guaranteed there would be "no change of existing [grazing] privileges to the detriment of current permittee[s]." There could, however, be no increase in the number of livestock permitted in areas contiguous to Bryce Canyon, and the Forest Service would continue to administer the permits and fees. Each permit holder would transfer 20 percent of his or her herd to other fee areas each year, with the elimination of grazing in the park as the long-range goal. President Herbert Hoover issued a proclamation in 1931 that softened the shift of grazing allotments by allowing stockmen the "right to drive their animals across the southwestern addition to the park."[51]

By 1935 grazing had been eliminated from Bryce Canyon's north-central region, and the two services moved ahead to faze it out in the rest of the park. The National Park Service encouraged the Grazing Service "to find nearby ranges on which stock then grazing in Bryce Canyon could be easily transferred." In 1940 only four park permit holders remained: Findlay Brothers, with 500 sheep for one month; John Johnson, 1,000 sheep for one month; Samuel Pollock, 824 sheep for one month; and the East Fork Cattle Association, with 802 cattle and horses for 10 percent of the year—most likely during the summer. Johnson sold his sheep in 1944 and went into cattle raising; the Findlays did the same in 1945, and Pollock sold his sheep in 1946, thus ending sheep grazing at Bryce Canyon. Johnson's cattle grazing came into question when he divided his forest grazing permit among several members of his family. The Forest Service policy prevented transfer of permits within the park area, and those permits were canceled. By 1953 only the Findlay Brothers (288 cattle) and the East Fork Cattle Association (484 cattle) retained grazing rights. The East Fork Cattle Association subsequently voluntarily phased out its cattle in the park.

The Findlay Brothers became somewhat of a problem. One of their main water sources was Riggs Spring on the Lower Podunk in the park, an area with very little forage and therefore subject to more long-range damage. After much trouble, the National Park Service appropriated funds in 1964 to pipe water from the spring to a trough located outside the park. The service then completed fencing the park boundary, thus ending livestock grazing in the park environs.[52]

Advancements in Garfield Communities

As mentioned, cooperative effort produced a fine new school for Cannonville. Just prior to that venture, area members of the LDS church worked together to build a beautiful new house of worship with a design reflecting both English and Scandinavian styles. The completed edifice included a chapel, classrooms, a bell tower, twenty tall, four-paned windows and a foot-pedal pump organ located on a raised dais where speakers and dignitaries sat. Artistic moldings and scroll work enhanced the exterior. Two years later, around 1912, residents also completed the Cannonville Recreation Hall. The townspeople pointed with pride to the main feature of the forty-by-sixty-foot building—its beautiful maple floor. The stage included rapidly changeable scenery panels perfect for theatrical and other productions.[53]

The people of Hatch had been gradually improving their own church building, which was virtually complete by 1910. However, the bishop, James B. Burrow, beginning in 1912, exhorted the ward members to finance the purchase of an organ. Many reminded him that no one in town could play an organ. Not to be swayed, Burrow had faith that if the members would contribute the Lord would provide an organist. By the time the new instrument was installed, William R. Riggs, Jr., had married Merle Snow of Kingston, and she became the organist.[54]

A little over a decade later, Hatch residents also contributed labor and money to build an amusement hall. In 1927 W.J. Peters, editor of the Garfield County News, suggested a celebration in honor of the building's completion and offered free advertising space in his paper to publicize the event. On 29 March people came in large numbers from neighboring towns to enjoy the concessions and dance. The following September the Panguitch LDS Stake Conference convened in the new social hall and church apostle Stephen L. Richards dedicated the building.[55]

After years of holding classes in homes or multipurpose one-room buildings, the school district decided to build a school for the children of Hatch. The district allocated one thousand dollars for the project. The two-room structure was designed and advertised for bid. William R. Riggs, Jr., received the contract to build the structure for $850. In the fall of 1913 the new school opened, with the versatile Riggs as the new principal and his new bride, Merle, as the teacher. This building served the town of Hatch in housing grades one through eight until it burned down in 1939.

The first schoolhouse built in Tropic in 1914. (Courtesy June Shakespear)

Throughout the county residents continued to focus on improving the education their young people received and upgrading area educational facilities. Elementary students in Escalante had been enjoying their new schoolhouse since returning from the Christmas holidays in January 1900. Voters in that town had agreed to bond the amount of $2,500 to finance the construction of the building, a brick, two-story edifice with room for four classrooms on each floor.[56] With Escalante's population increasing substantially, students would eventually fill up the space. Census figures indicate that by 1920 more than 1,000 people lived in the town.

The structure of education in the county changed substantially in 1915 when the state legislature mandated that all counties consolidate their schools into single districts. The following June Garfield County commissioners dissolved the old organization, created five precincts in the district, and also created a county board with a president and representatives from each precinct. J.B. Showalter served as the school district's first president. James Sargent represented Precinct 1, which included the north part of Panguitch and Bear Creek (Spry); Precinct

Garfield County's first high school opened to students in the fall of 1915.
(Utah State Historical Society)

2 included the south part of Panguitch, as well as Hillsdale and Hatch,
with Fred G. Gardner as its representative; Precinct 3 took in Tropic,
Cannonville, and Henrieville, with Maurice Cope from Tropic serving them; Marion King from Coyote (Antimony) represented Precinct
4, which also included the Widtsoe area; and Hyrum Gates served
from Precinct 5 and represented Escalante and Boulder.[57]

In 1914 construction on the first high school in the county began
in Panguitch. Previously, some high school classes had been held
within the community beginning in 1911. Garfield High School, a
commodious red-brick building on ten acres of land, opened to students at the beginning of the 1915–16 school year.[58] Other communities also desired high schools for their students. In 1920, Tropic
citizens rented and remodeled a building to begin their own high
school. Concerned that not enough students would enroll to justify
the county hiring a teacher, a town ordinance was passed requiring
school attendance for all students under eighteen years of age. June
Shakespear writes that "Even a few adults attended to make it go."[59]
Despite a leaking roof and a wood stove that smoked, Frank Riggs
taught twelve students in the building that year, and Tropic was
assured of a two-year high school for the future.

James Alvin Ott remembered being part of the first high school class held in 1920 and how great it felt to be among the "educational elite" when he completed first the ninth grade and then the tenth. He especially recalled the science field trips they took and the follow-up reports the students had to write. On one occasion, Riggs singled him out as having produced an exemplary report, boosting the ego of the shy lad.[60]

Ninth grade classes began for Escalante and Boulder students in 1920 in the local stone meetinghouse. There, too, facilities left much to be desired; however, their teacher Roy Lee reminded the young people, "Everything must have a beginning no matter how humble."[61] Of the twenty-two original students, six stayed in school to graduate in 1924. By then the school had moved to the old tithing office, where Lee, Cora Golding, and Principal Murray Shields taught all the classes except for sewing; Elsie Baker taught that course in the nearby William Mitchell home.

By the 1920s many Hatch families had become increasingly concerned about the education of their children beyond the eighth grade—a problem for most county parents. For a number of years many residents with children of secondary school age had resorted to sending them to such places as Beaver to attend academies during the winter. Some families even moved for the school year to towns with a high school, returning to their own homes in the spring. With the school year of 1926 less than a month away, parents from Hatch and Hillsdale took action. Sam Riggs agreed to put a good cover on his truck and transport the high school students to Panguitch each day. School Superintendent Fred Gardiner promised to help finance the endeavor on the condition that each student also pay part of the expense. Fourteen youths from the two areas pioneered the school bus transportation from Hatch to Garfield High School.[62]

Hatch parents also originated a hot-school-lunch program in the county. Students living in Panguitch could go home for the noon meal, but the commuters could not. Therefore Riggs purchased, then passed around from family to family, a one-gallon thermos jug to be filled with stew, chili, soup, or the like when it was their turn to furnish a hot dish. Each child brought his or her own bowl and spoon

Ruby's Inn during the 1930s. (Courtesy Ruby's Inn)

along with a sandwich. Once again, the pooling of resources and a spirit of cooperation provided a remedy to a recognized need.

Families in Antimony began bussing their secondary school children to Piute High School in Circleville beginning with the 1928–29 school year. Townspeople had Chester Allen and John Moore to thank for getting the service started, thus improving educational opportunities for their young people. Although parents had to pay for this transportation, they felt it worth the expense and was better than having to send their children away to further their education.

America during the 1920s has been characterized by some as the "Age of Play," a time when its citizens first became enamored with sports and sports heros. The automobile and especially the radio allowed more and more Americans to have access to sporting events. Such activities carried down to the local level throughout the country, and Garfield County did not deviate from the norm. Basketball became the acknowledged local favorite as high schools sprang up in county towns. Most of these institutions had relatively small student

Participants in the Utah Writers Project view Red Canyon about 1940. (Utah State Historical Society)

bodies, but they each still could put together a basketball team—all one needed was five players and a coach. Principal Murray Shields filled the position as the first basketball coach for Escalante's high school. He was followed shortly by Herb Adams, who fielded a team of seven players in 1925. Not long after that, the town also had a girls basketball team, coached by Bert Newman. Other schools in the county also soon had their own teams.

The crowning achievement in sports during this time period, however, came in 1924 when the Garfield High School boys basketball team went to Chicago to play in the All American tournament. To reach that pinnacle, the team won the district championship in Richfield and then went on to Salt Lake City and became state champions. Supporters held a pep rally for the team in Panguitch to help raise money for the trip. Four members of the team held an American flag by each corner and "passed [it] through the crowd and collected $1,000 in ten or fifteen minutes." Before the night was over, a total of $1,500 was raised "to send them on their way."[63]

Rudolph Church coached the team and Ben Lee managed it.

Team members included Captain Dwayne Henrie, Hayden Church, George Cooper, Clem Davis, Jesse Evans, Clyde Meecham, Elmo Richards, and Darrel Worthen. They won two games in the tournament and officials chose Henrie and Cooper as "All American Stars." The team from rural southern Utah received quite a write-up in Chicago newspapers. As one resident remembered, "I don't know of anything that ever happened in the schools of Panguitch that created as much excitement as this did."[64]

The enjoyment of sports was not confined to the high schools. Local LDS church congregations sponsored sports activities, and many southern Utah towns supported community teams in both basketball and baseball. Elijah Goulding coached one of these teams. He relocated his family to Henrieville in 1911 and eventually made his home in Widtsoe and Pine Lake. While there he began a town baseball team. One of his sons belonged to the team, his daughter Dessie was scorekeeper, and daughter Caroline Evelyn made the uniforms for the team.

The Growth of Widtsoe and Johns Valley

During this period, the community of Winder (Widtsoe), located on the west side of Escalante Mountain, was growing rapidly. Sawmills built in the canyon east of the townsite furnished the lumber necessary to construct the needed buildings. By 1916 the community boasted a social hall, two hotels, four stores, a confectionery, and a sawed-log, three-room meetinghouse with a bell that summoned townspeople to church meetings and school. Although this structure burned down in 1919, local citizens built a new, larger multifunctional facility in its place. The town also got a post office in 1916. The following year the postal service suggested the town change its name, since it was not the only community in the state called Winder. Residents settled on Widtsoe, named for dry-farming expert and future LDS apostle John A. Widtsoe, "who had helped in providing counsel on types of crops to be grown in this climate and altitude."[65]

As Widtsoe's population increased substantially, improvements on the mountain road to Escalante encouraged regular mail service between the two towns. George Davies procured the contract to carry the mail. A widower who had helped raise ten children, he moved from Escalante to Widtsoe, which was more central to incoming mail deliveries. *The Escalante Story* gives insight into the difficulties this sturdy man encountered:

> In the winter he had a carrier meet him at the foot of the moun-
> tain above Liston's ranch and bring back the Escalante mail, Davis
> [Davies] handling the difficult mountain stretch himself. He used
> horses for the first four years. With the beginning of a new con-
> tract he moved to Junction, and began using trucks. The road,
> though improved . . . changed to mud with every storm. [It] was
> rough and the trucks broke down, so that George and his son,
> Jimmy, had troubles.[66]

The U.S. Forest Service relocated the local office to Widtsoe from Panguitch beginning in 1919. For a time some even mentioned the possibility of moving the county seat to the young but thriving community. By 1920 about 1,100 people lived in Widtsoe and the surrounding homesteads. Twenty-five blocks, most with four homes per block, made up the town and surrounded a central city park. Residents also anticipated development at Pine Lake, a recreational site for Johns Valley settlers. Men set to work enlarging the lake and building an earthen dam to supply water for better irrigation of the Widtsoe lots and for a large ranch a new developer had purchased.

Just four miles to the north and slightly west of Widtsoe another colony began in about 1915. The settlers called their community Henderson in honor of William J. Henderson, a resident of Johns Valley who donated some of his land for a town center. Several home-steads increased the population of the settlement, and it too had a combination church/school building and a post office.[67]

As in other agriculture areas, the farmers of Widtsoe, Henderson, and other areas of Johns Valley suffered the uncertainties of nature and the market. But their situation was complicated by the high alti-tude and an apparent ten-year climatic cycle that produced either an abundance of water or an almost complete lack thereof—even insuf-ficient for dry farming. Residents recalled the good times when "the whole of Johns Valley [was] a waving field of grain," and when "alfalfa grew splendidly, also enormous crops of head lettuce" were grown there and shipped to Salt Lake City, Bryce Canyon Lodge, Cedar Breaks, and Grand Canyon.[68] At times Widtsoe's grain crop was greater than that grown in the rest of the county combined.

However, Frederika Hermansen Clinch remembered one of the dry periods. During the summer of 1920 they had no rain and the "crops burned in the fields." She recalled "the lines of worry beneath the dust on my father's face." One night she awoke to the sound of the wind blowing,

> flashes of lightning and rumbles of thunder. It was just getting light when the rain started to fall. I ran outside clapping my hands and singing. . . . Mother stood in the doorway and watched, her long braids hanging down over her shoulders. . . . That year there was a good harvest and the grain bins were nearly filled to the top of the cabin. There was just enough room for us to crawl between the grain and the roof. We slept on the grain, on straw ticks.[69]

These wild climatic swings caused Widtsoe first to produce a spectacular display of rapid advancement and then decline.

William F. Holt thought he could bring prosperity to Johns Valley. He arrived in 1924 from California, where he had made a reputation for himself in helping to irrigate the Imperial Valley. The people of Widtsoe and surrounding areas hoped he could do something similar for their region. Holt established a new community north of Widtsoe and Henderson which he named Osiris—for what reason, no one seems to know, but it proved to be apt: Osiris is the Egyptian underworld god who was killed and dismembered, and the town named after him had a short life-span.

Holt's development included a creamery (to which he induced many area farmers to ship their milk), a flour mill, several homes, a telephone exchange, and a ranch with a fine home, one-room cabins where his employees lived, granaries, and acres of land that yielded a substantial grain harvest during good years. Most importantly, he built a water-storage pond at Pine Lake and flumed water seven miles down to the valley. The venture, however, in which he invested hundreds of thousands of dollars did not succeed.

The town struggled until many settlers driven by drought from Widtsoe relocated there in 1920. The town then blossomed for a short time. However, groundwater was insufficient during drought years, and high-altitude lettuce proved to be the only consistently reliable crop in the valley. Holt, along with many other settlers, pulled up stakes and moved on.[70]

Tough times lay ahead for other Garfield County towns, as well. The Great Depression, World War II, and a restructuring of the livestock industry—always the county's economic mainstay—soon challenged the character, ingenuity, and will of Garfield citizens.

ENDNOTES

1. Effel Harmon Burrow Riggs, *History of Hatch, Utah, and Associated Towns Asay and Hillsdale,* 126–27.

2. M. Lane Warner, *Grass Valley 1873–1976: A History of Antimony and Her People,* 31.

3. Riggs, *History of Hatch,* 126–27. Riggs recalled this happening in June 1910. However, on 20 May the Halleys Comet came its closest to the Earth, 14 million miles away, and it is believed that the next day the Earth passed through the comet's tail.

4. See Riggs, *History of Hatch,* 118–23.

5. Quote from the *Panguitch Progress,* 29 May 1914 in Riggs, *History of Hatch,* 124–25; Ida Chidester and Eleanor Bruhn, *Golden Nuggets of Pioneer Days,* 311–12.

6. Riggs, *History of Hatch,* 246.

7. George W. Thompson "Cannonville History," 25.

8. Ibid., 28.

9. Vera Sevy Peterson Fotheringham, interview with Vivian L. Talbot, July 1996, Salt Lake City, tape in possession of authors.

10. Jean H. Henderickson's seventh grade class, "The Morrill Tragedy," Parowan, Utah, 1959 typescript, 7, copy in possession of authors courtesy of Barbara B. Burt. Information for this section comes from this source and from genealogy information in possession of author Linda K. Newell.

11. "The Morrill Tragedy," 7, 13.

12. Ibid., 7.

13. Ibid., 7–8. Rebecca Carson Miller visited Jean Hendrickson's seventh grade Parowan class in 1959 to tell the students what she remembered of her sister Emma's ordeal at Blue Springs. Much of the account here is taken from that section of the written class report.

14. Ibid., 9. The heading for this section of the document reads: "Copied by Barbara B. Burt April 16, 1976, from papers written in Clara

Matheson Benson's own writing, February 17, 1972, age 77, Parowan, Utah."

15. Ibid., 5.

16. Chidester and Bruhn, *Golden Nuggets,* 63–64, 292.

17. "History of John Whitehead Seaman," in possession of Helen Seaman Linford, Cedar City.

18. Virginia Smith, "History," 1983, 1, copy obtained by authors from Teora Willis of Henrieville.

19. Wallace Ott, interview, 1993.

20. June Shakespear, "Tropic," 4.

21. Nethella Griffin Woolsey, *The Escalante Story: 1875–1964,* 125.

22. Ibid., 188.

23. Lenora Hall LeFevre, *The Boulder Country and Its People,* 224.

24. Chidester and Bruhn, *Golden Nuggets,* 292–93.

25. J.W. Humphrey, "Notes, Comments, and Letters," as quoted in Nicholas Scrattish, *Historical Resource Study: Bryce Canyon National Park,* 15.

26. See Scrattish, *Bryce Canyon National Park,* 15–18.

27. Chidester and Bruhn, *Golden Nuggets,* 292–94; Scrattish, *Bryce Canyon National Park,* 16–19.

28. James A. Ott and Virginia S. Ott, "A History of the James Alvin and Virginia Spencer Ott Family," 16–17. Copy obtained from Marilyn Murdock. Herbert Hoover served President Wilson as head of food administration.

29. Janet M. Johnson Ott, "A Sketch of the Life of Joseph Alma Ott," 3.

30. Warner, *Grass Valley,* 30, 35.

31. "Eda Willis Quilter," 2, copy obtained by authors from Nancy Twitchell.

32. Woolsey, *Escalante Story,* 334–37.

33. Chidester and Bruhn, *Golden Nuggets,* 266–67.

34. Shakespear, "Tropic," 6.

35. Janet M. Ott, "Joseph Alma Ott." Ott evidently had been exposed to the disease about the time he was discharged from the army and only contracted a mild form of influenza. One of his army companions from Tropic, Woodruff Pollock, died from the disease.

36. June Shakespear writes that no one in town actually died of the disease. The Utah Bureau of Vital Statistics does not have a record of the number of deaths by community for that time period. It also could be that

Shakespear's and Ott's understanding of who actually lived within the confines of Tropic varies.

37. "Eda Willis Quilter."

38. Warner, *Grass Valley,* 35, 101.

39. Quoted in Karl C. Sandberg, "Telling the Tales and Telling the Truth: Writing the History of Widtsoe," *Dialogue: A Journal of Mormon Thought* 26 (Winter 1993): 99.

40. Ibid.

41. Chidester and Bruhn, *Golden Nuggets,* 340–41.

42. LeFevre, *Boulder Country,* 217–18.

43. Scrattish, *Bryce Canyon National Park,* 18.

44. Ibid., 21–2.

45. Ibid., 19–22. See also Chidester and Bruhn, *Golden Nuggets,* 294–95.

46. Scrattish, *Bryce Canyon National Park,* 61–73. The cost of the roads in Zion Canyon alone (including the tunnel) was more than $1.4 million. Another $456,000 of federal and state funds built the sixteen-mile section from Zion to Mount Carmel.

47. Ibid., 48–52.

48. Chidester and Bruhn, *Golden Nuggets,* 296–97.

49. Scrattish, *Bryce Canyon National Park,* 112–13.

50. Ibid.

51. Ibid., 108–9.

52. Ibid., 111.

53. Thompson, "Cannonville History," 29, 33.

54. Riggs, *History of Hatch,* 147.

55. Ibid., 189–90.

56. Woolsey, *Escalante Story,* 275–77.

57. Ibid., 277–79, and Chidester and Bruhn, *Golden Nuggets,* 78.

58. Woolsey, *Escalante Story,* 277–79 and Chidester and Bruhn, *Golden Nuggets,* 78–79.

59. Shakespear, "Tropic," 5.

60. Ott and Ott, "A History of the Ott Family," 15.

61. As quoted in Woolsey, *Escalante Story,* 282.

62. Riggs, *History of Hatch,* 226–27.

63. Chidester and Bruhn, *Golden Nuggets,* 84.

64. Ibid., 83.

65. Stephen L. Carr, *The Historical Guide to Utah Ghost Towns,* 122.

66. Woolsey, *Escalante Story,* 200. George Elisha Davies's son Wilford

told the authors that he had seen his father sign his name both Davies and Davis, which may be why it appears as Davis in the Woolsey book. The correct family name, however, is Davies. George Davies had been the first child born in Kanarrah, Iron County, in June 1861. After moving to Junction in 1919 he married his second wife, Emma Carson Morrill, widow of John Morrill, who froze to death near Blue Springs in 1916.

67. Carr, *Guide to Utah Ghost Towns,* 122.

68. Chidester and Bruhn, *Golden Nuggets,* 143.

69. In Sandberg, "Writing the History of Widtsoe," 95–96.

70. George A. Thompson, *Some Dreams Die: Utah's Ghost Towns and Lost Treasures,* 87; John W. Van Cott, *Utah Place Names,* 283.

CHAPTER 11

THE GREAT DEPRESSION TO POST-WAR RECOVERY

It was called the Great Depression, "great" referring to its magnitude, duration, and the social change that the economic depression of the 1930s wrought upon the United States and much of the industrialized world. The use of "great" also set apart that economic crisis from all others the United States had previously endured. Residents of Garfield County certainly felt its impact, but their experience differed from that of those living in more heavily populated and industrialized centers of the nation. Living in close proximity to supportive extended family members and being able to produce some of their own food sustained local citizens during those trying years. So too did cooperation on community projects and participation in recreational activities—both the traditional home-made variety and new, innovative ones.

County residents, however, also took advantage of relief programs offered by the federal government. President Franklin D. Roosevelt's New Deal, conceived to remedy the emergency, created an altered economic focus of government involvement in the lives of its citizens and a reorganization of the infrastructure in Garfield

County. This included the relocation of most citizens of one of the county's communities, thus hastening that town's demise. Additionally, World War II, which helped pull the nation and the county out of the Depression, introduced new challenges and a transformation of county life, as the population of the county declined considerably during the 1940s.

After the Stock Market Crash

For most residents of Garfield County the initial huge crash of the nation's stock market on 29 October 1929 held very little meaning. But the ensuing lean years of the Great Depression filtered down into their day-to-day lives substantially. Similar to most farming areas in the United States (except those affected by the Dust Bowl drought conditions), a majority of the people could raise the products with which to feed themselves. Utahns did this in spite of suffering through their own drought during portions of the early 1930s, 1934 generally being the worst year.[1]

The only bank in the county, the State Bank of Garfield, closed its doors within two years after the stock market crash, causing much hardship to investors and area stockmen.[2] Because many in the county lost their savings, they had to make do with old equipment and could not expand their land holdings. Even if they could raise additional crops or animals, markets for them were scarce or nonexistent. George Thompson recalled that times were indeed hard for many locals: "Some of the poor folks in Cannonville were forced to eat animal feed to survive. Ground wheat and cottonseed cake were common in the diet.... [W]ere it not for home produced fruit, vegetables, and meat the people could not have survived."[3]

Each individual old enough to remember can offer insight regarding this era. Alma and Mabel Ott of Tropic had not been married many years before the stock market crash. In recognizing her daughter-in-law's sacrifice and contribution to their family's well-being, Alma's mother wrote:

> There has been a depression on and it has been very hard to get the necessities of life. When I think of the nice comfortable home Mabel left and went out on the farm and worked side by side with

Tropic's new LDS Church in 1932. (Courtesy June Shakespear)

> her husband, helping him make a home and gain a livelihood from
> the soil! She has never failed in doing her part.[4]

People survived by helping each other out and by using the
barter system—a situation not so different from pioneer days. Others
simply made do with what they had until their situations improved.
Luetta Partner from Henrieville married Orlo Davenport in July
1928. They had begun to raise their family just when the Depression
hit. She wrote of the hard times they experienced living in a small
house at Orlo's homestead: "[We] lived mostly on boiled sagehens,
had no salt and no grease to fry them in. One day we walked up
where the cows had a salt lick and got a chunk off it to use for salt."
Eventually, after living for a time at Red Canyon, where Orlo worked
part-time at the sawmill and on road construction, the little family
moved to Panguitch. He secured sufficient lumber to build his family
a home of their own. They moved in as "soon as our frame was up
and boards over the top," Luetta wrote in her autobiography. "It had
no doors on and we put old quilts up to the windows. It rained quite

a bit that spring and summer of 1933. I would hold quilts up over the kids some nights to keep them dry. We finally got some shingles."[5]

Government statistics also testify to the hard times felt by the county's citizens. Garfield ranked second in the state in per-capita federal relief expenditures between 1932 and 1936. Many asked why this should be the case; the answers varied. In 1938, sociologists at the University of Utah came to some conclusions as to why the relief problem was so great in the county. To begin with, they found the region to be "poorly adapted for agricultural purposes, as less than one percent of the total land surface [had] even been sowed to crops and harvested, due principally to a lack of sufficient water." The data they collected also indicated that "increasing competitive individualism, decreasing co-operation, unintelligent land use, very limited natural resources, [and] an excessively high rate of natural increase" rendered the county unable to withstand a "prolonged depression."[6] County residents obviously didn't like such conclusions, and anecdotal evidence and some later natural resource development challenges some of the conclusions.

Soon after the onset of the Depression, the LDS church introduced its own welfare program to help meet the needs of its members during the economic crisis. However, evidence indicates it had little impact on the LDS families that made up more than 99 percent of Garfield's population. By 1939 the program had failed to remove anyone in the county from government relief.[7] Whether this was due to failings in the church program or to an unwillingness of county residents to leave government relief benefits is uncertain. Like many throughout the nation, most county residents only began to overcome their economic woes with America's entry into World War II.

Some Garfield communities had to deal with additional challenges during these hard economic times. The people of Antimony lost two ecclesiastical leaders within three days of each other in the summer of 1931. The first counselor in the ward bishopric, Mont Chesney Riddle, was helping the second counselor, Herbert S. Gleave, put up his hay when a rope suddenly broke and Riddle was severely injured.[8] A little over a week later he died. Meanwhile, Bishop Lawrence Gates suffered a ruptured appendix and died soon after. His funeral took place the day after Riddle's.

Almost a year to the day after these untimely deaths, a damaging flood struck Grass Valley. The home of Levi King, Jr., in Antimony suffered the worst damage, when mud and water thirty-four inches deep inundated the house. Many other homes also sustained considerable damage. The deluge either covered or swept away fences and sheds, washed out roads, bridges, and canals, and destroyed many crops. Damages were estimated to be in the tens of thousands of dollars.

Even more tragically, within six months of the flood outbreaks of spinal meningitis occurred in the community. The disease affected several families, causing death, deafness, and other afflictions to victims. Archie George and Stella Stoker Gleave and their three children had been in Antimony only a year when the epidemic hit their family. Their third child, Kenneth, died first. Archie described their ordeal:

> We were heart broken and I thought Stell would lose her mind, so I took her, Erwin, and Eldon [their two older children] to the sheep herd with me. While we were camped out with the sheep Eldon got spinal meningitis. We had the doctor come and he gave Eldon treatments; he tapped his spine and really worked hard to save his life. It left Eldon deaf. This was almost more than we could take. We later had our fourth baby boy, little David Phil. He died with pneumonia when he was thirteen months old.[9]

The Gleaves, like their neighbors and others in the county, came from pioneer stock and viewed tribulation much the same as their forebears did: one must get past personal tragedy and move on. Archie Gleave and his family moved away from Antimony for a time. When they returned, he played an important role in local politics and public service positions.

In Escalante the people took advantage of the ready labor supply during the Depression to get a new church built. A local dance hall had served the community for church services for some time. After securing a lot from the Twitchell family and clearing it of house, barn, and fruit trees, the community held a ground-breaking ceremony for their church in 1929. The men hauled rock and gravel to the building site, as well as bringing in the wood needed for heating the brick kilns.

The following spring construction work began. Perry Liston took charge of making bricks and Samuel Alvey molded the clay bricks to be fired. Willard Heaps managed the excavation, W.J. Osborn oversaw the freighting of cement from Marysvale to Escalante, and Arthur O. McInelly supervised general construction and roofing. Will Davis directed men in laying the brick and joined with Earl Woolsey in the carpentry, plastering, and painting of the structure. Members of the Relief Society presidency—Margaret Mitchell, Sally May King, Polly Spencer, and LaVern Woolsey—sponsored a ward banquet in the basement dining room of the nearly completed building on New Year's Day, 1932. They used the money earned from the dinner to furnish the kitchen and Relief Society room of the new structure. Ward clerk Earl Woolsey, together with Bishop Lorenzo Griffin and his counselors, Parley Porter and Ushur L. Spencer, proudly hosted the stake quarterly conference on 8 August 1932, at which time Apostle Richard R. Lyman dedicated the Escalante North Ward chapel.[10]

Other communities also completed new buildings. The previous year, on 31 May 1931, church members in Tropic dedicated a new chapel, which would serve that community for more than fifty years.[11]

Boulder residents found themselves with an unexpected building project. On 21 February 1935 school janitor Lorin Moosman lit fires in the two wood-burning box heaters before sun-up and then returned home. He wanted the building to be warm when the students arrived, but there was more heat than he bargained for. Nearby residents soon saw black smoke and flames coming from the schoolhouse. With telephone communication, word of the catastrophe spread almost as fast as the fire. When the crowd gathered, all they could do was watch the structure burn to the ground, unable to salvage one thing; "even the bell was found cracked open on one side when the rubbish was cleared away," wrote one.[12] For the rest of the year Boulder children attended school in the front room and kitchen of Chris Moosman's home.

Meanwhile, construction began on a new school. Arthur McInelly, Sr., of Escalante built the structure and David M. Woolsey and Earl Woolsey painted the building. When school began in the fall of 1935, Golda Peterson taught her class again in the Moosman home and Thomas Memmott taught the upper four grades in the Relief Society room of the church. However, by November teachers and students moved into the newly completed schoolhouse. Another room was added to the edifice in 1941.

Simultaneously with building a new schoolhouse, members of the LDS church in Boulder decided to erect a new chapel. Half the money for construction came from church headquarters in Salt Lake City. Each family was assessed an amount towards the building's completion that they could either pay in cash or in donated labor. Chris Moosman deeded one-quarter acre of land in central Boulder for the new church. Ernest Jackson of Teasdale secured the contract to build it. Much of the material had to be trucked in over the East End Road, which itself was still under construction by the Civilian Conservation Corps (CCC). Workers cooperated in assisting all travelers as they came to sections where men and equipment were working. With everyone's help and cooperation, the church's workers completed the basement by February 1936 and finished the $30,000 structure one year later, in February 1937.

The following August the local LDS stake conference convened in the new structure and Apostle Charles A. Callas dedicated the building for worship. That fall the community turned a work party into a town party. Men hauled in loads of wood for the meetinghouse furnace, and afterwards everyone sat down to a supper prepared by the women, Everyone then attended a dance in the structure's new recreation hall.[13]

Garfield County residents did not forget how to have fun even though resources were scarce. Ruby Moore remembered how the citizens of Henrieville and Cannonville took turns hosting weekly dances. According to custom, as people walked into the dance hall,

> the men went to the west side of the hall and the ladies to the east side. When . . . the music started playing, the men came across to their wives and the single men to their girl friends and started that way. Then they took turns dancing with everyone. . . . There was a dance manager so everyone had to act just right or they were escorted outside. . . . At the end of the dance the musicians started playing the Home Waltz and the boys found their girl friends and

The old showhouse (left) in Escalante was built by Lorin Griffin in 1938. In 1998 the Utah State Historical Society provided a grant to assist with the restoration of the showhouse facade. (Utah State Historical Society)

> the married men their wives and always danced that dance together.[14]

Few people in those communities had automobiles at that time, so they usually went by horse-drawn wagon to the dances. The girls often brought quilts in the wintertime to pad the bottoms of the wagons and to snuggle under.

A new form of entertainment helped county residents escape momentarily from the Depression-induced poverty. With the exception of Panguitch, no Garfield community had a movie house, but that did not keep residents from enjoying the cinema. Beginning in the fall of 1929, Kay Heywood came to Cannonville each week—weather permitting—with a movie projector powered by a small gasoline generator. The audience thrilled to the popular silent films of the day. They gained admittance by producing a dime or some product of their industry such as a squash, a bottle of fruit, or a freshly baked loaf of bread. George Thompson wrote that "one woman I talked with remembers picking a quart of dry beans up off the ground, to get a show ticket."[15]

Tropic had a similar situation. Levi Bybee would jack up the wheel of his old Model T and attach a small generator to it to run the silent films. June Shakespear remembered: "In February of 1934, the new town hall was filled to capacity as the first talking picture show was presented—'Sunset Pass' by Zane Grey."[16]

Escalante viewers attended the Star Dance Hall to see the silent movies. They also used a gasoline engine to power the projector. The films often would break, and if one couldn't be repaired immediately those in attendance received a ticket to come back next time. Audiences especially enjoyed a serial entitled *Stingeree* with Francis Bushman and could hardly wait for the next installment. Unfortunately the hall in Escalante was torn down in 1934, and the residents of both Escalante and Boulder had to wait four years for Lorin Griffin to build a new theater before they could once again attend picture shows.

Music had always played an important role in Garfield County society, whether it was for dances, funerals, church meetings, or patriotic celebrations. In the mid-1930s a new organization brought together ten women who shared a fondness for music and who produced a definitely new sound. These women formed the Panguitch Rhythm Band in 1936. The original members of the band included Eve Bell, Belle Boyter, Elinore Bruhn, Bell Cooper, Cora Cooper, Florence Houston, Isabell Ipson, Dean LeFevre, Rate Owens, and Lois Seaman-Maloney. Using tambourines, kazoos, washboards, sticks, triangles, drums, combs, tin plates, wooden spoons, always accompanied by a piano, these musicians played traditional songs as well as the latest compositions. The band proved to be an enduring organization, and it continues to perform to the present day. The women dress in vintage costumes and spruce up their instruments with ribbons, lace, and bows. No one can remember when they first played in the 24 July parade, seated on a decorated float, but the group has continued to appear in the parade each year.[17]

William Isabell had a hand in helping some Garfield residents forget their Depression woes during the Prohibition era. A Canadian, Isabell drifted into Boulder about the year 1930 after a short stay in Escalante. He established a camp for himself at Salt Gulch, where he installed a distillery near the bank of the Sweetwater inside a cellar that had belonged to the Gresham family many years before. He successfully—and stealthily—peddled his "good grade of whiskey" on horseback and pack mules to customers in Boulder, Escalante, and Wayne County despite frequent visits by Sheriff Frank Haycock of Panguitch, who could never seem to find sufficient evidence to justify arresting Isabell. For awhile he provided welcome refreshment across two counties, but his business ceased to thrive after national repeal of the Eighteenth Amendment to the Constitution by passage of the Twenty-first Amendment, ending Prohibition in 1932.[18]

Garfield residents could always find simple and inexpensive pleasure and recreation in their natural surroundings. Such untamed beauty attracted a young man from California during the mid-1930s. Everett Ruess—artist, writer and adventurer—spent several days at Bryce Canyon in November 1934. After spending a weekend in Tropic at the home of Maurice and De Esta Cope he left on Monday morning leading two burros. He walked down the street and east out the lane to Losee Valley toward the Pink Cliffs and on to Escalante. After having dinner with Clayton Porter at his sheep camp near the confluence of the Escalante and Colorado rivers, twenty-year-old Ruess left to explore the Indian cliff dwellings in the canyons south of the Escalante Desert and along the Colorado River. This was the last anyone saw of him.

Gale Bailey of Escalante later found Ruess's burros at the head of Davis Gulch where the young man had corraled them. The animals had little feed and no water, indicating that their owner had intended to return soon. Ruess's parents came to Escalante to help local citizens search for their son. But his disappearance has remained a mystery. In 1950 a book about Ruess, *On Desert Trails with Everett Ruess*, was published. It included some of his pictures, letters, and poems. Since that time Ruess and his works have increased in popularity and he has become the object of much interest. His life, his art, and his writings are the subjects of several publications.[19]

Garfield County and New Deal Programs

Measures embodied in the various programs of the Roosevelt administration's New Deal—most of which produced positive results—had a profound influence on life in Garfield County. Many agencies of President Franklin D. Roosevelt's administration became involved in the county, such as the Rural Electrification Administration (REA), the Works Progress Administration (WPA), and the Resettlement Administration (RA), but conservation programs perhaps had the most widespread effect. Some of these started when forest reserves came under federal government control around the turn of the century. Throughout most of the 1930s the Civilian Conservation Corps (CCC) was a popular and effective program that focused on conservation and reclamation projects.

The initial goal of the New Deal was to put people to work. The government paid men to reseed ranges and forests and to build range fences and flood-control structures, roads, and trails. One Cannonville resident recalled that they even built outhouses according to government specifications.[20] Perhaps the most appreciated projects involved establishing dependable culinary water systems. With the founding of county settlements in pioneer times, getting water to farms and residences was the most important priority. Culinary water for home use remained somewhat inadequate, however, until implementation of some New Deal projects.

Escalante residents had made strides to improve the situation by constructing cement-lined cisterns to store water for home consumption and using gasoline-powered pumps or gravity flow to pipe the water to individual houses. With the help of the WPA, town leaders saw an opportunity to improve their water system. They secured $90,000 from the federal government and put hometown men to work earning WPA wages of two to four dollars a day. Roy Lee spearheaded the plan to pipe water from mountain springs located some eighteen miles up Pine Creek Canyon. The town board under Mayor Alvey Wright secured permission from the Pine Creek Irrigation Company on 25 February 1934 to purchase needed water from Deep Creek and the springs that fed it. After trench digging, mostly by hand, and pipe laying through rocky hills and mountainsides, project superintendent Howard Clark of Panguitch brought the enterprise to a successful conclusion two years later. Local leaders held an impressive dedicatory service for the new water system on 23 May 1936. For almost three decades it delivered economical water that was reported by locals to be "pure, soft, and sparkling with no disagreeable flavor."[21]

Antimony also took advantage of the opportunity to secure a culinary water system through the WPA. A few people in the town had wells which provided pure water, but prior to 1938 most residents carried buckets of ditch water for household use. In September of that year WPA workers began laying pipe from a spring near Coyote Canyon. The community bonded for $20,000 for the project, while the federal government paid labor costs. When the project became operational only the thirty-five residences within the town proper benefited. Those living on the bench and in other outlying areas either had to continue carrying water or dig additional wells. With the outbreak of World War II there were no funds to extend the system.[22]

Even though the people of Tropic had built a canal long before to bring East Fork water to their community, they felt a need to build a reservoir. However, two early attempts resulted in dam failures. In November 1935 work began on a new reservoir as a federal relief project.[23] Robert A. Middleton of Henrieville was a foreman before becoming superintendent of the project. The completion of the reservoir helped residents somewhat, but problems of too much or too little water continued, with heavy seasonal rains followed by dry periods. A later installation of sprinkler-irrigation systems throughout the valley has remedied the situation for the most part. Tropic residents also benefited from the completion of a "Scout House" built by WPA workers.

During the mid-1930s when the unemployment picture appeared critical to county leaders, commission members headed by Walter B. Daly applied to the WPA for help in building an airport. After land was purchased from James P. Cameron on the East Fork of the Sevier River near Bryce Canyon, workers built roads and cleared the land for the hanger and runway. Daly and fellow county commissioners Jennings Allen and Sam Pollock supervised both the design and the construction. Ruby Syrett brought tractors from his Ruby's Inn resort and graded the 7,586-foot-long runway.

Civilian Conservation Corps workers cut the native ponderosa logs used to build the hanger as part of a program to control a black beetle infestation that was ravaging forests of southern Utah. Volunteers split and sawed the logs at the East Fork Sevier River sawmill and then hauled them to the airport site using horse teams and wagons. With much of the building labor also donated, the structure began to take the form of a barn, with "sheds" on either side. The log construction provided an intricate network of large timbers, many with the bark still on them, which supported a gabled tin roof. The finished structure measured 45 by 45 feet, with a row of double-sashed windows letting in light on both sides. Completed in 1937, wrote one,

> the building is truly an oddity, as many pilots from all over the world will testify. The barn-like construction of the native materials reflects the ranching-agricultural background of the men who built it. Having no previous experience in designing or building an airplane hanger, they built in the style they know with what they had.[24]

After the hanger was completed, the Lions Club of Panguitch hosted a countywide celebration and dance within the facility. This successful money-raising gala inspired the Lions and other civic organizations to hold similar events annually at the Bryce Canyon Airport to raise money for public projects.

The WPA funded labor for another building project that spawned a later enterprise. The people of Panguitch wanted to build a civic center. After they hosted several money-making projects, work on the building began. For various reasons, however, the project was abandoned sometime during the Depression. Later, after World War II, when the economy improved, the Panguitch Junior Chamber of Commerce began efforts to turn the incomplete building into a hospital. Members challenged each family in the county to donate twenty-five dollars to the project. Other civic clubs joined in the fundraising. They received a release from the federal government for the earlier work done by the WPA workers. Carnivals, auctions, races, and other events brought in thousands of dollars for the hospital. Finally the LDS church matched the collected funds to complete the facility. On 12 November 1946 LDS Presiding Bishop LeGrand

The Carnegie Library in Panguitch, 1938. (Utah State Historical Society)

Richards offered the dedicatory prayer at services conducted by local stake president Samuel Pollock.

The WPA provided another benefit for the schoolchildren of Boulder. In 1935 the agency launched a nationwide hot-lunch program in the schools. Surplus foods such as dried peas and beans came from the WPA to make soup. The school board furnished the dishes, utensils, and other equipment. In Boulder, Gertrude Moosman and Preston Porter cooked hot soup in Moosman's kitchen and served it to the town's fifty-five schoolchildren to supplement their sandwiches brought from home. The children either paid ten cents for the soup or brought meat and vegetables from home to contribute to the pot. As the government began to purchase a greater variety of surplus foods, the school-lunch program expanded until the children received a complete, well-balanced, hot meal. Schools in Antimony, Escalante, Panguitch, and Tropic also participated in the program.[25]

Public Health Nurses

The Public Health Nursing Service, administered and funded under New Deal agencies, became another program that benefited Garfield county children as well as adults when county nurses were appointed. These nurses had many duties, including monitoring the

general health of schoolchildren and securing needed medical attention for them. The government supplied each nurse with a five-gal-
lon can of cod liver oil to be used to dispense to needy families
without charge. Nurses also assisted local doctors and held pediatric
clinics in each community.

The first county nurse appointed in 1934 was Nelda Henderson.
Many competent women followed after her, serving in the various
towns.[26] Shanna Goulding of Henrieville described her duties—
which were typical—in this capacity:

> During those ten years I was in every home in town at different
> times for different illnesses, giving "shots," dispensing sulfa tablets
> or helping during the stress times of someone's loved one being
> called home. Sometimes I was the one to take patients to the doc-
> tor.[27]

Rural Electrification

Panguitch was the first Garfield town to have electricity. Citizens
received the service and hook-ups through the Teluride Power
Company after it reached Circleville in 1910–11. As more and more
lovely brick homes graced community streets throughout the county,
lighting them by modern means became a priority. Homeowners in
Escalante exported locally produced cheese to Salt Lake City, often
receiving in exchange barrels of coal oil and small glass lamps.
Eventually gas lights were installed in some homes.

By 1909 several Escalante citizens had organized a stock company
to finance the construction of a new flour mill to replace the now-
defunct one built by Isaac Riddle in 1892. The mill, east of town, had
been run by steam power, fueled by coal. In late 1919 the Escalante
Light and Power Company brought electricity to the town by
installing a generator at the mill, thus transforming it into an electric
plant. P. Orin Barker served as the firm's first president, Peter Shurtz
as vice-president, Joseph Larsen as secretary-treasurer, and F.L. Fisher
as director. They now could power the gristmill with an electrically
charged generator. By March 1920 the company had installed poles
and electric wiring to some local homes. Electrician Neils M.
Peterson of Richfield oversaw the operation, and lights were on the
following year, in April 1921. However, residents found they couldn't

yet put away their kerosene lamps for good. This early foray into electric power for Escalante had mixed success, but the pioneering effort anticipated better things in time.[28]

By the early 1930s the LDS church and recreation hall in Hatch had electric lights. Several nearby residences had this electric service extended to their homes for a monthly fee.[29]

One of the most exciting changes that came to Garfield County involved the Rural Electrification Administration, created by an act of Congress in 1935 to help bring electric power to areas of rural America. Much of the county's populace still depended at that time on kerosene or gas lamps and lanterns for lighting. A real step forward came with the organization of the Garkane Power Association on 8 July 1938, a cooperative venture involving several towns in Garfield and Kane counties. The association met and was organized in the office of Garfield County Attorney Warren W. Porter at Panguitch. Ten men and three women from the two counties comprised the first board of directors, with Ralph B. Blackburn as president, Harold Heaton as vice-president, and Luvera Covington as secretary.[30]

In order to get the federal REA money to bring electricity to its small towns, the county had to obtain a 135 subscribers to the service. Robert Middleton of Henrieville and others worked very hard to get the required number, going from home to home to sign people up. It cost each family five dollars, a lot of money during the Depression, and some folks had no cash. Middleton recalled one incident that illustrates the singular dedication the people had in completing the task: "I went to Serielda and Lee Savages home one evening and talked to them. They were both in bed so I sat on the foot of the bed and talked Garkane Power to them and got them to sign up while they were in bed."[31] With such persistence, organizers soon had the requisite number of subscribers.

Late in 1938 the organization received word that their REA loan for $1.5 million had been approved. Based on a recommendation of one of the directors, Leo Munson, the field representative for the agency, engineer Ben Crimm interviewed Middleton and hired him as supervisor of the project. The board approved his appointment. Edward P. Eardley of Salt Lake City became the construction engi-

A Henrieville resident drinking from culinary water barrels just before the arrival of piped water in 1941.

neer, Bessie Sandin was office secretary, and Warren C. Porter served as attorney.

The project took about a year to complete, including the installation of 110 miles of line and the building of an $80,000 generating plant. On 20 December 1939, residents of Hatch, Tropic, Cannonville, Henrieville, and Escalante, along with four towns in Kane County, received electricity at the same instant. Ruby's Inn and Bryce Canyon National Park also benefited from the project. A day-long and all-night celebration accompanied this momentous occasion. A program, barbecue, electrical demonstrations, and the turning of the switch to energize the lines took place in Hatch near the plant; festivities then moved to Tropic for a dance and more feasting.[32]

For the people in the communities served by the Garkane Power Company the coming of electricity conveyed the promise of a better life and new experiences. One resident wrote: "No one had the remotest idea of how to prepare or the possibilities that it brought us. We were modern and up-to-date if we had one light at the ceiling and one receptacle on any wall of the main rooms."[33]

Many humorous incidents accompanied the electrification of so many homes. When one turned off a gas lamp, the glowing mantle gave an extra few seconds of light. The afterglow gave some people time to walk across the room and get into bed before darkness engulfed the room. This didn't work with electric lights. It was written that "one man . . . was so surprised there was no lingering light when he turned the electric switch that he went back and turned it on again to see if he could beat it the next time."[34]

Local historian George Thompson reported that one unnamed resident of Bryce Valley applied for and received a General Electric dealership. Mostly through the barter system he managed to sell fifty-eight refrigerators in six months. People bought radios and other appliances from him as well. He accepted all kinds of livestock and other marketable items in exchange for the appliances and then peddled the items throughout the valley. As people realized the broad range of help electrical devices could be to them they purchased other appliances, which necessitated "an almost constant job of updating everyone's wiring to make it safe."[35]

Garkane electric power did not arrive in Boulder until 1947. In May 1946, company directors met with Boulder residents to discuss the possibility of bringing electricity to their community. Twenty-three homeowners contracted to pay $350 in advance or seventy dollars down and seventy dollars a year for five years to have the lines installed. Alton Talbot of Panguitch and Spencer and Lorin Moosman wired area homes. Residents had an additional reason to celebrate 25 December 1947, for that day they received electrical power along with other Christmas gifts.[36]

In 1946 Garkane employees worked with Antimony citizens to bring electricity to that community. The Ivan and Avera Montague home became the first to be hooked up, because that is where the workers stayed while they installed the lines. Daughter Peggy had the honor of flipping the first switch to turn on the lights. A handful of Salt Gulch families did not obtain electricity until 1953. Installation cost them each $1,000—paid in monthly installments over a ten-year period.

The Civilian Conservation Corps

Of all the federal programs to help fight the Depression, the Civilian Conservation Corps (CCC) was particularly important to President Franklin D. Roosevelt because of its dual role of providing jobs and conserving natural resources—both being his priorities.[37] The Civilian Conservation Corps also probably had more impact in Garfield County than did any other New Deal program. This agency employed jobless young men throughout the United States, provided them with room and board and paid them thirty dollars a month, most of which was required to be sent home to their families. By 1935 more than half a million young men had joined the corps. Since their main function involved reforestation, park maintenance, and erosion control, the men lived in camps close to the projects—sometimes in quite isolated locations. These camps operated under military discipline and organization. Locally the agency became important not only for the projects it undertook in Garfield County but also because it employed a number of young men in the area. However, many of their assignments kept the CCC men away from home for long periods of time. Periods of enlistment were six months, with the opportunity to reenlist. Enlistees could be sent anywhere in the country. Local experienced men (LEMs) were older men hired to supervise projects in areas in which they lived.

At Bryce Canyon, CCC work began in May 1934. The agency established a Bryce Camp NP3 in the same area the Union Pacific Company had their staging ground when they built part of the rim road. A spring used earlier by the Utah Parks Company provided the water for the camp. Many of the men came from a Zion National Park camp of Utah Company 962 and returned there for the winters. The CCC workers, who numbered over 200 that first summer at Bryce, took on a number of different projects: building new roads; controling erosion along existing roads; general roadside cleanup (particularly removing downed trees along them) and improvement; constructing or upgrading old horse, hiking, and fire trails; and putting up boundary fences.[38]

By the end of September 1935, the work force was reduced to about eighty. Except for a small group of twenty-five, most workers left at the end of October to work at Zion National Park for the winter, returning to Bryce with the warmer weather the next spring. Along with the depletion of the work force came drastic cuts in the Bryce camp's allotments for overhead, equipment operation and maintenance, and purchased materials.

The next two summers, however, saw improvements of the public campground at Bryce Canyon, including the dividing of it into individual campsites and the building of fireplaces and tables. Workers cut and split logs, positioned them around the campground lecture circle, and constructed a 500-foot walkway from the campground to the lecture circle. The new camping facilities opened to the public during the 1936 tourist season.

The CCC continued to keep workers at Bryce Canyon until the end of the corps in early 1942 building a "comfort station" at Sunset Point, several other pit toilets, a checking station at the park entrance, and an employee's dormitory and cabin. A beetle infestation caused the workers to turn their efforts to cutting and burning more than 3,000 Douglas fir and ponderosa pine trees over two seasons. They continued to improve roads and parking areas throughout the park as well as around the lodge, built cattleguards, and assisted the Garkane Power Company in erecting power lines to the park's residential area. These efforts helped the park handle the ever-increasing tourist traffic.[39]

As important as was the CCC work at Bryce Canyon, ending the profound isolation of the community of Boulder (known to some as "the last frontier in Utah") became perhaps the greatest contribution of the Civilian Conservation Corps in Garfield County.[40] This involved completing three good dirt roads. The first connected the Wayne County town of Grover to Boulder; the second was a dependable route between Escalante and Boulder by way of Posy Lake; and the third, which came a little later, was a new road at a lower elevation between Escalante and Boulder to provide year-round travel. The first and third of these roads anticipated the later Utah Highway 12.

To facilitate this construction, CCC camps sprang up by 1934 at both Escalante (Camp F-18) and Grover (Camp F-19, Company

1339), with spike camps later located in various places along the routes under construction. Work had begun in 1933 on what was called the East End Road from Grover, along the east side of Boulder Mountain. Forest Ranger Wilford Bently of Wayne County supervised the building of this road as it left Grover, and Neil Forsyth of Teasdale supervised construction of the road from Boulder toward Wayne County. As work progressed, the men established additional spike camps at Pleasant Creek, Wildcat Ranger Station, and the Boulder Ranger Station.

In the midst of construction, Forsyth and one of his crew on one occasion were using dynamite to remove ponderosa pine stumps. After laying the charge the two men scrambled away, the crew man climbing over a ridge with the battery. For reasons shrouded in mystery, Forsyth returned to the stumps and perished as the blast exploded. His accomplishments and those of the other workers, however, eventually produced a byway flanked by spectacular beauty that shortened considerably the travel time between Boulder and Wayne County. The two sections of the road, measuring a total of twenty-nine miles, finally met at Pleasant Creek, with work concluding in November 1935.

The second road—more difficult to construct but completed more quickly—involved the building of an overpass referred to as Hell's Backbone Bridge. The route went north out of Escalante along Pine Creek and veered to the west toward Posy Lake before it turned east and then south, traversing some treacherous terrain. Supervision of the crew for the road fell at first to Forest Ranger T. Carl Haycock, and later to John C. Tolton. The CCC workers started building the bridge long before an approach road reached it. Lionel Chidester took charge of its construction. Brothers with the surname of Liston packed in all the necessary supplies by mule train—including lumber, cement, and sand. The men worked under extremely dangerous conditions as they laid the bridge across an old mule trail that passed over a narrow sandstone ridge that skirted first the deep chasm of Death Hollow on the west side, then Sand Creek on the east. Those who operated the heavy equipment during this difficult construction included Kenneth Beckstrom and Martin McCallister of Panguitch and Wanless Alvey and Loral McInelly of Escalante.

Hell's Backbone bridge and road built by CCC workers in 1935 between Escalante and Boulder. (USDA Forest Service)

Meanwhile, additional CCC recruits cleared debris from approaching roads with hand tools. The men called the road that wound around the head of Death Hollow the "Poison Road: one drop—sure death."[41] The workers anchored huge ponderosa pine logs next to the rim of the gorge to inhibit vehicles from plunging downward. Amazingly, the bridge was completed by October, before many of the CCC men left for a winter camp in California. For more than a quarter century the bridge served travelers. (In 1960 Forest Service personnel replaced the old bridge with a new wider and longer structure.)

The road into Boulder, although not finished, was passable in the fall of 1933. By 1935 crews had completed construction on this good dry-weather road between the two communities. Because this road could not remain open during heavy winter weather, residents of Boulder and Escalante pleaded to have another route established. Work by the Civilian Conservation Corps on such a route began during the winter of 1934. It also presented some daunting challenges, as the men had to blast through sandstone ledges to the Escalante River and along the sheer canyon walls east of Calf Creek. Construction of the road included building a concrete bridge to span Escalante Creek. The twenty-nine-mile stretch of road cost more and took longer than anticipated. When CCC funds ran out, Forest Service, Division of Grazing, and Garfield County money went toward completing the bridge. Thanks to the leadership and work of men like Albert Delong, Dan Covington, Osro Hunt, Wanless Alvey, and many others, the road opened five years later.

Before the completion of the latter two roads, mail and supplies had to be hauled from Escalante to Boulder on pack horses and mules over Hell's Backbone or the Boulder Mail Trail—both precarious routes. Residents claimed that milk and cream Boulder residents sent to Escalante would often arrive as butter after being jostled along the trail. To celebrate the access provided by the three good dirt roads, local residents staged festivities on 21 June 1940 to honor visiting dignitaries and the builders themselves. With more than 600 people in attendance, the revelry began in Boulder and included a barbecued beef dinner (John King donated the meat and the local

The Escalante Dam on the North Fork, looking upstream through a break in
the dam in 1938. (Utah State Historical Society)

LDS Relief Society prepared the meal), a program, speeches, and
rodeo. It ended with an open-air dance in Escalante.

The outdoor dance hall in Escalante had been built in 1934 by
Leander Shurtz, who saw a need for places of recreation for both
townspeople and CCC men living in close proximity to the community. The hall doubled in winter as a skating rink. The facility
remained open until 1943, at which time the high school gymnasium
became the center for local social functions.

W. Kay Clark, in recalling his life in Henrieville, wrote about
dances held each Friday night in Cannonville and local clannishness
or mistrust of outsiders that has continued through the years. Some
CCC men camped near the community between 1936 and 1938, and
when they came to the dances Clark reported that "the Hometown
boys and husbands didn't want them to dance with the Hometown
girls and wives."[42]

Corpsmen at other CCC camps located within the county
worked on improving and building other roads and trails, installing
telephone lines, building ranger stations, and planting trees in forest

areas. A Dixie National Forest CCC camp, supervised by Treharne Leigh and located at Duck Creek, had a spike camp at Panguitch Lake. This group accomplished much in working on various conservation measures around the lake and surrounding area and also built several new roads. In 1938 an extensive reseeding program by the CCC enhanced range quality in areas of Upper Valley, Johns Valley, Cameron Wash, Reed Ranch, Duck Creek, Pine Valley, and Jones Corral.

The Demise of Widtsoe

Not all New Deal programs and relief efforts proved successful and beneficial to Garfield County residents, however. Although the community of Widtsoe showed great promise during its second decade of settlement, trouble loomed on the horizon. As mentioned in the previous chapter, one of Widtsoe's main problems involved securing a dependable source of water. Only 210 people remained in town by 1930; by 1935 only seventeen families were still living there. The Resettlement Administration moved in to purchase the land from the townspeople and homesteaders, most of whom were behind in paying their property taxes. The agency planned to return the land to public domain as a possible grazing area and help the inhabitants to relocate to more productive parts of the state. The citizens agreed with this strategy, but the plan went awry.

According to former resident Reed Beebe, the cost of administering the program more than doubled the money paid out for the land. Those who represented the Resettlement Administration also moved slowly in settling with the residents—usually taking months and years when it had promised it would only take weeks. Beebe's father died before reaching an agreement with the government—his son claimed the death was from a broken heart. A month after the elder Beebe's death, the Resettlement Administration came with their offer. Beebe described the situation: "interest on mortgages and delinquent taxes ate all the equity we had in our 3,000 plus acres of land. Vera [Beebe's sister] was relocated on a run-down fruit farm in Orem. I was given the choice of buying the farm of a cousin of the attorney for the government—or nothing. So ended our sojourn in Johns Valley."[43]

The government reportedly did not allow those who had been resettled to freely spend the money they received; their checks could not be cashed without being countersigned by someone in the Resettlement Administration office, another process that took time. Some resented the government methods, but the program was intended to benefit those who were already in the process of losing their land, which probably provoked some resentment in other tax-paying citizens that these people were being bought out at all.

The Resettlement Administration reportedly expended $81,300 to buy people out in Widtsoe. That sum, however, did not include the cost of administering the program. Those who did not receive funds from the government to relocate received supplemental loans to finance their move. When everyone had left, government personnel razed almost all of the buildings in town and placed the 26,143 acres under the supervision of provisions of the Taylor Grazing Act.[44] Some county residents still feel, however, that had there been diligent efforts undertaken by the Soil Conservation Service in those days, Widtsoe might have survived, even thrived.[45]

World War II

America's entry into World War II brought an even greater sadness to many Garfield residents. Because America's part in this war lasted so much longer than its fighting in World War I, the impact was far greater. Garfield County also provided a greater than average percentage of troops to fight in Europe and Asia.

The war altered population trends in the county. After almost steady growth from decade to decade, the county's population dropped between 1940 and 1950 by more than a thousand people—more than 20 percent. The young men and women who heeded the call to serve received assignments to military installations throughout the country for training. Most of them left home for the first time in their lives, and some came to believe that greater economic or social opportunities awaited them beyond the confines of their former homes. For others, the lure of a more temperate climate and comfortable lifestyle (such as that found in California) proved to be overwhelming. This held true for those who left to work in war industries as well.

The county seat, Panguitch, contributed about 350 young people to the war effort, including nurses and Women's Army Corps recruits, out of a population of just under 2,000. The women included June Haycock Kessler, Barbara Kenney, Edith Broadhead Lindsay, Mary Dickenson Calcara, Cleo Allen Henrie, Coris Slack, and Evelyn Marshall Roe. Ten young men lost their lives in the war. Julian Cherrington went down with his ship, the aircraft carrier *Saratoga*, in the Pacific. Carl Englestead, Earl Excell, and Homer Hatch also died in the Pacific theater. Erwin Kockerhans died in an army camp, while Ellis Adair and Arthur Dickenson lost their lives as the result of accidents in their respective camps. The body of one young man, Boyd Riding, never received a burial; the transport plane he was in went down in India, and he and the other sixteen on board were never found. Other Panguitch military men who died included Lindon Lemmons and Thomas Sevy. One young local soldier, Lt. Richard Haycock, son of Panguitch City Marshal and Mrs. J. Scott Haycock, saw duty during a significant event near the end of the war—while serving in Germany, he was an usher at the Potsdam Conference.

Hatch contributed fifty-four young men to the war effort, almost 18 percent of the town's population. Six of these men received Purple Hearts for valor—Ira Ray Barnhurst, Merrill Burrows, Mark C. Fallis, George H. Middleton, Ray Porter, and David G. Sawyer. Two lost their lives. Ira Ray Barnhurst died in France on 19 August 1944; his body was sent home for burial. Merrill G. Burrows was killed in action on the Pacific island of Tarawa on 20 November 1943.

From Antimony and surrounding farmlands forty-two men saw duty during the war. For a population of less than 300 in the area, this again was a large percentage. As many as four sons per family heeded the call of duty, and all served honorably. Three young men were killed in action: Ted Riddle died in the Battle of the Bulge in December 1944; Lark Allen first suffered injuries in Africa and then in Italy, and then both he and Arthur E. Twitchell met death during the invasion of Normandy.

Escalante had a population of 1,161 people in 1940 according to census records. When the United States went to war, 165 of the community's population served their country, more than 14 percent of

the citizenry. Among this number, four women enlisted—Evelyn
Barney, Ruby C. Cowart, Rosella Osborn, and Emma Spencer. In the
fall of 1944, some Escalante parents began receiving news of their
sons' deaths. Two local men died in October: Wallace Arnold Barney,
an aircraft gunner was killed in action in the Philippines and Milan
W. Cottam died in Pacific waters. In November Farlan L. Spencer
died in an airplane accident at McDill Air Base in Florida. The next
spring Gren McInelly died on the island of Luzon. Eldon Earnest
Griffin was killed in action near Tamboch, Germany, close to the end
of the war in Europe.

The communities in the upper Paria and Bryce valleys sent loved
ones to fight with the Allies as well. George Thompson sums up their
contribution: "Those in the service, due to their experience in handling problems and their skill with weapons and equipment, along
with their dependability and courage, advanced to officer ranks and
received the admiration and trust of their associates."[46] Out of a population of about 250 people, Cannonville sent twenty-eight young
men to the military during the war. Fortunately they all returned
home.

Henrieville sent thirty-three men to war out of a citizenry of
approximately 240. Only one did not make it back—Guy Nephi
Smith. He served aboard the USS Indianapolis. On its return from the
island of Tinian after it had delivered key atomic bomb components,
the vessel sustained heavy damage from a Japanese submarine tor-
pedo attack. The ship became the last U.S. naval vessel to be lost during World War II, taking 880 crew members—including young Guy
Smith—with her when she sank.[47]

Tropic also did its share in supplying young men for the military.
Forty-four men and one woman (Pearl Adair joined the women's
navy organization the WAVEs) went to war from a community of
about 500 people. Leon Barton paid the ultimate price for his patrio-
tism. Other valley war casualties included Eddie Henderson, Roy
Henderson, Jr., and Bernard Cope.[48]

Completing the catalog of Garfield participation in the military,
nine young men from Boulder served with distinction in World War
II. To add further perspective concerning the personal sacrifice of
county residents, it is interesting to note that four grandmothers liv-

ing within the county sent seventy-one grandsons and three grand-daughters to the cause: Elizabeth Smith of Henrieville had twenty-four grandsons, eight great-grandsons, and two granddaughters serving; Sarah Ann Shurtz of Escalante had eleven grandsons and grandsons-in-law who participated; Elizabeth Jolley of Tropic had twenty-three grandsons in the military; and Jane Haycock of Panguitch had thirteen grandsons and one granddaughter who served in the war.

On the Home Front

Supplying troops for the U.S. military was not the only measure of Garfield County loyalty during World War II. Many citizens volunteered to assist on local draft boards or to plan special occasions to honor those who served. As with the rest of the nation, county residents also took part in scrap drives, supported rationing programs, bought bonds when they could, and did without those items that were needed for the war effort.

Heber H. Hall taught high school in Boulder during the last school year that secondary classes were taught there (1941–42). He organized his pupils for a scrap collection. They visited the farms and ranches in the Boulder area and collected a small mountain of scrap iron. Horace R. Hall took the truckloads of metal to Salt Lake City. Among the items collected went the cracked bell from the burned-down schoolhouse.[49] In Antimony, Les Smoot volunteered to have his store be the depot for all iron scrap collected by citizens from throughout Grass Valley. Trucks then picked up the material to be taken to foundries for melting and recycling into war material. Since farmers could not buy new equipment during the war, Lloyd Marshall worked locally as a welder to help keep the farm machinery running.[50]

As in other localities of the country during the war, some of those involved in agriculture lacked needed labor at harvest time. Three men from Antimony found a ready source of workers to take up the slack. It had been the habit of Glenn Crabb, Charles Riddle, and Milo Warner to take their potatoes to the Phoenix area to sell throughout the winter months. In October 1943 Crabb and Warner stopped at some of the Navajo communities along the way to offer the people there jobs picking and hauling potatoes. Two truckloads of field workers returned with the men. This began a practice that lasted for more than twenty years.

The Navajo workers did such a good job and seemed so appreciative of the opportunity to earn the money that the next year they also went on to the sugar beet harvest in Sevier County after completion of the two-week potato harvest in Antimony and surrounding areas. Local residents learned about Navajo native customs while these men worked in their midst. They observed Native American habits of camp life, healing ceremonies that included sand paintings, and purification practices.[51]

Another source of labor came from the county's young people. Teora Newby Willis of Henrieville recalled that in 1942 when she was in the eighth grade she and her friends and siblings could get jobs picking and cutting potatoes and picking peas. This not only helped the farmers, but with the money earned the youths could buy their own school clothes. School let out for a few days each fall for potato picking and a few days in the spring for potato cutting.[52]

The lack of adequate health care during the war caused difficulties for Garfield County people. From Richfield on the north to Kanab on the south, locals had to do without the services of a doctor for most of the war years. They had to travel anywhere from 80 to 150 miles for hospital care in cases of serious illness or injury. When the war began, except for a few experienced in nursing and midwifery, all medical personnel left. Shortly before the war ended, with plans in the offing for a hospital in Panguitch, residents there persuaded Dr. Sims E. Duggins of Gunnison to relocate to their community.[53]

Memphis Sudweeks Talbot remembered when her husband, Russell, suffered an appendicitis attack. Dr. Duggins determined that he needed to get Talbot to the hospital in Cedar City, but he had used up all his gas-ration stamps and the Talbots did not own a vehicle. In desperation, Memphis Talbot went throughout the town to gather enough stamps to fill Duggins's gas tank, and the three of them finally took off for Cedar City for the emergency surgery.[54] For the Talbots and their county neighbors the completion of the hospital the following year came none too soon. Dr. George Monnet joined Dr. Duggins on the staff a few years later, followed by Dr. William L.

Mason. These physicians also held monthly clinics in various Garfield County towns.

From Country Schoolhouse to Post-war Modernity

In 1948 the *Salt Lake Tribune* decided to run a human-interest story regarding the old country schoolhouse in Antimony. They heard that the lcoal schoolchildren and their teachers had planned a three-day trip to Salt Lake City. The paper sent a photographer and reporter down to Antimony to gather background for the article. There the two found school still being held in a structure first built in 1883 that had since been enlarged to three rooms. Heat came from pot-bellied stoves in each room. The requisite school bell summoned students grade one through eight to school each day or back from recess.

On 5 May 1948 fifty excited children, their teachers, principal, and chaperoning parents boarded two Greyhound buses headed for the big city. After the children visited points of interest along the way, motorcycle policemen met them at the Point of the Mountain and escorted the entourage to the Hotel Utah, where they were guests. For the next three days the group saw urban sights and took a roller-coaster ride at Saltair Resort. They toured the *Tribune* headquarters and met and shook hands with Governor Herbert Maw in the Gold Room of the Utah State Capitol Building. They also met the president of the LDS church, George Albert Smith, visited Temple Square and the Cathedral of the Madeleine, and attended some water follies. The students even flew in a DC-3 airplane over Salt Lake City. Throughout their visit, the newspaper reporter and photographer followed them around and took pictures, later adding captions that gave the impression to some readers that the children from Antimony lived lives of deprivation. Not only did the state newspapers cover their activities, national news services also picked up the story. When the students returned home, most of the town turned out to meet them.[55]

This proved to be a marvelous experience for these youngsters; but the news stories promulgated a somewhat false impression of what it was like to live in a southern Utah rural area. By the end of the war, the majority of Garfield County residents were beginning to enjoy most of the same conveniences that their urban counterparts did. All communities had electricity, telephone service, much improved culinary water systems, indoor plumbing, and roads. The county had an up-to-date hospital, an airport, a consolidated public school system with improved facilities, and the beginnings of an infrastructure to accommodate a fledgling tourist industry. Increasing numbers of county citizens traveled regularly to Salt Lake City and other urban areas and had been exposed to life in other parts of the country and far-flung localities around the world. It was true that the county's population dipped during the immediate post-war period, but this trend soon abated. In future decades, Garfield County would begin to see increasing in-migration because of the unique quality of life it had to offer.

ENDNOTES

1. Vernon Davies, "Garfield County's Relief Problem," *Garfield County News,* 2 November 1938.

2. Ida Chidester and Eleanor Bruhn, *Golden Nuggets of Pioneer Days: A History of Garfield County,* 312–13.

3. George W. Thompson, "Cannonville History," 34.

4. Janet M. Johnson Ott, "A Sketch of the Life of Joseph Alma Ott," 6–7.

5. Luetta Partner Davenport, Autobiography, 2, copy obtained by authors from Nancy Twitchell.

6. Vernon Davies and Arthur L. Beeley, "The Survey of Relief and Rehabilitation in Garfield County, Utah; Results and Implications," in *Proceedings of the Utah Academy of Sciences, Arts and Letters* (Salt Lake City: Utah Academy of Sciences, Arts and Letters, 1939), 103.

7. Ibid., 104.

8. M. Lane Warner, *Grass Valley 1873–1976: A History of Antimony and Her People,* 52.

9. As quoted in Warner, *Grass Valley,* 72.

10. Woolsey, *Escalante Story,* 260.

11. June Shakespear, "Tropic," 7.

12. Lenora Hall LeFevre, *The Boulder Country and Its People: A History of the People of Boulder and the Surrounding Country,* 182.

13. Ibid., 211–12.

14. Ruby Moore, "Charles Luther and Ruby Moore," 2, copy obtained by the authors from Nancy Twitchell.

15. Thompson, "Cannonville History," 36.

16. Shakespear, "Tropic," 8.

17. "See *The Spectrum*, 23 July 1997, A1.

18. LeFevre, *Boulder Country*, 223–24.

19. Ibid., 261–62.

20. Thompson, "Cannonville History," 34.

21. Nethella Griffin Woolsey, *The Escalante Story: 1875–1964*, 202–3.

22. Warner, *Grass Valley*, 54–55.

23. Shakespear writes that this was a project under the Resettlement Administration; see "Tropic," 7. However, in a letter written to Utah Governor Calvin L. Rampton on 4 February 1970, Middleton states that it came under the WPA, which seems more logical. Copy of letter obtained by authors from Marilyn Murdock.

24. "Bryce Canyon Airport Hanger," *Bryce Canyon Country's Scenic Byway 12* (1992), 8-B, copy in possession of authors.

25. LeFevre, *Boulder Country*, 195; and Woolsey, *Escalante Story*, 293–94.

26. Woolsey, *Escalante Story*, 219–21.

27. Shanna Goulding, "My Early Memories of Henrieville," 2, copy obtained by authors from Nancy Twitchell.

28. Woolsey, *Escalante Story*, 206–7.

29. Effel Harmon Barrow Riggs, *History of Hatch, Utah and Associated Towns, Asay and Hillsdale*, 310.

30. Woolsey, *Escalante Story*, 207. Riggs, *History of Hatch*, 311, lists those in attendance at the first meeting; however, she records Blackburn as president and Warren Porter as secretary-treasurer.

31. Robert A. Middleton, "Life of Robert A. Middleton," 10, copy obtained by authors from Marilyn Murdock.

32. See *Garfield County News*, 14 December 1939; Robert A. Middleton to Governor Calvin L. Rampton, 4 February 1972; Woolsey, *Escalante Story*, 207; and Riggs, *History of Hatch*, 311–12.

33. Thompson, "Cannonville History," 36.

34. Riggs, *History of Hatch*, 312.

35. Thompson, "Cannonville History," 36–37.

36. LeFevre, *Boulder Country*, 269.

37. Paul S. Boyer et al., *The Enduring Vision* (Lexington, MA: D.C. Heath and Company, 1995), 546, 555.

38. Kenneth W. Baldridge, "Nine Years of Achievement: The Civilian Conservation Corps in Utah" (Ph.D. diss., Brigham Young University, 1971), 110.

39. See Nicholas Scrattish, *Historic Resource Study: Bryce Canyon National Park,* 153–63.

40. See LeFevre, *Boulder Country,* 231–34; Woolsey, *Escalante Story,* 191–94.

41. LeFevre, *Boulder Country,* 231.

42. W. Kay Clark, "Henrieville Town History," 2, copy obtained by authors from Nancy Twitchell.

43. Quoted in Sandberg, "Widtsoe Inside Out," 17.

44. Grant Nielsen, "'Mercy Death' for Towns," in *Johns Valley The Way We Saw It* (Springville, UT: Art City Publishing Co., 1971), 7; Carr, *Ghost Towns,* 122.

45. Chidester and Bruhn, *Golden Nuggets,* 143.

46. Thompson, "Cannonville History," 35.

47. Van Dorn Smith, *One and One Make Eleven* (Ogden, UT: n.p., 1993), 54.

48. The local high school yearbook paid tribute to these three young men along with Guy Smith and Leon Barton, but it is uncertain which communitics the three came from. See the *Brycconian,* 1946.

49. LeFevre, *Boulder Country,* 182.

50. Warner, *Grass Valley,* 56.

51. Ibid., 56–57.

52. Teora Willis, autobiography, 5. Although Willis's school days were spent in nearby Monroe, Utah, her experiences parallelled those of youths in Garfield County communities where growing potatoes was an important commercial enterprise.

53. Chidester and Bruhn, *Golden Nuggets,* 277.

54. Memphis Ula Sudweeks Talbot, interview with Vivian L. Talbot, August 1997, notes in possession of the authors.

55. Warner, *Grass Valley,* 59–60.

CHAPTER 12

GARFIELD COUNTY AT MID-CENTURY

P ost-World War II America enjoyed the longest sustained economic expansion in its history. Between 1940 and 1960 the nation's gross national production more than doubled, as did the number of households that moved into the middle-class bracket immediately following the war. Most residents of Garfield County also saw improvement in their financial well-being as well as greater convenience and comfort in their standard of living. However, in order to achieve this improvement, some men and women had to supplement their incomes with second jobs, particularly if they farmed for a living. With continued out-migration of their young people and their continued pursuit of livelihoods dependent on available natural resources, the economic future for most county citizens remained precarious.

Tourism would eventually take over as the leading money-making industry in Garfield as more and more people came to discover the scenic splendor of the county. But the monetary benefits from this industry fell unevenly on local people, and the jobs tourism fostered were usually seasonal and low-paying. Additionally, outsiders, whether representing government or private organizations, made greater inroads in defining public policy for rural southern Utah communities. Their agendas proved to have a detrimental impact on the county's livestock, lumber, and extractive mineral industries. Not only during the 1950s and 1960s but up to the present day, the debate is ongoing between traditional interests and outside influences.

Immediately following the war, optimism reigned among most Garfield residents. The Great Depression had finally dissipated as the fighting began, and, when the conflict ended, parents thought they no longer had to worry about their sons and daughters serving in far-flung locales under dangerous circumstances. The rationing of consumer products had been lifted and more and more labor-saving devices for home and farm appeared in stores and catalogs. Many could now afford to buy them because during the war they had saved their money. After all, there had been little available to purchase while the battles raged.

Shortly after VJ Day celebrating victory over Japan in August 1945 the citizens of Utah had another reason for celebrating: the centennial of the settling of their state. Many Garfield residents descended from those who had made that journey across the plains one hundred years before, and their posterity took pride in what had been accomplished since that time.

The approach of the Fourth and the Twenty-fourth of July each summer had always produced excitement among county residents. From their earliest beginnings each community could not let those dates pass without providing some celebratory activities. They normally included parades, programs, dances, rodeos, and even horse racing. As mentioned previously, many who resided in Panguitch and surrounding communities went to Panguitch Lake to celebrate, while those residing "under the dump" gravitated to Pine Lake in the Escalante Mountains for community campouts and chicken frys.

Girls in the county also looked forward to the July celebrations because they anticipated getting a new "Fourth" dress, some purchased on a recent visit to Richfield or Cedar City, others ordered from the catalog or sewn at home. Rather than receiving the traditional new spring outfit at Easter when temperatures remained low in much of the county, the young people appeared along the July

Fourth parade route or at the afternoon and evening dances decked out in their new warm-weather finery.

With the approach of July 1947, preparations for the centennial celebration occupied the thoughts of many county residents during the immediate post-war period. The LDS church encouraged each ward in the state to plan some special events to commemorate the 1847 arrival of pioneers into the Salt Lake Valley. The congregations and communities in Garfield County willingly complied. For instance, the townspeople of Hatch used the occasion to host a homecoming for all former residents under the direction of Bishop Earnest Riggs and his committee chairs, Ernal and Jennie Lyons. The men prepared a mutton fry with dutch-oven potatoes, while the women furnished the salads, rolls, and dessert—all free to the public. The LDS Primary organization sponsored a parade which, along with the dinner, became a tradition from that time forward.[1]

The Nation Takes Notice of Garfield County

Part of the Panguitch Pioneer Days festivities took place at the Bryce Canyon Airport.[2] The celebrants could not have been aware that within three months the nation's attention would be focused on that facility as tragedy struck. In October 1947 residents living in the eastern portion of the county observed a large DC-6 airplane on fire overhead. The pilot had turned back upon discovering the problem and was trying to land at the airport; but his craft crashed and burned before he could reach the runway, killing all fifty-two passengers and crew on board.

As federal officials from Washington, D.C., joined those from United Air Lines and Douglas Aircraft and relatives of the victims who converged on the airport and crash site, county citizens willingly and graciously extended their help and hospitality. Throughout the clean-up, retrieval of bodies, and investigation, local people and businesses performed a meritorious service for all concerned, and those they helped expressed their appreciation. For some weeks following the incident, the county, and Panguitch in particular, received a lot of attention from the press.

The following year, another event brought publicity to the county. A modern-day expedition party formed for the purpose of exploring the country en route to the Hole-in-the-Rock. The group consisted of *National Geographic* photographer Jack Breed; Arthur Crawford of the U.S. State Department of Publicity and Industrial Development; A.G. Kilbourne, a conservationist for the Extension Service under the U.S. Department of Agriculture; Don Moffat, representing the Taylor Grazing Service; and local county representatives Thomas Smith, Samuel Pollock, John Johnson, Wilford Clark, and Ralph Hunt. The September 1949 issue of *National Geographic* contained the article about this expedition, complete with breathtaking photographs.[3] For the first time the nation became aware of other scenic sights in Garfield County besides Bryce Canyon, which had been a national park since 1928. Such exposure would have an ever-increasing impact on the county's economic orientation and natural-resource management.

A tragedy receiving national coverage happened some years later along the route to Hole-in-the-Rock. National radio stations broadcast the story of an accident involving forty-five Utah boy scouts, their leaders, and a reporter. The group drove from the Salt Lake City and Provo areas on 10 June 1963 to meet a group of boaters floating down the Colorado River. While on the Hole-in-the-Rock road their truck did not make one of the treacherous curves in Carcass Wash, about fifty miles down the Escalante Desert. The vehicle rolled 125 feet downhill and dropped over a thirty-five-foot embankment, spilling its passengers. Several were crushed beneath the heavy truck, resulting in twelve deaths. Local citizens from the Boulder and Escalante area worked frantically to get the injured to the Panguitch hosptial 120 miles away, where one more victim succumbed two days later.[4]

Developments at Bryce Canyon

Although a committee called the "Associated Civic Clubs of Southern Utah" had petitioned Bryce and Zion national parks superintendent P.P. Patraw in 1934 for an independent Bryce Canyon administration, that did not happen until July 1956—twenty-two years later. The catalyst for that change was the National Park Service's "Mission 66."

Mission 66 was the brainchild of National Park Service Director

Bryce Canyon Lodge with a Union Pacific bus unloading visitors in the 1950s. (Utah State Historical Society)

Conrad L. Wirth, who in the mid-1950s implemented "an ambitious campaign to bring Park Service facilities throughout the country 'up to par' by the Service's golden anniversary in 1966." He asked each national park to produce a plan that would accomplish this. In 1955 Glen Bean had accepted the position of superintendent of Bryce Canyon under the condition that its administration would soon be separate from that of Zion. His reasons included increased visitation to Bryce; the need for massive physical development to be implemented by Mission 66; lack of attention to the park during winter months, especially with respect to roads and buildings; and renewed local pressure, supported by a petition, for a separate Bryce Canyon administration.[5]

Staff had been inadequate to handle the increased visitation to the park, which had risen steadily from 21,997 in 1929 (the first year records were kept) to 257,570 in 1956—with the exception of a considerable slump due to the rationing of gas during the World War II years.[6] Bean added a chief park ranger, a chief park naturalist, a park

Bryce Canyon Lodge employees in 1959. Most were high school and college students from Garfield and other Utah Counties. (Courtesy Carolee Reinhold Stout)

ranger, and converted a clerk position to administrative assistant at Bryce Canyon.

Although tourism swelled, the Utah Parks Company, which operated the lodge and inn, saw a decrease in its tour-bus business as automobile tourism became more popular. Its parent company, Union Pacific Railroad, ended summer-season trains between Lund and Cedar City in the spring of 1960, and the Utah Parks Company instead ran buses from Salt Lake City to Bryce, Zion, Cedar Breaks, and the North Rim of the Grand Canyon. That July Fred Warner stepped down from his position as Utah Parks Company general manager. Tom E. Murray replaced him and kept the company afloat amid a myriad of problems for twelve more years.[7]

As tourism increased, so did the need for culinary water at the park. When a record 300,311 people visited the park in 1965, it strained every available water source to satisfy their needs. The Utah Parks Company facilities consumed more than 75,000 gallons a day, and the National Park Service used an additional 30,000 gallons daily. In cooperation with the National Park Service, defective water lines were replaced and water-storage capacity increased. But other problems loomed.

The Utah Parks Company had maintained its facilities quite well over the years, but they had become inadequate to accommodate the increased visitation. In the fall of 1965 the National Park Service issued its Bryce Canyon master plan, which declared the Utah Parks Company units were "substandard" and called for their gradual removal. Public campgrounds were to replace the inn, lodge, and tourist cabins. The plan also charged that the Utah Parks Company transportation represented a "preferential franchise . . . obsolete in present day operations." However, a later National Park publication, *Historic Resource Study: Bryce Canyon National Park,* would term the 1965 master plan "a callous, narrow-minded document," concluding that "the Union Pacific's record at Bryce Canyon stands up well under scrutiny and that the company had "contributed enormously toward making Bryce Canyon a great national park."[8]

For decades, the Utah Parks Company had provided welcome summer jobs for county young people as well as other college students from across the state and even throughout the nation. They worked as busboys and waitresses, cabin maids and bell hops, cooks and kitchen help, horse-trail wranglers and wood choppers, curio-shop and soda-fountain sales clerks, as well as serving at the front desk and driving tour buses as "gear jammers."

The tourists were referred to by them as "dudes." Each day the hired help lined the front porch of the lodge for "Sing-away" as the loaded buses readied to leave. They entertained the dudes each evening by staging variety shows as well as organized choreographed performances. In the "Employee's Review" performance, the hired help explained their jobs in humorous song-and-dance routines set to well-known tunes. Another favorite with locals and visitors alike was "State Show," which featured songs of various states. It began and ended with the participants singing "I'm a Yankee Doodle Dandy" and culminated with "Uncle Sam" and the cast singing "This is My Country." Those who spent those summers at Bryce Canyon were rewarded not just with tips and small paychecks but with wonderful memories of friends and fun in one of the nation's most beautiful settings.

Waitresses Dione Peterson Williams and Linda King Newell at the Bryce Canyon Lodge in 1960. (Courtesy Dione Peterson Williams)

Throughout the decade of the 1960s the Union Pacific Railroad looked without success for a buyer for its Utah Parks concessions. Finally, in 1972 the company donated all its facilities and equipment at Bryce, Zion, Cedar Breaks, and the North Rim of the Grand Canyon, a laundry at Kanab, the Utah Parks Company complex in Cedar City, and the transportation fleet to the National Park Service. In September 1972 Trans World Airlines (TWA) was awarded the contract to operate the in-park concessions beginning in the 1973 season. On 18 December 1972 Tom Murray retired as manager of the Utah Parks Company, ending what many believe was the golden era of Bryce Canyon National Park and the Union Pacific Railroad's administration of the concessions there.[9]

Meanwhile, under the Mission 66 program, the National Park Service's employee housing was vastly improved with the building of seven three-bedroom houses in 1957–58, one two-bedroom house and a four-unit apartment building in 1957–58, and five two-bedroom houses in 1963–64. A new visitors center and entrance station were completed in 1960, costing $224,402 and $2,760, respectively. The erection of one new utility building and the extension of another, new maintenance shops, and additional equipment storage buildings were also part of the Mission 66 plan. The North and Sunset campgrounds got six new comfort stations; the latter also got a new campfire circle. The plan also provided $894,000 for construction and upgrading of roads and trails. Guard rails at some of the park's most scenic views were also installed. Nicholas Scrattish, in his 1985 *Historic Resource Study: Bryce Canyon National Park,* concluded: "Because of the [Mission 66] program local Utahns felt Bryce Canyon's facilities had finally been brought up to standards with Zion's. There is little doubt Mission 66 also created long lasting goodwill toward the Park Service in Salt Lake City.[10]

Natural Resources— The Basis for Local Economic Development

Since the beginning of settlement in Garfield County, the cutting and milling of timber have been important economic pursuits. To begin with, people had to have homes and out-buildings. Most of the early structures consisted of wood, either as logs or planks. But lumber also became important economically because the county has some of the state's largest forest reserves. The realization that the forests required proper management became more widespread just after the turn of the century under Theodore Roosevelt's presidency. The creation of forest reserves had implications relating to rangeland for livestock and watershed protection as well as the harvesting of trees for lumber.

Various acts passed by Congress since that time have dealt with such issues as pest control, allocating money to states for fire protection within the national forests, establishing multiple-use guidelines, and the setting aside of some reserves as wilderness areas where no development or harvesting is allowed. Especially during the early decades of forest management, personnel made periodic surveys of the reserves to assess the health of the trees and the rangelands within the forest boundaries.

During and following World War II, the timber industry increased in importance in the county. The government bought lumber to build bridges, barracks, ships, and packing crates. Lumbering became second only to livestock production as a source of wealth in Garfield County during the first post-war decades. Improved roads and means of transportation contributed to the industry's success. Such pests as porcupines, bark beetles, blister rust, and spruce budworms, in addition to periodic drought years, compromised forest vitality and were inherent in the lumbering business. Escalante, Hatch, Panguitch, and, to a lesser degree, Boulder had the most successful sawmills and lumber companies.

Development of the first large mill in the Escalante area began in 1943 along Pine Creek near Posy Lake.[11] T.H. Alvey and his son Forest started the business; later, another son, Wanlass, bought out his father's share. The Alvey brothers expanded their enterprise until they produced up to 16,000 board feet of lumber a day. They relocated their mill closer to town in 1959. Two years later they sold their business to H.M. Draper and Son of Salt Lake City. In 1962 the mill burned down, however, resulting in the loss of summer jobs for local residents when the owners decided against rebuilding.[12]

In 1946 Paul Steed went into the milling business in Upper Valley. For ten years he gradually improved his operation and then decided to move to a site just northeast of Escalante. Steed had several reasons for this move. First, he needed to comply with Forest Service policy, which discouraged operation of sawmills within the forests because of fire hazard. Second, warmer temperatures in the valley meant the possibility of almost year-round operation. Finally, the more central location promoted the harvesting of different timber stands from a wider area.

The community and county cooperated with Steed by building an oiled back road from the mill to the highway, thus making it more convenient for the logging and lumber trucks and less intrusive to the residents. At peak operation during the early to mid-1960s, Steed's Skyline Lumber Company employed between twenty-five and thirty-five men, with an annual payroll nearing $100,000. The Forest Service policy during the 1960s of increasing sales of mature timber for the stated improvement of forest conditions helped make possible Skyline's expanded operation. In June 1970 the mill closed down for a time, but it reopened after being completely renovated, including

Logging operation of the Mammoth Lumber Company near Hatch in the mid 1930s. (Utah State Historical Society)

the installation of new equipment. In September 1973 Skyline's owner, Paul Steed, died suddenly of electrocution in the pumphouse of the mill. After his death, the company reorganized and Steed's widow, Mary, became president of the firm.

The early locations of both Hillsdale and Hatch owed much to the establishment of sawmills. In 1936 Jess Wilson moved to Hatch, where he organized the Mammoth Lumber Company with six additional partners. They contracted with Nelson Brothers to do their log hauling. Disaster struck the promising enterprise in 1939, however, when the operation burned to the ground. Later that year, a new partnership included some of the original group plus additional men who planned to rebuild. This company was finally pared down to two partners, Jess Wilson and Eldan Porter, who assumed the indebtedness and operation of the mill. During the mid-1950s, the company reached its zenith of productivity and earnings, with annual payrolls exceeding $60,000. Health problems later plagued the partners and in 1962 they sold out to Croft Pearson Industries.[13]

Panguitch was never without sawmills from the time of its second settlement. But sawmill activity in the community vastly increased following World War II. The Croft family started their first

mill in northern Kane County on Cedar Mountain.[14] During the
mid-1940s they joined with the Pearsons to establish a mill on the
east fork of the Sevier River near the Tropic Reservoir. A few years
later, they moved their operation by Utah Highway 12 about three
miles west of its junction with Utah Highway 63 along the border of
the Paunsaugunt Plateau. Then, in 1955, they closed both their Cedar
Mountain and Highway 12 mills and relocated to Panguitch on property offered to them by the city on the west boundary of the community. The new Croft Pearson Industries (CPI) sawmill effectively
led to the closure of other small mills in and around Panguitch, but
jobs could be had at the new mill. The company not only processed
the timber but did most of its own logging, although it subcontracted
with independent loggers as well. The business grew and the company purchased additional land, until it occupied 106 acres on the
west side of Panguitch.

In 1966 the Kaibab Lumber Company bought out the Pearsons
and one of the Croft brothers. The firm had mills all over the West
and went into partnership with the remaining Croft brothers in
Panguitch. By 1969 Kaibab had bought them out as well. Devon
Owens of Panguitch managed the mill for much of the time it was
owned by Kaibab. He recalls that as many as 250 men worked for the
firm in Panguitch at one time. Most of the workers belonged to a
union and received some of the best wages being paid in the county.
Kaibab also had pension and insurance plans for its employees. The
mill ran two shifts and stayed open all year, although the logging
dropped off in the winter. Kaibab also ran a mill in northern Arizona
at Fredonia. The timber for the Fredonia mill came from the Kaibab
National Forest, while that brought into Panguitch came from the
Dixie National Forest.

On a much smaller scale, Boulder entrepreneurs engaged in the
lumber business. Two main mills operated in the area beginning in
the 1920s. Alma and Gertrude Wilson operated one of the mills on
Boulder Mountain during the summer months, but Joel Wilson
bought them out in 1935. By 1944 Wilson sold out to Truman Lyman
and Max Behunin, who relocated the mill to upper Boulder. This
business proved less than successful, so the partners sold everything

to E.H. Coombs. In 1954 Lyman once more took over the operation and moved it to his lumberyard on his ranch.

Samuel Coleman established the other mill in the foothills about three miles north of the upper Boulder ranches. On the east fork of Boulder Creek he constructed an enormous wooden waterwheel. Independent loggers obtained permits from the Forest Service to harvest small quantities of timber, which they brought to Coleman's mill for sawing. The mill also produced a good grade of shingles. In 1933 Coleman sold his operation to his son, Albert, and Kemner T. Memmott. The mill changed ownership several times after that until 1962.[15] No figures are available as to the output of these two mills or how many people they employed; however, they provided a much-needed service for local residents.

Sawmill employment and logging continued to be some of the highest-paying work in the county, even though it too was subject to changing markets, weather, and insect infestation. Some hoped to expand lumbering in the area. One economic study done in the late 1960s indicated that the county should promote the expansion of the lumbering and sawmill industry.[16] Others opposed such expansion, however; and optimism about expansion would prove to be unfounded.

Through the years other natural resources have shown some promise of bringing a degree of financial security to the county. In most cases, however, the confidence they at first generated vanished. With the ending of World War II came the beginning of the atomic age and with it the demand for the radioactive element uranium.[17] Uranium ore had been discovered as early as 1904 in the Henry Mountains in eastern Garfield County. However, the deposits did not attract hordes of prospectors until the Cold War time period after World War II when the United States and the Soviet Union vied for nuclear supremacy.

Geologists who visited the Circle Cliffs area to the north and east of Boulder and Escalante found large quantities of pitchblende, in which the richest uranium ore can be found. A number of men from these two communities were among the first to prospect for the element. Lawrence C. Christensen of Escalante filed the first claims on 21 December 1950, and Marion Jeppsen of Boulder joined him in the

This Hite ferry in 1951 during the uranium boom. (Utah State Historical
Society)

venture. Lorin Griffin along with sons and sons-in-law and William
L. "Billy" Davis also worked many uranium claims in the Circle Cliffs
area.

Using geiger counters, Clarion and Clifford Barney and Mohr
Christensen sought out the ore in the county's petrified forest area.
The numerous mines carried colorful names often associated with
western mineral strikes—Midas, Copperheads, Partners, Sneaky,
Black Widow, Rainy Day, Silver Spur, and Skud Horse Butt, among
others—most owned by Boulder men who formed the Circle Cliffs
Uranium Company. They included Leland and Otto Haws, Neil and
Bill Jepsen, and Kay Coombs. Fred Hines also built a large operation
called Hinesville at the head of Silver Falls. Its facilities included electric lights and an airstrip, and it offered employment to a number of
men.

The claims index at the county recorder's office indicates that
prospectors filed more than 3,000 claims, Escalante residents alone
accounting for about 900 of them. As the boom was getting started

the Bureau of Land Management and local stockmen cooperated in getting a road built from Boulder through Long Canyon to The Flats, an area in close proximity to where the major local strikes were located. As mining operations progressed, larger companies moved in and many local prospectors leased their claims to these entities. As a result, some made a little money for their trouble; a few made several thousands of dollars. Unfortunately for others, they turned down generous offers to sell out, and, before they knew it, the uranium boom ceased. In the mid-1950s the Atomic Energy Commission announced first a cut-back and later a complete cessation of uranium purchases. The bottom fell out of the market, and many local miners had reason to regret their folly. By 1957 most of the area mines ceased operations, although a few held on for several more years. Even today some optimists feel uranium might once more become an important commodity locally. Only four other states, all from the West, produce more of the element than does Utah.

Ticaboo

An ample and ready source of uranium attracted an eastern power company to southeastern Garfield County in the 1970s to build a uranium mill. Consumers Power Inc. anticipated major growth in electrical power needs within the state of Michigan. To meet the demand the company embarked on building the Midland Nuclear Plant, a twin-reactor generating station covering an area in central Michigan the size of a thousand football fields. After acquiring some uranium mines in Garfield's Shootaring Canyon, a subsidiary of the utility, Plateau Resources Ltd., built a state-of-the-art mill to process the uranium ore for the parent company's use in its expansion.[18]

In conjunction with this interest in uranium, in the late 1960s the Roy May family of Green River dreamed of creating a community along Utah Highway 276 to facilitate the needs of recreationists heading to the Bullfrog Marina of Lake Powell. With this in mind, May obtained a fifty-one-year lease on state-owned land about twelve miles north of the marina. Knowing that accommodations would be needed for its workers both during construction and after the mill's completion, Plateau Resources offered May a minor partnership in its mill and mining venture and financed the designing and building of his projected community.

They called the 640-acre town "Ticaboo," a word from the Ute language meaning "friendly place." Following May's plans, the town included many features to create what was hoped to be an ideal community: underground power and telephone lines; gracefully curved streets with concrete sidewalks and gutters; a 500,000-gallon water-storage tank buried from view on the top of a nearby mesa; a sewage lagoon and diesel generators to provide electricity, both installed behind a hill beyond the sight of the town's residents; a 160-pad mobile-home park, completely plumbed and wired; ninety-six single-family homesites, with all utilities visually separated from the mobile-home development; a platted secluded area for multiple-family housing; a family education center to accommodate grades kindergarten through twelve; and, on the drawing board and surveyed, a nine-hole golf course. Adjacent to the residential area was built a commercial strip mall and a two-story motel, an integral part of the Ticaboo Lodge, which included a laundromat, bar, restaurant, and convenience store. State officials anticipated that Ticaboo would become the county's second-largest community.

By 1982 Ticaboo was ready for occupation; however, economically disastrous events prevented May's dream from being realized. After pouring $2.1 billion into construction of its Midland Nuclear Plant, Consumers Power Inc. realized that the huge increased demand for nuclear power they projected was not going to materialize—thus they no longer needed the uranium supplied by the Plateau mines. On the brink of bankruptcy, the company was able to convert the plant to a facility fueled by natural gas. It opened in 1990 and has thus far proven financially viable.

The company still had an obligation to maintain the mill at Ticaboo, as specified by federal regulations. However, the $56 million mill operated for only two months before it was closed. People did not come to fill up the town, which had added another $15 million to the company's debt. After the decision was made to close, Consumers Power accepted responsibility for all the debt incurred, keeping only four employees at Ticaboo to do the required maintenance work. They, along with their families and the teachers who

worked at the one-room schoolhouse, made up Ticaboo's population, quite a change from the more than 800 occupants who lived
there during the building phase of the late 1970s and early 1980s.[19]

In December 1992 the company put the mines, mill, and townsite on the auction block. In September 1993 it found a buyer, of
sorts. Consumer Power *paid* U.S. Energy Corporation of Riverton,
Wyoming, $14 million to assume responsibility for the whole enter-
prise. It would have cost the Michigan firm even more to tear down
the mill. The company decided to cut its losses and move on. U.S.
Energy took over the operation because it anticipated a resurgence in
the demand for uranium within the next few years. The company
foresaw the world running out of stockpiled processed uranium in
the future. There were 423 nuclear reactors in twenty-six countries,
more than one-quarter of these within the United States. With only
four uranium processing mills in the country, when at one time there
had been forty-one, U.S. Energy figured the price of the material
would go up and planned to be prepared to meet the increased
demand.

In 1993, residents of Ticaboo had other reasons for optimism.
The motel had recently opened and added a swimming pool and
satellite dish to its facilities. Also, U.S. Energy hired Plateau's employees, and the new company anticipated the opening of a recreational-
vehicle park to further attract tourists.

At present, Ticaboo shows signs of living up to its original potential. U.S. Energy is poised to begin full operation of the uranium mill.
It has received clearance from all federal and state environmental
agencies except the Division of Environmental Quality (DEQ).
Director of the DEQ Diane Neilson toured the facility in February
1998, and clearance from that agency is expected. Although the future
need for uranium is unpredictable, the Ticaboo mine is one of only
four mines in the United States that has been cleared by government
agencies for future production.[20]

In the meantime, tourist and growth activity has increased. The
motel generally is filled throughout the summer months, the town
now includes a boat-storage facility, a new store has opened, twenty-
five to thirty mobile homes are occupied, seven new homes have been
built, and a real estate development company has plans to build

twenty more. The community also has filed for additional water for future growth.

Other Mineral Development

The geological make-up of eastern Garfield County also has indicated the possibility that oil could lurk deep in the stratified layers of canyon and mesa. As early as 1920 the Ohio Oil Company employed Escalante and Boulder men to build a road and haul equipment to the northeast Circle Cliffs area. The results of drilling begun in January 1921 did not prove successful, however, so the company abandoned the project. In 1949 the oil company returned and drilled some distance to the south on Wagon Box Mesa. Although it struck oil in Mississippian strata, the thick consistency made the oil unmarketable at the time. The company capped the well and moved on but continually renewed its lease in the area.

In November 1963 drillers for the Tenneco Oil Corporation struck high-grade oil at their No. 2 well in the upper valley near Escalante. They found the oil at the 6,650-foot level. This represented what was called "the first commercial find of oil in the permian formation in Utah."[21] Soon the well delivered 125 barrels a day, and then it steadily increased its output in the following weeks and months, reaching a maximum of 333 barrels per day. On 31 December 1963 the first tankload of oil left the well and headed north to the Woods Cross, Utah, refinery. The company also found oil at another well located about 1.5 miles to the south. Even though the first well they dug also delivered a good grade of oil, certain porous formations made it too difficult to access, so it was abandoned.

By 1967 Tenneco had a total of seven producing area wells and had increased its output to 1,500 barrels a day. By November 1968 it reached 50,000 barrels a day. Production kept eighteen drivers busy hauling the crude oil twenty-four hours a day, seven days a week. Although storage tanks were originally located near the wells, by the early 1970s the oil came by pipe from the fields to new tanks located in a ravine near but out of sight of the highway. The company did this to be in compliance with mandates of the Environmental Protection Agency and so drivers could avoid the steep, winding, hazardous roads from the wells. Other companies dug for oil in areas surrounding

Escalante, but none of the ventures proved to be as successful as Tenneco's. Even with the temporary closing of the Skyline lumber mill in 1970 local residents did not suffer from unemployment because of plentiful jobs generated by oil drilling and related activities.

Some Garfield residents also had access to another natural resource that supported oil-drilling operations. Bentonite, found in large beds in the upper Paria Valley, is a clay that has several industrial uses. It swells to several times its original size when wet and can be used as a fire retardant, in molding sands, in oil-well drilling muds, and to remove the color from oils. In 1960 Al Foster and Byron Davies started a bentonite mill near Tropic. During their ten years of operation, they supplied over 100,000 tons of the material to the oil companies operating locally. Another bentonite mine was located near Henrieville. The clay came down a chute at the point of the hill to a bin and then was hauled away by truck. Some have speculated that this product could have great potential and be accessed on a larger scale.[22]

Escalante is situated in an area with abundant high-quality coal reserves close at hand. However, for various reasons, extensive mining of the mineral hasn't occurred in eastern Garfield County. Just after the turn of the century most of the area mining activity took place in Coal Canyon. Locals including Don Shurtz, Lawrence Christensen, Johnny Davis, William Richards, the Schow brothers, Zetland Mitchell, William Moosman, George Alvey and his sons, the Twitchells, and the Munsons all tried their hand at coal mining over the years. George Frandsen came over from Panguitch and worked two mines, one being the Cherry Creek Mine and the other the Munson/Twitchell Mine. During the 1920s the federal government withdrew all public domain coal lands from potential private ownership, requiring that they only be leased. Most miners carried out their operations on a relatively small scale, and most either sold out to others or simply quit.

Perhaps the greatest obstacle most of these miners faced was hauling the coal out of the area. Economically, it just wasn't worth the time and effort. In the mid-1960s geologists and representatives of power companies carried out intensive explorations and testing of nearby coal deposits. Newspaper headlines declared that a huge power plant would be built within five years on the Kaiparowits Plateau, fueled by coal mined in the area east of Escalante. The *Salt Lake Tribune* quoted Utah State Engineer Wayne C. Criddle as saying, "It would be one of the biggest mine ventures in the history of the world's coal industry."[23]

The Kaiparowits plant never materialized, however, because of several factors. These included governmental bureaucratic red tape, environmental concerns leading to expensive litigation, and the cost of bringing the coal to market. However, a master plan study for the county published at the beginning of 1970 judged prospects hopeful for the future of coal and other mineral and oil development. As mineral finds occur, it asserted, "outside interests would be prepared to support any profitable venture."[24] However, as time would attest, the development of these resources proved far more complicated than those who prepared the study could have imagined.

Agricultural Developments

Agriculture had been the basis of Garfield County's economy since the time of white settlement, and figures for 1950—five years after the war ended—indicated that agrarian employment still dominated. Out of an employed work force of 1,137, 476 held agricultural jobs, a number greater by far than that of any of the other major employment groupings. This figure does not include family members who worked on farms and ranches without reported compensation.[25] An employment report for October 1947 from the Utah Department of Employment Security demonstrated the dominance of agriculture. Its figures included the self-employed, family workers, and hired labor. The agency noted that out of 1,725 jobs, 1,250 were agricultural.

Even though the county is the fifth largest in the state in terms of land area—with 5,158 square miles, or more than 3.3 million acres—only a small percentage of its land could actually be planted in crops. Three factors contributed to this situation: a short growing season due to the high elevation of much of the county; a frequent lack of dependable and accessible water; and generally rough topography. Much of the land, especially to the east, is composed of deep canyons, arid mesas, and various spectacular formations that are certainly pleasing to the eye but are impossible to farm. Therefore, farmers had to be creative and selective in what they planted. In some of the warmer areas to the east they raised corn and had fruit orchards that provided a livelihood for some. Nearly all residents had some type of kitchen garden adjacent to their homes even if they didn't farm for a living. Grains, hay, and alfalfa did well and complemented the live-stock industry that thrived early on with the ample pasturage. Potatoes also became an important crop.

During the early decades, the number of potatoes grown in the county was such that school in some areas would be let out several days in the spring so children could help cut and plant potatoes and again in the fall to harvest them. But growing potatoes could be dis-appointing. One writer observed that the population of Antimony by 1970 had dropped once again because farming became more difficult as the potato crop diminished "due to late frosts in the spring and early frosts in the fall making the growing season almost too short."[26]

Prior to mid-century the number of farms dwindled throughout Garfield. Again, as noted by Antimony's historian, "People were mov-ing to the cities because farming was becoming more costly for the small operator, and the price of equipment was rising, making prof-its hard to come by."[27] During the 1950s and 1960s the number of farms stayed constant but, as one study notes, "the composition has changed. There is a general decrease in small farms under eighty acres with an increase in farms with more acreage."[28] As people moved out of the county, not only was there a declining labor force, but far fewer people worked in agriculture. By the end of the 1960s, out of 1,120 county wage earners only 190 worked at agrarian jobs.[29] The number of livestock owned by farmers began to decline and has continued to do so, as will be discussed later.

For many residents, farming was what they loved or perhaps their only option if they wanted to remain living in the close-knit communities in which they were raised. Dewey and Teora Newby Willis, for example, both came from small southern Utah towns; they tried living along Utah's Wasatch Front during the early 1950s but wished to live out their days in Henrieville. When the opportunity came for them to return home to run Dewey's father's farm, they took it. They tried to buy additional fields to add to their acreage but had great difficulty clearing deeds and titles and securing loans. To help out financially, Teora wrote, "Dewey worked all kinds of jobs to go with it. He drove school bus, state road and road construction; anything he could get to supplement our farm income." She also describes how her husband "would pack his horses and go out on the range for 10 to 20 days at a time. These were drought years and the cattle did not do well. We never did make enough to pay for the time we were putting in." Teora also worked summers at nearby Bryce Canyon to bring in extra money.[30]

The Second World War enhanced the economic viability of agriculture throughout the nation; indeed, it accomplished for the farmer what none of the New Deal measures could. Large commercial farms and ranches benefited the most; but all food growers, including those in Garfield County, found a ready market for their produce. The demand for meat was especially great. Although the stock industry in the county was nothing like it had been during the first decades of settlement, some of the conservation measures instituted by government agencies and local stockmen were achieving desirable results.[31] Herds had been reduced to manageable sizes that the public rangeland could better support, which helped provide a more reliable food supply for the nation.

Ranchers began to have confidence in range-management techniques even though not all reseeding programs, combined with mandated herd reduction, proved successful. Along with range regeneration, many new water developments enhanced cattle-raising potential. The number of cattle in the county, after dipping substantially during the late 1930s and early 1940s, increased by 1950 and remained almost constant for another twenty years. Interestingly, however, the number of sheep being raised declined significantly. In 1935, tax figures indicate there were 100,571 sheep in the county; by 1969 the number had plummeted to 6,082 head. The fact that it became more and more difficult to hire men to herd sheep could have been a factor. Also, ranchers had to pay so much a head to graze their stock on national forest or BLM ranges. The costs for these permits grew from seven cents per animal unit month (AUM) to $1.25 per AUM. Ranchers felt they would receive a greater return on their investment by raising cattle, which offered dairying as an alternative and the sale of hides in addition to meat.

Branding cattle on the summer range near Boulder. (Courtesy Fay Jepson)

Interestingly, while the number of farms decreased from 491 in 1935 to 296 in 1969, much more acreage was involved. In 1935 all county agricultural land comprised 92,616 acres, while in 1969 cropland combined with pasture and range amounted to 264,531 acres. Pasture and range figures led planners in 1970 to conclude that there was an allocation of almost ten acres per head of cattle or sheep in the county and that this per capita figure could be raised. However, global market factors along with increases in costs and government regulations over the last three decades have discouraged more intensive stock raising in the county.

Planners also suggested that, taking all factors into consideration, especially the county's short growing season, Garfield crop growers might investigate the possibilities of hydroponic farming. Hydroponics is the science of growing crops without soil; that is, plants are grown in tanks filled with coarse sand, gravel, and water to which nutrients are added. However, scientists generally agree that growing plants in soil is still a much more dependable way to produce crops. Even if hydroponics were used, local producers would face stiff competition from abroad, where growing conditions are far superior and production less expensive.

The Burgeoning Tourist Industry

A number of federal government measures helped lead to Garfield County's increased emphasis on the tourist trade. In 1957 President Dwight Eisenhower signed the Interstate Highway Act of 1956 to create a national interstate freeway system. This thirteen-year program would be the most extensive public works project in U.S. history. Although the move had Cold War defense implications, many industries throughout the nation benefited from the new freeways, including tourism. No interstate highway traversed any portion of Garfield County, but the system improved visitors' overall access to the county's existing roadways, which the state and county gradually upgraded.

It was a long time after the federal government designated Bryce Canyon a national park before Garfield County had any of its other scenic wonders granted that status; but the next two were created within a much shorter time span. In 1964 a ruggedly beautiful area located mostly in western San Juan County received national park designation. The boundaries of the new Canyonlands National Park also spilled into eastern Wayne County along the Green River and to the northeastern tip of Garfield County in close proximity to the Colorado River. The park is divided into three distinct districts. The southern portion of the Maze district, comprising slickrock canyons and redrock formations, is located in Garfield County and is a very primitive area.

The next national park designation within the county involved greater controversy and complications. Residents of eastern Garfield County—and most of Utah, for that matter—received a shock on 20 January 1969 when President Lyndon B. Johnson signed a decree adding 215,000 acres (much of it in Garfield County) to the existing 39,173 acres making up Capitol Reef National Monument. This national monument in Wayne County had been created in 1937.[32] President Johnson had been assured by Secretary of the Interior Stewart L. Udall that this move would not be controversial. Instead, a violent outcry followed the announcement, and even the state's Democratic senator, Frank Moss, was caught unprepared by the magnitude of the increase. Stockmen from Boulder and Wayne County were most affected economically by the president's move and voiced their opposition. Over the ensuing two years, as Moss together with Republican Senator Wallace F. Bennett and Republican Congressman Lawrence J. Burton held hearings on the enlargement of the monument, it became obvious that many in other groups were equally outraged, including leaders of the BLM, U.S. Forest Service, and U.S. Soil Conservation Services. The Sierra Club, the Wasatch Mountain Club, and the Isaac Walton League, however, were among those who supported the expansion and hoped it would lead to the inclusion of all the Escalante River Basin in one great park or wilderness area.

Senator Moss and Senator Alan Bible of Nevada, chairman of the Senate Interior Committee, worked together to readjust the new boundaries. They eliminated from monument designation the Grand Gulch area used by Wayne County stockmen and the Circle Cliffs parcel used by Garfield County ranchers to graze their stock. They substituted for this land some 29,000 acres mostly to the north that included some of the area's most spectacular scenery. It reportedly had been omitted from the original designation in Johnson's haste to make an announcement before he left office.

Senator Moss next introduced legislation that changed both Capitol Reef and Arches in Grand County from national monument to national park status. Three years after Johnson's original decree, in January 1972, President Richard Nixon signed the bill creating Capitol Reef National Park. The park contained 241,671 acres, very little less than the original proposal.

By the early 1970s, Garfield County was well established as a tourist mecca. Garfield provided a gateway for much of southern Utah's and northern Arizona's most visited scenic sights. In addition, the county had one national park completely within its borders, shared another with Wayne County, still another with both Wayne and San Juan counties, and had part of the popular Glen Canyon National Recreation area along its eastern boundary. In 1972 the federal government created that recreational area, following the completion of the Glen Canyon Dam in 1964. Lake Powell, created as the dam backed up the Colorado River, is the second largest manmade lake in the nation. Even though neither the dam nor any of the lake's main marinas are located in Garfield County, some of the lake's most spectacular scenery is accessed by boating into some of Garfield's canyons, such as through Bullfrog Bay. The county also provides some of the vehicular passageways into the recreation area.

Working hand-in-hand with these developments, some local citizens began to provide accommodations for the influx of tourists. A dozen motels appeared in Panguitch between the end of World War II and 1970. Four eating establishments complemented these facilities—the Bryce Canyon Cafe, the Flying M, Orton's Cafe, and the Ru-Mil Cafe—although this last eatery, owned by Rula Houston and Mildred Riggs catered more to the local high school crowd than to out-of-town visitors.

Hatch residents operated two and sometimes three motels during this time period, and small cafes opened for varying lengths of time, usually changing ownership on a regular basis. Wanlass and Dena Alvey opened the first overnight accommodations in Escalante in 1937 to provide housing for some of the CCC men. Over the years they continued to add to their facilities, until they had created a motel complete with swimming pool and opened a cafe and service station. In the meantime, three other motels offered accommodations (the first one built by Leo Munson and later owned by Claron and Ruby Griffin), three cafes served home-style meals, and the Alveys also opened a drive-in eatery.[33]

Curio shops, selling such things as polished rocks, Indian crafts, and other handmade articles, attracted tourists. Panguitch had one such establishment on the south end of the town's retail district. Ron and Virginia Young in Hatch owned a shop in conjunction with their gas station. In Escalante, John and Lola Zenz opened a rock shop, where they made beautiful gifts from petrified wood found nearby. Even though John Zenz gradually lost his eyesight, he could still operate the necessary equipment. The couple not only served people who visited their shop but also had customers throughout the state and beyond.

In another effort to accommodate tourists, Mayor H.J. Allen of Escalante announced on 1 July 1966 the town's intention to create a new airport. Three entities provided funding for the project—the Federal Aviation Agency, the Utah State Aeronautics Commission, and the town of Escalante. At first it was intended to widen and lengthen an old existing runway, but community officials later decided to build a new one. Kelly Construction Company cleared and leveled the land, while the Mendenhall Company built the runway. Men in the town built the road from the airport to Utah Highway 12 and installed the necessary fencing. Don Kelly, who leased the airport facilities from the city after they were completed, built a reception center, office building, repair shop, and installed gas pumps. Dignitaries dedicated the $128,500 facility on 13 June 1970. A barbecue dinner and dance followed the ceremonies.

Garfield's natural wonders were not all that attracted outside visitors, and the coming of fall did not necessarily shut down tourist-oriented businesses. During the last two weeks in October deer hunters inundated local communities. Most came from Utah's Wasatch Front and from California. The annual deer hunt had become a celebration of sorts for locals as well as out-of-towners. Many towns hosted a deer hunters' ball on the night before opening day of the hunt. Motel rooms filled up and local restaurants and grocery stores did a brisk business.

Interestingly, this area did not have a great abundance of deer when the early settlers first arrived. Old-timers could not recall that the early settlers hunted deer very often, although wild game certainly augmented their regular diet. According to one early observer, "the sighting of two or three deer was considered significant in the old days."[34] Many argue that deer herds began to increase after the implementation of range reseeding programs and the reduction in domestic livestock. For whatever reason, the hunt became a real boost to southern Utah's economy.

Although it did not generate the concentrated excitement that the deer hunt did, fishing also continued to lure visitors. Panguitch Lake and other smaller lakes and clear mountain streams throughout the county promised great sport and an abundant yield to anglers. One fisherman, Chan Lee, caught an eighteen-pound trout in Panguitch Lake in the early 1940s; it was believed to be the biggest fish that the lake ever yielded. Recreational fishing stimulated the establishment of trailer parks and campgrounds. Because Otter Creek just over the county line in Piute County offered excellent fishing,

Bryant Riddle decided to purchase a store in Antimony from Wayne Delange during the 1960s and add a cafe and trailer park to it.[35]

Even if those who came to fish did not always have a lot of luck, the experience could be most satisfying. Clearly, Garfield County offered all visitors exceptionally beautiful and varied scenery in an atmosphere of utter tranquility, with western hospitality at its best. In turn, tourists could provide certain economic benefits to county residents that traditional industries no longer could. Jobs in the service sector and retail and government employment—all related to tourism—increased during the middle and later decades of the twentieth century as those related to agriculture declined. As mentioned, the Utah Parks Company as well as a prospering Ruby's Inn provided summer employment for many of the county's young people.

Garfield Citizens Experience the World and Beyond

Television as a communications tool played little importance until the late 1940s in the country. By the end of the 1950s, however, the majority of homes in America had television sets. Much of Garfield County did not enjoy television until the late 1950s and early 1960s. Panguitch received television transmission first as the signal came from a station installed on top of Bear Valley Mountain. Information is lacking as to when Hatch received TV reception, but presumably it did not come long after Panguitch.

The people of Escalante at first attempted to receive signals from a station on Griffin Top during the late 1950s. They reasoned that since this was the highest peak around it would provide a strong signal. Unfortunately, the efforts of Wilford Griffin, Lynn Gates, and Billy Davis proved futile in this first attempt. They then selected another site that allowed them to pick up signals from the Panguitch station. But further testing indicated that a stronger signal came from Wayne County at a station on Fish Lake Mountain. The men finally moved the station west, where they could get even better reception, on Rocky Lake Point, so named by Davis.

Finding funds for the tower, generator, and other needed equipment became a priority for townspeople. Gates, the president of the newly organized Escalante Lions Club, became chairman of the TV committee, and the club did much to raise money for the project.

They solicited several donations, and various activities, including a dance, brought in additional funding. Donations in labor were also important. Paul Steed, owner of Skyline Lumber, contributed men and equipment to build a road to Rocky Lake Point and level the area for the tower construction and generator. The cost of equipment came to about $35,000, and Escalante also paid Wayne County forty dollars a month for its maintenance work on the station. After completion, Escalante had access to the three national network television stations.

In 1965 an additional tower with a ten-foot-diameter dish was installed to receive public-television channels in the community. Arnold Alvey, an employee of Garkane Power, and Bill Kruska assisted in installing this addition. In May 1968 the Escalante town government took over TV service. City government continued to collect a two dollar per month fee from those receiving reception in their homes, and additional funding came from other sources; for instance, Boulder paid to use Escalante's signal.[36]

Other Garfield towns also received television reception during the early 1960s. Mayor Archie Gleave of Antimony and the town board labored hard to get service into their community. After first locating a tower on high land northeast of town, they found they could get better reception when they moved the tower to some hills just west of Otter Creek Reservoir.[37] The towns of upper Paria Valley, or Bryce Valley as it came to be called, all received television reception from a common source in 1962. Al Foster and Bill Davis, again with the help of the local Lions Club, got the project underway. Cannonville historian George Thompson explained the process:

> They took a small gas generator and a television set up to the top of the highest mountain around, found where the signal was strongest, put up the antennas and installed the equipment. It wasn't long until most families had T.V. and it seemed pretty good except, sometimes it was hard to tell the men from the horses, or Miss Kitty from Festus on "Gunsmoke," because of a snowy screen.[38]

June Shakespear noted that the mountain Thompson referred to was Canaan Mountain. Al Foster told Shakespear that he and Davis watched a ball game on a TV run by a protable generator on their first trip up the mountain to locate the strongest signal. Then Arthur Goulding, Vee (Gabby) Smith, and Foster hauled all the equipment up to the area on Smith's mule and three pack horses. Shakespear concluded, "Then on February 20, 1962, twelve TV sets were turned on in Al Foster's store and a large crowd watched John Glenn travel around the earth."[39]

Television opened up the world for many residents of Garfield County. Television programs were especially welcomed by older, homebound citizens, adding variety to their lives when they had little hope of traveling beyond the confines of their small communities. It became a learning tool for the elderly as well as for schoolchildren, as educational television was brought into the classrooms.

The coming of television also doomed the local movie theater in Panguitch, however. Managed by Russell and Memphis Talbot for almost twenty years, the theater provided jobs for their teenage children and other young people in town. After the mid-1950s the Allens and then the Wilcoxs ran the showhouse for brief periods. It finally shut down in the early 1960s. The theater no longer could attract crowds sufficient to pay for the latest movie release rentals. The show-house in Escalante suffered a similar fate. Gail and Reva Bailey ran the theater until it closed its doors, which was largely because of television. With no movie theater anywhere in the county today, there are numbers of Garfield residents who have never seen a movie in a theater. Rather than travel to Cedar City or Richfield, they simply wait for films to come out on video.

The Korean and Vietnam Wars

Exposure to world events did not always produce positive experiences. Conflicts in Asia—the Korean and Vietnam wars—would once again involve young people from Garfield County. Because the nature of these clashes differed from the two previous world wars, their impact was not as great on as many of Garfield's young people or their families; however, considering the county's reduction in population, the percentage of those serving in the conflicts was still substantial. Uncle Sam called up some of those who had already served in World War II to fight in Korea along with fresh recruits in the late

1940s and early 1950s. Some lost their lives, while others had to put their private aspirations on hold. Escalante sent more than ninety young men to Korea; one of them did not return—DeLoy Blood died in action on 13 July 1953. According to a monument in Panguitch that recognizes all those who have served in the armed forces from that community, 101 young people saw duty during the Vietnam era. Of this relatively large number, four lost their lives: Jim Jennings, Steven Moore, Paul Talbot, and David R. Veater.

During the Vietnam conflict of the 1960s and early 1970s thirty-five men served from the Escalante community, and one lost his life. Staff Sargeant Gary George Chestnut died of gunshot wounds on 2 December 1967 after having been wounded on four previous occasions during his four years in Vietnam.[40] Tropic resident Chris Munson was also killed in Vietnam. Henrieville had more than thirty men serve their country in the Korean and Vietnam wars. Thirty-eight men and one woman, Le Ann Hayes, from Hatch served in the military during this time period. Boulder sent a dozen young men to fight in Vietnam.

Schools and Churches

Life continued to evolve in positive ways as well, however. The look of each community changed as new building projects improved the infrastructure of the towns. Consolidation of schools closed some buildings but also brought improved and upgraded facilities to most schoolchildren. Indeed, a report released in 1970 found that "the present level of general education [in the county] is more than adequate to meet present needs," and further stated that the citizens "are stalwart and to be commended" in their financial commitment to their school system.[41]

Cannonville students had been traveling to Tropic for high school since 1920. Beginning in 1954 their younger counterparts would also travel to the new Bryce Valley elementary school at Tropic. Cannonville residents hated to see their well-constructed schoolhouse not being utilized, however. So, being resourceful, they moved the school across the street in 1963 and added it to their LDS chapel, with one new roof over all. After some additional remodeling and renovation, this provided a much needed cultural hall and additional classrooms for the church. Proud Cannonville residents rededicated the structure as part of their centennial celebration on 24 July 1976.

The construction of new buildings or the remodeling of existing LDS ecclesiastical structures also took place in Tropic, Antimony, Hatch, and Boulder. These included a new seminary building and the upgrading of recreational facilities. Residents of Boulder had to start from the ground up, as their Mormon church suffered a devastating fire in March 1960. Work began in 1961, and in October 1964 local residents hosted the Garfield LDS Stake conference in their new building. Apostle John Longden dedicated the new chapel at that meeting. Other new construction included a post office in Tropic, a tennis court, in Hatch and improved roads in and around Boulder. Both Hatch and Henrieville also completed much-needed improvements in their culinary water systems. With public cooperation and help from the federal government, Escalante completed the Wide Hollow Reservoir and various other conservation projects. These and other projects contributed to improvements in the quality of life for Garfield residents.

But the coming decades brought additional problems to some long-time county residents. According to census figures, after 1970 the population for most of the county had stopped its downward spiral. However, as the number of residents slowly started to increase in most towns, the make-up of the citizenry started to change: many of the newcomers had no historical connections with Garfield, and some were not members of the Mormon church, presenting an unusual, and to some, an unpleasant situation. Locals began to wonder how this would alter the feelings of community, so much a part of small-town life and cherished by long-time residents whose ancestors helped settle these villages.

Also, agencies and programs of the federal government had contributed much to the development of Garfield County, whether it was in the area of range revitalization, water projects, road building and maintenance, or numerous other much-needed enterprises. Local residents, however, objected to accompanying restrictions, particularly regarding the use and management of public lands, which they desired to use in traditional ways. How much control should Washington have in weighing environmental concerns against local economic development strategies? was one of the questions asked. Are the two, in fact, mutually exclusive? Mountain Area Planners of Salt Lake City, having been commissioned by county officials in the late 1960s to make an economic, population, and housing study, concluded that Garfield had many advantages. But it also possessed some disadvantages, none of which were insurmountable. The study concluded:

> Above all, the most important factor influencing the economic future of Garfield County is attitude. There are far too many individuals satisfied with things as they are, or who do not want to change things as they are, or who are defeatists with a conviction that it is futile to try. These attitudes must be changed for the better in order to hope for a better future.[42]

Could county residents prove these prognosticators wrong by rising above low expectations and defeatism? The next three decades would indeed prove to be challenging and interesting.

ENDNOTES

1. Effel Harmon Burrow Riggs, *History of Hatch, Utah, and Associated Towns Asay and Hillsdale*, 328–29.

2. Ida Chidester and Eleanor Bruhn, *Golden Nuggets of Pioneer Days: A History of Garfield County*, 348–49.

3. Jack Breed, "First Motor Sortie into Escalante Land," *National Geographic* (September 1949): 369–404; Chidester and Bruhn, *Golden Nuggets*, 350–51.

4. Lenora Hall LeFevre, *The Boulder Country and Its People: A History of the People of Boulder and the Surrounding Country*, 261.

5. Nicholas Scrattish, *Historic Resource Study: Bryce Canyon National Park*, 122–23.

6. Ibid., 116, 121.

7. Ibid., 134.

8. Ibid., 135–36.

9. Ibid., 138.

10. Ibid., 168–72.

11. See Nethella Griffin Woolsey, *The Escalante Story: 1875–1964*, 119–20; and Marilyn Jackson, "Escalante's Heritage, A Viable Cattle Industry," (1997), 14, 16, 17, 29, copy of paper in possession of authors.

12. Ibid.

13. Riggs, *History of Hatch,* 256–57.

14. Clark Frandsen, interview with Vivian L. Talbot, Panguitch, Utah, 25 September 1997, notes in possession of authors; Devon Owens, interview with Vivian L. Talbot, 26 September 1997, notes in possession of authors.

15. LeFevre, *Boulder Country,* 276.

16. Mountain Area Planners, "Economic, Population and Housing Study, Garfield County Master Plan Studies," 1970, 14, copy in possession of authors.

17. See Woolsey, *Escalante Story,* 184–85; LeFevre, *Boulder Country,* 253–54; and "Uranium," in *World Book Encyclopedia,* 1978 ed.

18. See Christopher Smith, "Boomtown Is Bust Before It Ever Boomed," *Salt Lake Tribune,* 28 December 1992, B1.

19. Ibid.; Christopher Smith, "Wyoming Company Bringing Utah Ghost Town Back to Life," *Salt Lake Tribune,* 4 September 1993, A1.

20. "Garfield County, Utah General Plan," 1995, D-4, copy in possession of authors.

21. Woolsey, *Escalante Story,* 180.

22. June Shakespear, "Tropic," 9; Smith, "One and One Makes Eleven," 66.

23. As quoted in Woolsey, *Escalante Story,* 178.

24. Mountain Area Planners, "Economic, Population and Housing Study," 14.

25. Ibid., 26.

26. M. Lane Warner, *Grass Valley 1873–1976: A History of Antimony and Her People,* 68.

27. Ibid., 61.

28. Mountain Area Planners, "Economic, Population and Housing Study," 29.

29. Ibid., 26.

30. Teora Newby Willis, autobiography, 12, copy obtained by authors from Nancy Twitchell.

31. Information and figures on stock raising in Garfield County from the 1930s through the 1960s came from Mountain Area Planners, "Economic, Population and Housing Study," 29–33; Jackson, "Escalante's Heritage," 14–15; and Woolsey, *Escalante Story,* 138–40.

32. See LeFevre, *Boulder Country,* 291–92; *Utah Atlas and Gazetteer* (Freeport, ME: DeLorme Mapping, 1993), 12.

33. Wanlass Alvey, interview with Marilyn Jackson, 29 April 1996, Escalante, Utah; Woolsey, *Escalante Story,* 160–62.

34. From an interview with Riley C. Savage in Jackson, "Escalante's Heritage," 5.

35. Warner, *Grass Valley,* 67.

36. Woolsey, *Escalante Story* supplement, (1974), 15–17.

37. Warner, *Grass Valley,* 64.

38. George W. Thompson, "Cannonville History," 37.

39. Shakespear, "Tropic," 7.

40. Woolsey, *Escalante Story* supplement, 69.

41. Mountain Area Planners, "Economic, Population and Housing Study," 43.

42. Ibid., 11, 14.

CHAPTER 13

CHANGE AMID CONTROVERSY

One of the most singular elements in Garfield County's recent experience has been controversy. For much of its history the county seemed insulated from strife regarding national issues. Perhaps the only exception to this was the early debate about polygamy and how its practice related to religious freedom. In the last three decades, however, the national agenda has come to revolve more and more around issues dealing with the environment and the management and use of public lands. It is perhaps inevitable that a county so rich in spectacular physical features, whose residents also wish to access its natural resources should find itself in the middle of a public debate on appropriate land use.

Some 89 percent of Garfield County's land area is controlled by federal government agencies. Clashes over its management have been inevitable. The same government that provided the means for many public improvements in Garfield has frustrated local leaders in their attempts to fund what they see as beneficial projects and programs for their constituents and still remain within federal and state planning guidelines.

Added to this are controversies relating to another national trend—urban flight. The increase in county population since 1970, although not great, has nevertheless been steady. For some communities the influx of new people has caused difficulties for lifelong residents, while for others the results have been positive or hardly noticed. As the county has wrestled with these and related issues, the one thing Garfield citizens have come to expect is change amid controversy.

Antimony Residents Want to Change Counties

A dispute that has reared its head on more than one occasion involves the location of Antimony within the boundaries of Garfield County. From its very beginning, the town has had a close social and economic connection with Kingston, fourteen miles to the west, which is firmly entrenched in Piute County. When the state legislature drew up the county boundaries in 1882 Antimony citizens found themselves south of the almost straight line defining Garfield County's northern border. Even today, in order for Antimony residents to gain access to U.S. Highway 89, the main thoroughfare through western Garfield County, they have to travel through Piute County by way of Kingston to Circleville. However, the community is also located in the north end of Johns Valley, and there is direct access going south out of Antimony to the eastern part of the county.

As a result, Antimony residents petitioned to be annexed by Piute County, and the issue appeared on the 1974 ballot. Town mayor Charles Brindley argued in favor of this annexation. He stated, "Our kids go to Piute County schools, our girls compete in Piute County beauty contests. . . . All of our activities are connected with Piute County, even though we are inside the Garfield County line by three or four miles."[1] A majority of the voters in both Garfield and Piute counties had to agree to the annexation for the measure to pass, however; and although there was a concerted effort to convince Garfield residents and its leaders that Antimony had a legitimate argument, voters defeated the proposal at the polls. Antimony petitioners brought up the controversy again two years later. Even though the vast majority of Antimony's voters supported annexation by Piute

County, the measure failed again, other Garfield County voters wanting to retain the tax base and population provided by the town.[2]

Women in Local Government

For more than two decades some Garfield County municipalities elected women mayors. Cannonville citizens elected Laurie Dea Holley in 1974. A native of Cannonville and former schoolteacher and postmistress, Holley served for twelve years as mayor.[3] Judging her town's culinary water system to be completely inadequate, she first turned her attention there. Holley knew that the federal government had grant and low-interest money available to update such systems in hard-pressed communities. She prevailed upon an engineer friend to study the town's water system, recommend changes, and take care of the paperwork necessary to obtain federal funding. By mutual agreement, he would be given the contract for the project if the monies came through, otherwise the city owed him nothing.

As soon as the application received approval, construction began. A spring near the Paria River became the main source of water. It flowed through a concrete spring box into a new line to a large concrete storage tank, where it was treated and then sent through additional lines to homes. Cannonville residents could now depend on water that had a flow of more than 100 gallons per minute, as compared to only six gallons per minute under the old system. Adequate water for fire fighting was a by-product of this improvement.

Mayor Holley next turned her attention to a community eyesore, the old local school lot, which was overgrown with weeds and littered with discarded trash. Through research Holley discovered that Cannonville had some money coming to it from both town and county tax sources. She persuaded the town to use these funds to create a park complete with lush green lawns watered by a newly installed sprinkling system, shade trees, "picnic tables, benches, grills, an open fire pit, playground equipment, a covered grandstand, lights and sanitary garbage disposal."[4] The park provides a center for outdoor community festivities and is an oasis for weary tourists as they travel through the scenic area.

One improvement called for another: the badly neglected lot across the street from the park also caught the eye of the mayor. By judicious management of funds, the city purchased the property. Town board member Michael "Jim" Clarke designed a community center in a Southwest architectural style, which blended beautifully with the surrounding natural landscape. The center features a wagon wheel over its entrance proudly emblazoned with the words "City of Cannonville." Its attractive visage and public restrooms complement the public park that it faces.

Also as a result of her search for government funding sources, Mayor Holley found money for street improvement. Augmented by donated time and equipment, the funds proved adequate to pave most of the dirt backstreets in the town.

Another innovation promoted by the mayor began a new tradition for Cannonville residents. The Utah Old Time Fiddlers Association had been performing in the city park each summer since 1978. That year, former mayor Jim Clarke organized the first concert with the cooperation of Karl Allred and Ron Lee, members of the association. In 1987 Mayor Holley scheduled the event between the Fourth and Twenty-fourth of July.

That same summer a bear from the nearby hills became a frequent visitor to local gardens and garbage cans. When the bear attempted to enter Robert and Mira Loy Ott's house, wildlife officer Charlie Greenwood reluctantly killed the 300-pound animal. On hearing of the incident, Mayor Holley contacted the Utah Fish and Game Department and persuaded officials to let the townspeople have the carcass. The head and pelt went to make a rug for the community center, and, in July 1987, local participants and those from far and wide came to the first Cannonville Old Time Fiddlers Bear Festival. Guests enjoyed playing and listening to music performed on traditional instruments and eating barbecued bearburgers on homemade buns, washed down with homemade root beer. The success of the festival exceeded all expectations and continues to be an annual affair—although the menu has since been altered somewhat.[5]

When the town of Boulder incorporated in 1958, Irene King served as the first president of the town council.[6] Beginning in 1978 the town successively elected three women mayors. Vivian Holmes Crosby, a horse rancher and relative newcomer (originally from Ohio), was the first. She brought order and consistency to city government by holding regular council meetings for the first time in Boulder's history. Under her administration the town also passed its first zoning laws. She obtained a grant to widen the town's culverts and oversaw the complete renovation of the old schoolhouse into a much-used community center. Another grant helped the town procure fire-fighting and playground equipment. Under Crosby's administration Boulder also received service awards from the state and county, including the prestigious Community Progress Award, netting the town $500, with which residents added another standard to the community basketball court.[7]

Residents of Boulder next elected Donna Moosman Wilson as mayor when Crosby could not run again because of personal considerations. Wilson, a native of Boulder, had become the first woman member of the town board in 1976 and served in that capacity for six years. She too secured grant money, this time to build a fire station and obtain uniforms and equipment to go with it. The grant stipulated that those servicing the station must be properly trained. She arranged for that training, with the understanding that ten individuals would take the course. When the class fell one short of the required number, Wilson joined the class herself. While mayor she and the council saw to it that all the roads in town were oiled along with some of those in lower Boulder.

Because of Wilson's work with local and state school boards, the community received public television programming for the first time, at no expense to the townspeople. While serving two terms, Wilson also represented other Garfield County mayors as a member of the regional association known as the Five County Association of Governments, which represents Beaver, Garfield, Iron, Kane, and Washington counties, focusing on promoting industrial growth and tourist travel in the five-county area. She continues to work for the community as a member of the planning commission.

Most recently, Julee Lyman, a native of Escalante and long-time farmer, became mayor through a different route. Lyman had no intention of launching a political career; however, in 1990 Boulder citizens voted her into office as a write-in candidate. Although she had no prior experience in government, Lyman accepted the responsibility. She made decisions based on the wishes of her constituents while implementing new municipal guidelines prescribed by the state.

A survey taken after she had been in office a short time indicated that most residents wanted to avoid growth and change in Boulder. Lyman said in 1993, "They want the town to stay like it is, with its rural atmosphere and respect for the heritage we have here."[8] As mandated by the state, the town drew up its own general plan, created a planning commission, and began the issuance of building permits with requisite inspections. It was among the first in the county to do the latter.

Despite the hopes of many locals, after long being an isolated community, Boulder has been "discovered." Tourism has escalated faster than anyone anticipated. The improvements on Utah Highway 12 and its designation as a Scenic Byway and the controversial paving of the Burr Trail (discussed in the following pages) have contributed to the influx of visitors. There also are those who have come to stay. Artists, summer residents, and those who wish to establish tourist facilities are gravitating to the community. Some of the newcomers want to see changes in Boulder, and therein lies a challenge for the mayor and those who will succeed her. Many of the new residents have higher incomes and are building more expensive dwellings than those of the long-time residents. Some of these residences are located within close proximity to forested areas, thus increasing their vulnerability to fire danger. Newcomers also often expect the town to provide the infrastructure and amenities to which they have been accustomed in urban locations, but the town does not have the tax base to provide all of these.

During her tenure Mayor Lyman has overseen some improvements, however. The city purchased a new fire truck, added a new kitchen to the town hall, and applied for land for a town park. With volunteer labor, the community has taken a garage formerly used to house the school bus, renovated and remodeled it into a commodious post office, and now leases it to the federal government.

Mayor Lyman and others also have been successful in getting the school district to build a new elementary school in Boulder. Now children from kindergarten through sixth-grade ages no longer have to travel to Escalante to attend classes. The quality of the education offered is excellent; in the 1990s Boulder children scored among the highest in the district in every subject.

With the increase in new residents additional problems have surfaced. For example, the owner of a tourist facility, who the city previously helped by putting approval of his establishment on a fast track, applied to the city to serve alcohol on his premises. Reflecting the wishes of the majority of Boulder citizens, local ordinances prohibit such activity. Now, for the first time in its history, the community faces a lawsuit, as the applicant has charged city authorities with discrimination. This is clearly an issue with a religious foundation, pitting established Mormon residents against non-Mormon newcomers, though some non-Mormons also wish to keep the community dry.[9]

The physical makeup of the town is also changing. As cattle allotments on public land are decreasing, local large land holders are subdividing their property into smaller lots, because these long-time residents see an opportunity to make extra money from their property. This is especially true in lower Boulder, where a number of young families who could not afford larger tracts of land have moved in. In spite of the wishes of many for Boulder to remain a small farm and ranch community, residents have found that the march of change seems inevitable and has its price.

Panguitch has also had the leadership of a woman mayor. Elaine Marshall Baldwin came to Panguitch around 1967.[10] This Minersville native then served on the city council for six years before her election to the mayor's office. She and the Panguitch City Council oversaw the completion of an extensive project spanning the tenures of three previous mayors—a sewer system for the city. Panguitch thus joined other Garfield communities, Escalante, Tropic, and Ticaboo, in providing facilities for wastewater disposal and treatment. At this writing, plans are underway for Panguitch to receive a natural-gas line. The service will most likely come through Dog Valley to the north of town. Once natural-gas service is in place in Panguitch, other towns along highways 89 and 12 will also receive it. This will certainly cut fuel costs for Garfield residents and provide greater convenience; however, controversy also surrounds this activity and will be discussed later in this chapter.

Another focus of Baldwin's administration has been one that seems incongruent with some common misperceptions of what life is like in rural southern Utah—ridding the town of drugs. In their determination to do something about this problem, the city council has worked with law enforcement and school personnel, leading to the arrest of seventeen drug dealers in a two-year period. The crackdown has forced others to leave town. Although some of the problem has been precipitated by newcomers, the offspring of long-time residents also have been implicated and involved in the drug trade.

An additional problem with which Mayor Baldwin has had to contend is the closing down of the area sawmill owned by Kaibab Industries. After opening operations first in Fredonia, Arizona, and then Panguitch, the company employed Garfield County citizens for thirty years. With a peak work force at one time of nearly 400 people, the sawmill had only about seventy-five employees on its payroll when it shut down. Several factors led to the closure: reduction of the company's timber allotment in both the Dixie and Kaibab national forests, pressure from environmentalists and from home owners whose property was located in close proximity to cut areas, and foreign competition.

Other mills have attempted to take up the slack in Panguitch. One is Frandsen Lumber, owned first by Lawrence Frandsen and now run by his son, Kevin. This business almost exclusively harvests trees infested with bark beetles and other pests.[11] But the mill employs only a handful of men, so it has only softened slightly the substantial economic impact of Kaibab closing. The mayor and other city officials are offering business management training and other related counseling services to help local small mill owners and other entrepreneurs run their businesses more successfully.

Garfield's Past Contributes to Its Future

To complement other local efforts, Panguitch downtown revitalization became another major endeavor during Baldwin's time in office. With the help and advise of state agencies, Panguitch has initiated a program of historical awareness and preservation on its Main Street. This includes assisting business owners to fix up or install new facades on their buildings.

Creating historical awareness and fostering preservation efforts in Garfield County are not limited to the study and heritage of mid-nineteenth-century white arrivals to southern Utah. Adjacent to the city of Boulder, far earlier county residents are in the spotlight. In 1958–59 archaeologists and students from the University of Utah began excavation of an Anasazi village, uncovering eighty-seven rooms. Considered to be the largest Anasazi village west of the Colorado River, this was home to approximately 200 members of the Anasazi culture, who occupied these dwellings more than 800 years ago, between about A.D. 1050 and 1200.[12]

Shortly after this first dig, the Utah legislature designated the area as a state park in 1960; but work halted at the site for a number of years. Then, in the early 1970s, construction began on a museum and visitors center, and in 1978 workers initiated a reexcavation and stabilization project at the site. Archaeologists still have much more of the six-acre park to explore. Park curator Todd Prince prepared a report documenting activities and discoveries at the site from the first dig to the present time.[13] Some of the artifacts unearthed include pottery, beans, squash, corn, handwoven sandals, and posts that supported the structures in which the "ancient ones" lived.

Besides the 4,000-square-foot visitor facility that now includes an auditorium, guests to Boulder's Anasazi Indian Village State Park can walk through a replica of an ancient Indian house and view the archaeological diggings in progress. Park Superintendent Larry Davis currently offers informative lectures laced with humor to visiting tourists. Since at least half of these visitors come from foreign countries, signs that explain features of the park are written in French, German, Dutch, Italian, and Spanish, as are also handouts for the foreign visitors. This shows the international appeal of Garfield County historic and natural sites and indicates the changing nature of the county's life and economy. The park, open all year, has become increasingly popular among travelers along Scenic Byway 12. Davis recalled the comments of one visitor. In all seriousness she asked him, "Would you tell me why these people built this village so far from Highway 89? We had to drive over 100 miles to get here."[14]

Reaching back still further in history another fascinating scenic attraction along Scenic Byway 12 awaits visitors. Just about one mile outside of town is the Escalante Petrified Forest. As paleobotanists continue to study the specimens within the park, it is expected that they will ultimately identify fossil remains of more than 150 kinds of terrestrial animals and plants. Sightseers not only will be awed by some of the finest and most beautiful examples of petrified wood to be found in the nation but also can enjoy staying at well-maintained campsites that include hot showers and flush toilets. Also, in close proximity to the park is the Wide Hollow Reservoir, offering visitors a full range of recreational activities. The ability to continue to lure visitors to these and other attractions in Garfield and to create additional inducements to prolong their stay undoubtedly will have an impact on the county's economic future.

Community-based celebrations and events contribute to this goal. Once again, the county's past plays a major role in such activities. For instance, in Escalante horse racing has long been a popular pastime. The town held races coinciding with the Kentucky Derby for many years. Today Escalante is the midpoint of the "Outlaw Trail Endurance Ride," a competitive race of five days of a sixty-mile ride each day. Participants traverse difficult trails from Teasdale, to Boulder, through Escalante, to Bryce Canyon, and on to Kanab. This competition attracts experienced riders from many western states. Local former forest ranger Millard "Crockett" Dumas supplies wit and humor to help participants and others "relive the days of Butch Cassidy and his outlaw gang," according to local observer Marilyn Jackson.

Economic Revitalization

In spite of a general improvement in the quality of life for Garfield County residents, in the late twentieth century the county continues to struggle economically. The county has an unemployment rate hovering around 12 percent, one of the highest in the state. Finding ways to remedy the situation is difficult. Adherents to the "New West" philosophy advocate a pronounced change in the county's economic focus, concentrating more on tourism, service industries, light manufacturing, and food processing with a more global focus. One proponent of this ideology declared, "there is now cold evidence that resource-based economies of the 'Old West' are becoming a thing of the past . . . [an] exercise in nostalgia."[15]

County officials realize that some changes in economic focus are necessary and assure critics that they are "committed to expanding a balanced mix of job opportunities." They also see the potential to more fully exploit tourism "by enhancing county recreational opportunities and developing destination-related activities."[16] On the other hand, however, they wish to preserve the heritage and culture of the area, which to them still includes holding on to traditional enterprises—raising livestock, timber extraction, and mining. Since the vast majority of the county is made up of public lands, such enterprises are subject to the often changing regulations of the federal government.

In recent years, even if one has the approval and cooperation of some federal agencies on any given project, another hurdle has to be cleared. In the past two to three decades, environmental awareness and concern has increased, as has the political power and influence of environmental groups, and the established industries of the county often run counter to their priorities. The lumber business is a case in point. The U.S. Forest Service planned in 1987 to harvest 26.4 million board feet of timber from the Dixie National Forest over a ten-year period. However, funds made available to administer sales increasingly had to be used for research and legal expenses as environmental groups tied up such sales in lengthy litigation. As a result, by 1992 the Dixie National Forest (DNF) yielded only 39 percent of its annual timber harvest projection. Dixie forest spokesman Mark Van Every reported, "The vegetation was available . . . but the money to process sales was not."[17] Such situations had a direct impact on the decision of Kaibab Industries in Panguitch to close.

Opponents of the sale contest the projected timber harvests, believing that sometimes government agencies like the Forest Service seek to please industry more than protect the forests, while traditional users see their livelihoods increasingly threatened or destroyed. Growing polarization of the citizenry is a result in Garfield County as throughout the West, and, indeed, in the United States in general.

The sawmill in Escalante once owned by Paul Steed closed in

1991 mainly due to the lack of access to timber. Since that time, however, the Forest Service claimed it had timber available that needed to be cut, much of it infested. Steed's eldest son, Stephen, then organized and built a smaller mill on farmland south of the community. Presently the mill employs seventy-four people and runs two full shifts.[18] Surviving lumber companies in Panguitch and Escalante have in recent years increasingly concentrated on harvesting only infested timber and now deal in timber by-products as well in their attempts to stay in business.

Stock raising is another industry locally under siege. Since the designation of the Grand Staircase–Escalante National Monument (details of which are addressed below) ranchers have sold off or anticipate selling off much of their stock because of concerns over a reduction in grazing permits. One long-time stockman, Obie Shakespear, recently voiced his concern as to the future of his industry and sound land stewardship within the new monument. In spring 1997 Obie and June Shakespear of Tropic received an award as the "Conservation Farmers of the Year" from the Canyonlands Soil Conservation District. A seventy-year veteran in the cattle business, Shakespear and his wife have leases on two state sections to run livestock in portions of the new monument. He observed that he and other ranchers in the area "helped improve the land and installed many beneficial improvements for livestock and wildlife." While operating in the region, they also "helped many stranded tourists." Shakespear feared that "an important way of life in the small communities in Garfield and Kane Counties will be lost" if cattle grazing is greatly curtailed.[19] Indeed, many argue that the increased tourist traffic to the monument area will cause greater environmental impact than would tightly controlled grazing of local herds.

As an alternative to traditional cattle and sheep ranching, some are raising stock of a different breed altogether. For instance, Robert and Louise Liston of Escalante have turned their family cattle ranch into an ostrich ranch. One of the reasons for the change is that ostriches don't need to be turned loose onto public grazing lands but can still subsist on alfalfa, a crop that does well in the county. To expand their operation, the Listons sold all their cattle in 1995–96 in

Neal Jepsen's Cattle on Boulder Mountain (Courtesy Fay Jepsen)

hopes that health-conscious consumers will realize that ostriches provide a low-fat meat with practically no cholesterol at a cost not much higher than beef.[20]

Another stock industry being introduced into Garfield County is still in its infancy. Just outside of Cannonville, Debby Urpani is raising alpacas on land adjacent to the Galloping Tortoise Bed and Breakfast establishment, run by herself and Jeff Parker. She reported that these animals are "inexpensive to raise because they eat little and are easy to shelter and fence . . . are incredibly healthy animals and cause little environmental impact."[21] Although alpacas prefer to browse and graze openly, five to ten can easily be accommodated on an acre of ground. The animals are shorn annually and their highly prized fibers produce yarns that bring a premium price. It is too early to predict whether or not alpaca raising will replace sheep herding as a viable economic venture in the county.

The extractive mineral business has had its ups and downs in Garfield County's history, but the potential remains for greater development. Producing oil wells continue to dot the landscape in the Upper Valley adjacent to Escalante, and some of the richest coal reserves in the nation rest in eastern portions of the county. However, the potential for an improved economic picture coming from mineral extraction was greatly compromised in the fall of 1996 with the designation of the Grand Staircase–Escalante National Monument.

Tourism has become Garfield's main industry. In 1994 the county formed the Garfield Travel Council to aid those seeking information about travel to the many scenic wonders the county has to offer. Bryce Canyon visitation has climbed steadily through the years. In 1997 nearly 2 million people traversed the park. New hotels and motels have sprung up, and older facilities have been remodeled and enlarged. Some Garfield citizens now have turned their historic houses into bed and breakfast establishments. The Ruby's Inn complex at the entrance of Bryce Canyon has grown steadily over the years. On 31 May 1984 a fire destroyed the historic inn and twenty guest rooms. It cost nearly $1.3 million to rebuild and resupply the establishment. Today it has 369 rooms and over 200 camp sites.

From the mid-1980s to 1997 rooms that accommodate tourists doubled countywide, bringing in over $473,000 of tax revenue to the county in 1997. Other businesses—restaurants, gas stations, stores of all kinds, banks, and others—all reap the rewards of tourism and contribute tax revenues to county coffers.

The Grand Staircase–Escalante National Monument

On Wednesday, 18 September 1996, President Bill Clinton, invoking the ninety-plus-year-old Antiquities Act, stood on a platform erected in Arizona at the south rim of the Grand Canyon and announced the creation of the 1.7-million-acre Grand Staircase–Escalante National Monument. Residents of Garfield and Kane counties, Utah, in which the monument would be located, were stunned. Indeed, the shock waves were felt throughout the state. Some hailed the act as a bold stroke to protect for future generations of Americans

a pristine and unique area from detrimental mineral and other economic exploitation. Others viewed the president's move as nothing
more than a bid for the national environmental vote in the upcoming
presidential election. Whether they were for or against the creation
of the monument, many Utahns criticized the manner and circumstances in which the president made the announcement. Soon after
the monument's designation, Dan Jones & Associates conducted a
poll of 606 Utahns regarding their feelings concerning the monument: 61 percent felt the process creating the monument was unfair,
with only 18 percent considering it fair; 22 percent had no opinion.
This compared with 49 percent against monument designation and
29 percent favoring it. In the following months, however, more
Utahns began to favor the creation of the monument.[22]

Word had first reached Utah Governor Michael Leavitt on
Sunday, 8 September. An article had appeared in the *Washington Post*
the previous day suggesting that a new national preserve in southern
Utah was in the works.[23] The next day, the governor called Interior
Secretary Bruce Babbitt to inquire as to the truth of the news story.
Babbitt denied knowing anything about it and suggested Leavitt call
the White House. Whoever the governor spoke to there also denied
knowing much about the subject but promised to get back to Leavitt.
When a White House staffer returned his call, Leavitt learned that
there had been a serious proposal, but that "there's no decision." The
staffer appeared vague on the issue of timing, which unsettled Leavitt,
so the governor made arrangements to meet with the president's
chief of staff, Leon Panetta, on Tuesday, 17 September. In the meantime, Representative Bill Orton of Utah met with Interior Secretary
Babbitt on 12 September. Orton said that Babbitt assured him that
"no decision was imminent" and that there had been no "specific
proposal for a national monument." Orton continued, "The White
House reiterated they would consult with me before any kind of
large-scale proposal for Utah's public lands would ever be submitted
by the current administration."[24]

Governor Leavitt met with Panetta and Kathleen McGinty, chair
of the president's Council on Environmental Quality. The governor
was unaware at the time that McGinty had promoted the idea of the
national monument. Leavitt made a forty-minute presentation to

them on a proposed "Escalante National Eco-Region," an idea he had been developing over a three-year period. Leavitt explained that his approach would be less restrictive, "allowing greater multiple use of the land while preserving certain areas as wilderness." Panetta assured Leavitt that there was still plenty of time for input regarding the president's decision. The governor expressed a wish to speak directly to Clinton because of the amount of land involved, just a few thousand acres less than the size of Rhode Island, Delaware and Washington, D.C., put together.[25]

The governor remained in the nation's capital overnight to wait for the president's call, even though he had to be in New York for meetings the next day. During the night, about 2:00 A.M., a call came from the president and Leavitt expressed his concerns about the rumors of the monument designation. He offered to send the president a memo outlining his proposal as an alternative and Clinton encouraged him to do so. Leavitt then wrote a long note, which he faxed to the president at 4:30 A.M.

Leavitt left for New York, and early that afternoon listened to President Clinton's speech at the Grand Canyon. There were no members of Utah's congressional delegation on the platform with the president that day, not even Orton (a member of the president's own party whose congressional district encompassed the monument) or any official government representatives from Utah or Arizona. Utah's governor had clearly been deceived as to the administration's intentions.

Monument designation had immediate and profound economic implications in at least two specific areas. Within the boundaries of the new preserve are 180,000 acres of Utah school trust lands. The state had hoped to extract minerals—most specifically coal, by some estimates worth $1 billion—from at least a portion of these lands for future revenues to help finance Utah's public school system. In addition, the multinational conglomerate Andalex Resources, Inc. owned leases of rich coal reserves on the Kaiparowits Plateau. The company was in the process of making the necessary applications to access the coal and of organizing mining and hauling operations when President Clinton made his announcement. Even though the area they proposed to mine was comparatively small and not located in close proximity to the monument's generally regarded most scenic features, the company decided to scrap its plans. This cost Garfield and Kane counties a projected estimate of up to 900 good-paying jobs, something that neither of these economically strapped counties wanted to lose and that were more important to many residents than the environmental or other social impacts such mining would have on the area. But Andalex knew that under the more strict environmental guidelines that came with monument designation their enterprise had a dim and uncertain future.

Even though news of the monument seemed devastating to many at the time, state and local government officials took heart in some of the promises and fine points of the president's announcement.[26] Most importantly, the administration of the new preserve would come under the jurisdiction of the Bureau of Land Management, an agency dedicated to foster multiple-use concepts of public lands, not the National Park Service, whose policies are much more restrictive. The BLM would conduct a three-year study of the new monument, inviting local and state input at public hearings before definite guidelines would be established as to its management. Previous hunting, fishing, and grazing laws would continue to be in effect, and water rights would remain under state law as they were before the monument designation. The boundaries of the monument were defined to exclude developed areas such as towns (otherwise Tropic, Cannonville, Henrieville, Escalante, and Boulder would have been within the proposed area), national forest lands, and state parks. The president also promised that any coal reserves on school trust lands would be traded for other reserves elsewhere.

In spite of all these assurances, the president's critics pointed out that the planning stage should have taken place before his announcement. They also contended that there are no other coal reserves as rich as those found within the monument and that Utah's school-children would never be fully compensated.

But the president's action also had its proponents and supporters. Hundreds of conservationists and environmental activists who were present at the Grand Canyon cheered Clinton's announcement. On the stand with the president and vice-president were former Utah first lady Norma Matheson, actor and Utah resident Robert Redford, and Utah writer and naturalist Terry Tempest Williams. Featured speaker Colorado Governor Roy Romer, the only western governor present, stated that the monument area was owned by the people of the United States and that the president had the responsibility to preserve the land.

Several environmental organizations have argued that the dispute between themselves and residents in southern Utah over social and economic ideologies has gone on for three decades. They cited local apathy about environmental concerns and lack of cooperation in helping define wilderness preserves as conditions that forced the president's hand. A spokesperson for one organization, the Southern Utah Wilderness Alliance, whose membership is composed of many living both within and outside the state, declared that, "The wilderness value far outweighs the commercial value here because we can get coal anywhere. Coal is abundant."[27] Environmentalists also contended that the ceremony at the Grand Canyon would not have been necessary if Utah's congressional representatives had been more reasonable concerning wilderness issues in Congress.

Some in the audience criticized Governor Leavitt, who prided himself on trying to be conciliatory on sensitive issues, for not being present on this occasion to pledge Utah's cooperation in managing the preserve, unaware that he did not know of the event and was not invited to attend. Environmental organizations also vowed they would not back down on their demand for 5.7 million acres of wilderness designated BLM lands in the state.[28] This amount far exceeds that favored by Utah's governor, the state's congressional representatives, and southern Utah county governments, whose counties make up most of the millions of acres earmarked by environmentalists for wilderness status. As Garfield County's General Plan states:

> the "ecosystem management" concept, as described by federal agencies tends to treat humans as intruders in the natural system. County leaders reject this supposition and will insist that natural resource management plans and/or "ecosystems" management plans for all county lands, public and private, consider humans as part of the system.[29]

A year after creation of the national monument the emotional ferment subsided somewhat, but controversy over its management continued unabated. Newly elected U.S. Representative Chris Cannon and residents of both Garfield and Kane counties complained that the BLM planning team established offices in Cedar City rather than in Kanab or Escalante. They feared the distance would make it more difficult for those most affected by the monument to participate in the planning process. But team manager Jerry Meredith noted that the BLM did not want to show favoritism in selecting one town over another during the planning stage; each community should have an equal opportunity to bid on providing the permanent headquarters for monument management. Meredith continued, "These are public lands, and everyone needs to be involved. Cedar City has air service, a university with satellite connections, the Utah Center for Rural Life. . . . It has a lot of things that make it easier for groups beyond the monument area."[30] Critics countered that team members earn substantial salaries and with their families would have had a beneficial effect on local economies in either Garfield or Kane counties.

At issue also is how the local governments will meet the expenses that monument designation has engendered. Both counties requested money from the federal government to help finance the planning and gathering of information on how the monument would affect and change local conditions and to help handle the influx of new visitors. But when the Interior Department presented Garfield County with $100,000, county officials, still smarting at the government's perceived duplicity, turned down the offer because of stipulations that accompanied the use of the funds. They seemed to be sending a message to Washington that rural southern Utahns did not trust federal officials to keep the government's promises. However, almost a year after the fact, Garfield County officials did reach an agreement with the BLM that will give the county $100,000 for law enforcement during 1997. The money went for search-and-rescue efforts in the monument—which had increased substantially and usually were expended on behalf of non-county residents—and to hire a sheriff's deputy for the Boulder area.[31]

The most controversial issue in the year following the monument designation was the BLM's decision to allow Conoco Incorporated to drill a second exploratory oil and gas well within the new monument.[32] Conoco first applied early in 1997 for state and federal drilling permits on lands within the monument's boundaries, where the company owned 111 leases. The state gave the company a go-ahead for drilling the well on their land. Both sites are located in Reese Canyon along a dirt road on the Kaiparowits Plateau in Kane County and are accessed from Escalante, about forty-five miles to the northwest.

A coalition of environmental groups tried to halt the drilling on two fronts. They petitioned the Interior Board of Land Appeals in Arlington, Virginia, to request that the BLM reconsider its decision. They also organized a grassroots protest against Conoco, which included a call-in blitz to the company and a boycott of their gas stations, encouraging customers to destroy their Conoco credit cards. To date there has been no indication if these efforts will produce the desired results.

Other companies also hold gas and oil leases within the monument, but Conoco has by far the major interests. The company felt pressure to begin the exploratory drilling in 1997 because their ten-year leases expired in November of that year and they needed to begin work to keep the leases active. Whether their wells will prove to be of commercial value or not remains to be seen. If they do, the State of Utah could then better assess the value of its school trust lands locked up within the monument, allowing Utah officials to bargain more effectively on what compensation is owed them by the federal government. Determining the value of mineral resources and how much mineral activity will ultimately be allowed within the monument will have a direct impact on Garfield County's economic picture.

Environmentalists are concerned about another activity they see taking place within the confines of the preserve—road cutting or enhancement. Under the government's "Revised Statute 2477" of 1866, states and counties are given rights-of-way across federal land unless it is already reserved for some other purpose. This law was repealed in 1977, but it still applies to roads existing prior to that year. Environmentalists fear that locals are actually creating new thoroughfares and are conducting unauthorized maintenance work on existing roads as an effective means of protesting monument or wilderness designation. Local thinking seems to be that the more dirt lanes that vein the area, "the more probable it becomes that at least those minimally developed patches will no longer qualify as wilderness," and would thus be subject to less scrutiny by the government.[33]

In an effort to curtail this activity, lawyers representing environmental groups convinced a federal judge to rule that before any road work can proceed on public lands the BLM must be given forty-eight hours notice. This would presumably give BLM officials time to assess whether or not such work is within the law. But it is difficult to police such a large area, and environmentalists fear that the ruling is being flouted.

A coalition of environmental groups are also concerned that, in the words of one, "rural Utah counties are fraudulently claiming many rights-of-way across public land for roads that either do not exist or are no longer used for a legitimate purpose."[34] Volunteers have been going into the new monument and other areas to investigate whether or not county roads that appear on maps actually exist. In some cases they have found legitimate thoroughfares, but in other cases they do not consider the road claims to be valid. A *Salt Lake Tribune* staff writer, however, wrote that the coalition's work is suspect, because "volunteers investigating road claims have preconceived biases in favor of wilderness and against roads" and few had scientific or analytical backgrounds.[35] Photographic documentation helps, but the issue promises to be controversial in the coming years as the two sides battle for their positions.

Controversy also took center stage as the Republican-dominated Congressional Resources Committee conducted hearings into the secretive circumstances behind the creation of the national monument.[36] Committee members called Kathleen McGinty to testify before the committee and requested that White House papers dealing with the president's proclamation be turned over to them. The administration complied by delivering more than one hundred documents; but they withheld twenty-seven others, invoking executive privilege in denying direct access to them for the purposes of the hearings. After repeated requests for these papers, the committee decided to push for contempt of Congress charges against McGinty.

Just before such action would have been taken, the White House released the additional documents.

The Resources Committee considered these papers important to determine the president's motives in creating the monument. Did he sincerely do this to protect a vital and unique ecosystem or was he merely trying to win environmentalists' support before the election? "If the documents show he included land that wasn't in need of protection," as provided by the Antiquities Act, "or that he drew the boundaries haphazardly or overly broad, it would help various groups now trying to either minimize or do away with the monument," wrote one reporter.[37] Regardless of what these papers reveal, citizens of Kane and Garfield counties believe they have a right to know what they include.

In the category of concern rather than controversy is the large influx of visitors to the Escalante and Boulder area since the creation of the national monument. One would think eastern Garfield residents would be enthusiastic about this, as it translates into tourist dollars; but, according to an Associated Press release, this isn't necessarily the case: "There is a certain irony, noticed perhaps by the locals who opposed President Clinton's ambush designation of the 1.7 million-acre Grand Staircase-Escalante National Monument, in that efforts to protect the land have resulted in attracting attention to it."[38]

Along the same theme, former rancher Paul Hansen chided environmentalists, "It's the attention that's going to bring the people. And people will do a lot more damage in the long run than the cows ever did." To be fair, grazing is not prohibited, and most environmentalists are more concerned with stopping large-scale mining and associated activities in the area. Local lodge owner Mark Austin contended that tourism has been on the increase steadily since the paving of Utah Scenic Byway 12. He said, "Monument status just turned the heat up."[39]

The visitor count by spring of 1997 to tourist attractions in close proximity to the preserve rose anywhere from 33 percent to double that reported the previous year. Visitors included two photographers from *National Geographic*, who were preparing a story about the new monument for the magazine's December 1997 issue, which, in turn, can't help but attract crowds of additional tourists.

In some respects, local leaders have noted a decline in controversy surrounding the monument designation. Beginning early in 1997, the BLM in cooperation with Garfield County commissioners and leaders of other interested entities have been holding a series of public meetings. These meetings have been part of the stipulated three-year planning process mandated by President Clinton. Most attendees have found these gatherings to be orderly and informative, with a prevailing desire among the participants to achieve an economic plan to sustain both the environment and those people living adjacent to the monument. Time will tell how successful all concerned will be in reaching this goal.

The Burr Trail Controversy

The Burr Trail is a scenic sixty-six-mile-long road, most of it graded dirt, which connects Boulder to the Bullfrog Marina on Lake Powell. The issue surrounding the road involves whether or not to maintain the "primitive character" of the road or to allow Garfield County to make certain improvements on the thoroughfare that county officials believe is in the interest of public safety and would further stimulate tourism. The debate has been ongoing since the mid-1980s when Garfield County, the National Park Service, and the BLM agreed on plans to pave the Burr Trail. At first the paving was held up by lobbying efforts of environmental groups when the county sought funds to carry out the project. Then in 1987 a coalition of conservation groups filed suit against the BLM "alleging that the County does not hold title to the road or, if title is valid, that the County's proposed activities exceed the scope of the right-of-way."[40]

This was the beginning of more than ten years of haggling over jurisdiction and maintenance of the road, including lawsuits and administrative appeals that have yet to be resolved. The courts have ruled in favor of the county in many of the past legal battles, enabling officials to make small improvements to the road. A ruling among federal agencies in March 1995 allowed for a "chip-seal" surface to be laid along the 30.7-mile stretch of the road from Boulder to the western boundary of Capitol Reef National Park; where the Burr Trail winds through the park the road will remain dirt, with only minor drainage improvements added and gravel laid in some clay areas where needed; a 7.8-mile section east of the park could be graveled and widened to twenty-six feet; and the remaining nineteen miles of road ending at Bullfrog will keep its chip-seal surface. (A "chip-seal" is a thin layer of asphalt atop a layer of gravel. It resembles a paved road but is not as durable.)[41]

Representatives of Garfield County challenged this decision because they felt the county had the right to select the type of paving material used since they had right-of-way claims as provided for in the 1873 Revised Statute 2477. The county also had the responsibility of maintaining the road and providing a safe thoroughfare for the public. Environmental interests argued that by retaining a dirt section within the park along the Burr Trail dramatic increases in traffic and resulting demands for services could be avoided.

In May 1996 the federal government took legal action against Garfield County. The National Park Service charged that the county's engineer, Brian Bremner, and county road crews on 13 February 1996 "trespassed and performed unauthorized work on a 1-mile section of the road inside of southern Utah's Capitol Reef National Park." The lawsuit claims that one section of the road "was widened by as much as 11 feet . . . and that crews caused 'extensive damage' to park resources, including the removal of a 30-foot-high hillside."[42] Garfield County officials claimed that the scope of the projected road work and the date it would commence had been discussed with National Park Service personnel well prior to 13 February and that this was to be an extension of approved maintenance begun the previous November.

The attorney representing the NPS argued that the Burr Trail right-of-way should only be twenty feet wide and also asked the court to order the county to pay for rehabilitating the damaged area in question and to cease all work on the road unless authorized by the Department of Interior. Utah's Assistant Attorney General Stephen Boyden agreed with county engineer Bremner that a twenty-foot right-of-way is far too narrow and wondered if the federal attorney meant just the road surface to be that wide. Bremner said that a wider right-of-way would allow for culverts to drain rainwater and "and let road crews landscape the cuts." Since Garfield County has been encouraged to economically exploit tourism to replace an emphasis on extractive industries, the county wants to facilitate the movement of motor homes over the trail, and many feel that what they call "a windy, twisty, mountainous road" will not meet their needs.[43]

The two sides in the lawsuit agreed to a court order that allowed county crews to repair portions of the disputed one-mile section of road in late September 1997. Unusually wet weather had washed out portions of the road and spread debris on others.[44] At least some of the damage could have been prevented and the resulting maintenance expenses reduced had the culverts been in place, county officials argued.

Because of all the complicated issues surrounding the paving, widening, and maintenance of the Burr Trail, U.S. District Judge Bruce S. Jenkins decided in May 1997 to view the surrounding area and travel the road before he made a final judgement concerning the lawsuit and future administration of the road. His goal was to come up with an all-encompassing decision concerning the Burr Trail rather than approach the problem piecemeal over an extended period of time. The Grand Staircase–Escalante National Monument designation has complicated the matter even more. Additional trails, some connecting to the Burr Trail, lay within the boundaries of the new preserve; questions must also be resolved concerning them. At the time of this writing, how all of this will be decided remains to be seen.

Argument and Accord

The issues surrounding the new national monument and the Burr Trail stole the spotlight from other Garfield County news as the county moved toward the twenty-first century. Garkane Power Association completed a major $1 million-plus upgrade of its services to its customers. As a result of this work, county residents received more reliable electrical service with fewer outages, a long-standing problem due to weather conditions.[45]

At this writing, Garkane Power is considering moving its utility headquarters from Richfield to Hatch, where a satellite office is already located. The company's board of directors currently favors the move, but this is not the first time a change has been considered. Previous attempts have failed. The board wants to move its headquarters so it will be within a community it serves; however, the Richfield City Council is trying to talk Garkane out of relocating. They argue that as utilities are deregulated over the next two years Richfield City, now a customer of Utah Power and Light Company, could easily "become one of Garkane's largest customers."[46] The relocation of company headquarters to Hatch, however, would give residents there an economic and psychological boost.

Another debate affecting southern Utah communities surfaced as Mountain Fuel Supply Company (now Questar Gas) prepared to bring natural gas to Garfield County, beginning with Panguitch. This issue was controversial because of the projected costs involved. With the small rural populations in Garfield, the high costs of hooking onto the main gas pipelines was cost-prohibitive to such companies as Mountain Fuel. Fortunately, another solution to fund access to natural gas was found.

A committee within the state legislature proposed that all Questar utility customers pay for expansion into these areas. It was estimated that the costs would amount to not more than $1 per customer per year for the next fifteen years if Questar cannot recover its costs with revenue from the Panguitch area consumers. Such a recommendation was consistent with the legislature's resolve to help revitalize economic development in rural areas. They argued that since the wildlands surrounding these small communities provide recreation for other citizens, thus limiting the economic uses of those lands, such a subsidy is not unreasonable.

Opponents to this suggestion argued that such arrangements are contrary to free-market ideals, that rate-payers would be subsidizing the expansion of a monopoly. But members of Utah's Public Utilities Commission wondered what could be done when the free market could not meet all the contingencies. There was also disagreement whether the considerable lower energy costs of natural gas could revitalize drooping local economies. Also, those who provide other energy fuels, such as propane, argue that government should not subsidize or favor one energy source over another. In spite of these concerns, during the 1998 legislative session, Representative Tom Hatch from Panguitch introduced and successfully pushed through a bill to bring the subsidized natural gas to Garfield County.

The current proposals would mean that present utility customers would pay for expansion into these areas. One proposal considered by lawmakers would be the creation of a "universal service fund" from which towns could borrow money to pay for such utility expansion. A surcharge to all present customers would establish the fund. Another proposal would permit a one-time rate increase among all present Mountain Fuel users. Opponents to both suggestions argue that such arrangements are contrary to free-market ideals, that rate payers would be subsidizing the expansion of a monopoly. But members of Utah's Public Utilities Commission wonder what can be done when the free market cannot meet all the contingencies.

There is also disagreement whether the considerably lower energy costs of natural gas can revitalize drooping local economies. Also, those who provide other energy fuels, such as propane, argue that government should not subsidize or favor one energy source over another. This is a controversy that is yet to be resolved.

The people of Henrieville also have a problem. In recent years they have been trying to restore and preserve their old school building, a structure that has been the center of community activity for more than one hundred years. It is perhaps the oldest structure in Garfield County east of the Sevier River. It began as a church/school facility in the 1880s, serving that function until a new church was built. It then functioned as a grade school until 1955. That year, Henrieville youngsters began attending classes in Tropic after county school reorganization.

Trying to get funding to restore the building is a problem. There are no commercial businesses within Henrieville, thus little money goes into the community's coffers. Through the Utah Historical Society, town leaders tried to get the old schoolhouse on the historical register to access available funding; however, modifications performed over the years prevented it from qualifying for such funds. Residents performed some restoration work and collected funds for additional renovation in an attempt to secure financing from government entities such as the Utah Community Impact Board (UCIB), but the amount they collected fell far short of what they needed. Also, the bids to do the restoration came in much higher than town leaders had estimated. The UCIB approved a grant of

$60,000 but is withholding the funds until the community has a signed restoration-work contract and has all of the necessary financing in place.

The two contractors who bid on the project are unwilling to sign anything tying them to a specific amount, however. Because of the structure's age there could be unexpected expenses involved. Adding to the price tag of the project is the need to meet the requirements of historic preservation. As an example, Henrieville Mayor Guy Thompson referred to the $900 cost of replacing three small historically accurate windows; ordinary windows would have only cost about $100.[47]

Some may regard this goal of Henrieville residents as just an "exercise in nostalgia"; however, historic preservation has come to be seen as a proven method of attracting tourists and inducing them to extend their stay in an area. The mayor and townspeople of Henrieville are committed to seeing this project completed, just as those who settled the area were committed to building their school in the first place. Such pioneer resolve lives on.

Garfield County's People—A Reason for Optimism

Garfield County boosters have said on numerous occasions that its most important resource is not its mineral wealth, its timber reserves, its stock-raising potential, or even its tourist attractions; it is its people. There is no doubt that these people are now being, and will continue to be, challenged by new circumstances as they move toward the next millennium. Although their progenitors suffered much and sacrificed greatly to establish homes and communities in a harsh environment, they lived out their lives against a more simple backdrop. Pioneer descendants are now confronted with an array of complexities their forebears could not have imagined. But in meeting present-day demands, Garfield's citizenry will need to emulate the determination and innovation of their ancestors.

In perusing a recent general plan created for the county by its elected leaders, one is daunted by how much needs to be done to maintain and upgrade the infrastructure of Garfield's communities. How will it all be paid for? How can the needs of all county residents be met? How can a change in economic focus best be accomplished and work in concert with environmental imperatives? How can Garfield's young people be induced to stay or to come back and help revitalize their communities? How can an influx of newcomers be a positive influence for good? The resolution of these and countless other questions rests with the composite group of individuals.

One can look at isolated examples to judge the caliber of individuals that Garfield has produced and will likely continue to produce. In a recent interview, Robert Linford, who grew up in Panguitch, recalled taking part in a graduation exercise at Southern Utah University in 1986 while he was still mayor of Cedar City. Linford observed that on this occasion the school bestowed two honorary Ph.D. degrees—one went to Walter DeVar Talbot, Utah's former Superintendent of Public Instruction, and the other went to J. Elliot Cameron, past president of both Snow College and Brigham Young University, Hawaii Campus. The representative from the Utah Board of Regents conferring the degrees was Clifford F. LeFevre. Linford noted that he and the other three men had all been members of the Garfield High School Class of 1941, where he served as student body president. The fact that just one class from a small county high school could produce individuals of such accomplishments is encouraging as residents now seek to find their way through a maze of complicated issues.

Steve Marshall, a Garfield resident who descends from pioneer stock, is looking toward the future without leaving the past behind. His grandfather opened the first drugstore in Panguitch in 1907; his father, Monte Marshall, returned to his hometown after serving in World War II to work with his father in the pharmacy. He later ran the business until his retirement in 1989. When Steve became involved in the family enterprise, he wanted to expand the store and provide space for additional shops, but he "hated the idea of [creating] a strip mall." After studying historic architectural structures and consulting specialists in the field, he built on Center Street a facility that, in his words, "depicts, in various ways, replicas of historic Panguitch structures such as the town's original tabernacle, an early LDS church and the old original social hall." Even the masonry is reminiscent of the brick manufactured in early Panguitch. According to a *Deseret News* reporter, Marshall "has brought new ideas to the business while combining it with old-style architecture, a formula he hopes will reap continued success for the Panguitch Drug Company."[48]

The newcomers, some with different ideas and lifestyles, many possessing a different heritage, must also be considered. The county's original pioneers came from many different cultures and were able to work in harmony and leave a worthy legacy to succeeding generations, although virtually all belonged to the Mormon church. Newcomers can make valuable contributions to the society. For example, in the late 1980s Wasatch Front residents Leon and Claudia Walkenhorst Crump were on their way home from a vacation driving along U.S. Highway 89 when they decided to make a stop in Panguitch. While in town, they took a self-guided mini-tour of the community. Their route took them past a deserted, dilapidated old brick home. Claudia Crump immediately fell in love with the place, and the couple soon owned it. After many months of work, the Crumps restored the home, said to be the first brick home built in Panguitch, to something resembling its original condition. Not long after they completed the renovation, they opened its doors to the public as a bed and breakfast establishment named for its original builder—the William Prince Inn. Local residents, and especially descendants of the Prince family, were ecstatic with the results.

Leon and Claudia Crump also purchased another home on Main Street, the Burns and Ruth Tebbs home, and created a quilt and needlework shop. Claudia Crump decided to name it The Snowed In Quilt Shop in honor of the heroic trek to Parowan made by seven Panguitch pioneers back in 1865 to bring back flour to grateful villagers threatened with starvation. In her shop Claudia Crump sells beautiful needlework items and hand-sewn articles by local women and also teaches classes in quilting. She has also become a member of the Panguitch Ladies Rhythm Band, probably their youngest member.

Certainly such activity has been and can be replicated in other towns throughout the county. Most newcomers are drawn to this southern Utah county because of its beauty, clean air, and less-hurried pace. Like the Crumps, they are weary of urban sprawl and all that it implies. With modern-day technology many can stay connected to their places of business and still enjoy the advantages of rural surroundings. Some of these public-spirited people enthusiastically participate in local governments and organizations. The majority of them want to preserve Garfield County's unique character; they value the quality of life it offers. Joining with those whose roots run deep into the county's past, they bring fresh perspective that can also provide solutions to local problems. In harmony together, both groups can leave a worthy legacy to posterity.

The sentiments of Henrieville resident Emma Allene Savage Riddle well express the reason why so many of Garfield's people choose to remain in the county:

> I have lived through two World Wars, not to mention the Korean War and Vietnam and a depression. I have seen presidents come and go, one [almost] impeached, one assassinated. Seen the water, electricity, indoor plumbing and television come. . . . Saw a man walk on the moon, rode in a [horse-drawn] flatbed wagon and the most modern car, bathed in a #3 tub, saw washing machines evolve from red worn hands to spin dry. Microwaves, dishwashers, but all in all, what is most important to me is to have lived in a town where people over the years still remained . . . loving, friendly, giving. People who still believe in prayer, in church, and in school, who believe in liberty, in doing their part. . . . The years I have lived in [Garfield] . . . were filled with happiness. . . . God does love this place . . . and so do I.[49]

Endnotes

1. *Richfield Reaper,* 3 October 1974.

2. *Richfield Reaper,* 30 September 1976.

3. See George W. Thompson, "Cannonville History," 61–65.

4. Ibid., 42.

5. Phil Chidester, "About Cannonville," *Daily Spectrum,* 11 December 1993, 3; J. Arthur Fields, "Bluegrass Fest Features Bear, Fine Fiddling," *Salt Lake Tribune,* 17 July 1995; Thompson, "Cannonville History," 43–44.

6. Lenora Hall LeFevre, *The Boulder Country and Its People,* 272.

7. Vivian Holmes Crosby, interview with Vivian L. Talbot, 11 October 1997, notes in possession of authors.

8. *Daily Spectrum,* 17 July 1993, 7.

9. Julie Christensen Lyman, interview with Vivian L. Talbot, 9 October 1997, notes in possession of authors.

10. Elaine Baldwin, interview with Vivian L. Talbot, 9 October 1997, notes in possession of authors.

11. Clark Frandsen, interview with Vivian L. Talbot, 25 September 1997, notes in possession of authors.

12. Reed L. Madsen, "Anasazi sandals walk viewers through history," *Deseret News*, August 1997, D11.

13. Todd Prince, "Coombs Site Excavation: 1970–1991," files, Anasazi State Park.

14. Bill McClure, "Anasazi: Ancient Ones," *Daily Spectrum*, 23 July 1993, B1.

15. Ken Miller, "The New West: Are Logging, Mining And Ranching Riding Into the Sunset?," *Salt Lake Tribune*, 17 June 1996, A1.

16. "Garfield County, Utah General Plan," 13 March 1995, 5–3.

17. Donna Brown, "Death of a small town," *Daily Spectrum*, 17 April 1994, A1, A4.

18. Information from Marilyn Jackson, Escalante, Utah.

19. *Garfield County News*, 3 April 1997, 1-A.

20. Jerry Spangler, "A new kind of 'cattle' on the hoof," *Deseret News*, 11 September 1997, A16.

21. *Garfield County News*, 10 April 1997, 1-A.

22. Brooke Adams, "Most Utahns opposed to designation," *Deseret News*, 19 September 1997, A1.

23. Karl Cates, "How Leavitt tried to stop Clinton's Escalante plan," *Deseret News*, 16 January 1997, A1.

24. "Teachers, politicos step up opposition to Escalante monument," *Spectrum*, 13 September 1996.

25. Cates, "How Leavitt tried," A17.

26. See Lee Davidson and Jerry Spangler, "Clinton makes it official: Monument now a reality," *Deseret News*, 18 September 1997, A2.

27. As quoted in Karl Cates, "Whose land is it?" *Deseret News*, 12 September 1996, A19.

28. Jerry Spangler, "Conservationists cheer creation of monument," *Deseret News*, 19 September 1996, A1.

29. "Garfield County, Utah General Plan," 3–3.

30. Lee Davidson, "Plans for monument offices angers Cannon," *Deseret News*, 16 January 1997, B5.

31. Reed L. Madsen, "Garfield to get $100,000 in Staircase aid," *Deseret News,* 7 September 1997, A19.

32. For information on this controversy see Karl Cates, "Plans for Escalante wells attacked," *Deseret News,* 12 February 1997, B1; Jim Woolf, "Monument Site Isn't Unique, Say Backers of Oil Drilling," *Salt Lake Tribune,* 23 April 1997, A1; and "Group protests decision to allow drilling in Staircase," *Deseret News,* 13 September 1997.

33. Jeffrey Kluger, "Deep Divide," *Time,* 10 February 1997, 65–66.

34. Brent Israelsen, "Wilds Lovers Hit Dirt To Erase Utah 'Roads'," *Salt Lake Tribune,* 21 April 1997, D1.

35. Ibid.

36. *Deseret News,* 23 October 1997, A1.

37. *Deseret News,* 28 October 1997, A12.

38. *Salt Lake Tribune,* 28 April 1997, D3.

39. Ibid.

40. "Chronological History of Boulder-To-Bullfrog ('Burr Trail Road') Road Improvement Project," obtained from Barbara Hjelle, St. George, Utah, 5 September 1997, 1.

41. See Jim Woolf, "Garfield to Fight Burr Trail Ruling," *Salt Lake Tribune,* 17 March 1995, C7.

42. Brent Israelsen, "Garfield County Hit With Suit Over Burr Trail," *Salt Lake Tribune,* 17 May 1996, B1.

43. Joe Bauman, "Judge set court date on controversy over widening Burr Trail," *Deseret News,* 20 May 1997.

44. *Deseret News,* 25 September 1997, A22.

45. Reed L. Madsen, "Garkane ends last phase of power-upgrade project," *Deseret News,* 31 July 1997.

46. Reed L. Madsen, "Board favors shift of Garkane's headquarters," *Deseret News,* 23 September 1997.

47. Reed L. Madsen, "Small Garfield County town fights to restore historic schoolhouse," *Deseret News,* 24 September 1997.

48. Reed L. Madsen, "Pharmacy get new quarters but keeps 91-year-old look," *Deseret News,* 1 March 1998, A20.

49. Emma Allene Savage Riddle, "A Lifesketch," 7, copy obtained by authors from Nancy Twitchell, Henrieville, Utah.

Appendices

Population*

PLACE	1890	1900	1910	1920	1930	1940	1950	1960	1970	1980	1990
County	2457	3400	3660	4768	4642	5253	4151	3577	3157	3673	3980
Antimony	na	na	na	na	na	245	187	161	113	94	83
Boulder	na	104	91	177	192	216	na	108	93	113	126
Cannonville	273	211	219	311	227	250	205	153	113	134	131
Escalante	667	723	846	1032	1016	1061	773	702	638	652	818
Hatch	na	na	na	250	274	294	244	198	139	121	103
Henrieville	na	181	158	170	207	241	114	152	145	167	163
Panguitch	1015	883	1338	1473	1541	1979	1501	1435	1318	1343	1444
Tropic	na	370	358	474	447	514	483	382	329	338	374

*Information obtained from Allan Kent Powell, ed., *Utah History Encyclopedia* (Salt Lake City: University of Utah Press, 1994), 432–438.

Elected Leaders

National Legislator

Wayne Owens, House of Representatives, 2nd Congressional District
One term—1972–1974
Three terms—1986–1992

*State Legislators—1896 to 1998***

Senators Representing Garfield County	Sessions Served
District 10	
R. W. Sevy	1909–1911
Quince Kimball	1917–1919
H. C. Tebbs	1921–1923
D. H. Robinson	1925–1927
William T. Owens Jr.	1929–1931
O. C. Bowman	1933–1935
Silas E. Tanner	1937–1939
McKinley Morrill	1941–1943
W. Wallace Houston	1945–1947
Lewis H. Larson	1949–1951
Roland H. Tietjen	1953–1955
Royal T. Harward	1959–1961
Vernon L. Holman	1961–1966
District 28	
Kendrick Harward	1967–1972
District 29	
Dixie L. Leavitt	1973–1976
Ivan M. Matheson	1977–1984
District 28	
Cary G. Peterson	1985

**Information obtained from Shelley Day, Public Information Specialist, The Office of Legislative Research and General Counsel, The State of Utah.

District 29
Ivan M. Matheson	1985–1988
Dixie L. Leavitt	1989–1992

District 28
Leonard M. Blackham	1993
Cary G. Peterson	1993
Leonard M. Blackham	1994–1998

Representatives from Garfield County

District 23
Andrew J. Hansen	1897
Jesse W. Crosby, Jr.	1899
George W. Johnson	1901
Alfred Luther	1903–1905
John N. Henrie	1907–1913
Thomas Sevy	1915
John King	1917–1919
W. J. Henderson	1921
C. E. Rowan Jr.	1923–1925
L. C. Sargent	1927
Lester Spencer	1929–1931
W. J. Henderson	1933
Milton Twitchell	1935–1941
Ambrose Myers	1943
M. V. Hatch	1945–1947
Walter B. Daly	1949
John H. Johnson	1951–1953
Parley Ipson	1955
Nathella K. Griffin	1957
J. Arthur Griffin	1959
Nathella K. Griffin Woolsey	1961
Daniel A. Tebbs	1963–1966

District 67
Royal T. Harward	1967–1970
Hyrum L. Lee	1971–1972

District 73

Calvin Black	1973–1974
Lloyd W. Frandsen	1975–1978
Charles Hardy Redd	1979–1982
James F. Yardley	1983–1994
Thomas Hatch	1995–1998

Garfield County Commissions***

Early Selectmen and Commissioners

Jesse W. Crosby
Ira Elmer
Andrew P. Schow
James Houston
Allen Miller
Erastus Beck
John Houston
Ira C. Schow
John T. Lufkin
Thomas J. Riddle
John L. Sevy
James T. Daly, Jr.
Perry M. Liston
A. F. Haycock
L. J. Willis
T. H. Cope
A. W. Carpenter
William Alvey
Josiah Barker
H. J. McCullough
Edward Twitchell
Edward Allen
James Little
Bernard Johnson

***Information obtained from Minute Books and Election Results found in the Garfield County Commission Offices, Panguitch, Utah.

Later Commissioners and Clerks
(First Commissioner listed served as Chair)
1908—John Ahlstrom
     David L. Heywood
     Ernest A. Griffin
     John F. Worthen (completed Griffin's term)
     John T. Partridge—Clerk
1910—John F. Worthen
     Ernest A. Griffin
     Ole Ahlstrom
     John T. Partridge—Clerk
1911—Ernest A. Griffin
     John F. Worthen
     Ole Ahlstrom
     John T. Partridge—Clerk
1913—William H. Tebbs
     P. Orin Barker
     Ole Ahlstrom
     James M. Sargent—Clerk
1915—No Change
1917—P. Orin Barker
     Elmer H. Jorgenson
     James N. Henderson
     Caesar Myers—Clerk
1919—James N. Henderson
     Vern Lyman
     Elmer H. Jorgenson
     M. V. Evans (completed Jorgenson's term)
     Ann Cooper Clark—Clerk
1921—Vern Lyman
     James N. Henrie
     Maurice Cope
     John T. Partridge—Clerk
1923—James N. Henrie
     P. Orin Barker
     John H. Johnson
     John T. Partridge—Clerk

1925—No Change
1927—No Change
1929—No Change
1931—James N. Henrie
      P. Orin Barker
      J. Austin Cope
      John T. Partridge—Clerk
1933—James N. Henrie
      Samuel Pollock
      Josiah Shurtz (became Chair upon Henrie's death)
      J. Frank Houston (completed Henrie's term)
      John T. Partridge—Clerk
1935—Walter B. Daly
      Samuel Pollock
      Heber J. Allen
      John T. Partridge—Clerk
1937—Heber J. Allen
      No Change for rest of Commission
1939—Thomas Dodds—Clerk
      No Change for rest of Commission
1941—Heber J. Allen
      J. Usher Henrie
      Samuel Pollock
      Thomas Dodds—Clerk
1943—J. Usher Henrie
      No Change for rest of Commission
1945—J. Usher Henrie
      Bernard A. Johnson
      Heber J. Allen
      Thomas Dodds—Clerk
1947—No Change
1949—J. Usher Henrie
      Samuel Pollock
      Earl Jolley
      Thomas Dodds—Clerk

1951—J. Usher Henrie
    Earl Jolley
    Herbert S. Gleave
    Thomas Dodds—Clerk
1953—Heber J. Allen
    John M. Cherrington
    Earl Jolley
    Thomas Dodds—Clerk
1955—Heber J. Allen
    Clarence I. Foy
    H. Alton Shakespear
    J. Ernest Riggs—Clerk
1957—Heber J. Allen
    Clarence I. Foy
    Malen A. Mecham
    J. Ernest Riggs
1959—William G. Bruhn
    Malen A. Mecham
    Heber J. Allen
    J. Ernest Riggs—Clerk
1961—LeGrand Farnsworth
    Heber J. Allen
    Samuel Pollock
    J. Ernest Riggs—Clerk
1963—LeGrand Farnsworth
    Samuel Pollock
    E. D. Haws
    J. Ernest Riggs—Clerk
1965—E. D. Haws
    Robert A. Middleton
    Sam Pollock
    J. Ernest Riggs—Clerk
    Vera Schow Wilcock—(Completed Riggs' term as Clerk)
1967—James Yardley
    Leland Griffin
    E. D. Haws
    Rea Dodds—Clerk

1969—James Yardley
        Leland Griffin
        Dale Marsh
        Rea Dodds—Clerk
1971—No Change
1973—No Change
1975—James Yardley
        Leland Griffin
        Dale Marsh
        Wallace Ott (Completed Griffin's term)
        Edra Miller—Clerk
1977—Jay Proctor
        Wallace Ott
        H. Dell LeFevre
        Edra Miller—Clerk
1979—George Middleton
        Wallace Ott
        H. Dell LeFevre
        Edra Miller—Clerk
1981—George Middleton
        H. Dell LeFevre
        Guy W. Thompson
        Edra Miller—Clerk
1983—No Change except Dawna Barney completed Miller's term
1985—H. Dell LeFevre
        Guy W. Thompson
        Thomas V. Hatch
        Hazel Houston—Clerk
1987—Thomas V. Hatch
        Sherrell Ott
        Louis Liston
        Hazel Houston—Clerk
1989—Thomas V. Hatch
        Sherrell Ott
        Louise Liston
        Hazel W. Rich—Clerk
1991—No Change

1993—No Change except Camille Anderton Moore
    completed Rich's term
1995—Louise Liston
    D. Maloy Dodds
    Clare Ramsay
    Camille A. Moore—Clerk
1997—No Change

Mayors or Town Presidents****

Name	Years Served
Antimony—Incorporated 1934	
J. Lester Smoot	1934–1939
Herber S. Gleave	1940–1943
Nad Riddle	1944–1947
Ward Savage	1947–1951
Laumaun Riddle	1952–1953
Archie Gleave	1954–1961
Lamaun Sorensen	1962–1964
Wayne Delange	1964–1967
Hal Jensen	1968–1973
Charley Brindley	1974–1981
Alma Lynn Savage 1982–1985	
Phil Allen	1986–1993
Shannon Allen	1994–1996
William Wiley	1996–
Boulder—Incorporated 1958	
Irene King Inglott	1958
(appointed by County Commission)	
Ivan Lyman	1958–1961
Cecil Griener	1962–1969
Obe J. Wright	1970–1973
John Meisenbach	1974–1977

****Information obtained from the various city offices and community representatives.

Vivian Holmes Crosby	1978–1981
Donna Moosman Wilson	1982–1989
Julie Christensen Lyman	1990–1997
Keith Gailey	1998–

Cannonville—Incorporated about 1933

Wilford Clark	abt. 1933
George Anderson	Dates unavailable
Ernest Mangum	" "
Jack Seaton	" "
George W. Thompson	abt. 1948
Byron Davies	Dates unavailable
June Nelson	1962
Irving Johnson	abt. 1966
Edgar Dunham	abt. 1970
Laurie Holley	1974–1985
Jim Clarke	1986–1989
John Matthews	1990–1997
A. E. Stone	1998

Escalante—Incorporated 1903

Alfred Luther	1903
Alfred Sherman	1918
Rufus H. Liston, Jr.	1921
Joseph Larsen	Dates unavailable
John Spencer	" "
William Mitchell	" "
Alvey Wright	1934
Sherman Eyre	1940–1945
J. Clyde Spencer	1946–1949
Dale Marsh	1950–1957
Claron Griffin	1958–1965
William L. Davis	1966–1973
Mohr Christensen	1974–1977
Dale Marsh	1978–1981
Mohr Christensen	1982–1985
Wade Barney	1986–1989
Clem Griffin	1990–1993

Wade Barney	1994–1997
Howard Miller	1997
(completed Barney's term)	
Sandie Hitchcock	1998–

Hatch—Incorporated 1934

David Hyrum Evans	1934–1937
Rudolph I. Luker	1938–1941
Elliott L. Barney	1942–1945
Rudolph I. Luker	1946–1947
Neil Clove	1947–1949
A. Wiley Huntington	1950–1953
Karl Lowder	1954–1957
Orlas Riggs	1958–1961
Robert Evans	1962–1965
Robert L. Henderson	1966–1969
Karl Lowder	1970–1979
Mervin Barnhurst	1980–1989
LaVal Sawyer	1990–1997
Nile Richard Sawyer	1998

Henrieville—Incorporated

James Goulding
Guy W. Thompson
Robert Patterson
Riley Miller
Les Barker
Elmo Bushnell
Doyle Neilson
Ralph Chynoweth
David Rose
Oscar Willis
Leland Griffin
David Quilter
Darrel Blackwell
Bart Smith
Thorley Johnson

Panguitch—Incorporated 1899

John Houston	1899–1901
Ira W. Hatch	1902–1903
Thomas Haycock	1904–1905
John Houston	1906–1907
Thomas Sevy	1907–1909
John E. Myers	1910–1911
Joseph Houston	1912–1913
H. Clement Tebbs	1914–1915
Thomas Sevy	1916–1917
Fred E. Eldridge	1918–1919
Beny Cameron, Jr.	1919–1921
James M. Sargent	1922–1925
Rudolph Church	1926–1927
J. Frank Houston	1928–1931
Parley Ipson	1932–1933
Jed E. Cooper	1934–1935
W. Earl Marshall	1936–1943
M. Vee Foy	1944–1947
Reed S. Henderson	1948–1949
William G. Bruhn	1950–1957
Daniel A. Tebbs	1958–1961
Norman T. Henrie	1962–1963
M. Kay Heywood	1964–1973
Wallace G. Lee	1974–1981
Jon Lee Torgerson	1982–1989
Jake Albrecht	1990–June 25, 1991
D. Maloy Dodds	1991–1994
John Ward Houston	1994–1995
Elaine M. Baldwin	1996–1997
Jon Lee Torgerson	1998–

Tropic—Incorporated 1902

Andrew J. Hansen (resigned 23 May 1904)	1902–1904
Thomas H. Cope	1904–1905

John Ahlstrom	1906–1910
(died 22 August 1910)	
Ole Ahlstrom	1910–1913
Thomas H. Cope	1914–1915
James R. Ott	1916–1917
Elias H. Smith	1918–1923
Frank Ahlstrom	1924–1927
John F. Pollock	Dates unavailable
Samuel Pollock	" "
John H. Johnson	1932–1941
James A. Ott	1942–1943
Earl Jolley	1943
(completed Ott's term)	
Malen Mecham	1944–1947
Wallace Ott	1948–1949
Malen Mecham	1950–1953
Earl Jolley	1954–1959
Afton Pollock	1960–1963
Weldon Sudweeks	1964–1965
Arnold Adair	1966–1973
Mondell Syrett	1974–1980
(resigned 24 July 1980)	
Reed LeFevre	1980–1981
Evan Chynoweth	1982
(resigned October 1982)	
Douglas Ahlstrom	1982–1983
Jay Littlefield	1984
(resigned 16 August 1984)	
Ella Adair	1984–1985
Rick Bybee	1986–1987
Robert Bradley	1988–1993
Jean Seiler	1994

Selected Bibliography

Adovasio, James M. "Fremont Basketry," *Tebiwa* 17, no. 2 (1975): 67–76.

———. "Prehistoric Basketry." In *Handbook of North American Indians*, William C. Sturtevant, gen. ed., vol. 11, *Great Basin*, Warren D'Azevedo, ed. Washington D.C.: Smithsonian Institution, 1986, 194–205.

Aikens, Melvin C. *Fremont-Promontory-Plains Relationships*. University of Utah Anthropological Papers 82. Salt Lake City: University of Utah Press, 1966.

———. *Hogup Cave*. University of Utah Anthropological Papers 93. Salt Lake City: University of Utah Press, 1970.

———. "The Far West." In *Ancient Native Americans*, Jesse D. Jennings, ed. San Francisco: W.H. Freeman and Co., 1978.

Alexander, Thomas G. *Utah, The Right Place*. Salt Lake City: Peregrine Smith, 1995.

Ambler, Richard J. *The Anasazi*. Flagstaff: Museum of Northern Arizona, 1987.

Anthropology of the Desert West: Essays in Honor of Jesse D. Jennings. University of Utah Anthropological Papers 110. Salt Lake City: University of Utah Press, 1986.

Armstrong, John Christopher. Diary. LDS Church Archives, Salt Lake City, Utah.

Bailey, L.R. *Indian Slave Trade in the Southwest*. Los Angeles: Westernlore Press, 1966.

Baldridge, Kenneth W. "Nine Years of Achievement: The Civilian Conservation Corps in Utah." Ph.D. dissertation, Brigham Young University, 1971.

Baker, Pearl. *The Wild Bunch at Robbers Roost*. New York: Abelard-Schuman, 1965.

Betenson, Lula Parker (as told to Dora Flack). *Butch Cassidy, My Brother*. Provo, UT: Brigham Young University Press, 1975.

Bradley G. Hill, and S. Robert Bereskin, eds. *Oil and Gas Fields of Utah*. Utah Geological Association Publication 22, 1993.

Breed, Jack. "The First Moter Sortie into Escalante Land," *National Geographic* (September 1941): 369–404.

Brewerton, George D. *Overland with Kit Carson: A Narrative of the Old Spanish Trail in 1848*. New York: Coward, McCann, 1930.

Brooks, Juanita. *Jacob Hamblin: Mormon Apostle to the Indians*. Salt Lake City: Westwater Press, 1980.

———. *John Doyle Lee: Zealot, Pioneer Builder, Scapegoat*. Glendale, CA: Arthur H. Clark Company, 1973.

Brown, John. Journal. LDS Church Archives, Salt Lake City, Utah.

Brown, Vernal A. "The United States Marshals in Utah Territory to 1896." Master's thesis, Utah State University, 1970.

Campbell, Robert L. Journal. LDS Church Archives, Salt Lake City, Utah.

Carter, Kate B., compiler. *Our Pioneer Heritage*. Salt Lake City: Daughters of Utah Pioneers, 1968.

Carr, Stephen L. *The Historical Guide to Utah Ghost Towns*. Salt Lake City: Western Epics, 1972.

Chidester, Ida, and Eleanor Bruhn. *Golden Nuggets of Pioneer Days: A History of Garfield County*. N.p.: Daughters of Utah Pioneers, 1949.

Christensen, J. Oral. "The History of Education in Garfield County, Utah," Master's thesis, University of Utah, 1949.

Chronic, Halka. *Roadside Geology of Utah*. Missoula, MT: Mountain Press Publishing Company, 1990.

Cleland, Robert Glass and Juanita Brooks, eds. *A Mormon Chronicle: The Diaries of John D. Lee, 1848–1876*. Salt Lake City: University of Utah Press, 1983.

Cooley, John R. *The Great Unknown: The Journal of the Historic First*

Expedition Down the Colorado River. Flagstaff, AZ: Northland Press, 1988.

Corbett, Pearson. *Jacob Hamblin, Peacemaker.* Salt Lake City: Deseret Book Company, 1973.

Cordell, Linda S. *Prehistory of the Southwest.* Orlando, FL: Academic Press, 1984.

Crampton, C. Gregory, ed. "Military Reconniassance in Southern Utah," *Utah Historical Quarterly* 32 (Spring 1964): 146–61.

Creer, Leland Hargrave. *The Founding of an Empire: The Exploration and Colonization of Utah, 1776–1856.* Salt Lake City: Bookcraft, 1947.

Dalley, Gardiner F., and Douglas A. McFadden. *The Archaeology of the Red Cliffs.* Cultural Resource Series 17. Salt Lake City: Bureau of Land Management, 1985.

Daly, Walter Kirk. "The Settling of Panguitch Valley, Utah: A Study in Mormon Colonization." Master's thesis, University of California, 1941.

Durrah, William Culp. *Powell of the Colorado.* Princeton: Princeton University Press, 1951.

Ellsworth, S. George. *Utah's Heritage.* Salt Lake City: Peregrine Smith, 1992.

Eubank, Mark. *Utah Weather.* Salt Lake City: Weatherbank, Inc., 1979.

Fish, Rick J. "The Southern Utah Expedition of Parley P. Pratt: 1849–1850." Master's thesis, Brigham Young University, 1992.

Fremont, John C. *Report of the Exploring Expeditions to the Rocky Mountains in the Year 1842 and to Oregon and North California in the Years 1843–44.* Washington, D.C.: Gales and Seaton, 1845.

Gilbert, Grove Karl. *Report on the Geology of the Henry Mountains.* Washington, D.C.: Government Printing Office, 1880.

Gottfredson, Peter. *Indian Depredations in Utah.* Salt Lake City: Skelton Publishing Co., 1919.

Greenwell, Scott L. "A History of the United States Army Corps of Topographical Engineers in Utah, 1843–1859." Master's thesis, Utah State University, 1972.

Gregory, Herbert E. "Scientific Explorations in Southern Utah." *American Journal of Science* 248 (October 1945): 527–49.

―――. *A Geologic and Geographic Sketch of Zion and Bryce Canyon National Parks.* N.p.: Zion-Bryce Natural History Association, 1956.

Hauck, F.R. *Cultural Resource Evaluation in South Central Utah, 1977–1978.* Salt Lake City: Bureau of Land Management, 1979.

Hinton, Wayne K. *The Dixie National Forest: Managing an Alpine Forest in an Arid Setting.* Cedar City, UT: United States Forest Service, c. 1987.

Jackson, Marilyn. "The Unraveling of a 'Shurtz Tale' and an Epoch of Escalante Excitement." Unpublished typescript, 1992.

Jennings, *Jesse D. Glen Canyon: A Summary.* University of Utah Anthropological Papers 81. Salt Lake City: University of Utah Press, 1966.

————. *Prehistory of Utah and the Eastern Great Basin.* University of Utah Anthropological Papers 98. Salt Lake City: University of Utah Press, 1978.

Jenson, Andrew. Encyclopedia History of the Church of Jesus Christ of Latter-day Saints (Salt Lake City: Deseret New Publishing Company, 1941).

Johnson, Diana. "The First White Men Come to Henrieville." Unpublished manuscript, no date.

Jones, Dewitt, and Linda S. Cordell. *Anasazi World.* Portland, OR: Graphic Arts, 1985.

Jones, Raymond S. "The Last Wagon through the Hole-in-the-Rock," *Desert Magazine* (1954): 22–25.

Journal History of the Church of Jesus Christ of Latter-day Saints, 750 vols. LDS Church Archives, Salt Lake City, Utah.

King, Larry R. *The Kings of the Kingdom: The Life of Thomas Rice King and His Family.* Orem, UT: Larry R. King, 1996.

Kelly, Charles. *The Outlaw Trail, A History of Butch Cassidy and His Wild Bunch.* New York: Bonanza Books, 1959.

Kluger, Jeffery. "Deep Divide," *Time,* 101 February 1994, 65–66.

Knowlton, Ezra C. *History of the Highway Development in Utah.* Salt Lake City: State of Utah, n.d.

Larson, Stan, ed. *Prisoner for Polygamy: The Memoirs and Letters of Rudger Clawson at the Utah Territorial Penitentiary, 1884–87.* Urbana: University of Illinois Press, 1993.

LeFevre, Lenora Hall. *The Boulder Country and Its People: A History of the People of Boulder and the Surrounding Country, One Hundred Years— 1872–1973,* Springville, UT: Art City Publishing Co., 1973.

Lindsay, Lamar. "Unusual or Enigmatic Stone Artifacts: Pots, Pipes and Pendants from Utah," *American Antiquities Section Selected Papers* 2, no. 8 (1976): 107–17.

Lipe, William D. "Anasazi Communities in the Red Rock Plateau." In *Reconstructing Prehistoric Pueblo Societies,* William A. Longacre, ed., 84–139. Albuquerque: University of New Mexico Press, 1970.

————. "The Southwest." In *Ancient Native Americans,* Jesse D. Jennings, ed., 326–401. San Francisco: W.H. Freeman, 1978.

Lister, Robert H., and Florence C. Lister. *Those Who Came Before.* Globe, AZ: Southwest Parks and Monuments Association, 1989.

Little, James A. *Jacob Hamblin: A Narrative of His Personal Experiences, as a Frontiersman, Missionary to the Indians and Explorer.* 1881. Reprint. Freeport, NY: Books for Libraries Press, 1971.

Lyon, Thomas, and Terry Tempest Williams, eds. *Great and Peculiar Beauty: A Utah Reader.* Salt Lake City: Peregrine Smith, 1995.

Madsen, David B. "Dating the Paiute-Shoshone Expansion in the Great Basin," *American Antiquity* 40, no. 1 (1975): 82–86.

————. *Exploring the Fremont.* Salt Lake City: Utah Museum of Natural History, 1989.

————. "The Fremont and the Sevier: Defining Prehistoric Agriculturalists North of the Anasazi." *American Antiquity* 44, no. 4 (1979): 711–22.

Madsen, David B., and Michael S. Berry. "A Reasessment of Northeastern Great Basin Prehistory," *American Antiquity* 40, no. 4 (1975): 391–405.

Malmgren, Larry H. "A History of the WPA in Utah." Master's thesis, Utah State University, 1965.

Martineau, LaVan. *Southern Paiutes: Legends, Lore, Language and Lineage.* Las Vegas: KC Publishing, 1992.

Marwitt, John P. *Median Village and Fremont Culture Regional Variation.* University of Utah Anthropological Papers 95. Salt Lake City: University of Utah Press, 1970.

Matlock, Gary. *Enemy Ancestors.* Flagstaff, AZ: Northland Publishing, 1988.

May, Dean L. *Utah: A People's History.* Salt Lake City: University of Utah Press, 1987.

Meeks, Priddy. Journal. Typescript. Utah Historical Records Survey, 1937.

Miller, David E. *Hole-in-the-Rock.* Salt Lake City: University of Utah Press, 1959.

Moffitt, John. *The History of Public Education in Utah.* Salt Lake City: Utah Department of Education, 1946.

Morss, Noel. "The Ancient Culture of the Fremont River in Utah," *Papers of the Peabody Museum of American Archaeology and Ethnology* 12, no. 3 (1931).

Nielsen, Grant. *Johns Valley: The Way We Saw It.* Springville, UT: Art City Publishing Co., 1917.

Parker, Kathleene. *The Only True People: A History of the Native Americans of the Colorado Plateau.* Marceline, MO: Walsworth Press, 1991.

Peterson, Charles. *Utah: A Centennial History*. New York: W.W. Norton & Company, 1977.

———. *Utah: A History*. New York: W.W. Norton & Company, 1997.

Pierson, Lloyd M. *Cultural Resource Summary of the East Central Portion of Moab District*. Salt Lake City: Bureau of Land Management, 1981.

Pike, Donald G. *Anasazi: Ancient People of the Rock*. New York: Harmony Books, 1974.

Pointer, Larry. *In Search of Butch Cassidy*. Norman: University of Oklahoma Press, 1977.

Powell, Allan Kent, ed. *Utah History Encyclopedia*. Salt Lake City: University of Utah Press, 1994.

Powell, John Wesley. *The Exploration of The Colorado River and Its Canyons*. 1895. Reprint. New York: Penguin Books, 1989.

———. *Report on the Lands of the Arid Region of the United States, With a More Detailed Account of the Lands of Utah*. Washington, D.C.: Government Printing Office, 1879.

Pratt, Parley, P. *Autobiography of Parley Parker Pratt: One of the Twelve Apostles of the Church of Jesus Christ of Latter Day Saints, to the People of England*. Manchester: James Jones, n.d.

Rabbit, Mary C. "John Wesley Powell: Pioneer Statesman of Federal Science." *The Colorado River Region and John Wesley Powell*. Geological Survey Professional Paper 669. Washington, D.C.: Government Printing Office, 1969.

Riggs, Effel Harmon Burrow. *History of Hatch, Utah, and Associated Towns Asay and Hillsdale*. Beaver, UT: Hatch Camp of Daughters of Utah Pioneers, 1978.

Roberts, Brigham H. *A Comprehensive History of the Church of Jesus Christ of Latter-Day Saints*. 6 vols. Reprint. Provo, UT: Brigham Young University Press, 1965.

Rusho, William L. *Powell's Canyon Voyage*. Palmer Lake, CO: Filter Press, 1969.

Sandberg, Karl C. "Telling the Tales and Telling the Truth: Writing the History of Widtsoe," *Dialogue: A Journal of Mormon Thought* 26 (Winter 1993): 93–105.

Schaafsma, Polly. *The Rock Art of Utah*. Cambridge, MA: Peabody Museum, Harvard University, 1971.

Schroedl, Alan R. "The Archaic of the Northern Colorado Plateau," Ph.D. dissertation, University of Utah, 1976.

Scrattish, Nicholas. *Historic Resource Study: Bryce Canyon National Park.* Denver: National Park Service, 1986.

Smart, William B. *Old Utah Trails.* Salt Lake City: Utah Geographic, 1988.

Smith, Shelley, Jeanne Moe, Kelly Letts, and Danielle Paterson. *Intrigue of the Past: Investigating Archaeology.* Salt Lake City: Bureau of Land Management, 1992.

Smith, Van Dorn. *One and One Make Eleven.* Ogden, UT: n.p., 1993.

Stegner, Wallace. *Beyond the Hundredth Meridian: John Wesley Powell and the Second Opening of the West.* Lincoln: University of Nebraska Press, 1982.

———.*Clarence Edward Dutton: An Appraisal.* Salt Lake City: University of Utah Press, 1936.

Stokes, William Lee, *Geology of Utah.* Salt Lake City: Utah Museum of Natural History/Utah Geological and Mineral Survey, 1988.

Thompson, George A. *Lost Treasures on the Old Spanish Trail.* Salt Lake City: Publishers Press, 1986.

———.*Some Dreams Die: Utah's Ghost Towns and Lost Treasures.* Salt Lake City: Dream Garden Press, 1982.

Thompson, George W. "Cannonville History." Unpublished manuscript, 1994.

U.S. Bureau of the Census. *County and City Data Book.* Washington D.C.: U.S. Department of Commerce, various years.

U.S. Bureau of the Census. *United States Census of Agriculture.* Washington D.C.: U.S. Department of Commerce, various years.

U.S. District Court, case files for the Territory of Utah, 1870–1896. Family History Library, Salt Lake City, Utah.

Utah Agricultural Statistical Report. Salt Lake City: Utah State Department of Agriculture, various years.

Utah Atlas and Gazetteer. Freeport, ME: DeLorme Mapping, 1993.

Utah High Schools Activities Association Handbook 1997–98. Salt Lake City: Utah High Schools Activities Association, 1997.

Utah Statistical Abstract, various years. Salt Lake City: Bureau of Economic and Business Research, University of Utah.

Van Cott, John W. *Utah Place Names.* Salt Lake City: University of Utah Press, 1990.

Van Wagoner, Richard S. *Mormon Polygamy: A History.* Salt Lake City: Signature Books, 1989.

Warner, M. Lane. *Grass Valley 1873–1976: A History of Antimony and Her People.* Salt Lake City: American Press, 1976.

Winkler, Albert. "The Ute Mode of War in the Conflict of 1865–68," *Utah Historical Quarterly* 60 (Fall 1992):300–18.

Woolsey, Anne I. "Agricultural Diversity in the Prehistoric Southwest," *The Kiva* 45, no.4 (1980):317–35.

Woolsey, Nethella Griffin. *The Escalante Story: 1875–1964.* Springville, UT: Art City Publishing Co., 1964.

Index

Adair, Ellis, 309
Adair, Jedediah, 207, 210
Adair, Julia Ann, 210
Adair, Orson, 210
Adair, Pearl, 310
Adair, Samuel, 68
Adair, Thomas, 61
Adairville, 210
Adams, Daniel, 136
Adams, David B., 131, 141
Adams, David R., 136, 172
Adams, Herb, 275
Adams, Lydia Catherine, 131, 141
Adams, Rob, 173
Agriculture, 78–79, 336–39
Ahlstrom, James, 201
Ahlstrom, John, 201, 206
Ahlstrom, Ole, 201, 202, 206, 207
Airplane Crash—1947, 319
Albright, Horace, 268
Allen, Beulah, 259
Allen, Chester, 274
Allen, Edmund, 135
Allen, H.J., 342
Allen, Isaac, 136

Allen, Jennings, 294
Allen, Lark, 309
Allen, Lucy, 131
Allen, Philo, 131, 135
Allen, Robert, 136, 171, 172–73
Allred, Beth, xii
Allred, Karl, 355
Alpacas, 364–65
Alvey, Arnold, 345
Alvey, Dena, 342
Alvey, Forest, 326
Alvey, George, 335
Alvey, Mary Elizabeth Heaps, 131
Alvey, Samuel, 288
Alvey, T.H., 326
Alvey, Wanless, 303, 305, 326, 342
Alvey, William, 131, 171, 215
Alvin, Seth, 201
American Antimony Company, 122
Anasazi Indian Village State Park, 25, 360
Anasazi Peoples, 25–29, 31–32
Andalex Resources, 367
Anderson, Mark, 250
Anderson, Oliver, 113

Anderson, Sarah D., 213
Andrus, James, 67–74, 29
Angrove, John, 198
Animals, 16
Antimony, x, 117–123, 173, 175, 194, 233, 254–55, 258, 274, 294, 309, 313, 353–54
Aquarius Plateau, 14, 104
Archaic Period, 23–24
Arthur, C.J., 157
Arthur, Chester A., 178
Arze, Maurice, 42
Asay, Aaron, 114, 117
Asay, Amos, 114
Asay, Eleazer, 113
Asay, Jerome, 114, 172
Asay, Joseph, 113, 213
Asay, Sarah Ann Pedric, 113, 213
Atlatl, 23–24
Austin, Mark, 373
Automobiles, 246–49
Avertt, Elijah, 70, 73

Babbitt, Bruce, 366
Bailey, Gail, 346
Bailey, Gale, 292
Bailey, Reva, 346
Bailey, T.C., 103
Baker, Amanda Jensen, 185
Baker, Elsie, 273
Baker, George, 183–84, 185, 188, 189
Baker, Henry, 185
Baker, William, 185, 188
Bamberger, Simon, 260–61
Bankhead, John, 49
Barker, Alice Woodhead, 130
Barker, James, 130
Barker, Josiah, 130, 132, 135, 136
Barker, Mariah, 130
Barker, Mary Alice, 130
Barker, Orin, 249, 297
Barker, Peter, 130
Barker, Robert, 260
Barker, Tom, 249
Barker, William, 130
Barney, Alma, 83, 86, 130, 246
Barney, Clarion, 330

Barney, Clifford, 330
Barney, Evelyn, 310
Barney, Frank, 215
Barney, George H., 218
Barney, Henry, 222, 256
Barney, Joseph S. 136
Barney, Newton, 246
Barney, Vird, 258
Barney, Wallace Arnold, 310
Barnhurst, Anna Marie Jensen, 117, 172, 213
Barnhurst, Ira Ray, 309
Barnhurst, J.C., 172
Barnhurst, Samuel, 117
Barton, Leon, 310
Bateman, Lavar, 267
Beaman, O.E., 101
Bean, George, 117
Bean, Glen, 321
Bean, Victor, 136, 190
Bear Creek, 123
Beck, Erastus, 171
Beckstrom, Kenneth, 303
Beebe, Reed, 307
Beebe, Vera, 307
Beebee, Albert, 70
Behunin, Max, 328
Bell, Eve, 291
Bell, Lizzie, 174
Bennett, Wallace F., 341
Benson, Clara Matheson, 242–43
Benson, Philip, 242
Bentley, Wilford, 303
Bentonite, 335
Berry, Louise, 128
Berry, William S., 127
Best, Christian, 256
Betenson, Lula Parker, 228, 229
Bible, Alan, 341
Bishop, Francis Marion, 96, 101
Black Hawk War, 62–74
Black, Esther Clarinda King, 120, 175
Black, George, 120, 175
Black, Nephi, 258
Blackburn, Ralph B., 298
Bliss, Orley Dwight, 143
Blood, DeLoy, 347

Blue Spring Canyon, 87
Boreman, Jacob, 179
Boulder, x, 181–91, 260, 288, 300, 302, 310, 355–58
Boulder Grazing Association, 219
Boulder Mountain, 14, 43, 72
Bowman, H.I., 263
Boyden, Stephen, 375
Boynton, John F., 142
Boyter, Belle, 291
Bradley, George, 95
Breed, Jack, 320
Bremner, Brian, 375
Brick kilns, 84
Brindley, Charles, 353
Brinkerhoff, Willard, 182, 183–84, 185
Bristlecone Pine, 17
Bromide Mine, 198
Brothers, Findlay, 269
Brown, John, 47, 49, 50
Bruhn, Elinore, 291
Bruhn, Fred, 242
Bryce Canyon Airport, 294–95
Bryce Canyon Cafe, 342
Bryce Canyon Lodge, xi
Bryce Canyon National Park, x, xi, 10–11, 40, 102–3, 249–53, 320–25; creation of, 260–68; lodge, 265–66, 321, 322, 324; grazing rights, 268–69
Bryce Valley, 69; CCC work, 301–2;
Bryce, Bill, 153
Bryce, Ebenezer, 143–45
Bryce, Mary Ann Park, 143–45
Buffalo, 16
Bullock, Gertrude Young, 258–59
Bullock, Robert, 158
Burr Trail, 374–76
Burrow, James B., 175, 214, 270
Burrows, Merrill, 309
Burton, Lawrence J., 341
Bushman, Francis, 291
Butler, Caroline, 90
Butler, Jack, 198
Butler, James, 66
Butler, John, 61, 79
Butler, John Lowe II, 76
Butler, Phoebe Melinda, 78

Butler, William, 79
Bybee, George, 205
Bybee, Levi, 291
Bybee, Louisa, 205

The Cactus, 181, 208
Calcara, Mary Dickenson, 309
Callas, Charles A., 289
Cameron, Benjamin, 220
Cameron, David, 68, 171
Cameron, J. Elliot, 380
Cameron, James P., 294
Campbell, John R., 210
Campbell, Moses Usher, 245
Campbell, Robert Lang, 47–49
Camperson, Sadi, 220
Cannon, Chris, 370
Cannon, George Q., 144, 156
Cannonville, x, 143–50, 176, 194, 238, 310, 347, 354–55
Canyonlands National Park, 5, 340
Capitol Reef National Monument, 340
Cardenas, Garcia Lopes de, 39
Carnegie Library in Panguitch, 296
Carnegie, Andrew, 208
Carson, Hannah Waggle, 239
Cassidy, Butch, 224–29
Cassidy, Mike, 225–26
Cataract Canyon, 98
Cenozoic Era, 10–14
Centennial History Project, vii
Chamberlain, Solomon, 51, 53
Chatwin, Ida, 245
Chatwin, Will, 201
Cheese Making, 137
Cherrington, Joe, 247
Cherrington, Julian, 309
Chestnut, Gary George, 347
Chidester, John F., 192
Chidester, Lionel, 303
Chidester, Sabina, 204
Christensen, Hans, 59
Christensen, Lawrence C., 329, 335
Christensen, Magdelina, 59
Christensen, Mohr, 330
Chubs, 194
Church, Charles, 265

Church, Hayden, 276
Church, Rudolph, 275
Chynoweth, Jeanie, xii
Chynoweth, Sampson, 153
Civilian Conservation Corps, 289, 293, 301–7, 343
Clark, Cecil, 245
Clark, Howard, 293
Clark, Lorenzo, 79
Clark, R. Garn, 245
Clark, Riley G., 79, 80, 220
Clark, W. Kay, 306
Clark, Wilford, 320
Clarke, Michael "Jim," 355
Clayton, Albert, 120
Clayton, Ed, 145
Cleveland, 123
Clifton, 151
Climate, 15
Clinch, Frederika Hermansen, 278
Clinton, Bill, 365, 367, 374
Clove, Mary Ann, 174, 211
Clove, Neils Ivor, 172
Clove, Neils Peterson, 115–16, 210
Clove, Sophia Rasmussen, 115–16
Coal, 9, 335–36
Coleman, Albert, 329
Coleman, George, 131, 136
Coleman, Jane, 131, 138
Coleman, Maria, 131
Coleman, Samuel, 329
Collett, Ephraim, 157
Collett, Reuben, 136, 142, 159
Collett, Sylvans, 218
Colorado Plateau, 2, 14
Colorado River, 2
Consumers Power Inc., 331
Coombs Village, 25 see also Anasazi Indian State Park
Coombs, E.H., 329
Coombs, Kay, 330
Cooper, Bell, 291
Cooper, Cora, 291
Cooper, George, 276
Cooper, Seguine, 87
Cooper, Wise, 182
Cope, Bernard, 310

Cope, De Esta, 292
Cope, Matilda, 248
Cope, Maurice, 202, 248, 268, 272, 292
Cope, Thomas R., 206
Cottam, Milan W., 310
Covington, Dan, 305
Covington, Luvera, 298
Cowart, Ruby C., 310
Cowles, Harry N., 219
Cox, Orville, 156
Cox, Phoebe, 204
Coyote Creek, 117–18
Crabb, Glenn, 311
Crawford, Arthur, 320
Criddle, Wayne C.,336
Crimm, Ben, 298
Croft Pearson Industries, 327
Crosby, Jesse, 68, 79, 84, 86, 170, 199
Crosby, Vivian Holmes, 355
Crossing of the Fathers, 43
Crump, Claudia Walkenhorst, 381
Crump, Leon, 381
Cuyler, Lillie Zabriskie, 258

Dalton, Edward, 58
Daly, Kirk, 267
Daly, Walter B., 294
Dame, William H., 57, 58, 75, 80
Dameron, Joe, 175
Dance Hall Rock, 162–63
Dances, 124, 133, 162, 189, 192, 289, 306
Dart, John, 51, 53
Davenport, Orlo, 285
Davies, Bryon, 335
Davies, George, xi, 244, 276–77
Davies, Jimmy, 277
Davies, John Henry, 127–28
Davis, Emma Carson Morrill, xi
Davis, Clem, 276
Davis, Johnny, 335
Davis, Joseph C., 79
Davis, Larry, 360
Davis, Mary Elizabeth Fretwell, 158
Davis, Will, 288
Davis, William L. "Billy," 330, 344, 345–46
Decker, Anna Maria Mickelsen, 162

Decker, James B., 158, 162
Decker, Lena Deseret, 162
Deer Hunt, 343
Delange, Wayne, 344
Dellenbaugh, F.S., 97, 101, 103
Delong, Albert, 130, 131, 171, 305
Delong, Dicy, 114
Delong, Gladys, 208
Delong, Winnie, 208
Dern, George, 266–67
Deuel, Kate, 138
Deuel, William Henry, 134, 142
Dickenson, Arthur, 309
Dickenson, James, 76
Dickenson, Sarah Jane Snyder, 76
Dickson, John, 145
Digger Indians, 44
Dinosaurs, 8, 10
Diphtheria, 207
Dirty Devil River, 98, 104–5
Division of State History, vii
Dockstader, George, 120
Dockstader, Inez Forrester, 120
Doctor Bill, 66
Dodds, George, 85, 176, 177, 188
Dodds, James, 256
Dominguez, Francisco Atanasio, 41–42
Draper, H.M., 326
Drew, J.J., 251
Duggins, Sims E., 312
Dumas, Millard "Crockett," 361
Duncan, John C., 158
Dunn, William "Bill," 95, 99,
Dunning, Debbie, 181
Dunning, John M., 171, 176, 177, 181, 206, 208
Dunning, Lydia, 181
Dunton, Harvey, 158
Durfrey, Alma, 182
Dutton, Clarence E., 105
Dutton, George, 149
Dutton, James, 117
Dutton, William, 149

Eager, William W., 109
Eagle City, 198–99
Eagle Valley Mission, 113

East Fork Cattle Association, 269
East Fork Irrigation Company, 200
Eber, Frank, 120
Eber, Kate Effie, 120
Edmunds Act of 1882, 178
Education, 174–77, 271–72 (see also schools)
Eisenhower, Dwight, 340
El Escalante Hotel, 262
Elder, Jim, 238
Elder, Rainy, 238
Elder, Theda, 238
Eldredge, Fred, E., 208
Electrification, 297–301
Elmer, Elijah, 79
Elmer, Ira B., 150, 170
Englestead, Carl, 309
Erastus, 199
Escalante, x, 172, 175, 194, 271, 287, 290, 293, 309–10, 342
Escalante, Silvestre Velez de, 41–42
Escalante Basin, 14
Escalante Cattle and Horse Growers Association, 219
Escalante Dam, 306
Escalante Light and Power Company, 297
Escalante Lions Club, 344
Escalante Petrified Forest, 361
Escalante River, 14, 100–1, 103, 129
Escalante School, 137
Evans, David, 80
Evans, Jenkins T., 58
Evans, Jesse, 276
Evens, Blue John, 224
Excell, Earl, 309

Fallis, Leonard, 260
Fallis, Mark C., 309
Firmage, Richard A., xii
Fish industry, 88
Fish, Franklin R., 80
Fish, Joseph, 67, 69–70
Fisher, F.L., 297
Five County Association of Governments, 356
Fletcher, Joe, 149

Fletcher, K.A., 200
Flying M, 342
Fordham, Joseph, 136, 139
Forest Reserves, 217–20
Forshey, Jim, 173
Forsyth, Neil, 303
Fort Sanford, 65, 123
Foster, Al, 335, 345–46
Fotheringham, Vera, 239
Fourth of July Celebrations, 86, 154, 318
Foy, Mamie, 114, 208
Foy, Martin W., 78, 136, 171
Francis, Joseph, viii
Frandsen, George, 335
Frandsen, Kevin, 359
Frandsen, Lawrence, 359
Fredrick, David, 109
Fremont, John C., 45–46, 54
Fremont Peoples, 29–32
Fremont River, 104–5
Fuller, Craig, viii, xii

Garcia, Lagos, 42
Gardner, Fred G., 272, 273
Garfield County, area; 1; landscape today, 14–16; climate, 15; birth of, 168–70; name, 170; boundaries, 170; county seat, 170; courthouse, 209; attempt by Antimony to leave county, 353–54
Garfield County News, 208, 270
Garfield High School, 272, 380; boys basketball team in 1924, 275
Garfield Mountain States Telephone and Telegraph Company, 220
Garfield Travel Council, 365
Garfield, James A., 168–69
Garkane Power Association, 298–301, 302, 376
Gates, Hyrum, 216, 272
Gates, Lawrence, 286
Gates, Lynn, 344
Gates, William Henry, 130
Gavin, Fred M., 208
Gem Theater, 239
Geologic History, 3–14

Georgetown, 156
Gibson, Richard, 113
Gilbert, Grove Karl, 102, 105
Gillmore, Mike, 88
Gleave, Archie George, 287, 345
Gleave, David Phil, 287
Gleave, Eldon, 287
Gleave, Elizabeth Barrowmen, 120
Gleave, Herbert S., 286
Gleave, Stella Stoker, 287
Gleave, Walter, 120
Glen Canyon, 98–99, 341–42
Glenn, John, 346
Gold Mining, 198–99
Golding, Cora, 273
Goodman, Frank, 95
Goodwin, Betsy, 136
Goshute Indians, 32–33, 44–45
Gould, John C., 242, 244
Gould, Samuel, 48
Goulding, Arthur, 346
Goulding, Caroline Evelyn, 276
Goulding, Daniel, 143, 152–53, 156
Goulding, Dessie, 276
Goulding, Dorie, 258
Goulding, Elijah, 276
Goulding, Elizabeth Pratten, 152–53
Goulding, Fanny Pratten, 152–53, 154
Goulding, Jim, 258
Goulding, Kenneth, 229
Goulding, Shanna, 297
Grand Staircase-Escalante National Monument, 365–74
Grass Valley, 117–23
Great Depression, 283–86
Green River, 2, 14
Greenwood, Charlie, 355
Gresham, Cal, 187
Gresham, Josepha Shefield, 187
Grey, Zane, 291
Griffin, Albert, 215
Griffin, Claron, 342
Griffin, Eldon Earnest, 310
Griffin, Elizabeth, 138
Griffin, Jody, 249
Griffin, Laura Lay, 260
Griffin, Lorenzo, 288

Griffin, Lorin, 291, 330
Griffin, Ruby, 342
Griffin, Theron, 249
Griffin, Wilford, 344
Grimes, Oliver J., 252, 260–61
Gristmills, 79, 134
Guida, Donna, xii
Guiser, Albert, 118, 119
Gunn, Thomas, 58

Hadden, Alfred, 58
Hadden, Mary Caroline, 58
Hagglestead, Frank, 193
Haight, Isaac C., 48, 80
Hakes, Collins R., 65
Hall, Andy, 95
Hall, Charles, 136, 159–61
Hall, Heber H., 311
Hall, Horace R., 311
Hall, Job, 132, 136
Hall, Jobe, 238
Hall, John, 160–61
Hall, Mary Elizabeth, 132
Hall, R.F., 222
Hall, Reed, 160–61
Hamblin, Jacob, 99–101, 118, 129
Hancock, Levison, 201, 204, 206
Hanks, Arthur E., 263
Hanks, Charley, 198–99
Hanks, George E., 192, 246
Hansen, 199
Hansen, Andrew James, 199, 200, 201,
    205, 206
Hansen, Caroline, 201
Hansen, Franklin, 190
Hansen, Paul, 373
Harriman, Elizabeth Hobbs, 158
Harris, James, 135
Harris, Llewellyn, 135
Haslem, Jane Ellen 131
Hatch, (see also Hatchtown) x, 210–14,
    238, 270, 309
Hatch-Hillsdale Cattlemen's
    Association, 219
Hatch Farmers Improvement
    Association, 212, 220
Hatchtown Reservoir, 210–14, 234–37

Hatch, Elida, 239
Hatch, Homer, 309
Hatch, John, 61, 199
Hatch, Julia, 117
Hatch, Lyle, 239
Hatch, Mary Ann Ellis, 115, 117, 174
Hatch, Meltiar, 76, 78, 114–15, 117,
    178, 212
Hatch, Permelia Snyder, 115
Hatch, Tom, 377
Hatch, Weltha Maria, 115
Hatchtown, 112–17, 172, 174, 210–14
Hatton, Andrew, 101
Hawkes, Ephraim, 133, 136
Hawkes, Joshua, 133, 136
Hawking, William "Billy" Rhodes, 95
Hawley, C.B., 252
Haws, Franklin, 182, 185–86, 188, 190
Haws, John, 187
Haws, Leland, 330
Haws, Otto, 330
Haws, Ralph, 186
Haws, Sariah Hilman, 187
Haws, Wilhemine (Minnie) Smith,
    185–86
Haycock, Albert, 87
Haycock, Frank, 292
Haycock, George, 114
Haycock, J. Scott, 309
Haycock, Jane, 311
Haycock, Richard, 309
Haycock, T. Carl, 303
Haycock, Thomas, 259
Hayes, Le Ann, 347
Haywood, James B.,209
Head, Franklin H. 63–64
Heaps, Eleanor, 130
Heaps, Henry, 130, 131
Heaps, Susannah Turner, 131
Heaps, Susannah Goldthorpe, 130
Heaps, Thomas, 129, 130, 131, 136
Heaps, Willard, 288
Heaps, William, 131, 147–48
Heaton, Harold, 298
Hell's Backbone bridge and road, 303–4
Henderson, 277
Henderson, Edie, 310

Henderson, Lydia, 110
Henderson, Nelda, 297
Henderson, Roy, 310
Henderson, William J., 145, 149, 150, 153, 200, 277
Henrie, Carrie, 121
Henrie, Cleo Allen, 309
Henrie, Dwayne, 276
Henrie, James, 76, 78, 79, 84, 151, 170
Henrie, John N., 209
Henrie, Myra Mayall, 58, 84
Henrie, S.O., 220
Henrie, Samuel, 78, 79, 87, 129
Henrie, William, 47
Henrieville, x, 151–54, 173, 257, 310, 378
Henry Mountains, 12–13, 16, 72–73, 98, 105, 198–99
Henry, James, 79
Henry, Joseph, 73, 85
Henry, Rebecca, 178
Herrell, David, 181
Heywood, James B., 171, 174–75
Heywood, Joseph L., 76, 77
Heywood, Kay, 290
Heywood, Mary, 83
Higbee, John M., 80
Hillers, J.K., 97, 99
Hillsdale, 172, 194
Hilton, Hyrum, 202, 205, 206
Hilton, Joseph, 202, 206
Hines, Fred, 330
Historical Preservation, 359–60, 379
Hobbs, George B., 158
Hodget, William, 79
Hole-in-the-Rock Expedition, 121, 157–64, 209, 320
Holley, Laurie Dea, 354–55
Holt, William F., 278
Hoover, Herbert, 253–54, 269
Horse racing, 361
Houston, Dorothy, xii, 84
Houston, Florence, 291
Houston, James, 171
Houston, John, 68, 171, 189, 209, 210, 220
Houston, Joseph, 171

Houston, Rula, 342
Houston, Wallace, W., 87
Howell, Edwin E., 102, 105
Howland, Orvel G., 95, 99
Howland, Seneca, 95, 99
Huff, James, 120, 122
Huff, Sophia, 120
Humphrey, W.H., 249–50, 251–52
Hunt, Joseph, 118
Hunt, Osro, 305
Hunt, Ralph, 320
Hunter, Archie M., 120, 121
Huntington, Dimick, 47
Huntington, Julia, 213
Huntley, Lydia Webb, 120
Hyatt, John, 76
Hyatt, Walter, 118

Ice cutting, 188
Imlay, James, 79, 83, 87, 90, 193
Imlay, John, 87
Influenza Epidemic of 1918–1919, 256–60
Ingram, Alex G., 64
Ingram, George, 145
Ingram, John, 145
Ingram, Joseph, 156, 173
Ingram, Melissa, 156, 173
Ingram, Will, 149
Interstate Highway Act of 1956, 340
Ipson, Hans P., 208
Ipson, Isabelle, 291
Ipson, Niels Peter, 87
Irrigation, 79, 106, 134–35, 146–47
Isaac Walton League, 341
Isabell, William, 291–92
Isom, George, 70
Ives, Joseph C., 95

Jackson, Clarence, 78
Jackson, Ernest, 289
Jackson, Marilyn, ix, xii, 216, 361
James Andrus Military Expedition, 67–74
James, Frank, 223
James, Jesse, 223
Jenkins, Bruce S., 376

Jennings, Jim, 347
Jennings, Schyler, 50
Jensen, Andrew, 194
Jensen, Anna Marie, 117
Jensen, 120
Jensen, Josephine, 120
Jensen, Kareen Marie, 115
Jensen, Louisa Mahitable, 120
Jeppsen, Marion, 329
Jepsen, Bill, 330
Jepsen, Fay, xii
Jepsen, Neil, 330
Jessup, Tom, 114
Johns Valley, 277–78
Johnson, Alvin Seth, 204
Johnson, Anna P., 124
Johnson, Anthony, 110
Johnson, Drusilla, 150
Johnson, George, 206, 207
Johnson, Janet Fife, 124
Johnson, Joel, 79, 112
Johnson, Joel H., 111, 124, 147, 156
Johnson, John, 202, 269, 320
Johnson, Lyndon B., 340
Johnson, Maiben, 149
Johnson, Margaret Thrylkeld, 124
Johnson, Martha Jane Stratton, 180
Johnson, Nephi, 111, 149
Johnson, Nicoli, 182
Johnson, Sena Schow, 201
Johnson, Seth, 86, 111–12, 117, 172,
    173, 178, 180, 202, 207
Johnson, Susan Bryant, 124
Johnson, W., 97
Jolley, George, 258
Jolley, Henry, 202
Jolley, Jesse, 245
Jolley, John Reuben, 258
Jolley, Kate Effie Wilcox, 122
Jollyn, Lydia Ann Johnson, 207
Jolley, Udell, 150
Jolley, William, 202, 205, 206
Jones, Buck, 88
Jones, Dan, 50
Jones, J.C., 120
Jones, John, 113
Jones, Kumen, 158

Jones, S.V., 101
Judd, Annie Dowler, 83
Judd, Arza, 259
Judd, Emily Adams, 83
Judd, Frederick, 84, 85
July 4th celebrations; 1876: 133
Justet, Dan, 130, 131
Justet, Nellie, 131

Kaibab Industries, 359, 362
Kaibab Lumber Company, 328
Kaiparowits Coal Fields, 9, 336, 367
Kaiparowits Plateau, 69
Kanarra Cattle Co-op, 127, 143
Kanarrah, 51–53
Kartchner, William, 79, 171
Kelly Construction Company, 343
Kelly, Charles, 227
Kelly, Don, 343
Kenner, Beaugard, 218
Kenney, Barbara, 309
Kessler, June Haycock, 309
Kilbourne, A.G., 320
King, Culbert Levi, 119, 179–80
King, Delilah, 179
King, Eliza Syrett, 120, 179
King, Esther Clarinda King, 120
King, Forrest, 120
King, George 120
King, Helen, 119, 120
King, Henry, 109
King, Irene, 175–76, 355
King, John, 182, 187, 305
King, John Rice, 119, 120
King, John Robinson, 179
King, Levi, 287
King, Lucy White, 179
King, Marion, 272
King, Mary Ann Henry, 179
King, Matilda, 179
King, Murray E., 204
King, Sally May Stringham, 187, 288
King, Thomas Edwin, 179
King, Thomas Rice, 119–20, 178–79
King, Volney, 120
King, William, 179
Klinginsmith, Philip, 80

Knight, Brigham, 87, 109
Kockerhans, Erwin, 309
Kodachrome Basin, x, 69
Korea, 346–47
Kruska, Bill, 345

Lake Powell, 341–42
Lameroux, Bert, 87
Lancaster, Samuel c., 265
Laramie, Alice, 131, 139
Laramie, Henry, 139
Laramie, Onizime (Lacey), 131, 136,
    139, 145
Larsen, Joseph, 297
Larson, John Rio, 162
Larson, Mons, 162
Larson, Olivia Ekelund, 162
Lawler, Frank, 199
Lay, Joe, 135, 142
Lay, John Taylor, 68, 129
Lay, Rachel, 138
Lay, William V., 219
Leavett, Dorothy, xii
Leavitt, Michael, 366–67, 369
Leavitt, Percy, 249
Lee, Alma, 87
Lee, Ben, 275
Lee, Chan, 343
Lee, John D., 51–52, 53, 80–82, 209
Lee, Robert E., 224
Lee, Ron, 355
Lee, Roy, 273, 293
Lee, Sarah Carolina Williams, 80, 140
Lee's Ferry, 158, 224
LeFevre, Clifford F., 380
LeFevre, Dean, 291
LeFevre, Henry, 256
LeFevre, Peter, 255
LeFevre, Thomas, 80
LeFevre, William, 78, 124–25
Leigh, Treharne, 307
Lemmons, Lindon, 309
Lemon, Alexander, 48
Leroy, Dan, 114
Lewman, William, 200, 201
Liberal party, 171
Lime kilns, 84

Lincoln, Abraham, 178
Lindsay, Edith Broadhead, 309
Linford, Joseph Henry, 214–15
Linford, Luella Rowena Orton, 215
Linford, Robert, 380
Linford, Vee, 216–17
Link, Bill H., 120
Lions Club of Panguitch, 295
Liston, Alberta, 134
Liston, Louise, xii, 363–64
Liston, Martin, 135
Liston, Mercel, 260
Liston, Perry, 288
Liston, R.H., 222
Liston, Robert, 363–64
Liston, Rufus, 135, 219
Little, James, 113
Littlefield, David O., 143, 145, 152
Littlefield, Edward, 145
Littlefield, Edwin, 152
Littlefield, Louisa, 152
Littlefield, Sam, 145, 152
Littlefield, Sarah Francis, 152
Littlefield, Sidney, 61, 76, 86, 87, 152
Littlefield, Waldo, 245
Longden, John, 348
Losee, 156–57
Loseeville, 156
Losee, Isaac, 156
Louder, Emily, 61
Louder, Jesse, 58, 61, 65–66
Louder, John, 61, 64, 65, 86
Louder, Zilpha, 86
Lowell, Simon, 79
Lyman, Amasa, 182–84, 188, 189
Lyman, Julee, 356–57
Lyman, Richard R., 288
Lyman, Rosanna, 182, 184, 187
Lyman, Truman, 328
Lyman, Vern, 182, 184
Lynn, Henry, 86
Lyons, Ernal, 319
Lyons, Jennie, 319

McCallister, Elizabeth Ann, 119
McCallister, Martin, 303
McCartney, Margaret Aveline, 187

McCartney, Warren, 187
McCarty, 224, 226
McClasky, Adolph G., 175
McClellan, 202
McCullough, Eliza Esther, 119
McCullough, Henry J., 173
McCullough, Levi Hamilton, 173
McEdwards, Angus, 120
McEdwards, Edward, 120
McEwen, Douglas, 256
McGath, Ben, 187
McGinty, Kathleen, 366, 372
McInelly, Arthur O., 288
McInelly, Gilbert, 260
McInelly, Gren, 310
McInelly, James, 134, 136
McInelly, Loral, 303
McInelly, Mildred, 260
McIntyre, Robert, 68
Mabey, Charles R., 262
Macomb, J.M., 94–95
Mail Service, 171–73, 190
Mammoth Lumber Company, 327
Mangum, Carl H., 210
Mangum, Orin, 201
Manwell, John F., 201
Marshall, Jim, 225
Marshall, Joseph, 79, 171
Marshall, Lloyd, 311
Marshall, Mary A., 58–59
Marshall, Monte, 380
Marshall, Steve, 380
Marshall, Thomas, 267
Marshall, William, 205
Mason, William L., 312–13
Mather, Steven, 262, 268
Matheson, Alexander, 58, 61, 64
Matheson, Norma, 368–69
Matheson, Simon A., 242–43
Mathews, Joseph, 47
Maw, Herbert, 313
May, Roy, 331–32
Mecham, Emery, 200
Mecham, Henry, 200, 201
Mecham, Lizzie, 204
Mecham, Morrison, 145
Mecham, William B., 201

Medical Care, 244–45, 296–97
Meecham, Clyde, 276
Meeks, Priddy, 51, 53
Meeks, Sarah, 114
Meeks, William, 182
Memmott, Kemner T., 329
Mendenhall Company, 343
Meredith, Jerry, 370
Merril, Mary E, 153
Mesozoic Era, 5–10
Meteorite, near Antimony in 1910, 233
Middleton, George H., 309
Middleton, Robert A., 294, 298
Midwives, 139, 140, 213
Miller, Allen, 79, 87, 171, 205
Miller, Becky Carson, 242
Miller, Glen, 256
Miller, James L., 260
Miller, John C., 259
Miller, Joseph, 259
Miller, Lovisa, 209, 259
Miller, Ninian, 79
Miller, Rebecca Carson, 240, 241
Minchey, Jacob, 109
Mission 66, 320–21, 324–25
Mitchell, Margaret, 288
Mitchell, William, 273
Mitchell, Zetland, 335
Mix, Tom, 88
Moccasin Bill, 155
Moffat, Don, 320
Monnet, George, 312
Montague, Avera, 300
Montague, Ivan, 300
Montague, James Shepherd, 87, 191
Montague, Peggy, 300
Montague, Sarah Jane, 86
Moody, Etta, 139
Moody, Jane, 131, 139
Moody, John, 131, 139
Moore, Amelia, 224
Moore, Audry, 257
Moore, Billy, 153
Moore, Camille, xii
Moore, Elige, 153, 223–24, 229
Moore, John, 274
Moore, Steven, 347

Moore, Thomas, 224
Moosman, Christian, 187, 189, 289
Moosman, Gertrude, 296
Moosman, Lorin, 288, 300
Moosman, Mary Justett, 187
Morgan, Silver Tip, 224
Morrill Anti-Bigamy Act of 1862, 178
Morrill, Belle, 239, 241, 243
Morrill, Ben, 239
Morrill, Cair, 239
Morrill, Emma Carson, 239–44
Morrill, John "Jack" D., 239–44
Morrill, LaBaron, 239, 240
Morrill, Melvin, 239
Morrill, Mildred, 239
Morss, Noel, 29
Mortensen, Mary, 90
Moss, Frank, 340–41
Moss, Riley, 58, 76
Mossman, William, 335
Mount Ellen, 12–13, 105
Mount Ellsworth, 12–13
Mount Hillers, 13
Mount Holmes, 13
Mount Pennell, 12–13, 105
Mountain Air Planners, 349
Mountain Fuel Supply Company, 377
Mountain Meadows Massacre, 80
Mountain States Telephone &
    Telegraph, 220
Movies, 290–91, 346
Muddy Creek, 104–5
Muddy Mission, 113
Mumford, George, 59
Mumford, Lydia, 59
Munson, Chris, 347
Munson, Hortense Cope, 204
Munson, Leo, 298, 342
Murdock, Gideon, 118
Murray, Eli H., 170
Murray, Tom E., 322, 324
Musser, A.M., 74–75
Myers, John, 170–71

National Geographic, 320
Navajo Indians, 64, 128–29, 148–49,
    312

Neilson, Diane, 333
Neilson, Jens, 58
Nelson, Peter, 120
New Deal Programs, 292–308
Newell, Jack, xii
Newell, Linda King, xi, 324
Newman, Bert, 275
Nicholes, Dave, 120
Nicholes, Josiah, 120
Nielsen, Maren, 90
Nielson, August, 182
Nielson, Neilsanna Anna Johanna, 115
Nielson, Niels, 120
Nixon, Richard, 341
Norton, Albert, 85
Norton, John W., 79, 83, 85, 172
Numic Peoples, 32–34, 42
Nunn, L.L., 226

Ogden, Harry, 227
Ogden, Margaret, 190–91
Ogden, Warren, 187
Ohio Oil Company, 334
Oil, 334–35, 370–71
"Old Sow," 86
Olsen, Daniel, 119
Olsen, Delilah, 119
Orton, 123
Orton, Bill, 366–67
Orton, Owen, 265
Orton, William, xi, 124
Orton's Cafe, 342
Osborn, Harriet Elmer, 187
Osborn, Rosella, 310
Osborn, W.J., 288
Osborn, William, 187,
Ostrichs, 363–64
Ott, Alma, 284
Ott, David B., 203
Ott, James, 257
Ott, James, A., 203, 207, 273
Ott, James Robert, 201, 203
Ott, Janet M. Johnson, 203, 207, 257
Ott, Joseph, 201, 253–54, 257
Ott, Mabel, 284
Ott, Mira Loy, 355
Ott, Robert, 355

Ott, Wallace, 205, 224, 229, 246–47
Outlaw Trail Endurance Ride, 361
Owens, Devon, 328
Owens, Rate, 291
Owens, William T., 192

Pace, James, 87, 153, 171
Packer, Jonathan, 145, 150
Packer, Nephi, 145
Packer, William, H., 76
Page, J.J., 220
Paiute High School, 274
Paiute Indians, 32–34, 41, 44–45,
    51–52, 62, 64, 68, 70, 104, 128, 185,
    192, 193
Paleo-Indian Period, 20–23
Paleozoic Era, 3–5
Panetta, Leon, 366–57
Panguitch, x, 69, 194, 358; first
    settlement, 57–62; second
    settlement, 74–76, county seat, 170;
    mail service, 171; schools, 174;
    influenza epidemic, 259; Carnegie
    Library, 296; World War II, 309
Panguitch Cooperative Mercantile and
    Manufacturing Institutions, 78
Panguitch Drug Company, 381
Panguitch Junior Chamber of
    Commerce, 295
Panguitch Ladies Rhythm Band, 381
Panguitch Lake, 51, 54, 75, 87–88, 106,
    191–94, 318
Panguitch LDS Stake Tabernacle, 85
Panguitch Progress, 208
Panguitch Rhythm Band, 291
Panguitch Valley, 13, 53
Paradox Basin, 3–4
Parker, Ann Gillies, 225, 229
Parker, Jeff, 364
Parker, Maximillian, 225
Parker, Robert LeRoy, 224–29
Parley P. Pratt Expedition, 46–51
Parmer, Sally, 58
Parowan, 54
Partner, Luetta, 285–86
Partridge, Gwen, 222
Patraw, P.P., 320

Pendleton, Alta Carson, 240
Pendleton, C.C., 57
Pennellen Pass, 105
People's party, 171
Perea, Estevan, 39
Perkins, Andrew, 201
Perkins, Jesse, 109
Peters, Billy J., 208
Peters, James C., 187
Peters, Ruth Rio, 187
Peters, W.J., 270
Peterson, Amanda, 249
Peterson, Canute, 120
Peterson, Golda, 289
Peterson, James E., 180
Peterson, Neils, M., 297
Peterson, Sophia, 84
Phelps, William W., 47
Phipps, Washington, 142
Pine Creek, 103
Pine Lake, 154, 318
Pinney, Charles, 70, 86, 204
Pinney, R.C., 171
Pioneer Day, 155, 192, 318
Piute County, 353–54
Place, Etta, 228
Plant Life, 17
Plateau Resources Ltd., 331–32
Pollack, Hyrum, 68, 70
Pollock, Allen, 260
Pollock, Dan, 201, 215
Pollock, Emma Roe, 260
Pollock, Jack, 204
Pollock, John F., 201, 203, 206
Pollock, Samuel, 245, 269, 294, 296, 320
Pollock, William, 204, 206
Polygamy, 85–86, 177–81
Porter, Clayton, 292
Porter, Eldan, 327
Porter, Eliza Alvey, 260
Porter, Emmitt, 249
Porter, Hyrum, 222
Porter, J.R., 136
Porter, Joseph, 222
Porter, Parley, 288
Porter, Preston, 296
Porter, Ray, 309

Porter, Warren W., 298
Potato Valley, 71, 129
Powell, Allan Kent, viii, xii
Powell, Clem, 101
Powell, Emma, 101
Powell, John Wesley, 3, 72, 93–106
Powell, Walter, 95
Pratt, Parley P., 47–51
Pratt, Sarah, 119
Pratt, Teancum, 109
Pratten, Elizabeth, 152–53
Pratten, Fanny, 152–53
Prehistoric Peoples, 20–32
Prince, William, 84, 87
Prince, Louisa Lee, 84
Prince, Todd, 360
Prince, William, 193
Proctor, Martha, 256
Proctor, Merlin, 256
Proctor, William, 78
Public Health Nurses, 296–97

Questar Gas, 377
Quilt Walk, 60–61
Quilter, David, 255, 257–58
Quilter, Eda Willis, 257–58
Quinarrah, 51–53

Ramsey, Elizabeth, 186
Ramsey, Jane Mills Paxton, 6
Ramsey, John, 66
Rasmussen, Sophia, 115
Red Lake, 66
Redford, Robert, 368–69
Resettlement Administration, 293,
    307–8
Revised Statute 2477, 371
Reynolds, Cliff, 256
Reynolds, Cyrus, 87
Reynolds, Enoch, 87, 171
Reynolds, Lizzie Pollock, 204
Rice, Ann Morris Butler, 140
Richards, Elizabeth, 131
Richards, Elmo, 276
Richards, Florence, 256
Richards, LeGrand, 295–96
Richards, Morgan, 131, 136

Richards, Stephen L., 270
Richards, Thomas, 61
Richards, William, 256, 335
Ricketts, Thomas, 258
Rico, Mable, 193
Riddle, Bryant, 344
Riddle, Charles, 311
Riddle, Emma Allene Savage, 229, 382
Riddle, Isaac, 118, 179–80, 209, 297
Riddle, Isaac J., 118
Riddle, Leona, 259
Riddle, Mont Chesney, 286
Riding, Alfred, 85
Riding, Boyd, 309
Riding, Frank, 205
Riding, Heber, 205
Riding, Miriam Adelia, 245
Riggs, Earl, 256
Riggs, Earnest, 236, 319
Riggs, Effel, 177, 222, 236
Riggs, Frank, 272–73
Riggs, Merle, 270
Riggs, Mildred, 342
Riggs, Priscilla, 236
Riggs, Sam, 236, 273
Riggs, William R., 270
Riggs, William Sears, 153
Robbers' Roost, 226
Robinson, Cornelia, 59
Robinson, Jane Coupe, 58
Robinson, John R., 58
Robinson, Julia Ann, 58, 59, 61, 67
Robinson, Richard Frederick, 258–59
Robinson, Timothy, 58, 59, 67
Rock Art, 21–22, 31
Rodgers, Samuel G., 80
Roe, Evelyn Marshall, 309
Romer, Roy, 369
Roosevelt, Franklin D., 283, 293, 301
Roosevelt, Theodore, 217, 325
Roundy, Almeda, 153
Rowan, Charles E., 120
Rowley, Samuel, 159
Ruby's Inn, 264–67, 274, 365
Ruess, Everett, 292
Rugg, Frederick, 70
Ru-Mil Cafe, 342

Rural Electrification Administration, 293, 297–301

Safely, John, 189
San Juan Mission, 157–64
Sandberg, Karl C., xii
Sandin, Bessie, 299
Santick, 65
Sargent, Fred, 247
Sargent, James M., 267, 271
Sargent, L.C., 260
Sargent, Maria L., 85
Sargent, Willard S., 259
Sargent, William P., 84–85, 170, 174
Savage, Ebenezer, 153
Savage, Lee, 298
Savage, Moroni, 153
Savage, Neil, 153
Savage, Serielda, 298
Saw Mills, 326–29, 359, 362
Sawyer, David G., 309
Sawyer, Levi, 212
Sawyer, Margaret, 211
Sawyer, Thomas B., 211, 212
Scarlet Fever, 207
Schools, 84–85, 121–22, 155, 174–77, 187–89, 238, 270–76, 288–89, 313, 347–48, 357–58
Schow, Andrew, 129, 130, 135, 138, 141, 159, 170, 178, 215, 260
Schow, Annie Hansen, 131
Schow, Annie Jeppesen, 130
Schow, Ira C., 206
Schow, James, 129, 131
Schow, Mariah, 245
Schow, Mary Ann Perry, 130, 133, 138, 141
Schow, Mike, 215
Schow, Susannah, 260
Schvwits Indians, 99
Scrattish, Nichols, 325
Seaman, John Whitehead, 246
Seamon-Maloney, Lois, 291
Seaton, John, 150
Seibert, Percy, 228
Sevier Lake, 1
Sevier Orogeny, 8

Sevier River, 1–2, 13
Sevy, George W., 75, 76–79, 83, 84, 85–86, 87, 178
Sevy, John L., 220
Sevy, Margaret Nebraska Imlay, 86, 90
Sevy, Phoebe Melinda, 58, 83, 86
Sevy, Thomas, 220, 309
Sevy, Warren, 87
Sevy, William, 170
Shakespear, Brandon, 259
Shakespear, David, 76
Shakespear, George, 201, 205
Shakespear, Hannah Brandon, 244–45
Shakespear, Joseph, 203, 205
Shakespear, June, xii, 272, 291, 345, 363
Shakespear, Obie, 363
Shakespear, Richard, 205
Shakespear, William, 84, 205, 247–48
Shefield, Sam, 183–84, 189
Shegump, 65
Sherman, Al, 248
Shields, Murray, 273, 275
Shipp, Ellis Reynolds, 140
Shirts, Darius (Di), 131, 139
Shirts, Margaret, 131
Showalter, J.B., 271
Showalter, James, 214, 220
Shurtz, Ambrose, 222
Shurtz, Cal, 249
Shurtz, Chester, 260
Shurtz, Don, 335
Shurtz, Don Carlos (Carl), 131, 133, 134
Shurtz, Elizabeth (Betsy) 131
Shurtz, Ellis, 256
Shurtz, Josiah, 222
Shurtz, Leander, 222, 306
Shurtz, Mary Alice, 140, 162
Shurtz, Sarah Ann, 311
Sierra Club, 341
Siler, Andrew S., 109
Simons, Dora, 187
Simons, Fred, 187
Simons, G.J., 201
Skougaard, Lizzie Carson, 242
Skyline Lumber Company, 326–27, 345
Slack, Coris, 309

Slade, William, 87
Smith, Ada, Olivia, 164
Smith, Arabella "Belle" Coombs, 163–64
Smith, Elias, 249
Smith, Elizabeth, 153, 311
Smith, Elroy, 163
Smith, George A., 57, 64, 74
Smith, George Abraham, 164
Smith, George Albert, 313
Smith, Guy Nephi, 310
Smith, James, 153, 220
Smith, Jedediah, 42
Smith, Jesse N., 58
Smith, John Calvin Lazell 51, 53
Smith, John L., 51
Smith, John Paul, 61
Smith, Joseph, 45–46
Smith, Joseph Stanford, 163–64
Smith, Lydia Ann, 111–12
Smith, Mary Julia, 111–12
Smith, Mary Susan, 153
Smith, Seth Alvin, 111
Smith, Silas Sanford, 65, 159
Smith, Thomas, 320
Smith, Vee (Gabby), 346
Smith, Virginia Hardy, 246
Smoot, Aurella, 176, 258
Smoot, John, 120, 176
Smoot, Les, 311
Snow, Erastus, 67, 74–75, 170
Snow, Lorenzo, 115, 179, 190
Snow, Merle, 270
Snyder, C.W., 205
Snyder, Charles, 201
Sorenson, Christian, 120
Southern Paiutes (See Paiute Indians)
Southern Utah Wilderness Alliance, 369
Spanish Trail, 42–44, 45–46, 158
Spencer, Emma, 310
Spencer, Farlan L., 310
Spencer, Guernsey, 220
Spencer, Joseph H., 131, 133, 145
Spencer, Polly, 288
Spencer, Ushur L., 288
Spenlove, John, 201, 204, 206
Spenlove, William, 201

Spry, 123–24
Spry, William, 123–24, 236
Star Dance Hall, 291
State Bank of Garfield, 284
Steed, Paul, 326–27, 345, 362–63
Steed, Stephen, 363
Steele, John, 51,53, 85
Steele, John A., 206
Steele, M.M., 84, 85, 170, 177
Steele, Mahonri M. Jr., 205, 208, 220
Steen, John, 120
Steiner, J.J., 245
Stevens, Arthur W., 251
Stevensen, Catherine Justet, 130–31
Stevensen, David, 130–31
Stewart, J.F., 101
Stock Raising, 214–17, 363
Stokes, Jeremiah, 139
Stokes, William Lee, 3–4
Stratton, Martha Jane, 111–12
Sudweeks, Claude, 251
Sumner, Jack, 95, 198
Swensen, John C., 176–77
Syrett, Alice, 236–37
Syrett, Clara Armeda (Minnie), 251–53, 254, 261–62, 263–65
Syrett, Fred C., 237
Syrett, Reuben (Ruby) Carlson, 243, 251–53, 254, 261–62, 263–65, 294
Syrett, Sarah D., 259

Table Cliff Plateau, 69
Tahdah'heets, 89
Talbot, Charlotte Newman, 60, 76
Talbot, Jane, 120
Talbot, Memphis Sudweeks, 312, 346
Talbot, Paul, 347
Talbot, Russell, 312, 346
Talbot, Vivian L., xi
Talbot, Walter DeVar, 380
Talbot, William, 60, 61, 76, 83
Tanneries, 79
Tantalus Creek, 105
Taylor Grazing Act of 1934, 224
Taylor, John, 84, 131
Tebbs, Burns, 381
Tebbs, Daniel F., 123, 124

Tebbs, Ruth, 381
Tebbs, Susan B., 172
Tebbsville, 123
Television, 344–45
Tenneco Oil Corporation, 334
Thompson, Almon H., 93, 99, 101–6,
    129, 182
Thompson, Brig, 152
Thompson, Dave, 152
Thompson, George, 284, 290, 300, 310,
    345
Thompson, George W., 148, 149
Thompson, Guy, 379
Thompson, Jack, 152
Thompson, James, 152
Thompson, James Brigham, 145, 153
Thompson, James L., 145
Thompson, Jim, 152
Thompson, John Orson, 145, 154
Thompson, Louise, 187
Thompson, Matilda Willis, 148–49
Thompson, Samuel, 145
Thompson, William Samuel, 145, 156,
    173
Thompson, Willis, 136, 187, 189
Thurber, Albert K., 117
Ticaboo, 331–34
Tillahash, Tony, 89
Timber Industry, 325–29
Tippets, John, 210
Tippets, Joseph A., 206
Tolton, John C., 303
Tourism, 340–44, 362, 373
Tourist's Rest, 261–62, 263
Trans World Airlines, 324
Tropic, x, 199–207, 257. 310, 347
Tropic and East Fork Irrigation
    Company, 202
Turnbow, Isaac, 129, 131
Twitchell, Adelbert, 136
Twitchell, Arthur E., 309
Twitchell, Edwin, 130, 131–132, 141
Twitchell, Monroe, 136
Twitchell, Nancy, xii

U.S. Energy Corporation, 333
Udall, Stewart L., 340

Underwood, Gilbert Stanley, 265
Union Pacific Railroad, 262–63, 322
United Order, 119–20
Ur, 199
Uranium, 329–31
Urpani, Debby, 364
Utah Antimony and Smelting
    Company, 122
Utah Centennial County History
    Council, vii-viii
Utah Center for Rural Life, 370
Utah Community Impact Board,
    378–79
Utah Highway 12, 302, 360
Utah National Park, 266
Utah Old Time Fiddlers Association,
    355
Utah Parks Company, 262, 322–23
Utah State Automobile Association, 252
Utah State Historical Society, 290, 378
Utah State Legislature, vii-viii
Utah Statehood, 193, 207
Utah Writers Project, 275
Utah's New Wonderland, 252–53
Ute Ford, 43
Ute Indians, 32–34, 41, 44–45, 64

Van Every, Mark, 362
VanLeuven, Levert, 109
Veater, David R., 347
Vietnam, 347

Wakara, 49
Wardle, Enoch, 67, 68, 76
Wardle, Mary Mortensen, 76
Wardle, Saul, 61
Wardle, Solomon, 86
Warner, Christina Brown, 120
Warner, Fred, 322
Warner, Margaret, 59
Warner, Matt, 224, 226
Warner, Milo, 311
Warner, Mortimer W., 120
Wasatch Mountain Cub, 341
Waterpocket Fold, 104
Weather, 15–16
Webb, Catherine Wilcox, 120

Webb, Helen Matilda, 119
Webb, Mack, 182
West, May, 88
West, William, 65
Weyss, John E., 102–3
Whatcott, Alfred, 61–62
Whatcott, Isabella Paxton, 61, 66
Wheeler, George M., 102–3
White, C.D., 207
White, Henry, 109, 141, 142
White, Susannah, 142
Whitmore, James M., 68
Whitney Francis T., 51, 53
Wide Hollow Reservoir, 361
Widtsoe, 209–10, 258, 276–77, 307–8
Widtsoe, John A., 276
Wilcock, Edward, 131, 134, 136, 139, 214
Wilcock, Lydia, 131
Wilcox, Franklin Henry, 120
Wilcox, John D., 120, 122, 173, 176, 179–80
Wilcox, Kate Effie, 258
Wilcox, Mary Theodotia Savage 120
William Prince Inn, 381
William, George, 203
William, James V., 109
Williams, Dione Peterson, 324
Williams, James A., 110
Williams, James Y., 78, 84
Williams, Sylvester (Vet), 135
Williams, Terry Tempest, 369
Willis, Dewey, 337–38
Willis, Myron, 223
Willis, Teora, xii, 312, 337–38
Wilson, Alma, 328
Wilson, Dick, 136
Wilson, Donna Moosman, 356
Wilson, George, 79, 112
Wilson, Gertrude, 328
Wilson, Joel, 328
Wilson, Rebecca, 114, 174
Wilson, Rob, 135
Wilson, Woodrow, 253
Winder, 210
Winder, John R., 210
Windsor, Lucy, 174

Winn, Thomas, 80
Wint, 193
Wirth, Conrad L., 321
Wolfskill, William, 43–44
Woodard, George, 256
Wooden Shoe, 151
Woodruff, Wilford, 180
Woods, Joseph, 87
Woolf, Walter M.,177
Woolley, Franklin Benjamin, 69, 71, 72, 73, 90, 103
Woolsey, Brigham, 131, 134
Woolsey, David M., 216, 288
Woolsey, Earl, 288
Woolsey, LaVern, 288
Woolsey, Nethella Griffin, 142
Workman, Abram Smith, 116, 117, 172, 174, 200, 211
Workman, Dave, 116–17
Workman, Julia Hatch, 213
Works Progress Administration, 293, 295–96
World War I, 253–56
World War II, 308–13, 338
Worthen, Darrel, 276
Worthen, Elizabeth, 208
Worthen, Frank, 243
Worthen, Fred, 265
Worthen, James A., 171, 176
Worthen, Samuel, 84, 85, 87
Wright, Alvey, 293

Yardley, Gilbert, 256
Young Ladies Mutual Improvement Association, 84
Young, Brigham, 46, 64, 66, 74–75, 113
Young, Joseph A., 82–83
Young, Ron, 342
Young, Virginia, 342
Yount, George C., 43–44

Zabriskie, Adella, 258
Zabriskie, George, 258
Zabriskie, Orrel, 258
Zenz, John, 342
Zenz, Lola, 342